Zeba A. Crook
Reconceptualising Conversion

Beihefte zur Zeitschrift für die neutestamentliche Wissenschaft

und die Kunde der älteren Kirche

Herausgegeben von
James D. G. Dunn · Carl A. Holladay
Hermann Lichtenberger · Jens Schröter
Gregory E. Sterling · Michael Wolter

Band 130

Walter de Gruyter · Berlin · New York

Zeba A. Crook

Reconceptualising Conversion

Patronage, Loyalty, and Conversion
in the Religions of the Ancient Mediterranean

Walter de Gruyter · Berlin · New York

BT
780
.C76
2004

☉ Printed on acid-free paper which falls within
the guidelines of the ANSI to ensure permanence and durability.

ISBN 3-11-018265-3

Bibliographic information published by Die Deutsche Bibliothek

Die Deutsche Bibliothek lists this publication in the Deutsche Nationalbibliografie; detailed bibliographic data is available in the Internet at <http://dnb.ddb.de>.

© Copyright 2004 by Walter de Gruyter GmbH & Co. KG, D-10785 Berlin
All rights reserved, including those of translation into foreign languages. No part of this book may be reproduced or transmitted in any form or by any means, electronic or mechanical, including photocopy, recording, or any information storage and retrieval system, without permission in writing from the publisher.
Printed in Germany
Cover design: Christopher Schneider, Berlin

This work is dedicated to three teachers who, though they might be surprised to learn this, shaped me as a scholar:

my mother Rithea who taught me to inquire into all things;

my father Patrick who taught me to distrust traditional answers;

my coach Dr. D. B. Clement who taught me to risk aspiring beyond my reach.

Acknowledgements

My first debt of gratitude must be extended to Professor John S. Kloppenborg, my doctoral advisor. His ability and care as a scholar in such a wide array of areas never ceases to amaze me, and he acted as mentor and model for me. What can I say about this scholar that has not been said already by a "cast of thousands"? Professor Kloppenborg sought to control my propensity for excess and to strengthen my weaknesses; would that we were all so lucky as to have advisors of this quality.

In addition, Professors J. M. Bryant, T. L. Donaldson, B. H. McLean, and A. F. Segal were generous and helpful readers, commentators, and examiners. Professors Leif Vaage, Colleen Shantz, and Stanley Porter read parts of this work at various stages, and reined me in methodologically at several points. Professor David Bossman encouraged me both warmly and forcefully to finish this work when it was a dissertation, and in that probably had a greater influence on me than he realises. I also gratefully acknowledge the encouragement, guidance, and diligence of Professors Gregory Sterling, Gustavo Benavides, and Kocku von Stuckrad, and of Dr. Claus-Jürgen Thornton at De Gruyter.

I would like to thank the Social Sciences and Humanities Research Council of Canada, Ontario Graduate Scholarship, the Catholic Biblical Association, and the University of St. Michael's College, whose generous financial support made timely completion of the doctoral process possible.

It strikes me as inadequate to even attempt to enumerate the myriad ways in which my partner, Professor Kelly Quinn, has helped me in this project. At every stage I have burdened her with my questions and concerns. Though our respective fields complement each other, I suspect strongly that the benefits that are to be had from the attention of a critical eye and keen intellect flow more in my direction than in hers. She is *mea patrona inimitabilis*.

Table of Contents

Acknowledgements vii

Abbreviations and Editions xiii

Introduction 1

Chapter One: The Influence of Psychology on Contemporary Society and Scholarship 13

1.0 Introduction 13
1.1 The Early Influence of Psychology 15
    1.1.1 The Influence of Psychology on New Testament Studies 17
1.2 Psychology and the Study of Conversion 22
    1.2.1 Movements Away from Psychological Approaches
    to Conversion 28
1.3 A Critique of the Cross-Cultural Psychological Model 31
    1.3.1 The Self as Culturally Constructed 34
    1.3.2 Emotion and Culture 39
    1.3.3 New Testament Social Scientific Criticism 47
1.4 Conclusion 49

Chapter Two: General Reciprocity Among Humans and their Gods 53

2.0 Introduction 53
2.1 A Taxonomy of Reciprocal Exchange 54
    2.1.1 Marshall Sahlins 54
    2.1.2 Stegemann and Stegemann 56

2.2 Defining our Terms: Patronage vs. Benefaction 59
  2.2.1 Stephan Joubert 60
2.3 Human Patronage and Benefaction 67
  2.3.1 Social Patronage 67
  2.3.2 Literary Patronage 74
2.4 Divine Patronage and Benefaction 76
2.5 Divine Patronage and Benefaction in Hellenistic Judaism 79
  2.5.1 Septuagint 80
  2.5.2 Flavius Josephus 82
  2.5.3 Philo of Alexandria 85
2.6 Conclusion 88

Chapter Three: The Rhetoric of Patronage and Benefaction 91

3.0 Introduction 91
3.1 The Call of the Patron/Benefactor 93
  3.1.1 Human Patronage and Benefaction 93
  3.1.2 Divine Patronage and Benefaction 97
3.2 Persuasion and Philosophical Conversion 100
  3.2.1 Philosophy and Religion 101
  3.2.2 Philosophy and Persuasive Rhetoric 104
  3.2.3 The Call of the Philosopher-Patron 107
3.3 Prayer, Praise, and Proselytism 108
  3.3.1 Prayer and Praise 108
  3.3.2 Patronal Proselytism 112
3.4 Patronal Synkrisis 117
  3.4.1 Human Patronage and Benefaction 119
  3.4.2 Divine Patronage and Benefaction 122
  3.4.3 Philosophical Patronage and Benefaction 124
  3.4.4 Patronal Synkrisis in the Septuagint, Philo, and Titus 128
3.5 The Χάρις of the Patron/Benefactor 132
  3.5.1 Meanings of χάρις 132
  3.5.2 Moffatt, Manson, and Conzelmann on χάρις 136
  3.5.3 Χάρις and Patronage and Benefaction 139
3.6 Conclusion 148

Chapter Four: The Rhetoric of Patronage and Benefaction in Paul's Conversion Passages 151

4.0 Introduction 151
4.1 First Corinthians 9:1, 16–17; 15:8–10 155
    4.1.1 Patronage and Apostleship 164
4.2 Galatians 1:11–17 170
4.3 Philippians 3:4b–11 179
4.4 Paul and the Patronage of Philosophy 186
4.5 Conclusion 192

Chapter Five: Patronage and Benefaction, Loyalty, and Conversion 199

5.0 Introduction 199
5.1 The Nature of Loyalty 201
5.2 Loyalty and Patronage and Benefaction 215
    5.2.1 Imperial Loyalty 217
    5.2.2 Manumission Loyalty 226
    5.2.3 Philosophical Loyalty 234
5.3 Loyalty, Conversion, and Paul 243
5.4 Conclusion 250

Conclusion 251

Bibliography 257

Index of Primary Sources 287

Index of Names and Subjects 303

Index of Modern Authors 307

Abbreviations and Editions

Abbreviations of all Classical authors follow the conventions of *The SBL Handbook of Style*, (ed. Patrick H. Alexander, et al.; Peabody, Mass.: Hendrickson, 1999), and the editions used are those of the Loeb Classical Library Series unless otherwise noted immediately below.

The following inscription and papyrus abbreviations follow the conventions of Bradley McLean, *An Introduction to Greek Epigraphy of the Hellenistic and Roman Periods From Alexander the Great Down to the Reign of Constantine (323 B.C.–A.D. 337)* (Ann Arbor: University of Michigan Press, 2002), and John F. Oates, et al. (eds.), *Checklist of Editions of Greek and Latin Papyri, Ostraca and Tablets* (4th ed.; Atlanta: Scholars Press, 1992) respectively, but are provided below for convenience.

Aelius Aristides:	W. Dindorf, *Aristides*. Hildesheim: Georg Olms Verlagsbuchhandlung, 1964; C. A. Behr, *Aelius Aristides and* The Sacred Tales. Amsterdam: Adolf M. Hakkert, 1968.
BDAG	*A Greek-English Lexicon of the New Testament and Early Christian Literature*. W. Bauer, F. W. Danker, W. F. Arndt, and F. W. Gingrich; Revised and Edited by F. W. Danker. Chicago: University of Chicago Press, 2000.
BGU	*Aegyptische Urkunden aus den Königlichen Museen zu Berlin: Griechische Urkunden*. 11 vols. Berlin: Weidmann, 1895–1968.
Ceb. Tab.	J. T. Fitzgerald and L. Michael White, *The Tabula of Cebes*. Chico: Scholars Press, 1983.
CIL	*Corpus Inscriptionum Latinarum, Consilio et Auctoritate Academiae Litterarum Regiae Borussicae Editum*. Berolini: Reimer, 1863–1974.
CIRB	*Corpus Inscriptionum Regni Bosporani*. Moscow and Leningrad: Nauka, 1965.
Dig	*The Digest of Justinian*. Edited by Theodor Mommsen, P. Krueger. English translation edited by A. Watson. Philadelphia: University of Pennsylvania Press, 1985.
IAssos	*Die Inschriften von Assos*. Edited by R. Merkelbach. Bonn: Habelt, 1974.
IBM	*The Collection of Ancient Greek Inscriptions in the British Museum*. Oxford: Clarendon, 1874–1916.
IDelos	*Inscriptions de Delos*. Académie des Inscriptions et Belles-Lettres. Fonds d'Epigraphie Grecque. Fondation du Duc de Loubat. 7 vols. Paris: Boccard, 1926–76.
IG II²	*Inscriptiones Atticae Euclidis anno anteriores*. Edited by J. Kirchner. 4 vols. Berolini: Reimer, 1913–40.
IG IV²	*Inscriptiones Epidauri*. Edited by F. Hiller von Gaertringen. Berolini: Reimer, 1929.

IG XI[4]	Inscriptiones Deli. Decreta, foedera, catalogi, dedicationes, varia. Edited by P. Roussel. Berolini: Reimer, 1914.
IG XIV	Inscriptiones Graecae. Siciliae et Italiae, additis Graecis Galliae, Hispaniae, Britanniae, Germaniae inscriptionibus. Edited by G. Kaibel. Berolini: Reimer, 1890.
IGRR	Inscriptiones graecae ad res romanas pertinentes. Edited by R. Cagnat. Roma: L'Erma, 1964.
IKret	Inscriptiones Creticae: Opera et Consilio Friderici Halbherr collectae. Edited by M. Guarducci. 4 vols. Rome: Libreria dello Stato, 1935–50.
IKyme	Die Inschriften von Kyme. Edited by H. Engelmann. Bonn: Habelt, 1976.
ILS	Inscriptiones latinae selectae. Edited by Hermann Dessau. 3 vols. Berolini: Weidmann. Reprint Dublin: Weidmann, 1974.
ISardH	Peter Herrmann, "Mystenvereine in Sardeis." Chiron 26 (1996): 315–41.

Justin Martyr: J. C. M. van Winden, *An Early Christian Philosopher: Justin Martyr's Dialogue with Trypho, Chapters One to Nine. Introduction, Text and Commentary.* Philosophia Patrum 1. Leiden: E. J. Brill, 1971.

Liddell, Scott, Jones: *A Greek-English Lexicon.* Compiled by Henry George Liddell and Robert Scott. Revised and Augmented by Sir Henry Stuart Jones. Oxford: Clarendon Press, 1996.

Louw and Nida: Johannes P. Louw and Eugene A. Nida, *Greek-English Lexicon of the New Testament Based on Semantic Domains.* New York: United Bible Societies, 1988, 1989.

LXX	Septuaginta. Edited by Alfred Rahlfs. Stuttgart: Bibelgesellschaft, 1959.
NewDocs	New Documents Illustrating Early Christianity. Vols. 1–5 edited by G. H. R. Horsley; vols. 6–9 edited by S. R. Llewelyn. North Ryde, Aus.: Ancient History Documentary Research Centre, Macquarie University, 1981–94.
OGI	Orientis graeci inscriptiones selectae. Edited by W. Dittenberger. 2 vols. Leipzig: Hirzel, 1903–1905. Reprint Hildesheim: Olms, 1986.
P. Fay.	Fayûm Towns and their Papyri. Edited by B. P. Grenfell, A. S. Hunt, and D. G. Hogarth. London: Egypt Exploration Fund, 1900.
P. Giss.	Griechische Papyri im Museum des oberhessischen Geschichtsvereins zu Gießen. Edited by O. Eger, E. Kornemann, and P. M. Meyer. Leipzig and Berlin: Teubner, 1910–12.
P. Grenf.	New Classical Fragments and other Greek and Latin Papyri. Edited by B. P. Grenfell and A. S. Hunt. Oxford: Clarendon Press, 1897.
P. Hib.	The Hibeh Papyri. Vol. I edited by B. P. Grenfell and A. S. Hunt. London, 1906. Vol. II edited by E. G. Turner and M.-Th. Lenger. London: Egypt Exploration Society, 1955.
P. Lips.	Griechische Urkunden der Papyrussammlung zu Leipzig. Edited by L. Mitteis. Leipzig: Teubner, 1906.
P. Lond.	Greek Papyri in the British Museum. 7 vols. London: British Museum, 1893–1974.
P. Mich. Zen.	Zenon Papyri. Edited by C. C. Edgar. Ann Arbor: University of Michigan Press, 1931.

P. Oxy.	*The Oxyrhynchus Papyri.* 84 vols. London: Egypt Exploration Society, 1898–2001.
P. Petr.	*The Flinders Petrie Papyri.* Edited by J. Mahaffy and J. G. Smyly. Dublin: Academic House, 1891–1905.
P. Teb.	*The Tebtunis Papyri.* 4 vols. London: Egypt Exploration Society, 1902–1976.
Porphyry	Mark Edwards, *Neoplatonic Saints: The Lives of Plotinus and Proclus by their Students.* Liverpool: University of Liverpool Press, 2000.
PSI	*Papiri greci e latini.* Edited by G. Vitelli, M. Norsa, et al. 15 vols. Florence: E. Ariani, 1912–79.
SEG	*Supplementum Epigraphicum Graecum.* 39 vols. Amsterdam: Gieben, 1923–92.
SIG	*Sylloge inscriptionum graecarum.* Edited by W. Dittenberger. 4 vols. Leipzig: Hirzel, 1915–24. Reprint Hildesheim: Olms, 1960.
SVF	*Stoicorum veterum fragmenta.* Edited by H. von Arnim. 4 vols. Leipzig: Teubner, 1903–24.
Syll³	See *SIG.*

Introduction

It is a risky practice, to be sure, to open a work of this length with a negative statement, but doing so may help to clarify the intent of this work. This work is not about Paul, the Apostle to the Gentiles. It is, to state it positively, about how we understand conversion in the ancient world. Nonetheless, I have found Paul's conversion a useful point of comparison for two reasons. By situating Paul in a work that is about ancient conversion, I seek to stress that contrary to the claims of the Christian tradition, only some of which are implicit, Paul was not a paradigm-setting convert who was without peer or parallel in the ancient world. Paul was like his peers when it comes to how he talked about and how he envisioned his conversion experience. The second reason Paul's conversion is useful is because, quite simply, his is the most accessible example of conversion from the ancient world. Practically everybody, Christian or otherwise, knows about "Paul the convert." The phrase "Damascus road" has become axiomatic in English-speaking cultures to refer to people changing convictions or opinions in an unpredictable, transformative and emotionally traumatic manner.

This book brings together two trajectories of New Testament scholarship: the study of and interest in Paul's conversion, fuelled as it is by a desire to understand the relationship between the man and the event; and social scientific criticism, in turn fuelled by its desire to understand the relationship between (wo)man and his/her surrounding cultural values and institutions. The resulting combination strives to situate Paul and his conversion within the culture that housed the man and that provided the framework within which his conversion was understood. This study also takes as its point of departure from other studies of ancient conversion the seminal observation of social scientific criticism that the culture and constellation of social institutions of the New Testament world is not the same as those of the modern western world. To miss this important difference between the two worlds is to act as if culturally embedded features of the ancient world were interchangeable with culturally embedded features of the modern world, and such could not be further from the truth. It is a fact that needs to be reckoned with fully that the cultural institutions of the ancient Mediterranean and the modern West are different. Such a *fact* as this must have a greater influence on how we understand the setting of the New Testament and its characters than simply providing us with new sets of questions and new answers we think are helpful. It should compel us to re-open questions and fields of inquiry we thought were closed in order to see if things we thought we knew, things that have perhaps reached the status of "common knowledge," need to be analysed anew. Paul's conversion, and conversion in the ancient Mediterranean world in general, is one such topic that needs to be re-opened in light of recent work in the social sciences.

The study of Paul's conversion has commanded a great deal of scholarly and popular interest. There are long and short studies on Paul's conversion that attempt either to understand the conversion better or to discuss its relationship to other features of Paul, such as his teaching, personality, or theology. Early studies on this topic were, as we shall see in Chapter One, explicitly psychological; they were either a direct outgrowth of the work of William James, or they *were* the work of William James.[1] In some later studies this reliance on James's psychological foundation to the study of conversion was implicit, part of the cultural baggage of the author and thus unrealised.[2] This can in part be traced to the great attraction of the west to the psychological paradigm and of the influence of psychology over Western ways of thinking about and of framing the world. The formative stages of the relationship between 'West' and 'Psychological' was truly a dialectical one — the sense of individualism that sets Westerners off from much of the rest of the world led to a system of framing the world and the self that in turn affected the development of the Western personality and of the Western *individual*. The subtlety of this dialectic might explain why, despite the fact that scholarship on Paul's conversion has moved away from explicitly psychological explanations, much of it has remained implicitly grounded in a psychological framework, often attempting unsuccessfully to make a clean break with past psychological approaches.

The landmark study that illustrates best this attempt to move scholarship on Paul's conversion away from psychologising explanations is Krister Stendahl's essay on "Paul and the Introspective Conscience of the West."[3]

---

[1] William James, *The Varieties of Religious Experience* (New York: Penguin, 1902).
[2] Arthur D. Nock, *Conversion: The Old and the New in Religion from Alexander the Great to Augustine of Hippo* (London: Oxford University Press, 1933); Ramsay MacMullen, *Christianizing the Roman Empire: A. D. 100–400* (New Haven: Yale University Press, 1984).
[3] K. Stendahl, "Paul and the Introspective Conscience of the West," *HTR* 56 (1963): 199–215.

Stendahl was arguing against a long-standing tradition that within Christian interpretation that Paul had been driven to Christianity (sic!) because of guilt or some psychological trauma incurred as a Jew. Yet it is Stendahl's *methodological* contribution and observation that is of greater interest here. His claim that introspection was not a feature of Paul's world but rather that it is a characteristic of modern Western consciousness should have radically altered academic approaches to Paul's conversion in particular and Pauline biography in general. Instead, New Testament scholarship on conversion appears to have taken up only Stendahl's clarion call concerning Paul's robust and healthy Jewish faith, though this too was in need of correction. Stendahl's point regarding the lack of an introspective conscience in Paul appears to have been largely unheeded within many conversion studies, and thus assumptions about parallels between ancient and modern psychology continue in much scholarship on Paul's conversion as they did before Stendahl's essay appeared in 1963.

This tendency to assume parallels between ancient and modern psychological perspectives has been vigorously challenged, both directly and indirectly, by the results of social scientific approaches to the New Testament and to cross-cultural analysis. A familiarity with anthropological approaches has given social scientific criticism the keen awareness that there are not only differences among global cultures (and therefore temporally separated cultures as well), but that these differences have serious consequences for how individuals within different cultures construct and understand their worlds. This has led to some influential observations concerning the interaction of ancient characters in terms of dyadic personality structures and honour and shame, for example, but has not yet been applied to ancient human interactions with the gods, especially with respect to the issue of conversion in the ancient world. The cultures of the New Testament and of the modern West respectively have vastly different constructions of the self; they understand the relationship of individual to society differently; and they understand the realm of emotions differently. This is not to say, "completely differently," as if there are no points of contact between ancient and modern humans on a whole range of matters concerning the human condition. Nonetheless, there are very real differences between the ancient and modern human experience of the world, and these need to be understood fully even before we could hope to appreciate properly the similarities. The problem with how we have been talking about conversion for the last century of scholarship is that we have either not been aware of these differences, or we have not taken them adequately into account in our work. It stands to reason that cultures with such different views of the self will frame and understand their social and religious experiences differently. Yet the assumption has always been one of sameness. I will return to this point of sameness shortly.

This is, in effect, the conclusion drawn by the work undertaken in Chapter One. Many areas of biblical scholarship, like other academic fields and like the West in general, have answered the siren song of psychologism. Psychologism is the assumption that all people share the same basic psychological structure, and that cultural difference leads to little more than differences in how psychological experience is expressed. Thus, in our field, it has led to the assumption that Paul's psychological experiences are accessible and understandable to us because we can use ourselves analogically. But increasingly, as cultural anthropologists and psychologists struggle with the primary experience of difference among cultures, this assumption of sameness is being undermined. The emerging consensus is that while emotion, as an example of a central feature of psychological experience, is universal (all people have them), emotions themselves are highly culturally specific. And while conversion is not an emotion, nor has anyone ever claimed it to be, I show in Chapter One that the foundational works on conversion in the field of Christian Origins have, in line with the general imagination of the West, either explicitly or implicitly defined and measured conversion in emotional and thus psychological categories.

The problem, then, that fuels the first chapter of this book is that if conversion is cast in emotional terms, and if emotional experience does not lend itself to cross-cultural transfer, how then are we of all people to empathise with the conversion experiences of ancient characters like Paul? The conclusion drawn at the end of Chapter One is that if we are to understand Paul's conversion experience, we need to overcome the psychologising tendencies of studies of conversion and approach the issue from another direction. The direction I propose in this study, therefore, involves a model that is more intrinsic to Paul's own world, one that seeks to overcome the challenges and weakness of cultural ethnocentrism. A better understanding of Paul's conversion will give priority not just to his words, but to his world. The overwhelming body of ancient sources, literary and material, suggests that people in Graeco-Roman antiquity framed their experiences of conversion in the language of ancient patronage and benefaction, and that as one formed wholly by his culture, Paul did so as well.

The Mediterranean institution of patronage and clientage has been studied in many works by classicists, historians, and New Testament scholars alike, and I do not seek to contradict that body of knowledge. There are three ways, however, in which I hope to contribute to our understanding of patronage and clientage in the ancient world, which I undertake in Chapter Two. First, it is widely acknowledged that patronage and clientage is one of the foremost keys for interpreting human interaction in an ancient Mediterranean setting. Studies on this alone abound, and studies that presuppose this research are increasing. It is a slightly less common observation, on the other hand, that Graeco-Roman human interaction with the gods was understood in the same framework as human interaction, and an even less common claim that the God of the Hellenistic Jews was framed in the same manner. We might call this divine patronage and benefaction, since it involved the exchange of benefactions and reciprocity between humans and their gods. Illustration of these claims is not, in the interest of space, handled directly, but rather can be seen from the total collection of texts and examples provided throughout this work. If we can understand the relationship and continuity between human and divine patronage and benefaction, we are that much closer to understanding the ancient world from an ancient perspective. In short, there appears to have been a pan-Mediterranean framework within which worshippers typically viewed their interactions with the gods, and it matters little whether that God was Isis, Asclepius, or the God of Israel. Second, in Chapter Two I situate the practice of patronage and benefaction within a model of ancient exchange, thereby differentiating it from other forms of exchange that I hope people will find helpful. Third, I hope to supplement our understanding of ancient patronage and benefaction by drawing attention to the form and function of the rhetorical conventions that are the subject of Chapter Three.

The description of patronage and benefaction in Chapter Two is more detailed than many will require, since an increasing number of New Testament scholars are familiar with it. The level of detail in Chapter Two is important, however, in order to ensure the detailed arguments and observations in Chapter Three do not presuppose knowledge the reader does not have, or has to go elsewhere to attain. The focus of Chapter Three is on how participants in divine and human relationships of patron-client exchange (and mostly clients) expressed themselves, and thus it requires a full and fresh familiarity with the model of patronage and benefaction. In other words, it is on the rhetoric of patronage, as opposed to the structure of patronage, that is the focus of the third chapter.

There are five rhetorical conventions that occur consistently within what we can call the rhetoric of patronage and benefaction, and what is doubly noteworthy is that these conventions are used regardless of whether the patron/benefactor is human or divine. The first of these rhetorical conventions is the call of the patron. Here we find the claim (sometimes it is true and sometimes it is simply claimed) that clients were approached by a patron, as opposed to approaching the patron themselves, in order to be benefited. It is an interesting feature of patronage and benefaction that clients were not solely responsible for establishing a patronal relationship, since the facts of poverty and necessity would have placed the burden of effort squarely on the shoulders of clients. That patrons human and divine were reputed to have called their clients into relationships of benefaction warrants a closer look in association with conversion and the common motif of "the call" by gods and philosophers.

The second convention is quite different from the first; it has to do with the philosopher's teaching and rhetorical delivery as a benefaction in and of itself. It was quite common for disciples and sympathetic writers to refer to philosophical teachers and their teachings, and at times to philosophy "herself," in the language of patronage and benefaction. A philosopher's lessons were a benefaction to humanity, designed to save people from ignorance and death. Philosophy in the abstract is spoken of as benefactor of all humanity, giver of all that is good and right in the world. What is more, it is not only philosophers that fall into the pattern of patronage and benefaction, but also the students/disciples whose conduct consistently reflects that of any other client. If interaction with philosophy and with the gods is framed in similar terms, then an understanding of ancient conversion needs to account for this relationship.

The third convention of the rhetoric of patronage includes three aspects, namely prayer, praise, and proselytism. We might think of these as three aspects of "Honouring Discourse," for lack of a better phrase. Within a context of patronage and benefaction, prayer and praise should require little explanation. Prayer and praise work hand in hand and were the primary way for a client to communicate with a patron or benefactor. Further, prayer is both a way of honouring the divine patron, and a way of making a request. The third element, proselytism, is less self-explanatory and much more fascinating as a phenomenon. It was expected behaviour of clients of human patrons to publicise the generosity of a patron in an attempt both to increase the reputation of the patron and to attract new clients, the logic behind this being that the more clients a patron had the greater the patron's public honour. Clients boasting about their patrons in an attempt to convince others is found when the patrons are wealthy people and when they are philosophers/teachers. It appears to have worked the same way when their patrons were divine:

spreading the good news of a divine patron's or benefactor's wonderful deeds, and thus attracting clients and increasing the number of worshippers, in effect 'patron evangelisation,' served to honour the god and was not uncommon behaviour in a client/worshipper. Prayer, praise, and proselytism were three interrelated ways in which a client could express his or her all-important client reciprocity.

The fourth convention of the rhetoric of patronage and benefaction I have come to call patronal synkrisis. Synkrisis is the simplest of rhetorical tropes — it means comparison. Typically it was used in encomiastic writing to compare the subject of a *bios* to a great man in the past, thus drawing a portrait of greatness by association, but it was also used in philosophical protreptic as a method of comparing life before and after one's encounter with philosophy. Yet, I have found that synkrisis commonly appears in the very specific setting of patron- or benefactor-oriented rhetoric. Clients were given to comparing their lives before and after their encounters with their patron in a way that always honours the current patron. They might describe their past as death, as darkness, as exile. Sometimes these descriptions are literal, sometimes obviously not; yet what matters is that the client is crediting the patron with some profound change in the quality of life. As a result we have here a type of synkrisis that I call patronal synkrisis; it offered a client an additional way to articulate the relationship of reciprocity and gratitude that was the moral and social obligation of a client towards a patron or benefactor.

A final feature of the rhetoric of patronage and benefaction is an important and still overlooked element of the vocabulary of ancient patronage: the term χάρις. Of course, the term is almost always translated as 'grace,' but the term 'grace' is so infused with Christian theological overtones that we have lost sight of the Graeco-Roman context that provided the first level of meaning for the term, namely 'benefaction.' ('Favour' is a useful translation because it reflects both a concrete and an abstract sense, but I prefer the concrete emphasis of 'benefaction,' lest we fall back into the trap of theological abstraction that 'grace' has become.) While χάρις in the New Testament can sometimes be translated as gratitude, in the majority of instances it could be simply translated as benefaction, and doing so often serves to highlight effectively Paul's relationship with his God. It is a relationship of client to divine patron, and much of Paul's language and conduct reflects exactly this.

There sits behind these five conventions of the rhetoric of patronage and benefaction a moral imperative. Each of them together and individually was designed to accomplish three goals: to give thanks to a patron, to praise a patron, and to secure future benefactions. These three goals summarise the moral and social duty of the client towards the patron, whether human or divine. Recalling that the sole duty of the client was to increase the honour of the patron (in exchange for benefactions received or the promise of benefactions), the rhetoric of patronage and benefaction refers to the patterns of articulation most commonly invoked by the client in order to increase the honour of the patron. What is more, each of these is visible in one way or another in Paul's conversion passages, as I shall illustrate in Chapter Four. In other words, Paul's own rhetoric of conversion, like that of his ancient Mediterranean peers, is a rhetoric of patronage and benefaction. Absent in conversion narratives, Paul's included, are introspective or emotional markers; what we find in their place are the markers of patronal exchange, benefactions and gratitude. With the exception of the rhetoric of the philosopher as patron, each of these conventions of the rhetoric of patronage and benefaction appear explicitly in Paul's conversion passages (1 Cor 9:1; 9:16–17; 15:8–10; Gal 1:11–17; and Phil 3:4b–11), and Chapter Four illustrates how this is the case.

This chapter closes with a look at the parallels between philosophy as an area of patronage and Paul as one who might well have been mistaken for a popular philosopher by his Hellenistic audiences. Parallels between Paul and the Graeco-Roman philosophers have long been pointed out and their significance debated. My goal in this discussion is not to argue that Paul was himself a "card-carrying" member of any philosophy, but only to point out that understanding the parallels between the earliest Jesus movement and the indigenous philosophies will help us to understand the phenomenon of conversion better. That is, it is widely held now that philosophy and not ancient religion was the domain of ancient conversion, and understanding how earliest Christianity fits into this cultural matrix can only complement our knowledge.

Recognition that ancient narratives about interaction with the gods and with philosophers was framed in the rhetoric of patronage and clientage is a profoundly important step in acknowledging that ancient conversion cannot be understood analogously with modern conversion. Chapter One problematises the assumptions that Paul can be transported into a modern cultural setting, that we can speak about his personal experiences and features as if he were one of us; Chapters Two through Four establish the extent to which Paul's conversion narratives were consistent with his cultural paradigm, a relationship that serves only to accentuate the differences between him and us. The intent of these chapters, supplemented ultimately by the final chapter, is to provide a workable and meaningful alternative to the dominant psychological reading of Paul's conversion experience, not simply to undermine that reading.

Lest one begin to think that ancient conversion involved automatons computing benefits and costs and changing patrons or benefactors (converting) on that basis alone (the "what's in it for me" principle), the final chapter introduces loyalty into the equation. Loyalty is an important feature of the model of ancient conversion, for without it, it appears that conversion in this cultural context was nothing more than a form of rational choice theory—that human actors behave as if the world is a market in which decisions are made rationally based only on perceived outcomes and benefits. We ought not over-emotionalise or over-sentimentalise ancient conversion; if much in conversion narratives emphasises what is to be gained by joining a certain patron, we should assume that the balance sheet was a factor in ancient conversion. We should take them at their word. This does mean that clients were apt to choose patrons based on the benefits they stood to gain. There can be no doubt that a feature of Paul's preaching to new Graeco-Roman converts involved drawing their attention to the benefactions to be gained from association with his God. Yet once inside, there was more dynamism to conversion than that. The life-blood of conversion, the dynamism, the way we know there was something at stake for all parties, is contained in an understanding of loyalty within the patron/benefactor and client bond. There is ample evidence that the bond that united some clients to their patrons went considerably beyond what can be accounted for by a sort of rational choice theory. Loyalty helps us to bridge that gap; it adds dynamism to a change in the patronal relationship that might otherwise be mistaken as entirely sober.

There lies at the root of this work an attempt to reverse a long-standing fallacy of contiguity that has resulted from the language we use—English language and psychological language. The use of the term 'conversion' in studies of the ancient world creates the illusion that conversion meant and represented then what it means and represents in the modern West. It is wholly natural that the Western (and English) hearer will hear the term 'conversion' used and assume she knows precisely what is meant. Or, conversely, the scholar can fall into similar patterns and assumptions by using the same term; the scholar's use of the term as an item of convenience inevitably becomes a statement of similarity. Our minds naturally work by analogy. What would be best is if we could come up with an alternative term. Some attempts have been made towards this (I have in mind here Beverly Gaventa's three types of conversion that arise in my Chapter One, of which the type "transformation" best describes Paul[4]). It appears, however, that no other term has been able to take the place of 'conversion.' It may well be that the reason 'conversion' has not been replaced is because no other term so well embodies the psychological assumptions that attend the term. Whatever the case, neither have I been able to come up with a different term to describe ancient 'conversion,' so I offer this work as a step towards acknowledging that there are perhaps more differences than similarities between the two cultural constructs of conversion, ancient Mediterranean and modern Western. Despite the fallacy of contiguity that is created when we use the term 'conversion,' we should avoid facilely assuming that the ancient counterpart can be understood by using the modern counterpart as an analogical model, whether deliberately or otherwise. It turns out we have been talking about conversion in the ancient Mediterranean all this time with the wrong language—our own.

While on the topic of the fallacy of contiguity created by the use of similar terminology, I have one additional item to discuss. It is still common idiom, based largely on our modern separation of church and state, firstly to differentiate the religious from the secular domains of social life, and from there to imagine that religion is a social entity discrete from other social entities, such as kinship, politics, economics. Such distinctions work well in our culture, but remarkably poorly in other cultures. With respect to the ancient Mediterranean, religion did not exist as a discrete social entity independent of other social entities, but rather was embedded within them. What we have in the ancient Mediterranean is political-religion, kinship-religion, and economic-religion, the point being that religion did not exist alone but was inexorably tied up in other social institutions. In order to facilitate against the confusion of sharing misleading terminology, I endeavour to use the words 'cult' and 'cultic' where we usually use 'religion' and 'religious'—that is to describe activities having to do with human interaction with the gods. Where I lapse back into familiar terminology, it is due to the smoother idiom offered by the familiar, and should not be taken as an indicator of shared features. And indeed it is not simply a matter of using appropriate terminology, for it is probably the perpetuation of this false

---

[4] Beverly R. Gaventa, *From Darkness to Light: Aspects of Conversion in the New Testament* (Philadelphia: Fortress Press, 1986). Alan F. Segal also uses this term, though with a different meaning [*Paul the Convert: The Apostolate and Apostasy of Saul the Pharisee* (New Haven: Yale University Press, 1990)], but despite its use by two influential scholars, the term has not caught on.

dichotomy between religious and secular life in the ancient world that has led to the continued misunderstanding of ancient conversion.

This study, then, seeks to establish that ancient and modern people talk differently about conversion because they are very different people, constructed differently by their cultures, and thus are prone to experience life—their interactions with each other and with their gods—differently. While we are certainly enriched by noting similarities between different cultures and people, we can be equally enriched by understanding, accepting, and honouring the differences without trying to homogenise everything. The ultimate challenge lies not in knowing that differences exist, but in actually using that knowledge to change how we think about ourselves and others.

Chapter One

The Influence of Psychology on Contemporary Society and Scholarship

1.0 Introduction

Psychology, with its emphasis on the emotional and introspective features of human experience, provides the default framework within which the modern West tends to analyse and describe conversion.[1] This claim does not assume that psychology is the only way people understand conversion, but that its pride of place is so natural to so many that its value is infrequently challenged. That the psychological approach is the default one is true despite the fact that one can study different *aspects* of conversion that are not psychological or that would not appear to lend themselves to psychological commentary or assumptions. For instance, one might focus on social aspects of conversion, looking into peer, network or community pressures, or into the dynamics of changing communities of faith, friends, and family. Similarly, one might focus on theological aspects of conversion, looking into the nature of the unique message or into the attainment of a higher religious truth.

Though some studies may well focus on aspects of conversion, they will naturally and necessarily presuppose a conversion experience that stands

---

[1] The terms "West" and "Western" are a little imprecise, but they are convenient and widespread. Studies of cultures in terms of individualism and collectivism (terms that will be defined later) illustrate two important things. The first is that individualism-collectivism is a linear range, not a pair of binary opposites. There is no clear demarcating line at which one culture is collectivist and the other individualist. Nonetheless, and this is the second point, certain geographical areas predominate at either ends of the spectrum—countries in North America (excluding Mexico), Europe, Australia/NZ are clustered at the individualistic end and countries in South America, Africa, and Asia are clustered at the collectivistic end. See table 5.1 in Geert Hofstede, *Culture's Consequences: Comparing Values, Behaviors, Institutions, and Organizations Across Nations* (2nd ed.; Thousand Oaks: Sage Publications, 2001), 215. The significance of this for the present study should be clear: Biblical scholars are overwhelmingly enculturated at the individualistic end of that spectrum.

behind whatever aspect they happen to study. It is this inaugural experience, and not necessarily the various aspects of conversion, which our culture tends strongly towards framing in psychological categories: personal, introspective, individualistic, and emotionally tumultuous (to varying degrees). The West overwhelmingly understands conversion as an event marked more by its internal effects and features than it is by its external effects and features.

This perspective, however, is not *only* psychological; it is also modern and Western, in other words encompassing a very narrow perspective both temporally and geographically. These three categories—psychological, modern, and Western—are so closely related as to be almost synonymous, but it is important and useful to differentiate among them. For instance, we shall see that a construction of the self that is individualistic and egocentric is decidedly Western and modern, and that such a construction of the self stands in sharp contradistinction to non-Western constructions of the self and self-identity. In and of itself, however, this is not psychological. Yet, the construction of psychological models was founded upon the egocentric and individualistic self that dominates Western society. These are not, incidentally, value laden terms, but rather anthropological terms distinguishing Western personality constructions from non-Western ones.

Psychology is such an organic (that is, implicit and tenacious) part of the cultural Western landscape, and it so thoroughly informs how Westerners understand and articulate human experience, that one might nearly *predict* that psychology would be the default manner for understanding conversion.[2] Indeed, given our profoundly psychological cultural setting, one could be forgiven for feeling that such an approach to understanding ancient conversion is wholly natural. Such, however, is not the case. Understanding conversion psychologically is not *natural* but rather precisely and narrowly *cultural*. It is neither self-evident nor obvious that psychology provides the best way for understanding conversion, but it is our culturally prescribed way for (and hence a very convenient way of) doing so.

---

[2] See, for instance, William R. Woodward, "Professionalization, Rationality, and Political Linkages in Twentieth Century Psychology," in *Psychology in Twentieth-Century Thought and Society* (ed. M. G. Ash and W. R. Woodward; Cambridge: Cambridge University Press, 1987), 295–309; Ellen Herman, *The Romance of American Psychology: Political Culture in the Age of Experts* (Berkeley: University of California Press, 1995); R. Hagendijk and H. Helms, "De invloed van de psychologie op andere disciplines: een kwantitatieve verkenning," *Nederlands Tijdschrift voor de Psychologie en haar Grensgebieden* 50 (1995): 257–66.

Of course, our first task must be to define psychology, for the term itself includes a startling variety of meanings and areas of research. The arrival of psychology as a modern academic discipline was marked by the "experiential" and structuralist psychology of Wilhelm Wundt in the 1870s. For Wundt, psychology was a "science of immediate experience," where experience refers to "such phenomena as sensations, perceptions, feelings, and emotions."[3] Despite the development of sub-disciplines and specialisations since the birth of modern psychology just over a century ago, the basic interest of Wundt in the mental and emotional states and introspective activities of the individual and the individual's mind continues to characterise the interest of the various schools of psychological study. It is this admittedly narrow though equally predominant aspect of psychology that the term "psychology" implies when it appears throughout this chapter: the thoughts, memories, feelings and emotional experiences of human beings.

In what follows, I shall map out (very briefly) the influence of psychology on various academic disciplines, moving quickly towards an analysis of its influence on Religious and New Testament Studies. From there I shall narrow the focus, looking at studies of conversion, which themselves cover modern, ancient, New Testament, and Pauline conversion. The purpose there shall be to identify the often subtle and implicit psychological assumptions in these works. Throughout this section, my intent is only to illustrate, where possible, the psychological or modern orientation of each work, not to assess the work (as a work on conversion) critically. I shall then lay out in some detail the limitations of applying the modern Western psychological model to texts and characters (ancient and New Testament) that were formed in a cultural environment that is neither modern nor Western. This chapter will close by suggesting an alternative model that is more sensitive and responsive to the cultural milieu of the ancient Mediterranean, and that will be illustrated and applied in subsequent chapters.

1.1 The Early Influence of Psychology

Almost from its inception as an academic discipline, psychology has influenced other fields of study, particularly within, but not limited to, the humanities and social sciences: those fields of study in which people and their social life figure prominently. Psychology had a rapid and profound

---

[3] Fred S. Keller, *The Definition of Psychology* (New York: Appleton-Century-Crofts, 1973), 19.

effect on sociology, anthropology and religious studies.[4] The combination of psychology with religious studies and anthropology appears to have always been appealing, evidenced by the fact that many of the landmark studies in psychology are also landmark studies in anthropology and religious studies—James H. Leuba and E. D. Starbuck, William James, Franz Boas, Bronislaw Malinowski, Émile Durkheim, and later Sigmund Freud and C. G. Jung.[5] The inevitability of cross-fertilisation is suggested by the academic genealogy: Franz Boas, arguably the founder of modern cultural anthropology, as well as such seminal contributors as Émile Durkheim and Bronislaw Malinowski, were each pupils of Wilhelm Wundt; Boas passed on the psychological torch to his students Margaret Mead and Ruth Benedict.[6]

William James pioneered the combination of psychology and the study of religion, and his influence, even through those whose work is even more well known, is still considerable: Sigmund Freud, C. G. Jung, Abraham Maslow, and S. G. F. Brandon.[7] These scholars were psychologists by training

---

[4] J. M. White, "Psychological Anthropology," in *The Social Sciences Encyclopedia* (ed. A. and J. Kuper; London: Routledge, 1996), 687–88; Philip K. Bock, *Rethinking Psychological Anthropology: Continuity and Change in the Study of Human Action* (New York: W. H. Freeman, 1988).

[5] Sigmund Freud, *The Origins of Religion: Totem and Taboo, Moses and Monotheism and Other Works* (ed. and trans. J. Strachey and A. Dickson; Pelican Freud Library 13; London; New York: Penguin, 1990); C. G. Jung, *Psychology and Religion: West and East. Collected works of C. G. Jung vol. 11* (ed. H. Read et al.; trans. R. F. C. Hull; London: Routledge & Kegan Paul, 1958); Bronislaw Malinowski, *Magic, Science and Religion: and Other Essays*. Selected and with an introduction by R. Redfield (Boston: Beacon Press, 1948); idem, *The Foundations of Faith and Morals: An Anthropological Analysis of Primitive Beliefs and Conduct with Special Reference to the Fundamental Problems of Religion and Ethics* (London: H. Milford; Oxford University Press, 1936); James H. Leuba, *The Psychology of Religious Mysticism* (New York: Harcourt Brace, 1925); idem, *The Psychological Origin and the Nature of Religion* (London: Constable, 1921); Émile Durkheim, *The Elementary Forms of the Religious Life* (trans. J. W. Swain; London: G. Allen & Unwin, 1915); Leuba, *A Psychological Study of Religion, its Origin, Function, and Future* (New York: MacMillan, 1912); Franz Boas, *The Mind of Primitive Man* (New York: MacMillan, 1911); William James, *The Varieties of Religious Experience* (New York: Longmans, Green, and Co., 1902); E. D. Starbuck, *The Psychology of Religion* (New York: Charles Scribner's Sons, 1899).

[6] Margaret Mead, *Coming of Age in Samoa: A Psychological Study of Primitive Youth for Western Civilization* (New York: W. Morrow, 1928); idem, *Sex and Temperament in Three Primitive Societies* (New York: William Morrow, 1935); Ruth Benedict, *The Chrysanthemum and the Sword: Patterns of Japanese Culture* (Boston: Houghton Mifflin, 1946).

[7] Abraham H. Maslow, *Religious Values, and Peak-Experiences* (Columbus: Ohio State University Press, 1964); S. G. F. Brandon, *Time and Mankind: An Historical and Philosophical Study of Mankind's Attitude to the Phenomena of Change* (London:

with a side interest, at times hostile, in religion. More illustrative of the influence of psychology on the study of religion, and the New Testament more specifically, are scholars trained in religion but with a side interest, at times hostile and at other times latent, in psychology.

1.1.1 The Influence of Psychology on New Testament Studies

Given the incursion of psychology into other academic fields and especially its influence on our culture and society, it would be surprising to find that New Testament studies had been untouched by the influence of psychology.[8] Because of their status within the early Christian movement, both Jesus and Paul have been the frequent subject of psychological evaluation. Jesus attracts psychological attention because of what is understood as his charismatic personality, his ostensibly having no human father, and probably because of his death as something of a rebel.[9] People likely consider Paul no less

---

Hutchinson, 1951). For a survey of such landmarks in the psychology of religion, see J. W. Heisig, "Psychology of Religion," in *Encyclopedia of Religion* (ed. Mircea Eliade; 17 vols.; New York: MacMillan, 1987), 12:57–66.

[8] In his introduction to D. Andrew Kille's *Psychological Biblical Criticism* (Guides to Biblical Scholarship, ed. Gene M. Tucker; Minneapolis: Fortress Press, 2001), Gene Tucker writes, "Psychological language and presuppositions are deeply embedded in contemporary culture. . . Indeed, one could argue that a leading theme if not the defining concern of modern western culture is the human psyche. . . Psychological interests abound in scholarly circles as well and certainly are not limited to the disciplines of psychology and psychiatry. . . It should not be surprising, therefore, that biblical scholarship should turn to psychological interpretation" (ix). A similar sentiment to that expressed here is found in W. G. Rollins, *Soul and Psyche: The Bible in Psychological Perspective* (Minneapolis: Fortress Press, 1999), 66. It may be fitting at this point to indicate that Psychological Biblical criticism, which these two scholars represent, along with the Society of Biblical Literature group with which they work, is different from the psychological approaches that I am discussing in this chapter (though Tucker's comments do not seem to reflect an understanding of this difference). Psychological Biblical criticism is hermeneutically oriented, and as such is closely related to Reader Response criticism. The psychology which is more problematic and with which I am primarily concerned is exegetically oriented, in that it makes psychological assessments of the texts and characters of the ancient world. Conversely, a hermeneutic approach looks for ways in which text and reader are engaged in psychological ways.

[9] While it would be interesting to look at psychological studies of Jesus, this would take us too far beyond the necessarily more narrow focus on Paul in this chapter. Such a study would include: Peter Malone, *The Same as Christ Jesus: Gospel and Type* (London: St. Paul's, 2000); Hal Childs, *The Myth of the Historical Jesus and the Evolution of Consciousness* (SBLDS 179; Atlanta: Society of Biblical Literature, 2000);

charismatic, but he is additionally attractive psychologically because of his having experienced a conversion of some sort.[10] We also have in his letters the original writings of a person whose personality, it has been maintained, permeates the letters and can be reconstructed from close examination of them. That we can reconstruct elements of Paul's personality based on what he writes in his letters is stated explicitly in one study;[11] for the most part, however, it is simply presupposed. For example, T. Callan reconstructs a psychological personality portrait of Paul based on a survey of Paul's language of competitiveness and boasting, as well as his dim outlook on sexuality, his parents, and death.[12]

Donald Capps, *Jesus: A Psychological Biography* (St. Louis: Chalice Press, 2000); Alan Watson, *Jesus: A Profile* (Athens: University of Georgia Press, 1998); Jack Dominian, *One Like Us: A Psychological Interpretation of Jesus* (London: Darton Longman and Todd, 1998); Heike Bee-Schroedter, *Neutestamentliche Wundergeschichten im Spiegel vergangener und gegenwärtiger Rezeption: Historisch-exegetische und empirisch-entwicklungspsychologische Studien* (SBB 39; Stuttgart: Katholisches Bibelwerk, 1998); John W. Miller, *Jesus at Thirty: A Psychological and Historical Portrait* (Minneapolis: Fortress Press, 1997); Eugen Drewermann, *Jesus von Nazareth: Befreiung zum Frieden* (Zürich: Walter-Verlag, 1996); Hubertus Mynarek, *Jesus und die Frauen: Das Liebesleben des Nazareners* (Frankfurt am Main: Eichborn, 1995); Christoph Kähler, *Jesu Gleichnisse als Poesie und Therapie: Versuch eines integrativen Zugangs zum kommunikativen Aspekt von Gleichnissen Jesu* (WUNT 78; Tübingen: J. C. B. Mohr [Paul Siebeck], 1995); Stevan L. Davies, *Jesus the Healer: Possession, Trance, and the Origins of Christianity* (New York: Continuum, 1995); Eugen Drewermann, *Discovering the God Child Within: A Spiritual Psychology of the Infancy of Jesus* (trans. P. Heinegg; New York: Crossroad, 1994); Margaret G. Alter, *Resurrection Psychology: An Understanding of Human Personality Based on the Life and Teachings of Jesus* (Chicago: Loyola University Press, 1994); Mariann Burke, *Advent and Psychic Birth* (New York: Paulist Press, 1993); Steven A. Galipeau, *Transforming Body and Soul: Therapeutic Wisdom in the Gospel Healing Stories* (Jung and Spirituality; New York: Paulist Press, 1990). In a class apart from these and certainly a step in the right direction in the creation of a social psychological approach to ancient texts, see Andries van Aarde, *Fatherless in Galilee: Jesus as a Child of God* (Harrisburg, Pa.: Trinity Press International, 2001), and "Jesus as a Fatherless Child," in *The Social Setting of Jesus and the Gospels* (ed. W. Stegemann, B. J. Malina, and G. Theissen; Minneapolis: Fortress Press, 2002), 65–84.

[10] On this point, note that several people argue that Jesus too underwent a conversion at the Baptism by John: Miller, *Jesus at Thirty*, 28; Capps, *Jesus*, 134; and Marcus J. Borg, *Conflict, Holiness and Politics in the Teachings of Jesus* (New York: Edwin Mellen Press, 1984), 27.

[11] See, for example, A. Vanhoye, "Personnalité de Paul et exégèse paulinienne," in *L'Apôtre Paul: personnalité, style et conception du ministre* (ed. A. Vanhoye; BETL 72; Leuven: Peeters, 1986), 3–15.

[12] T. Callan, *Psychological Perspectives on the Life of Paul: An Application of the Methodology of Gerd Theissen* (SBEC 22; Lewiston, N. Y.: Edwin Mellen Press, 1990). Cf. Klaus

Attention to Paul's personality, however, figures most prominently in studies about Paul's troubled relationship with the Torah and Torah obligations. Romans 7 is central to scholars who seek to make this argument. For instance, C. H. Dodd focuses on Paul's resentment with his unattractive appearance (from the *Acts of Paul and Thecla*), and on his short temper and penchant for emotional outbursts (Galatians and 2 Corinthians), and derives from these a psychoanalytic assessment of the Paul of Romans 7.[13] Dodd argues that Paul knew instinctively that the law was a yoke, but repressed such feelings. Dodd even suggests that Paul's positive statements concerning the Law (Rom 7:22) evidence nothing more than the degree to which he repressed his anxiety—"As the boy [Paul] matures, the repression is not merely administered from without: it is inwardly accepted."[14] Finally, Dodd associates Paul's repressed emotions (anxiety concerning the Law coupled with his patent desire to excel as a Jew) with his persecution of the earliest Christians.

> Now when a severe conflict exists within the self, one way of relief is to externalize the conflict by identifying that which one detests in oneself with some other person or body of persons... Now Paul found relief in persecuting the Nazarenes.[15]

Berger, *Historische Psychologie des Neuen Testaments* (Stuttgart: Katholisches Bibelwerk, 1991) and Pierre-Marie Beaude, "Psychologie et exégèse paulinienne," in *Paul de Tarse* (ed. J. Schlosser; LD 165; Paris: Éditions du Cerf, 1996, 101–18.

[13] C. H. Dodd, "The Mind of Paul: A Psychological Approach," *BJRL* 17 (1933): 91–105.

[14] Dodd, "Mind of Paul," 98. Michael Reichardt does something similar with Paul's positive statements concerning the Torah, in his case by associating them with different periods of Paul's life. To the dominant position that Phil 3:6 far more represents Paul's view of the Torah than does Romans 7, Reichardt contends that the former reflects "das Bewußtsein des vorchristlichen Paulus" while the latter reflects "den zu dieser Zeit unbewußten Konflikt mit dem jüdischen Gesetz" (M. Reichardt, *Psychologische Erklärung der paulinischen Damaskusvision: Ein Beitrag zum interdisziplinären Gespräch zwischen Exegese und Psychologie seit dem 18. Jahrhundert* [SBB 42; Stuttgart: Katholisches Bibelwerk, 1999], 337).

[15] Dodd, "Mind of Paul," 100. See also George B. Cutton, *The Psychological Phenomena of Christianity* (New York: Charles Scribner's Sons, 1908); Robert L. Moore, "Pauline Theology and the Return of the Repressed: Depth Psychology and Early Christian Thought," *Zygon* 13 (1978): 158–68. S. Tarachow, "St. Paul and Early Christianity," *Psychoanalysis and the Social Sciences* 4 (1955): 223–81, argues that Paul's conversion was brought on by intense guilt over witnessing and doing nothing to stop the murder of Stephen.

Of course, the language of repression and projection belongs firmly to the field of psychoanalysis, and Dodd is certainly not alone among biblical scholars in finding that terminology fruitful.

Dodd's approach to Paul is imitated and extended by two subsequent and important scholars, Gerd Theissen and Jerome Murphy-O'Connor. Like Dodd, Theissen sees in Romans 7 Paul's discomfort with the Torah and with being subject to it.[16] According to Theissen, "The demonstrative pride in the law of Paul the Pharisee was the formation of a reaction to an unconscious conflict with the law, in which the law became a factor eliciting anxiety."[17] Theissen understands the tensions between Philippians 3 and Romans 7 to represent, in the first instance, "the consciousness of the pre-Christian Paul" and in the second, "a conflict that was unconscious at the time . . . of which Paul became conscious only later."[18] Theissen resolves the tension between these two passages based on the benefits of depth psychology, showing that he understands psychological theories, and human emotional experience, to be universal.[19] Theissen does not claim that Paul was exactly the same as a modern person, but accounts for the differences between Paul and modern counterparts by appealing to the evolutionary approach to psychology: Paul and other ancient writers reflect "preliminary stages" of later advanced psychological theories.[20]

The psychological experience of emotional repression figures largely in the recent work of Jerome Murphy-O'Connor, particularly in his assessment of Paul's pre-conversion years in *Paul: A Critical Life*.[21] Murphy-O'Connor depicts Paul as young bright and independent student leaving Tarsus to do

---

[16] According to Theissen (G. Theissen, *Psychological Aspects of Pauline Theology* [trans. John P. Galvin; Edinburgh: T & T Clark, 1987]).

[17] Theissen, *Psychological Aspects*, 242. This same position is represented in, among others, D. M. Davies, "Free From the Law: An Exposition of the Seventh Chapter of Romans," *Interpretation* 7 (1953): 156–62; P. Carrington, *The Early Christian Church* (2 vols.; Cambridge: Cambridge University Press, 1957); and more recently R. L. Rubenstein, *My Brother Paul* (New York: Harper and Row, 1972).

[18] Theissen, *Psychological Aspects*, 235. Such a claim is also made more recently by Michael Reichardt, *Psychologische Erklärung der paulinischen Damaskusvision*.

[19] Theissen presumes a universal psychological and emotional human response when he writes, "It is the paradox *of culture* that the more intensely a person identifies with its requirements, the greater the danger becomes that these requirements will be joined to a destructive energy that can endanger the culture itself" (Theissen, *Psychological Aspects*, 229; emphasis mine).

[20] Theissen, *Psychological Aspects*, 43.

[21] Jerome Murphy-O'Connor, *Paul: A Critical Life* (New York: Oxford University Press, 1996).

graduate work in pharisaic studies in Jerusalem.[22] He insists on the likelihood that Paul was married based on three pieces of evidence. First, that is what typical young Jewish men did, and by Murphy-O'Connor's understanding, Paul was a typical Jewish young man. Second, Murphy-O'Connor appeals to the ambiguous nature of 1 Cor 7:8, namely "Λέγω δὲ τοῖς ἀγάμοις καὶ ταῖς χήραις, καλὸν αὐτοῖς ἐὰν μείνωσιν ὡς κἀγώ." Murphy-O'Connor reads this to say that Paul had a wife, though of course it is famously unclear from this passage whether Paul was unmarried or a widower. And third, Murphy-O'Connor appeals to Paul's persecution of the early Christians. This final point requires some attention, for it is the most problematic of Murphy-O'Connor's three rationales.

Murphy-O'Connor reasons that since other Pharisees disagreed with Christians but did not persecute them as Paul did, some other explanation for Paul's activity must be sought. For Murphy-O'Connor, this "something" had to be traumatic (presumably in order to account for the alleged vehemence of Paul's persecutions). The source of the required trauma for Paul, Murphy-O'Connor suggests, was the death of his wife in Jerusalem. He cites no evidence for when or under what conditions this would have taken place, only that Jerusalem "cannot have been immune to the domestic tragedies" (earthquakes, fires, and buildings collapsing) that occurred elsewhere. According to Murphy-O'Connor, Paul the Pharisee could not have directed his anger at God for his wife's death, and thus had to repress it and eventually redirect it: "If his pain and anger could not be directed against God, it had to find another target."[23] Christians, he contends, were that target.

Of note in Murphy-O'Connor's depiction of Paul is how thoroughly modern and Western Paul sounds. Here is a Paul who left home after high school to pursue graduate studies,[24] who would have felt restricted by the lack of opportunities afforded him in Tarsus, who repressed and channelled emotions, and who felt God was beyond rebuke (despite the fact that at least some expressions of Jewish piety, Amos, Job, and the writers of the Psalms, felt no such sense of restriction). Murphy O-Connor's unselfconscious use of psychoanalysis to work in reverse from Paul's "rage" (which is itself also a psychological assessment that takes some interpretive liberties) against early Christians to an earlier trauma and repressed emotions clearly implies a

---

[22] Murphy-O'Connor, *Paul*, 52.
[23] Murphy-O'Connor, *Paul*, 65.
[24] 'Graduate studies' is not Murphy-O'Connor's term, but it is essentially what he implies.

conviction that Paul was no different from modern people. It shall become clear later what is problematic with such a position.

1.2 Psychology and the Study of Conversion

There are number of works on ancient and New Testament conversion that are widely esteemed treatments of the subject—those of William James, Arthur Darby Nock, Ramsay MacMullen, Beverley Gaventa and Alan Segal. It is upon these works that I shall focus my attention both because of their status in the field, and because of the quality of their work. In other words, they warrant a critical analysis most decidedly not because they are the worst works on conversion but because they are the best, especially, as we shall see, the most recent two.[25] What I seek to do with each author is assess the extent to which she or he has either presupposed a modern and/or a psychological framework in their treatments of ancient and New Testament conversion, or where s(he) has not gone far enough in avoiding to do so.

William James, who opened the twentieth century with his foundational work *The Varieties of Religious Experience* (1902), remains the single strongest influence on our understanding of conversion. His work on conversion was fuelled thoroughly by his study of psychology as well as his own personal experience of psychological illness. For James, conversion refers to that

> process, gradual or sudden, by which a self hitherto divided, and consciously wrong inferior and unhappy becomes united and consciously right superior and happy, in consequence of its firmer hold upon religious realities.[26]

James's definition of conversion is psychological in several ways. At the centre of his definition of conversion lies the problem that conversion seeks to solve: the divided self. A self divided presupposes introspective self-awareness on the part of the convert to discern an inner tension in need of relief, which in turn presupposes an introspective individual. The "divided

---

[25] For a thorough, though dated, bibliography of many different approaches to conversion, including the psychological, see Lewis R. Rambo's bibliographical essay, "Current Research on Religious Conversion," *RSR* 8 (1982): 146–59.

[26] William James, *The Varieties of Religious Experience* (New York: Penguin, 1984), 189.

self" is the singular phrase most commonly associated with William James, and this concept was the foundation of his very image of religion.[27]

The second part of the definition refers to the before-and-after state of the convert that associates conversion with emotional wholeness and well-being. This, as we shall see in Chapter Four is in sharp contrast to the before-and-after state Paul presents in Gal 1:11–17 and Phil 3:4b–11, which will emphasise his relationship with God rather than his emotional wholeness. Rather, it is precisely in the area of the emotions that James would have assessed conversion to happen. The effectiveness of conversion was its ability to cure the divided self or sick soul, and the emotions were the sole measure of that effectiveness.

Indeed, the emotions play a central role throughout his discussion of conversion, including when James comments on the conversion of Paul in the very same psychological language.[28] James relates that he was interested primarily in "striking instantaneous instances" of conversion, of which he considered Paul's example to be "the most eminent, and in which, often amid tremendous *emotional excitement* or *perturbation of the senses*, a complete division is established in the twinkling of an eye between the old life and the new."[29] Two aspects of this definition warrant comment. The first is James's association of emotional crisis with conversion—"tremendous emotional excitement" and "perturbation of the senses"—, an aspect of conversion that James builds on throughout both of his two chapters on conversion.[30]

---

[27] Richard M. Gale, *The Divided Self of William James* (Cambridge: Cambridge University Press, 1999). See also the June 23, 2000 edition of the *Times Literary Supplement*, which gave a cover reference to a review of this book, suggesting that William James is still news-worthy one hundred years after his seminal contributions to academia.

[28] James, *Varieties*, 195–210.

[29] James, *Varieties*, 217, emphasis mine.

[30] James, *Varieties*, 189–258. See also R. O. Ferm, who, for one, enthusiastically took up James's notion of psychological *crisis* being central to the conversion experience (R. O. Ferm, *The Psychology of Christian Conversion* [Old Taplan, N. J.: Revell, 1959]). *Crisis* also remained one of the central features of Lewis Rambo's model of conversion, which combined elements of the sociological (i.e., the role of community) with psychological elements such as this (Lewis R. Rambo, *Understanding Religious Conversion* [New Haven: Yale University Press, 1993]). Finally, Rambo's model has been taken up most recently by Scot McKnight, *Turning to Jesus: The Sociology of Conversion in the Gospels* (Louisville: Westminster John Knox Press, 2002). The primary problem with McKnight's treatment, at least in terms of our present concerns, is that throughout his book he derives his model for understanding conversion in the Gospels through the conversion testimonies of several of his present-day students, raising the problem, which I shall address later in this

Secondly, James's usage of "life" later in the passage might just as well have read "self," for what James means is that conversion results in a complete division between the old self, which is diseased and divided, and the new self, which is whole and right.

A deliberate focus on the self is crucial for James's understanding of religion and of conversion as healing, but that self is only the modern Western individualistic self with which James would have been familiar, for, as we shall see later, other constructions of the self will behave very differently. James builds his study on stories of people's conversion experiences and, tellingly, he includes Paul among them, as if Paul too were simply one of his modern interviewees. The evidence of Paul's diseased and divided self is found, not surprisingly, in Romans 7, which James claims reflects Paul's "self-loathing" and "self-despair." He also claims that in Paul, no differently from his modern examples, the "interior is a battle-ground for what [one] feels to be two deadly hostile selves."[31] William James was a psychologist of religion, which might explain his interest in religious *experience*, not the least appealing of which was conversion, and his tendency for framing that experience in exclusively psychological terms. His approach, his language, and the way he imagines conversion to have "worked" exhibit a psychological cognitive framework from within which he views the experience and effects of conversion.

Arthur Darby Nock was not a psychologist of religion, but rather a scholar of antiquity, and his work on ancient conversion is still an excellent resource.[32] But his work *Conversion* fits very well into the pattern established by James. In his landmark study, Nock distinguishes ancient cults from ancient philosophies. They are differentiated by the fact that religious cults did not teach or preach about lifestyle, life and death, and the nature of the divine, and nor did they require exclusive loyalty. Cults were unlikely to contradict or compete with each other, and hence one tended to participate in several at a time. Says Nock, "The gods of a region were, so to speak, permanent residents who had a natural right to the worship of any human occupants and whom in any event it would be unwise to neglect."[33] This is reflected in Sophocles' *Oedipus at Colonus*. When a citizen of Colonus informs Oedipus, a foreigner, that he is walking on hallowed ground, Oedipus is

---

chapter, concerning the cross-cultural parallels between ancient and modern conversion experiences.

[31] James, *Varieties*, 171.
[32] Arthur D. Nock, *Conversion: The Old and the New in Religion from Alexander the Great to Augustine of Hippo* (London: Oxford University Press, 1933).
[33] Nock, *Conversion*, 6.

well-warned and begs him, "Tell me the awesome (σεμνόν) name I might invoke."[34]

Nock argued that in contrast to the ancient religions, the philosophies were very much concerned with teaching and exhortation, for they required strict behaviour and discipline on matters of diet, sex, money, work, and friendships. The philosophies gave adherents answers to life's questions—the nature of the divine, the origin of life and meaning of death—and they focussed on lifestyle and worldview, while ancient religions were about practical needs and ritualised behaviour. The philosophies, according to Nock, evoked emotions while religious cults were primarily functional and pragmatic with little need for emotion. Nock claims that "A man *used* Mithraism, he did not belong to it body and soul,"[35] and of the religious cults, he claims that "Usually we have simple adhesion involving little emotion."[36] The implication of course is that the philosophies did involve body and soul, and involved emotional commitment, not only adhesion.

Herein lies Nock's debt to the Jamesian psychological tradition: his emphasis on emotion as the central and defining characteristic of conversion. Emotion for Nock is what differentiates between conversion and mere adhesion. Greeks *adhered* to religions and cults, according to Nock, they were not emotionally or psychologically bound to them, and for this reason one cannot talk about, nor does one find, conversion within them. Because the cults did not require loyalty, and thus would not have evoked emotional bonds, conversion is absent from Greek cultic life. On the other hand, the experience of conversion existed, according to Nock, among the philosophies, for that is where he found the sense of a past being rejected for a glorious and new present reality, as well as the frequent attestation of the discomfort and dislocation so typical of modern conversion narratives. For instance, it is hard not to see that Plato's well-known Parable of the Cave describes a conversion in this sense (*Resp.*, book VII).

Nock's definition of conversion echoes James's definition to a remarkable extent. Both definitions revolve around the concept of crisis, and where there is crisis, emotional duress is not far removed. Indeed, the level of emotional

---

[34] Sophocles, *Oed. col.*, line 41. Oedipus is a Theban in exile at Colonus, a town near Athens.

[35] Nock, *Conversion*, 14, emphasis mine. A. Deissmann made a similar observation in describing ancient religion as "a business transaction, *do ut des*, between man and a fetish" (A. Deissmann, *Light from the ancient East* [trans. L. R. M. Strachan; New York: Harper & Brothers, 1927], 161).

[36] Nock, *Conversion*, 36.

tumult is for Nock what distinguishes between conversion and other less authentic religious experiences, and in this conversion is necessarily painful and unsettling, and, thereby, an obviously psychological experience. Nock's definition also presupposes a convert with Western individuality. Conversion is "the reorientation of the soul of an individual, the deliberate turning from indifference or from an earlier form of piety to another, a turning that implies a consciousness that a great change is involved, that the old was wrong and the new is right."[37]

Conversion here is a personal choice made by a bounded individual who is being governed solely by his or her own psychological needs. This, as we shall see below, is an image of the self that is limited to the modern Western world. Nock never claimed either to reject or to accept the psychological approach to conversion. I believe he was writing before such a concern would have been expressed. Nonetheless, it is revealing that although he does not explicitly invoke a psychological framework he implicitly relies on one to define his subject. His approach to, understanding, and definition of conversion are psychological.

When it comes to conversion *per se*, Ramsay MacMullen's *Christianizing the Roman Empire* is difficult to assess, for it is not really about conversion, but rather about the growth of the movement through conversion.[38] His focus is the growth of Christianity, which he accounts for in several ways: the attraction of converts through the impressive performance of miracles, the inspiring example of martyrs, and, eventually, monetary rewards (tax breaks, employment and promotion opportunities) and coercion. MacMullen does say of his study that "The process we are tracing, of the slow but gigantic growth of a community of believers, seems thus to have had at its heart a psychological moment. . . ."[39] So, it is the growth of the movement that he seeks to understand, but he acknowledges that at the root of it all stands the initial psychological moment that was conversion into the early Christian movement.

At first glance, MacMullen and Nock appear to represent different ways of understanding conversion. MacMullen argues that Nock's understanding of conversion is built upon "the fundamental assumption that religious belief does not deserve the name unless it is intense and consuming."[40] In contrast to this, MacMullen seeks to include as examples of authentic conversion

---

[37] Nock, *Conversion*, 7.
[38] Ramsay MacMullen, *Christianizing the Roman Empire: A.D. 100–400* (New Haven: Yale University Press, 1984).
[39] MacMullen, *Christianizing*, 3–4.
[40] MacMullen, *Christianizing*, 4.

many experiences that Nock considers mere adherence, such as conversion via monetary rewards, family pressure, and martial or social coercion. By calling attention to Nock's exclusive emphasis of the "intense and consuming" experience, MacMullen appears to imply that Nock's understanding of conversion is too psychologically limited. It is true that Nock focuses on experiences situated at the high end of a psychological or emotional scale (those involving high emotional turbulence). But could one argue that MacMullen rejects altogether the psychological scale that Nock uses?

MacMullen does not reject Nock's psychological scale, only his parameters. MacMullen expands Nock's psychological scale to incorporate a broader range of experiences, but he appears to accept implicitly the psychological scale as a tool for measuring conversion experiences. In fact, by arguing as he does that conversion must also include a "broad range of psychological phenomena," MacMullen implies a reliance upon and endorsement of that same scale.[41] This is echoed also in another instance, in which MacMullen suggests that whether conversion "was warmly or little *felt*," and whether it was a profound or surface experience, depends on the instance and cannot be a limiting factor in defining conversion.[42] So for example, he compares several instances of conversion that appear to differ from each other by the intensity of the emotional commitment that follows—conversion by the laying on of hands with no attending instruction[43] and the post-conversion declaration of the apocryphal Acts of John in which loyalty is proclaimed loudly and passionately.[44] In each of these instances, the reader can be forgiven for feeling that the psychological and emotional scale remains present and useful. The difference between Nock and MacMullen lies in how that scale is calibrated, not in what it measures. The scale by which MacMullen measures the extremes of conversion is still a psychological scale, though it is less obvious than in Nock's case because the additional experiences that MacMullen includes as conversion sit lower on the psychological and emotional scale.

---

[41] MacMullen, *Christianizing*, 5.
[42] MacMullen, *Christianizing*, 5; emphasis added.
[43] See MacMullen, *Christianizing*, 123 n. 6.
[44] *Acts of John* 41–42. See MacMullen, *Christianizing*, 3 and 123 n. 8.

1.2.1 Movements Away from Psychological Approaches to Conversion

Psychological studies of New Testament conversion abounded in the 20th century, though in truth none of these were tremendously influential.[45] Nonetheless, they did reflect a cultural environment very comfortable with psychology. Equally, however, there was a growing awareness that psychological assessments of ancient texts and characters were problematic, and two studies of conversion should be acknowledged for expressing these first objections. Beverley Gaventa and Alan Segal both explicitly disapprove of the limitations of looking at New Testament or Pauline conversion from a modern and psychological perspective.[46] And both scholars take important steps towards understanding conversion outside of the psychological paradigm. Gaventa argues that modern notions of conversion tend to assume a single type of conversion. Gaventa's work is important for her challenge of the notion that conversion can be understood as a single type of event. Indeed, she finds in the New Testament three different types of conversion. The first type of conversion involves a change that results in a pendulum-like swing from one extreme to another, and that involves the wholesale rejection of the convert's past. Pendulum-like conversions are found in Luke's portrayal of Paul (Acts 9, 22, 26), especially in his change from violent persecutor to passionate supporter. The terminology for the second type of conversion she borrows

---

[45] Rambo, *Understanding Religious Conversion*; Warren S. Brown and Carla Caetano, "Conversion, Cognition, and Neuropsychology," in *Handbook of Religious Conversion* (ed. H. N. Malony and S. Southard; Birmingham: Religious Education Press, 1992), 147–58; Serge Moscovici and Gabriel Mugny, *Psychologie de la conversion: Études sur l'influence inconsciente* (Fribourg: Delval, 1987); C. B. Johnson and H. N. Malony, *Christian Conversion: Biblical and Psychological Perspectives* (Rosemead Psychology Series; Grand Rapids: Zondervan, 1982); J. G. Gager, "Some Notes on Paul's Conversion," *NTS* 27 (1980–81): 697–704; Walter E. Conn, ed., *Conversion: Perspectives on Personal and Social Transformation* (New York: Alba House, 1978); Raymond F. Paloutzian, S. L. Jackson, and J. E. Crandall, "Conversion Experience, Belief System, and Personal and Ethical Attitudes," *Journal of Psychology and Theology* 5 (1977): 103–109; R. L. Rubenstein, *My Brother Paul* (New York: Harper and Row, 1972); J. L. Cheek, "Paul's Mysticism in the Light of Psychedelic Experience," *JAAR* 38 (1970): 381–89; Ferm, *The Psychology of Christian Conversion*; W. S. Reid, "Psychology of Conversion," *EQ* 28 (1956): 33–42; Tarachow, "St. Paul and Early Christianity"; G. J. Inglis, "The Problem of St. Paul's Conversion," *ExpTim* 40 (1928–1929): 227–81; George B. Cutton, *The Psychological Phenomena of Christianity* (New York: Charles Scribner's Sons, 1908).

[46] Beverly R. Gaventa, *From Darkness to Light: Aspects of Conversion in the New Testament* (Philadelphia: Fortress Press, 1986), 8. See also Alan F. Segal, *Paul the Convert: The Apostolate and Apostasy of Saul the Pharisee* (New Haven: Yale University Press, 1990), 285–300.

from sociologist of religion R. V. Travisano[47], who named it "alternation." This is a change in religious affiliation that is more intellectual than emotional; it is a change made because of external pressures (though not necessarily coercive pressures). Alternation is represented in the New Testament by the Ethiopian eunuch in Acts 8 and by Cornelius in Acts 10. Finally, Gaventa labels the third type of conversion "transformation," which she defines with reference to Thomas Kuhn's well-known formulation of the paradigm shift. This may well involve a radical change, but the convert's past is not rejected, but rather reinterpreted. According to Gaventa, Paul represents this third type of convert. The letters of Paul, Gaventa argues, present a person who has *reinterpreted* his past and certainly not rejected it, and thus can be called transformed.

Alan Segal's *Paul the Convert* was and remains a critical contribution to our understanding of Paul's conversion. Segal pointedly replaces the psychological approach to conversion with a sociological approach. Segal's sociology of conversion stresses the importance of the convert's socialisation into a new community of faith and the role that the new community plays in the convert's construction of her or his past and conversion experience. Hence, Segal looks at the effects Paul's move from one community of faith to another had on his understanding of his conversion experience and his theology. Paul drew the meaning and content of his conversion from the Merkabah mystical community into which he moved, one which understood conversion as having to do with transformation. Segal assumes that the sociology of conversion touches on aspects of conversion that are universal, even while allowing for the fact that each culture defines by itself what conversion entails.

It is unfair in many ways to fault a scholar for what she or he has not done. In the case of Gaventa's and Segal's attempts to divorce the study of conversion from its dominating psychological assumptions, however, it is precisely in what they have not done that cracks appear in their impressive works. Given the pervasive psychological assumptions that shape the western mind, I would like to suggest that it is not enough to look at conversion in another way. One needs to look closely at *why* the psychological approach to understanding ancient conversion is inappropriate and potentially misleading. Gaventa and Segal do reject the psychological approach to conversion, but there are hints in their treatments that they do so for the wrong reasons. Clarity on this matter can only help.

---

[47] R. V. Travisano, "Alternation and Conversion as Qualitatively Different Transformations," in *Social Psychology Through Symbolic Interaction* (ed. G. P. Stone and H. A. Farberman; Waltham, Mass.: Ginn-Blaisdell, 1970), 594–606.

Gaventa claims that "we cannot seek a psychological explanation for Paul's conversion" because the texts "are concerned only with Paul's apostolic task."[48] Along similar lines, Segal says that "it is inappropriate to psychoanalyse a man who gives us little evidence of his psychological development."[49] Both, in fact, are correct, but they imply that it is simply a matter of sources that makes psychoanalysis of Paul inappropriate. They point out that Paul says very little about what led to his conversion, and he appears to have had quite a "robust conscience" as a believing and practising Jew.[50] As a result, there is not enough psychological data in what Paul says to allow any sort of psychological analysis. Gaventa and Segal appear to be saying that psychological analysis might have been possible had Paul been more self-revealing. As we shall see shortly, however, there are strong reasons why psychological analysis of Paul is questionable, but it has little to do with his apparent vagueness concerning his psychological experience.

Further, both studies also need to be more careful about their use of terminology, and here again because of the psychological paradigm from within which most of their readers will digest their work. There is language in both studies that will strike a psychologically informed reader as perfectly self-evident, which only serves then to undermine the stated goals of both authors to not support a psychological reading of Paul or of ancient conversion. A few examples stand out. Segal claims that the Hellenistic world was individualistic,[51] even stressing the "importance of individualism in the first century."[52] Also, Segal characterises Paul as a religious quester, describing Paul as undertaking a "personal religious quest"[53] and Josephus as a "religious quester."[54] The religious quester acts as an individual, driven only by his or her individual and spiritual needs and searches for religious fulfilment—a description quite in keeping with Segal's characterisation of Josephus from his *Vita* 7–12.

The problem is that Segal works with a sense of individualism that is more nuanced than the typical western reader will appreciate. Segal is certainly correct in pointing out that the Graeco-Roman world at this point was

---

[48] Gaventa, *From Darkness*, 20.
[49] Segal, *Paul the Convert*, 5.
[50] This, of course, is Stendahl's classic phrase, with which Segal fully agrees (Krister Stendahl, "Paul and the Introspective Conscience of the West," HTR 56 [1963]: 199–215).
[51] Segal, *Paul the Convert*, 32.
[52] Segal, *Paul the Convert*, 33.
[53] Segal, *Paul the Convert*, xi. So too Philo and Josephus: Segal, *Paul the Convert*, 32.
[54] Segal, *Paul the Convert*, 82.

opening up to individual freedom of choice when it came to religious and philosophical affiliation. Becoming a Cynic, after all, involved rejecting socialised conduct and acting often against the wishes of family (e.g., individually).[55] Yet, Segal would also agree that this did not make them individualistic in the sense that modern western readers of his book are individualistic. Hence, one needs to describe one's categories more carefully lest the western reader assume parallelisms that do not exist in reality or in the writer's mind.

The same holds true for Segal's most problematic claim that Paul was a "convert in the modern sense of the word."[56] Segal means this claim to be understood within the sociological model he is working with. He relies on modern sociological studies of conversion and community formation. But since conversion "in the modern sense of the word" is, as we have seen, precisely psychological and not sociological, the phrase practically invites the reader to misunderstand Segal, and to assume that a psychological model is either being assumed or upheld.

Gaventa and Segal made important advances in moving scholarship away from the psychological understanding of ancient conversion, and they did so in part by offering alternatives. I hope I can contribute to the process they started by doing the only thing they did not: looking closely at precisely why the psychological approach to ancient conversion needs to be avoided. I will also provide an alternative model that allows us to get at the ancient experience of conversion, which should ease the process of ridding scholarship of psychologising assumptions.

1.3 A Critique of the Cross-Cultural Psychological Model

The use of the (modern and Western) psychological framework for understanding New Testament texts, characters, and conversion, has a parallel to a practice equally common in other fields. It is called cross-cultural psychology. It is not merely a question of methodological trends that we should avoid importing psychological presuppositions into our study of ancient conversion. There are crippling problems with cross-cultural psychology, at least as it

---

[55] Joseph M. Bryant, *Moral Codes and Social Structure in Ancient Greece: A Sociology of Greek Ethics from Homer to the Epicureans and Stoics* (New York: State University of New York Press, 1996) illustrates that after the decline of the polis Hellenistic culture was increasingly individualistic.

[56] Segal, *Paul the Convert*, 6.

tends to be practised by scholars of religion. As an intellectual approach, cross-cultural psychology is the practice of taking what we have learned from the field of psychology (general psychology[57]) and applying it to people in other cultures. Cross-cultural psychologists seek to illuminate the experiences and analyse the behaviour/customs of others, from non-western urban elites in Japan to non-western rural elites in Morocco, and further afield to non-western hunter and gatherer tribes in Africa or on Pacific islands, using models and analogies derived from the practice of Western psychology.

Clearly, in order to implement such a study one must assume certain things about peoples in different cultures, namely that they share something fundamental that makes such comparison both possible and meaningful. For cross-cultural psychologists, people can be distinguished by cultural and local differences, such as language, dress, and customs, but stripped of such surface differences, people are essentially the same.[58] It is hard, usually on an emotional level, not to feel the allure of this notion. With racism and homophobia in many societies continuing to inhibit people from accepting what is foreign or different, it is hard not to be touched by the argument that our differences are only skin deep. But an acceptance of others that seeks to homogenise all forms of difference (global, cultural, sexual) creates as many problems as it seeks to solve. The fact is, for all that unites us as human beings, cultural difference effects more than interesting and humorous travel anecdotes about odd cuisine and social *faux pas*. We will be better served, socially and academically, not to seek to eradicate all difference, but to embrace and understand what these differences entail.

The belief that 'below surface differences people are the same wherever you go' has not actually been (and perhaps cannot be) proven. It is rather an activating presupposition of cross-cultural psychology, and, more importantly, one that has been increasingly challenged by cultural psychologists and anthropologists. It has been called 'the presupposition of psychic unity',[59] that is, that Western and non-western peoples (a categorisation that works as well for modern and ancient peoples) are united by a similar psychological "hardware" that enables them to think in similar ways, to act in similar ways and for similar reasons, and to experience emotion similarly. Cross-cultural

---

[57] General psychology is simply modern Western psychology developed and practised in a modern Western setting on modern Western clients.

[58] See, for example, M. H. Segall et al., *Human Behavior in Global Perspective* (New York: Pergamon Press, 1990), 53.

[59] Richard A. Shweder, *Thinking Through Cultures: Expeditions in Cultural Psychology* (Cambridge, Mass.: Harvard University Press, 1991), 73.

psychology shares with general psychology the belief that beneath personal or cultural differences there lies within people a "central (abstract and transcendent = deep or interior or hidden) processing mechanism inherent (fixed and universal) in human beings, which enables them to think (classify, infer, remember, imagine), act (strive, prefer, choose, evaluate), and learn" in identical ways.[60] Belief in the existence of universal psychological experience can be strongly challenged based on work done in two areas: the cultural construction of the self, and the culturally conditioned experience of emotion. These observations are culled from recent important work in an emerging field known as cultural psychology—the name implying that other's cultures have psychologies, but that cultures do not share psychologies in any extensive sense, and that at any rate, psychological difference needs to be recognised fully before similarities can be meaningful.

Before I embark on a critique of cross-cultural psychology, it may be helpful to make a clarification concerning the claims of differentiation that follow. What is wrong with cross-cultural psychology are its assumptions about psychic unity, and the two sections that follow will illustrate some ways in which this assumption is not valid. In the process I shall be working in broad generalisations concerning human behaviour and personality structure in an attempt to show that ancient and modern people are not the same. I cannot emphasise strongly enough that this is not a claim that ancient and modern people or Western and non-Western people share nothing in common psychologically. I will argue that modern/western people are individualistic, monadic and bounded, while ancient and many non-Western people are collectivistic, dyadic and unbounded. These are heuristic categories, not absolute descriptions, and we are thus not helped by searching for examples that contradict the pattern since we are working with general tendencies.

The general pattern of antiquity concerning personality and the self is different from the general pattern of modernity. Though similarities undoubtedly exist, it is important to understand as thoroughly as possible what a difference the differences make, for this will allow one to appreciate better what is similar. It is perhaps useful to imagine the model I am constructing as a linear model, at the ends of which sit the completely individualistic and the completely collectivistic person respectively. Modern and ancient cultures are situated somewhere between these two extremes; the ancient tends towards one extreme and the modern towards the other, but these are relative categories not absolute ones, and not binary opposites. It is not that ancient

---

[60] Shweder, *Thinking Through Cultures*, 77.

people were incapable of making self-centred decisions, nor that modern people never care what others think of them. We have a general pattern of self-construction, however, that differs markedly in degree from that of antiquity, and this has to be the starting point for understanding the other.

1.3.1 The Self as Culturally Constructed

What we know about people and their psychological features is the result of the study of individuals from a single (and thus very narrowly conceived) cultural and geographical area, namely the modern industrial West. There is nothing cross-cultural (or pan-cultural) about how psychological discoveries have been made, which is not a problem for general psychology practised on Western individualistic people, but should immediately strike one as problematic for the application of psychology across cultures. Western psychology is built entirely upon the study of a single notion of the self that is not only not shared across cultures, but that is quite unique among global cultures. Typically, yet so often unwittingly, Westerners assume a single human model of the self. There has developed in the industrialised West a sense of the self that is distinct from the past Western understandings of the self as well as distinct from that of contemporary non-Western cultures. What we are talking about is not the *creation* of the self in the modern (or early modern) era, as if there were before that no sense at all of the self. Indeed, all cultures have (had) some sense of the self, and all languages have a way of expressing and distinguishing 'self' from 'other,' if in no other way at least bodily.[61] Yet not all cultures conceive of the self in the same way, and these differences have profound implications for how we understand the behaviour of non-Westerners, as well as for the applicability and helpfulness of psychology to understanding their experiences and their behaviour.

That there are significant (and not simply curious) differences in the way different cultures construct reality and self-understanding is the lasting contribution of Kluckhohn's and Strodtbeck's Values Orientation Model (VOM).[62] What their model establishes is that while all cultures share similar

---

[61] Gerald M. Erchak, *The Anthropology of Self and Behaviour* (New Brunswick, N. J.: Rutgers University Press, 1992); Brian Morris, *Anthropology of the Self: The Individual in Cultural Perspective* (Boulder, Colo.: Pluto Press, 1994).

[62] Florence Rockwood Kluckhohn and Fred L. Strodtbeck, *Variations in Value Orientations* (Evanston, Ill.: Row, Peterson and Company, 1961). Useful and reliable summaries of the model can be found at http://www.collegeofbusiness.fau.edu/peterson/Culture%20Dimension%20Toolbook%20R2.htm (June 10, 2004); and

values (or as we are about to see, sometimes 'value pairs'), nonetheless they arrange their orientations differently. By "orientation" Kluckhohn and Strodtbeck were referring to five basic questions or relationships, the orientation of each person to something else—the question of human nature (evil, neutral/mixed, good), the relationship of the person to nature (subject to, in harmony with, and mastery over), the question of temporal focus (past, present, future), the modality of human activity (being, being in becoming, doing), and finally, and most significantly, the person's relationship to other people (linearity, collaterality, individualism). In effect, the first of each of these value orientations together describes, for all intents and purposes, the biblical world and ancient Mediterranean, while the third of these value orientations together describe the culture of North America and Europe.[63]

Kluckhohn's and Strodtbeck's observation concerning the relational value orientation (linearity, collaterality, individualism) was developed into the Individualism-Collectivism construct by more recent cultural anthropologists, and it is this construct that has proven to be the most enduring in anthropology because of its ability to answer the most questions concerning cultural differences in behaviour, even while recognising that it works with such broad generalities.[64] Because the construct of Individualism-Collectivism refers to the culture as a whole, in keeping with Kluckhohn's and Strodtbeck's attempt to delineate culture blocks, Triandis and company coined the very fruitful terms *idiocentric* and *allocentric* to describe the people who, respectively,

---

T. Gallagher, "The Value Orientations Method: A Tool to Help Understand Cultural Differences", *Journal of Extension* 39 (2001), online at http://www.joe.org/joe/2001december/tt1.html (June 10, 2004).

[63] For useful applications of the Values Orientation Model to the New Testament, see J. J. Pilch, "Marian Devotion and Wellness Spirituality," *BTB* 20 (1990): 85–94; idem, *Introducing the Cultural Context of the New Testament* (Hear the Word, vol. 2; New York: Paulist Press, 1991); Bruce J. Malina and Jerome H. Neyrey, *Portraits of Paul: An Archaeology of Ancient Personality* (Louisville: Westminster John Knox Press, 1996); Jerome H. Neyrey, "Prayer, in Other Words: New Testament Prayer in Social Scientific Perspective," in *Social Scientific Models for Interpreting the Bible: Essays by the Context Group in Honor of Bruce J. Malina* (ed. J. J. Pilch; Biblical Interpretation Series 53; Leiden: E. J. Brill, 2001), 349–80.

[64] For example, by Geert Hofstede, *Culture's Consequences*. See also Harry C. Triandis, "Individualism and Collectivism," in *The Handbook of Culture and Psychology* (ed. D. Matsumoto; Oxford: Oxford University Press, 2001), 35–50.

inhabit individualist and collectivist cultures.[65] Even allowing for differences within collectivist and individualistic cultures[66] and for a linear gradation to the differences between them, there emerges from study of these categories some basic and real differences between what amounts to Western and non-western cultures. That is, Western and non-Western cultures engender different, and hardly compatible, senses of the self.[67] Although we are dealing with generalities here of the sort anyone should be suspicious of, it is striking that the differences described below have been replicated in myriad independent and differently constructed studies.

The individualistic and collectivist construct is built upon four relational issues: "the definition of the self as independent (in individualism) or interdependent (in collectivism), the primacy of personal or in-group goals, the primary emphasis on attitudes or norms as the determinants of social behaviour, and the importance of exchange or communal relationships."[68] Of course, there are different ways of expressing each of these. Marcel Mauss, for instance, contrasts "personhood" with "selfhood."[69] With the term "personhood," Mauss refers to ancient and non-Western cultures and the way people live in them collectively. In contrast to "personhood," Mauss believes that "selfhood" is a relatively new and limited (in terms of geographical proliferation) development. That is, the Western notion of the individualistic self set apart from its social context, as free and autonomous, is limited to the West in terms of modern global cultures, but also in temporal terms, dividing the modern West also from many of the cultures of the past.

---

[65] Harry C. Triandis, K. Leung, M. Villareal, and F. L. Clack, "Allocentric versus idiocentric tendencies: Convergent and discriminant validation," *Journal of Research in Personality* 19 (1985): 395–415.

[66] Triandis came to further divide individualist and collectivist cultures into vertical and horizontal dimensions. Based on the categories he uses, the ancient Mediterranean would be vertical collectivistic, combining the verticality of the patronage and clientage/honour and shame systems with the allocentric identities of ancient personalities. See Harry C. Triandis, *Individualism and Collectivism* (Boulder, Colo.: Westview Press, 1995).

[67] Christine Griffin, "More Than Simply Talk and Text: Psychologists as Cultural Ethnographers," in *Culture in Psychology* (ed. C. Squire; London: Routledge, 2000), 19.

[68] Triandis, "Individualism and Collectivism," 36.

[69] Marcel Mauss, "A Category of the Human Mind: The Notion of Personhood; the Notion of the Self," in *The Category of the Person: Anthropology, Philosophy, History* (ed. M. Carrithers, S. Collins and S. Lukes; Cambridge: Cambridge University Press, 1985), 1–25. See also Harry C. Triandis, "The Self and Social Behavior in Differing Cultural Contexts," *Psychological Review* 98 (1989): 506–20.

Clifford Geertz has worked among the Javanese, Balinese, and Moroccans, three cultures that are distinct from each other and yet are part of a larger shared cultural pattern that distinguishes them markedly from the West. Geertz observes that

> the Western conception of the person as a bounded, unique, more or less integrated motivational and cognitive universe, a dynamic center of awareness, emotion, judgement, and action organized into a distinctive whole and set contrastively both against other such wholes and against a social and natural background is, however incorrigible it might seem to us, a rather peculiar idea within the context of the world's cultures.[70]

What goes for differences among modern cultures also goes for differences between ancient and modern cultures. In other words, we should never assume a continuity of self-understanding between ourselves as modern Western biblical readers and the biblical characters we study. We should assume, no less, that differences in how the self is constructed will affect how the self interacts with others, how the self experiences the world, and how the self understands its own interactions with that world (and the world beyond).

The difference between allocentric and idiocentric selves is of more than just abstract interest. It does not merely have to do with how people see themselves, and to whom they see themselves tied. Hofstede shows that

> "The relationship between the individual and the collectivity in human society is not only a matter of ways of living together, it is intimately linked with societal norms.... It therefore affects both people's mental programming and the structure and functioning of many institutions aside from the family: educational, religious, political, and utilitarian."[71]

How one understands the self shapes how people understand each other. Shweder and Bourne show that allocentric people think of other people not

---

[70] C. Geertz, "On the Nature of Anthropological Understanding," *American Scientist* 63 (1975) 48. Interestingly, Price connects the presupposition of individualism among modern scholarship on antiquity with a tendency towards Christianising assumptions, but we should assume that what he means is Western Christian assumptions (S. R. F. Price, *Rituals and Power: The Roman Imperial Cult in Asia Minor* [Cambridge: Cambridge University Press, 1984], 11–15).

[71] Hofstede, *Culture's Consequences*, 210.

in relation to what is unique about them as individuals (she is aggressive and hostile; he is friendly) but in relation to a concrete social context (he swears at his grandfather; she brings cakes to my family).[72] Allocentric (non-western) peoples see themselves as part of a collective, not as bounded individuals (that is, individuals tied to no one but themselves). This does not mean that allocentric people are incapable of discerning between their own person and others. It means they tend not to be motivated by individually centred (that is egocentric or idiocentric) expectations. Their own value as people is directly related to their contribution to the functional society, and to the execution of their duties.

Behaviour in non-western cultures tends to be conditioned by social and cultural relationships, and less so internally or sub-consciously. Rather than using the terms "personhood" and "selfhood," Shweder and Bourne refer to sociocentric and egocentric behaviour. The sociocentric person is unbounded; she is tied in time as well as place and in a particular set of social relationships and not to herself. Conversely, the egocentric person is "bounded"; she is an individual, an autonomous self, a closed unit relying on no other to define her identity.

That Western and non-western selves differ in how they are conceived is important for two reasons. First, assumptions about individual experience and motivation that presuppose a Western construction of the self as universal, say that all people are motivated by personal desire to get ahead in the world, or that people feel limited by the career opportunities supplied them by their village, are potentially misleading. Any assessments about how other people experience life need to take into account their relationship to their society. Hofstede, summarising a number of other studies, concluded that "our cognition, emotion, and motivation all differ depending on whether our culture had provided us with an independent or an interdependent 'self-construal'."[73] Secondly, the application of observations made on one culturally constructed self (general psychology) to another different construction of the self (cross-cultural psychology) is potentially misleading. That psychological observations are universally applicable cannot be taken for granted. This is true also with respect to emotion.

---

[72] With the exception of the gender balanced language, these phrases reflect what respondents, Western and non-Western respectively, told Shweder and Bourne when asked to describe people they knew. See Richard A. Shweder and Edmund J. Bourne, "Does the Concept of the Person Vary Cross-Culturally?" in Shweder, *Thinking Through Cultures*, 113–55.

[73] Hofstede, *Culture's Consequences*, 210.

1.3.2 Emotion and Culture

The assumption that other people are just like us or more specifically that they think like we do is often found in close proximity to the sentiment that other people *feel* like we do, that is that the experiences of emotions are universal. Of course, it would be futile and misguided to argue that some emotions, say grief and anger, are not in some way universal. What is required, however, is not the generalisation that other people do not feel emotions like grief and anger, but rather the more subtle observation that just because they do feel such emotions does not mean they experience them in the same way or for the same reasons, nor that they understand their source or deal with them in similar ways to us.[74] In short, even to say that some emotions must be in some way universal requires so much qualification as to be almost a meaningless observation.

Such an assumption is made by Meyer Fortes, for example, whose classic study of West African (Talensi) religion followed the tradition of Frazer's *The Golden Bough* in finding the ancient myths of Oedipus and Job in other cultures.[75] The myth of Oedipus represents the notion of a fate that no one can avoid, and the myth of Job represents the notion of divine justice that people must operate within, but cannot (nor, dare not) transcend. Yet, Fortes contends that simply finding parallels, as interesting as it might be, is not sufficient. One must seek to understand them, and in order to understand them "we must take into account the common intellectual and emotional dispositions of mankind."[76] For the most part, what Fortes undertakes is social psychology, which is to say he seeks to understand the behaviour and beliefs of the individual in relation to the society in which the individual is

---

[74] For a survey of landmark studies illustrating both the universality of emotion and on some of the cultural differences, especially concerning the effects of individualism–collectivism (IC) on emotional recognition and expression, see Nathan Yrizarry, David Matsumoto, Chikako Imai, Kristie Kooken, and Sachiko Takeuchi, "Culture and Emotion," in *Cross-Cultural Topics in Psychology* (ed. L. L. Adler and U. P. Gielen; Westport, Conn.: Praeger, 2001), 131–47. The limitation of this article is that it mostly discusses the universality of emotion through facial recognition, and thus cultural difference is seen only in some patterns of recognition. The study does not touch on the cultural specificity of emotions themselves, but it alludes to it in several places. Nonetheless, the fact that in the vast majority of instances, emotional expressions are universal certainly suggests that the experience of emotion is shared across cultures.

[75] Meyer Fortes, *Oedipus and Job in West African religion* (Cambridge: Cambridge University Press, 1959).

[76] Fortes, *Oedipus and Job*, 2.

embedded. Fortes's social psychology emphasises that Talensi society is exclusively structured on the institution of kinship, and that all other things, especially religion and personal identity, operate within it. Also very interesting is Fortes's attempt to understand how Talensi religion functions to regulate Talensi lives, and he rightly states, "we must see religious ideas and rites in the context of the situation, the context of personal history and the context of social relationships."[77]

While Fortes is generally very successful at relating his explanations to the sociocentric society he is studying, too often he lapses into explanations that presuppose psychological and emotional universality between the Talensi and himself (a Westerner). For instance, the Talensi have taboos that inhibit contact between the patriarch and his adult eldest son (the next in line to take over), for they recognise that the fates of the father and the eldest son are at odds with one another. Fortes interprets this through Western eyes when he suggests that the relationship between father and adult eldest son "gives rise to suppressed hostility and opposition"[78] and "latent opposition"[79] because the son yearns for independence and autonomy. Fortes argues that the "hostility that this might generate is drained away in the ritual avoidances binding on an eldest son."[80] It is an emic characterisation to claim that the father's and son's destinies are enemies, which is one thing; but it is ethnocentric to suggest that these have to do with a latent desire for independence, especially in collectivistic cultures. In the end, Fortes's functionalism is not only social, but also emotional, serving to assuage the destructive emotions that life among the Talensi generates. The problem with stressing the emotional state of the Talensi is not necessarily that Fortes is wrong (that would be exceedingly difficult to assess), but that he *assumes* the emotions of the Talensi operate and are understood by them as they are by us. At the very least, he needs to indicate how we know this to be the case, and should not assume that cross-cultural continuity exists just because the Talensi experience emotions and appear to have ways of dealing with them. Put another way, Fortes's assessment rings true for a Western father and son, but we need to stop and wonder whether individual autonomy and the suppression of emotional hostility in the absence of such autonomy makes sense in a non-Western setting. I am not, I should be clear, claiming that they are not, but rather warning against the *assumption* that there is parallelism in the area of human emotion.

---

[77] Fortes, *Oedipus and Job*, 10.
[78] Fortes, *Oedipus and Job*, 11.
[79] Fortes, *Oedipus and Job*, 12.
[80] Fortes, *Oedipus and Job*, 13, see also page 22.

Anger as an emotion might appear to be universal, but it would be a mistake to assume that it is perfectly parallel cross-culturally. Michelle Rosaldo has argued in fact that "anger" is not a universal emotion at all, in that it is not understood, caused, or experienced in the same way across cultures. How emotion is experienced, what it means and how it is understood is culturally derived.[81] For example, Rosaldo witnessed a drunken brawl between two Ilongot brothers. She suggests that Western psychological culture would have understood this as the surfacing of repressed anger. What is more, the next day, there were no traces of hostility between the two brothers. According to the Ilongot, the fight was not the result of bottled emotions finding expression, but rather solely the result of the consumption of alcohol. It was perfectly natural, then, that the following day, in the absence of the alcohol, there would be no hostility, whereas from a Western perspective, this would likely serve as warning signs to the further dangerous repression of emotions. It would be ethnocentric to argue, Rosaldo claims, that the brothers simply went back to repressing their emotions. Rosaldo admits to the attractiveness of psychoanalysing this scenario quite easily, but goes on to say, "what is difficult to understand, as long as Ilongot 'anger' is construed within our analytic frame, is how and why the Ilongots concerned could be content with what to me appeared the sort of outcome that could only lead to renewed conflict."[82] The Ilongot are capable of "forgetting" their anger in a way Westerners would consider unhealthy, but that in Ilongot culture "works."

A second illuminating example comes from the work Rabia Malik has done on depression among Pakistanis.[83] According to Malik, the relationship between culture and psychological experiences has been underplayed, and this results in misunderstanding depression in different cultures. In the typical model of cross-cultural psychology, "culture is the 'thin' layer concealing the 'thick' biological and psychological unity of human kind."[84] Malik points out that emotions are not understood in similar ways cross-culturally; the West understands them as completely internal and psychological phenomena, whereas many non-Western cultures see emotions or emotional states as external and

---

[81] Michelle Z. Rosaldo, "Toward an Anthropology of Self and Feeling," in *Culture Theory: Essays on Mind, Self and Emotion* (ed. R. A. Shweder and R. A. LeVine; Cambridge: Cambridge University Press, 1984), 137–57.
[82] Rosaldo, "Toward an Anthropology of Self and Feeling," 144.
[83] Rabia Malik, "Culture and Emotions: Depression Among Pakistanis," in *Culture in Psychology* (ed. C. Squire; London: Routledge, 2000), 145–62.
[84] Malik, "Culture and Emotions," 147.

social phenomena. In the West, emotions tend to be "psychologised" (which is to say internalised, subjected to introspection, and often pathologised) even though theorists recognise that Western emotions too have a social context.

Malik shows three important ways in which "depression" among Pakistanis differs from depression in the West. First, and most importantly, depression in Pakistan is not pathological, which is to say it is not an unnatural feature of life, it is not an illness; second, it is not treated individually (as in therapy) but through communal religion or social relationships; and third it is conceived of somatically (emanating physically from the heart), not psychologically (emanating from the mind). She states that "these cross-cultural differences in depressive 'state' and 'symptoms', which serve as criteria for defining and treating depression in Western psychiatry, cast doubt on the universality of the syndrome of depression."[85] In effect, if "depression" among non-western peoples is so differently understood and so differently treated, and especially if it is not even considered a sickness, is it even fair to call it "depression," which is not only a Western term (lacking in Urdu) but encapsulates a Western view of the self and medicine? Put another way, the cultural specificity of emotions and emotional states makes the names of emotions nearly technical terms. Depression becomes a technical term implying pathology and the need of medical attention that is limited by its technical nature to the West. This opens the possibility that other emotions might be best understood as technical terms with limited cross-cultural applicability.

The anthropological and social-psychological conclusions of Rosaldo and Malik respectively have been confirmed in the work of two scholars whose work is independent of each other and yet related in interesting ways—a philologist and an ethno-linguist. I shall take up each in that order. Classicist David Konstan illustrates how emotions do not enjoy a one-to-one relationship across cultures or time, comparing the modern West with ancient Greek documentary sources. He argues that emotions differ across cultures in much the same way as colour does; colour is seen, experienced, verbalised and understood differently depending entirely on cultural context. Recent study has shown that while *colour* is real, and all cultures have and recognise colour, *colours* are not real, by which I mean that colours are not primary and concrete items to be observed, but are interpreted through experience and then coded in language. At the same time, however, what language can

---

[85] Malik, "Culture and Emotions," 150.

express is finite, which means that to a certain extent, colour is also "the product of the lexical and grammatical structure of particular languages."[86]

Konstan argues compellingly that the cross-cultural relationship between colour and colours offers a useful analogy for distinguishing between emotion and emotions. *Emotion*, that is the general fact that all people appear to recognise and experience that life has an emotional component, is universal, but *emotions*, the experience, naming and understanding of emotions, is not universal at all. In two unpublished (but forthcoming) papers, Konstan looks at anger, hatred and jealousy as emotions and tries to establish whether they meant in the ancient world what they mean today. In other words, will a modern reader naturally understand what is being felt and why when she comes across reference to an emotion or emotional state in (most commonly translated) ancient writing? Aristotle claims that anger is a desire for revenge for a perceived slight from a social equal. Anger is *not* a response to harm done, but a response to belittlement, to treating someone worse than their social standing dictates. The anger that Achilles feels, and that propels him to seek revenge in Homer's *Iliad* supports this: it is a response to having been shamed, not harmed, by Agamemnon.

Likewise, the ancient Greeks lacked a term for, and even the concept of, the modern emotion of jealousy. Furthermore, jealousy does not appear among the emotions that Aristotle lists. According to the Stoics, ζῆλος is more akin to malice or spite than it is to jealousy. Ancient jealousy arises when someone else has something that we too have; it is not, as it is for us, nearly synonymous with envy, but closer in meaning to hoarding. ζηλοτυπία seeks to have something only so that someone else cannot have it, which is why ancient jealousy might be closer to our notion of spite.

Konstan's contribution to the discussion is clear: emotions are not the same between ancient Mediterranean culture and the modern Western world. They are not defined similarly, they are not motivated by the same things, and they are not understood to derive from the same source. Calling them by the same name only creates a sense of similarity, but close examination reveals that the similarity is illusory. About all that is shared between ancient and modern people is that there are emotions, and that most people feel them.

Anna Wierzbicka is an ethno-linguist who has studied the question of language and emotion.[87] I shall not deal with her solution to understanding

---

[86] David Konstan, "The Emotions of the Ancient Greeks–Anger and Hatred." Unpublished Paper (2001).

emotions across cultures, but rather look at what motivated her to reach her solution. Wierzbicka distinguishes between 'emotion' language (anger, sadness) that is too rooted in a particular cultural location and 'feeling' language that is truly cross-cultural (feel, want, know, think, do, say, happen, etc.) which Wierzbicka calls the "Natural Semantic Metalanguage." Words like anger or sadness are too rooted not only in English language but in English speaking culture, and Wierzbicka argues that it is a fallacy to assume that emotion words will have one-to-one translations in all other languages. Worse yet, she argues, is for an outside observer to claim that a culture that lacks a word for sadness, for instance, must still *feel* sadness nonetheless. Wierzbicka writes

> It is ethnocentric to think that if the Tahitians don't have a word corresponding to the English word *sad* . . . , they must nonetheless have an innate conceptual category of 'sadness'; or to assume that in their emotional experience 'sadness'—for which they have no name— is nonetheless more salient and more relevant than, for example, the feelings of *tōiaha* or *pe'ape'a*, for which they do have a name (although English does not).[88]

What one call things matters immensely, and here Wierzbicka makes a point that really is directly relevant to my arguments concerning the nature of the word "conversion" and its cultural background. She writes: "Words provide clues to other people's conceptualizations. . . . it is words, more than anything, which allow us access to the 'emotional universe' of people from another culture."[89]

These studies illustrate, each in its own way, that what we are dealing with here is not a claim that non-Westerners have no emotional life, nor that their experience of emotions is completely and utterly foreign to us. Yet, despite real and apparent commonalities between the Western and non-western experience and understanding of emotions, the differences are what make all the difference. The point has its classic formulation in an observation that is at once painfully obvious and yet under-appreciated. Although recognising that people across cultures are not totally without common elements when it comes to the emotions, Michelle Rosaldo is forced to observe that

---

[87] Anna Wierzbicka, *Emotions Across Languages and Cultures* (Cambridge: Cambridge University Press, 1999).
[88] Wierzbicka, *Emotions Across Languages and Cultures*, 26.
[89] Wierzbicka, *Emotions Across Languages and Cultures*, 28–29.

"the Balinese no more feel 'guilt' than we feel 'lek'."[90] While some things are universal—an insult followed by a bad feeling is probably universal—other things are not universal—*what* one feels (shame, rage, anger, tension, whatever) depends on *how* one understands what happened. The phenomenon of the insult is universal; what is insulting is cultural. Emotion is universal; emotions are parochial.

A useful example of the important difference between ancient and modern experience of emotions, and one that is especially pertinent for New Testament scholars, is the concept of shame. Modern Western readers see the word 'shame' mentioned in the New Testament and naturally believe they know precisely what is at stake. This is fair enough on the one hand; the phenomenon of shame is not limited to the ancient Mediterranean. But is the "shame" in the New Testament the "shame" that readers associate it with? Is there a presumption of parallelism created by the sharing of terminology (one in translation and the other indigenous)? In the modern world shame is an emotion, exclusively. This, unfortunately, is not the most helpful way of understanding shame as it functioned in the ancient Mediterranean. Honour and shame can be fruitfully understood in two ways, as commodity and as social judgement—note that both are external phenomena, already setting them apart from shame as emotion.

As a commodity, honour was a limited good, which made it highly sought after; conversely shame among elite males was a negative commodity, something no one wanted to accumulate. Alternatively, honour had to do with a public claim of worth, one's reputation; shame, on the other hand, was a demotion in one's reputation, or depreciation in the eyes of the public court of reputation. Shame among the males with honour, thus, was not an *emotion*, but a *demotion*. Being demoted in the eyes of public court of reputation may very well have evoked emotional feelings, but it was not itself an emotion, just as reputation is not an emotion, though emotions might be associated with the gain and loss of reputation. Likewise for females, whom we believe represented positive shame, shame was the proper conduct in keeping with gender expectations—again, not an emotion but a standard of activity. Even when terminology is shared between cultures (in translation!), and even when emotions might well be associated with both, it cannot be assumed that they were psychologically analogous, or that assuming psychological parallelism is a helpful approach.

---

[90] Rosaldo, "Toward an Anthropology of Self and Feeling," 142.

The psychological analysis of people from the distant past has received its harshest blow from D. E. Stannard.[91] What we described above as "psychic unity" (the sentiment that people are the same wherever you go) Stannard calls "historical presentism." Historical presentism, like the assumption of psychic unity is necessary for psychohistory to work, for if people

> were not always essentially the same, the behavior of many past individuals (to say nothing of whole cultures) would be psychoanalytically unintelligible. Their actions and motives would be operating at a level beyond the reach of psychoanalytic concepts and suppositions, which are products of the direct study of primarily urban, post-industrial, literate, twentieth-century, Western individuals.[92]

What anthropologists have already come to learn, and what historians were just starting to learn when Stannard wrote this book, some scholars of the New Testament appear yet to take seriously enough. New Testament scholarship on conversion, and often as well Pauline biography, has been slow to understand that temporal distance creates as much of a gulf between cultures as can geographical distance. If I might redirect Stannard's words to historians to those New Testament scholars who presuppose psychic unity between themselves and their objects of study, these scholars "have before them the task of more carefully structuring their conceptual arguments, in a sense from the inside out to conform with the recognition that they do not share a reciprocity of cognitive perspectives with their subjects."[93] If we do not share a cognitive perspective with first-century Mediterraneans, then it becomes exceedingly doubtful that insights derived from and germane to our own cognitive perspective, both psychological and emotional, can be transferred to another vastly different cognitive perspective. Put another way, since we do not share a cognitive perspective with ancient and Mediterranean cultures, we should not assume that their behaviour or experience of the world will be intelligible to us based on the analogy of our own modern Western cognitive perspective.

All this recent work by anthropologists, cultural psychologists, and historians allows us to draw several conclusions about a psychic unity that is believed to cross cultural and temporal thresholds. It appears that, while of course some common features must exist across cultures, the mental and

---

[91] David E. Stannard, *Shrinking History: On Freud and the Failure of Psychohistory* (New York: Oxford University Press, 1980).
[92] Stannard, *Shrinking History*, 121.
[93] Stannard, *Shrinking History*, 143.

emotional experiences of humanity cannot be separated from the cultural context in which they exist. In other words, "culture and psyche make each other up."[94] Cultural psychology, though it is not my goal to attempt it, is possible, but only within "a deeper understanding of the relationship between psychology and the cultural domain."[95] And, finally, assumptions about the psychic unity of humanity over all time are based on wishful thinking at best and Western twentieth-century ethnocentrism at worst; psychology and the insights it has gained are not obviously nor self-evidently transferable to non-western and ancient cultures; despite the fact that the personal experience of emotion is universal, what those emotions mean, how they are interpreted and dealt with, differs.

1.3.3 New Testament Social Scientific Criticism

A small number of New Testament scholars have been making many of the same points expressed above for over twenty years. For example, cross-cultural psychology has been challenged by various social-scientific critics of the New Testament, though to varying extents. J. J. Pilch argues that cross-cultural psychology errs when it assumes that features derived from a Western setting are self-evidently universal.[96] He also says, in characteristically strong language, that "applying these monocultural insights to other cultures proves disastrous."[97] Yet ultimately Pilch does not deny the possibility of a successful attempt at cross-cultural psychology. He allows that there might be common processes that make comparison possible, even if the differences between cultures problematise such an attempt.

Conversely, Bruce Malina seems less hopeful. People in the ancient (as well as modern) Mediterranean thought in allocentric (social) terms; they did not, as we do, think in idiocentric (psychological) terms.[98] Malina's main reason for being suspicious of cross-cultural psychology is that our understanding of the individual and the self is so different from that of ancient peoples (with Mauss and Stannard). Over the course of many different

---

[94] Shweder, *Thinking Through Cultures*, 99.
[95] Christine Griffin, "More Than Simply Talk and Text," 17.
[96] J. J. Pilch, "Psychological and Psychoanalytical Approaches to Interpreting the Bible in Social-Scientific Context," *BTB* 27 (1997): 112–16.
[97] Pilch, "Psychological and Psychoanalytical Approaches," 114.
[98] Bruce J. Malina, "The Individual and the Community—Personality in the Social World of Early Christianity," *BTB* 9 (1979): 126–38; "Is There a Circum-Mediterranean Person? Looking for Stereotypes," *BTB* 22 (1992): 66–87.

articles, Malina has made the same important point: the way the modern world understands and sees the self is so different from how the self was understood in the ancient world that many *assumptions* about continuity between them and us simply must be abandoned.[99] The primary difference between the ancient and modern world is that ancient individuals were dyadic, whereas the modern Western individual is monadic (yet another way of differentiating sociocentric and idiocentric individuals). Dyadism is about stereotyping; when you know someone's family, or their ethnic origin, you know all you need to know about them.[100] By contrast, with a modern and monadic personality, you can only truly know another individual when you know her individual character, that is, when you know what lies within. In our world we try to avoid stereotyping, but in the ancient world, that is how one knew others. Unlike the modern West,

> ancient people did not know each other very well in the way we do, i.e., psychologically, individually, intimately and personally. . . . this means that they knew or cared little about psychological development, psychological motivations and introspective analyses. . . . The whole point is that in this aspect of their culture, they were not like we are at all. Hence to infer psychological states of some person on the basis of our texts would be a highly questionable and anachronistic enterprise.[101]

Of course the ancient world knew of the individual (the human; the biological entity), and it knew the "person" (individual as agent; the sociological entity) in male gender form only; by contrast, the modern world knows the individual, the person in all gender forms, and knows in addition the individualistic self (the individual as locus of human experience; the psychological entity).[102] This self, to say it again, does not exist in a universal form cross-culturally.

---

[99] Bruce J. Malina, "Dealing with Biblical (Mediterranean) Characters: A Guide for U.S. Consumers," *BTB* 19 (1989): 127–41; with Jerome H. Neyrey, "First-Century Personality: Dyadic, not Individual," in *The Social World of Luke–Acts* (ed. J. H. Neyrey; Peabody: Hendrickson, 1991), 67–96; with Jerome H. Neyrey, *Portraits of Paul*; Malina, *The Social World of Jesus and the Gospels* (London: Routledge, 1996).

[100] See Malina, "Is There a Circum-Mediterranean Person?" 68–75, for a thorough exposition of ancient physiognomonia.

[101] Malina, "The Individual and the Community," 131.

[102] See Malina, "Is There a Circum-Mediterranean Person?" 76–77, following the typology of Grace Gredys Harris, "Concepts of Individual, Self, and Person in Description and Analysis," *American Anthropologist* 91 (1989): 599–612, for a further explanation of the categories of individual, person, and self.

Malina's and Neyrey's *Portaits of Paul* offers a number of challenges to mainstream Pauline scholarship when it comes to their understanding of ancient personality. They outline the practical differences between ancient and modern personality, as evidenced for example in the ancient encomium and also in ancient physiognomics, noting how people defined and honoured each other. They also helpfully outline many of the various ways in which ancient and modern personality differences would have been manifested in the difference between collectivist and individualist cultures. Their most interesting chapter, at least for our purposes, is on Paul and how understanding Paul's status as apostle and prophet changes when one is equipped with a proper understanding of personality and culture. Most telling of all is that Malina and Neyrey go out of their way to avoid using the term "conversion" of Paul at all. They write evocatively:

> The obvious change in Paul's behaviour from persecutor to preacher ... was not the result of individual investigation or study. It did not derive from his individual and personal anguish, anxiety, uncertainty, distress, or any other psychological state that we normally associate with soul searching decision making or "conversion."[103]

Malina and Neyrey claim this not, in keeping with Stendahl, because Paul had a "robust conscience" as a Jew (though they would not likely disagree with that contribution), but because "Paul simply had no individualist 'soul' to search."[104] They go on to suggest very briefly that the event was external and had to do with God's patronage.

1.4 Conclusion

The rise and influence of the psychological cognitive perspective of Western culture has everything to do with the development of the idiocentric (individualistic) self and far less to do with actual (as opposed to perceived) universal human experience. It is not accidental that psychology as "science" and as a *Weltanschauung* did not arise in non-western (sociocentric or collectivistic) cultures, nor that it did not arise until the autonomous individual and self became the central feature of Western culture and

---

[103] Malina and Neyrey, *Portraits of Paul*, 206.
[104] Malina and Neyrey, *Portraits of Paul*, 206.

society.¹⁰⁵ This fact is not merely a point of interest along the trajectory of the history of thought but has profound implications, as many are beginning to realise, for the application of such a narrowly defined and conceived understanding of the self to the broader collection of global and historical cultures. Philip Bock writes, "The failure to recognise the origins of Western psychology in our own cultural tradition, with its own unconscious values, biases, and habits of thought, is the crudest kind of ethnocentrism."¹⁰⁶

One can always object that ancient people were underdeveloped when it came to introspective or psychological awareness, and that it is our gift to them to be able to understand them in ways they did not have available. At best such a position can only be assumed, not proven, and recent work on cross-cultural psychology suggests that such a position in fact should not be assumed. Likewise, one might object to the notion that we cannot apply modern psychological theory to ancient people because it is modern with the observation that physics and biology are also modern. Surely, ancient people lived by the laws of physics, and surely they were constructed biologically as we are.¹⁰⁷ Yet, psychology is not a science in the same sense as these pure sciences, though some psychologists would certainly object to this. Further, the objects that physics and biology study are not culturally constructed as is the object that psychology studies; the physical body and nature are not created by culture as the "self" and self-identity are created. The difference therefore does not lie in whether an approach is modern or ancient, but whether the approach in question is wholly reliant on the modern construct of the Western idiocentric self.

Finally, there is an important clarification that needs to be made and that I hope is not too late. To say that we cannot talk about Paul's emotional state, or that we cannot look for what motivated him internally, is not meant in any

---

¹⁰⁵ This is not a claim of causality—the rise of the autonomous individualistic self *resulted* in the creation of psychology—but rather one of necessary condition—the rise of the autonomous individualistic self created the necessary conditions without which psychology could not have come about.

¹⁰⁶ Philip K. Bock, *Rethinking Psychological Anthropology: Continuity and Change in the Study of Human Action* (New York: W. H. Freeman, 1988), 212.

¹⁰⁷ One might argue that homosexuality is a better example, since how we understand it, like gender and unlike physics, *is* culturally constructed. There are two problems with assuming parallels between ancient and modern homosexuality, however. There was no term for "homosexual" until the 19th century; the absence of vocabulary suggests the absence of the concept. And, secondly, the concept did not exist because homosexuality was something one *did*, it was not something one *was*. In other words, it had nothing to do, as it does now, with identity.

way to imply that he was a rigidly emotionless automaton. It is unlikely that ancient people did not share some of the same emotions we have, though it is also likely that they knew emotions we do not, and vice versa. To say that we cannot talk about Paul's emotions is, rather, to claim that we cannot use ourselves as the model from which to draw parallels with his experience of those emotions. In too many different ways we have seen how ancient and modern, Western and non-western, people are different. We cannot assume that such different beings experience life and emotions in similar ways. And if they do not experience life and emotions in similar ways, we should not imagine that psychology, which (allegedly) can help us understand our own lives, will be a helpful or illuminating way to understand their lives. For example, behaviour in the ancient world was governed *externally*, by honour and shame, more than it was governed *internally*, by guilt. Yet, as we saw above, just because the modern world knows the feeling and vocabulary of shame, we should not assume that we can empathise with an ancient person's experience of shame.

The goal of this chapter has emphatically *not* been to argue that psychology has nothing at all to offer neighbouring fields of study, and I tentatively include New Testament studies among them. It has been, rather, to show that the influence of psychology across fields of study is not only more pervasive than is typically acknowledged, but also far more problematic. There is a myth of self-evidence that people are essentially the same when you remove the cultural baggage, and this has been strongly challenged by recent psychological critical writing. Time and again it is found that the Western psychological framework is not helpful, and worse, can distort and misrepresent non-western emotional and behavioural phenomena (Shweder, Malik). The goal of this chapter has been to illustrate the need for an approach to understanding ancient people and ancient experience that does not implicitly assume a Western psychological framework or modern Western constructions of the self. Yet we also need a framework that is supported by the abundance of ancient sources.

There is certainly nothing inherently inappropriate about using etic categories to understand other people or cultures. Etic categories of analysis, which social scientific models frequently are, can be very useful heuristically, even though they may be quite foreign to the culture being studied. But given the fact that Western psychological analysis is terribly underqualified to make psychological assessments of ancient and non-Western characters, it is debatable whether there is any heuristic value to the psychological model. Even if this is too pessimistic a view of psychology, however, it is at least the case that we will be better served by such etic categories if we can first achieve as full an understanding as possible of other people and cultures in their own (emic) categories first.

This book is intended to offer that emic category and an alternative to the dominant psychological paradigm with which the West typically approaches conversion. As we will see, ancient social interaction was profoundly shaped by notions of reciprocity, with the social, political and religious structures of life framed within an understanding of general reciprocity—the institutions of patronage-benefaction and clientage. In the following chapters I shall present the model, derived from ancient primary sources, and illustrate the extent to which Paul's language reflects and presupposes it.

Chapter Two

General Reciprocity Among Humans and their Gods

2.0 Introduction

The practice of exchange and concerns of reciprocity are hardly the unique domain of any one culture, and yet the types of exchange that exist are complex and varied. Exchange and reciprocity in different contexts, both within and among cultures, results in different relationships and expectations. Some relationships are inaugurated, confirmed, or completed through exchange, and different types of exchange carry with them different expectations of both giver and recipient. It will be worth while then to map out the different types of exchange that are found in the ancient Mediterranean.

A number of attempts have been made to develop a model of exchange in the ancient world, and based on these we are able to delineate the dominant framework of exchange in the ancient Mediterranean. The structure and expectations of general reciprocity, embodied in the social institutions of patronage and benefaction, supply the conceptual and practical framework within which Graeco-Romans, including Hellenised Jews like Philo and Josephus, expressed their understanding and their experience of their interactions with their gods.

This chapter and the one that follows are closely related. In this chapter I would like to discuss types of exchange, especially as they pertain to the ancient Mediterranean, and review in detail the structure and social role of ancient patronage and benefaction. Though this latter information has been offered in many other places,[1] there are a number of reasons why it is

---

[1] Bruce J. Malina, "What is Prayer?" *TBT* 18 (1980): 214–20; Frederick W. Danker, *Benefactor: Epigraphic Study of a Graeco-Roman Semantic Field* (St. Louis: Clayton Publishing House, 1982); J. H. Elliott, "Patronage and Clientism in Early Christian Society: A Short Reading Guide," *Forum* 3 (1987): 39–48; Bruce J. Malina, "Patron and Client: The Analogy Behind Synoptic Theology," *Forum* 4 (1988): 2–32; H. Moxnes, "Patron–Client Relations and the New Community in Luke–Acts," in *The Social World of Luke–Acts: Models for Interpretation* (ed. J. H. Neyrey; Peabody: Hendrickson, 1991), 241–68; J. K. Chow, *Patronage and Power: A Study of Social Networks in Corinth* (JSNTSup 75; Sheffield: Sheffield Academic Press, 1992); R. A.

valuable to do so here as well. First of all, the present work relies on a detailed understanding of ancient patronage and benefaction; it is better that the information be provided here rather than forcing the reader to go elsewhere. Secondly, attention to this detail will confirm the extent to which patronage and benefaction were of a piece with ancient personality, a point stressed in the previous chapter. Thirdly, a full understanding of human patronage and benefaction allows the numerous parallels with divine patronage and benefaction to stand out clearly. And finally, the model of patronage and benefaction is still relatively new to a large and slowly advancing field of Biblical Studies, and there will be many readers for whom this is new material. These four rationales also prepare us for the chapter that follows, in which I shall present a number of rhetorical conventions that typically and regularly appear in the discourses of patronage and benefaction, both human and divine.

2.1 A Taxonomy of Reciprocal Exchange

2.1.1 Marshall Sahlins

In pre-modern economic exchange, "material flow underwrites or initiates social relations."[2] That is to say, all forms of exchange inaugurate a social relationship. Karl Polanyi called this reciprocity, a concept that Marshall Sahlins broke down into several different types, which he called generalised reciprocity, balanced reciprocity, and negative reciprocity.[3] Generalised reciprocity involved disinterested giving, that is giving without ulterior motives of profit or control. Further, generalised reciprocity allowed for a delayed return, not an immediate return as you would have for example in a market place exchange. Under exchanges of generalised reciprocity Sahlins includes the "pure gift," hospitality, help, and generosity. There is an expectation of

---

Horsley (ed.), *Paul and Empire: Religion and Power in Roman Imperial Society* (Harrisburg, Pa.: Trinity Press International, 1997); David A. deSilva, "Patronage and Reciprocity: The Context of Grace in the New Testament," *ATJ* 31 (1999): 32–84.

[2] Marshall Sahlins, *Stone Age Economics* (New York: Aldine Publishing Company, 1972), 186.

[3] Sahlins, *Stone Age Economics*, 191–96. See also Karl Polanyi, *Primitive, Archaic, and Modern Economies: Essays of Karl Polanyi* (ed. G. Dalton; New York: Doubleday and Company, 1968).

reciprocity, but it is an open ended one, "not stipulated by time, quantity, or quality: the expectation of reciprocity is indefinite."[4]

Balanced reciprocity entailed interested giving with immediate and balanced return. There is direct exchange involved here, wherein the value of the goods or services is equivalent. Belonging to this category of exchange might be trade, commerce, certain types of gift exchange, but also peace agreements and friendship. The first two categories in this list in some ways preclude an open-ended time frame for reciprocity, though Sahlins does not, as far as I know, discuss debt or credit as a form of balanced reciprocity. Obviously, balanced reciprocity is less personal and more economic in nature, and the exchange is one in which "the material side is at least as critical as the social."[5]

Sahlins set up his three forms of reciprocity on a continuum of extremes. Where generalised reciprocity was "selfless," and balanced reciprocity was commercial but balanced, his third category, negative reciprocity, was entirely self-interested and profit motivated. Types of exchange that fall under negative reciprocity include bartering, haggling, gambling, and theft. The point is to get something for nothing, or to cheat the other party out of a balanced exchange. It stands to reason that Sahlins considered this the least personal form of exchange, since "the participants confront each other as opposed interests," rather than as human counterparts.[6]

For as useful and illuminating as Sahlins's model of exchange was, it has certain limitations. In the first instance, it is too general to be useful in a broad spectrum of societies. That is to say, there are not enough categories of exchange to be able to apply to actual examples of exchange. Secondly, it is doubtful that any giving is ever entirely selfless, so that category of exchange is questionable. In fact, the main problem with the model as a whole is that it is founded on an understanding of the degree of (self-)interest on the part of the giver to discern between these types of reciprocity. This means one must assess the level of interest or self-interest on the part of the giver, which is surely next to impossible to assess in people to whom we have no access.

---

[4] Sahlins, *Stone Age Economics*, 194.
[5] Sahlins, *Stone Age Economics*, 195.
[6] Sahlins, *Stone Age Economics*, 195.

2.1.2 Stegemann and Stegemann

Stegemann and Stegemann adapt and improve Sahlins's model by focusing on two features other than the selflessness of the giver. The Stegemanns focus on the social status of the interlocutors rather than their apparent level of interest in return, and secondly they focus on the nature of what is exchanged and how. In the first instance, this allows the Stegemanns to distinguish between kinship and extra-kinship exchange (more on this shortly), for example, and in the second, it allows them to distinguish between gift exchange and patronage, which also (and confusingly) involves the allocation of gifts. Nonetheless, they are clearly indebted to the general structure of Sahlins's model of exchange.

The Stegemanns identify four types of reciprocity-oriented exchange: familial reciprocity (*Familiäre Reziprozität*), balanced reciprocity (*Ausgeglichene Reziprozität*), general reciprocity (*Generelle Reziprozität*), and negative reciprocity (*Negative Reziprozität*).[7] As the name suggests, familial reciprocity occurs within the family, though of course the family in antiquity comprised quite a larger unit than its modern counterpart. What is more, familial exchange could occur within families, but also between families within a single clan, and between clans within a single tribe. The social status was egalitarian, though that term needs to be heavily qualified. It is not that each member of the family had equal status; clearly they did not. The claim suggests rather that the family formed a unit within which there would be equality relative to those outside the family unit. Another way of putting this is that the giving and receiving that occurred within the family was not the source of tensions nor the arena of agonistic contests. These sorts of exchanges, then, were quite naturally different from exchanges that occurred outside of the kinship unit.

Balanced reciprocity occurs outside the family unit, though could, we must imagine, occur between families within clan and tribe. The primary characteristics of balanced reciprocity is that it takes place between social equals and that it involves the mutual exchange of gifts with balanced value—e.g., gift exchange and loan allowance and repayment. In gift exchange, what is exchanged *must* be of equal or greater value; if one makes a gift and receives in return something of less value, the relationship is thrown out of

---

[7] E. W. Stegemann and W. Stegemann, *Urchristliche Sozialgeschichte: Die Anfänge im Judentum und die Christusgemeinden in der mediterranen Welt* (Stuttgart: Kohlhammer, 1995), 43; ET *The Jesus Movement: A Social History of Its First Century* (trans. O. C. Dean Jr.; Minneapolis: Fortress Press, 1999).

balance and begins to break down. It is likewise, with loans, which too must be repaid (often with interest); failure to repay breaks down the balance, and the relationship naturally becomes antagonistic. We also see balanced reciprocity in commercial transactions, where too we expect goods equal in value to be exchanged, such as another good, or a service, or currency worth equivalent value. It is important to understand that balanced reciprocity does not refer to the parties doing the exchanging, but to the value of what is exchanged. However, where it concerns the relative social status of the exchanging parties, there are two options within balanced reciprocity. On the one hand, balanced reciprocity necessitates that social status is equal. In gift exchange, for instance, it is expected that parties of equal status exchange goods or service. Two features of this kind of reciprocity keep the relationship from developing into one of patron–client: that the exchanging parties are of equal or near equal social status, and related, that they have the means to exchange gifts of equal or greater value. On the other hand, however, social status is not relevant to commercial exchange, which are also balanced, but in which one party purchases a good or service from another. It may be that the consumer is of a higher social status, and the seller lower, but this does not influence the nature of the exchange. We can say then that in balanced reciprocity, the relative social status of giver and receiver is benign—it either works positively (as in gift exchange) or neutrally (as in commercial exchange). This is not so in general reciprocity.

Balanced reciprocity stands in sharp contrast to general reciprocity in two ways. First, general reciprocity is grounded in the unequal social status of the parties involved. Secondly, general reciprocity involves the exchange of goods or services that do not share equal value. Rather, general reciprocity requires repayment not in kind but by "homage and loyalty or political support or information."[8] In general reciprocity, the absence of balance, at least strictly speaking, results in an on-going and open ended relationship. In the balanced reciprocity of commercial exchange, the relationship ends with the transaction; there is no lingering responsibility of either party to the other. Although gift exchange, also a form of balanced reciprocity, does entail an on-going relationship, the fact of balance results in a very different dynamic than with general reciprocity. Here a different relationship is entered into precisely because both parties do not have equal access to goods or services; hence one party is the recipient, and enters into a relationship of subservience to the

---

[8] Stegemann and Stegemann, *The Jesus Movement*, 36.

giver, where their reciprocity is marked not by balanced exchange but by honour and gratitude.

General reciprocity occurs primarily in the relationship of exchange between patrons or benefactors and their clients.[9] A gift is not a benefaction, since receiving a gift does not make of one a client. A gift must be reciprocated, but it must be reciprocated with another gift of equal or greater value. Thus the cycle remains unbroken because there is balance, or as theorists note, at least the promise of balance. Conversely, a benefaction by definition can never be repaid with another benefaction; it must be repaid with honour, gratitude, and loyalty. Otherwise it would be a gift, and there would be no client since the "client," it turns out, would have equal access to the means and resources to repay a gift. And reciprocating a benefaction on the part of a client does not result in an ontological shift in which patron or benefactor suddenly becomes client and vice versa. Ideally, reciprocity on the part of a client encourages a patron to give again, knowing she or he can count on well-behaved clients, but it does not shame the patron into giving, nor place the patron at the mercy of the client. If these references seem oblique, they shall become clear when I discuss patronage and benefaction in detail below.[10]

The exchange that occurs between patrons and clients and between benefactors and recipients falls under the category of general reciprocity. This must be allowed to include exchange relationships between powerful individuals and their needy clients, literary patrons and their writers, the Emperor and those he appoints to various offices, the Emperor and the people who receive games, streets, buildings, tax breaks, the Emperor and his client kings, philosopher-teachers and their disciple-students, and last but not least, the Graeco-Roman gods and those they benefit through healings, revelations, guidance, and salvation. All of these, though unique in their own ways, share the common element that they are *reciprocal* (goods and services are exchanged for honour, gratitude and loyalty), they are to varying degrees *personal* and of some *duration*; and they are *asymmetrical*.[11]

---

[9] See also S. R. Eisenstadt and L. Roniger, "Patron–Client Relations as a Model of Structuring Social Exchange," *Comparative Studies in Society and History* 22 (1980): 42–77.

[10] The fourth form of reciprocity, negative reciprocity, occurs between strangers, regardless of social status, and is characterised by "self-interest and profit" (Stegemann and Stegemann, *The Jesus Movement*, 35). It need not delay us here.

[11] These are the three primary elements named by Saller as comprising patronage and clientage. See R. P. Saller, *Personal Patronage under the Early Empire* (New York: Cambridge University Press, 1982), 1.

There are a number of benefits to using the category of general reciprocity first rather than moving immediately to the more popular category of patron–client. On the one hand, it addresses a justified complaint of Frederick Danker to the effect that "It is unfortunate that the narrow term 'patron–client relationship' should have entered the discussion rather than the more comprehensive term 'reciprocity system' of which 'patron–client' more accurately describes an ancient Roman subset."[12] Generalised reciprocity is, of course, a further subset of Danker's reference to the broader "reciprocity system," and hence I believe an even more useful distinction. On the other hand, starting with the broader category of generalised reciprocity helps us to locate the different exchanges that occur between people (and their gods) with varying social statuses and relationships and in various social settings. Thus, we are able to acknowledge that patron and client exchanges and exchanges of benefactions are not precisely parallel types of giving. And yet, we are simultaneously encouraged to recognise that despite their differences, they share much in common precisely because they are both forms of generalised reciprocity. It is for this reason that I refer to the social institution under analysis as patronage and benefaction: not because I think they are the same, but because from the perspective of the rules, expectations, and obligations of generalised reciprocity, they have more in common than they have differences. It is worth looking closely, however, at this very issue.

2.2 Defining our Terms: Patronage vs. Benefaction

Our entry into ancient conversion must begin with the recognition that in order to understand ancient conversion, one needs to understand ancient human interaction and relationships with the gods. The experience of conversion is going to be an extension of the experience of exchange and of loyalty to the gods and to philosophers. As we shall see shortly, ancient writers and inscribers continually framed their relationships with the gods and with their philosophical teachers in the language of patronage and benefaction.

These terms, however, patronage and benefaction, have recently come under some discussion. It is worth while pausing at this point to engage in

---

[12] F. W. Danker, "Paul's Debt to the De Corona of Demosthenes: A Study of Rhetorical Techniques in Second Corinthians," in *Persuasive Artistry: Studies in New Testament Rhetoric in Honour of George A. Kennedy* (ed. D. A. Watson; JSNTSup 50; Sheffield Academic Press: Sheffield, 1991), 262–80.

this debate, in order to explain the use of my terminology throughout this book. At the outset, it can be stated categorically that patronage and benefaction are not perfectly synonymous terms; they do not describe precisely the same practices, but rather very closely related ones. Clearly distinguishing between them based on primary sources is nearly impossible, unfortunately, since the language ostensibly of the one is frequently used in settings having to do with the other.[13] The issue of how patronage and benefaction differ from one another has been raised recently by Stephan Joubert and Alicia Batten.[14]

2.2.1 Stephan Joubert

Though time consuming, it is worth closely engaging Joubert's work, for in doing so many helpful points emerge concerning the challenges one encounters when attempting to strongly demarcate patronage from benefaction. Joubert defines patronage as a "pervasive, voluntary form of interaction between socially disproportionate individuals, as well as between socially disproportionate individuals and groups involved in a reciprocal exchange of material goods and services."[15] The primary characteristics of patronage for Joubert are that it is a close and personal relationship, and that there is an element (or at least the relationship lends itself to the possibility of) exploitation. Hence, examples of patronage for Joubert include the exchange relationships of landlords to tenants (it is unclear why this is not an example of balanced reciprocity), patrons to freedpersons, Emperors to client-kings, Emperors to senators and other elites, and finally the patron to the *collegia* or voluntary

---

[13] Likewise, Harrison, in the process of warning against conflating Greek benefaction with Roman patronage admits that the vocabulary of each begins to overlap in the Greek East (James R. Harrison, *Paul's Language of Grace in its Graeco-Roman Context* [WUNT 2.172; Tübingen: Mohr Siebeck, 2003], 16).

[14] Stephan Joubert, *Paul as Benefactor: Reciprocity, Strategy and Theological Reflection in Paul's Collection* (WUNT 2.124; Tübingen: J. C. B. Mohr [Paul Siebeck], 2000); idem, "One Form of Social Exchange or Two? 'Euergetism,' Patronage, and Testament Studies," *BTB* 31 (2001): 17–25. Alicia Batten, "God in the Letter of James: Patron or Benefactor?" (paper presented at the annual meeting of the Society of Biblical Literature, Toronto, 2002). She generously shared her work with me, and I acknowledge here that that work was likely very much 'in progress' when I heard and then read it. My focus in this following section will be upon Joubert, and I shall point out the places where Batten has made a similar point.

[15] Joubert, *Paul as Benefactor*, 23; also idem, "One Form of Social Exchange or Two?" 19.

association. And finally, he calls patronage "a system of social control," likely owing to the phenomenon of exploitation in addition to the practice of patrons conferring political office and securing loyalty.[16] In short, because the relationship of clients to patrons is so close, so personal, and involves such an obvious imbalance of power, Joubert argues that exploitation is both inherent to and characteristic of the relationship.

As a rule, the absence of exploitation in relationships of benefaction is what differentiates benefaction from patronage. Benefaction, or as Joubert calls it *euergetism*, is found in two forms. The first he calls collective or public benefaction, that is between a noble and wealthy giver and groups of people whose individual identity is not relevant and where the individuals do not enter into a relationship with the giver. Joubert argues that the collective benefactor is represented best by Aristotle's "magnificent" man (*Eth. nic.* 4.2), who gave the right amount at the right time with the right motivation, and is contrasted with the person who gives ostentatiously (vulgar giver) or who gives little thinking he or she is giving a lot (miserly giver). The second form of benefaction Joubert calls private benefaction, or giving between two individuals. In *Paul the Benefactor* he claims that the giving, at least according to Aristotle's portrait of the "great-souled" man (*Eth. nic.* 4.3), occurs between people of equal status and involves the calculation of honour based on a better memory for what one has given than for what one has received.

There are a number of problems with the use of Aristotle's different types of man for this purpose. First with respect to Aristotle's "magnificent man," while he does discuss ways of giving, he does not claim to be writing about benefaction. Rather Aristotle is talking about characteristics of giving that he tries to make fit into the ideal of his principle of the mean between two extremes. It is unclear that this characterisation of a type of giver can be taken as a description of a collective benefactor. As for Aristotle's "great souled man," Joubert is surely incorrect in marshalling that as an example of a form of benefaction. For one thing, like with his treatment of the 'magnificent' man, Aristotle is describing a character that he idealises in terms of the mean. The greater problem for Joubert here, however, is that the type of exchange that Aristotle describes is far more consistent with balanced reciprocity, and gift exchange in particular, than it is with general reciprocity and benefaction. Exchange that occurs between parties of equal status and that involves a memory of exchanges is a form of balanced reciprocity. Conversely, benefactions exchanged between people of equal status would by definition be

---

[16] Joubert, "One Form of Social Exchange or Two?" 19.

gifts, not benefactions, since benefactions require one party to enter into a relationship of subservience to the other, something that would not be part of an exchange involving people of equal status.

In his attempt to contrast benefaction from patronage, Joubert also relies heavily on Seneca's *De beneficiis*. The most important principle that Joubert distils from Seneca is that giving must be selfless, with no motivation for gain on the part of the giver. Based on the title of Seneca's work, Joubert concludes that benefaction is selfless and that patronage is, therefore, exploitative.[17] Joubert's use of Seneca as an illustration of benefaction specifically seems to overlook two potentially important issues. First, *De beneficiis* has all the appearances of prescriptive writing, with Seneca's fantastic calls for people to give even after being dishonoured by an ungrateful recipient, though Joubert seems to read the work as a simple description of ancient "benefactorism."[18] Further, Seneca, seems to be criticising common tendencies in exchange relationships and establishing an ideal as opposed to describing benefaction as it happens. Secondly, it is not always clear whether Seneca is writing only about "Greek" benefaction, as Joubert must have it, or whether he is writing about "Roman" patronage as well. Most likely, Seneca is writing more broadly about reciprocity between parties of unequal status, which includes both benefactions *and* patronage and is meant to prescribe *ideal* behaviour concerning both. After all, Seneca is writing in Latin (thus the term *euergetism* would have been foreign to him) and as one firmly ensconced within the practices and institution of Roman patronage.

Joubert's attempt to distinguish between patronage and benefaction encounters further problems when his focus turns away from sources and towards trying to characterise the behaviour and motivations typical of each. Initially, he recognises that there are a number of characteristics in common with both patronage and benefaction. Both patronage and benefaction, in Joubert's portrait, can be directed at individuals or at groups, both can result in long term relationships and can even be hereditary, and both can involve reciprocity expressed in similar forms to each other: honorary decrees

---

[17] So too Batten, "God in the Letter of James."
[18] See also his similar treatment of Seneca in Stephan Joubert, "Coming to Terms with a Neglected Aspect of Ancient Mediterranean Reciprocity: Seneca's views on benefit exchange in *De Beneficiis* as the framework for a model of social exchange," in *Social Scientific Models for Interpreting the Bible: Essays by the Context Group in Honor of Bruce Malina* (ed. J. J. Pilch; Biblical Interpretation Series 53; Leiden: E. J. Brill, 2001), 47–63.

Defining our Terms: Patronage vs. Benefaction 63

(inscriptions), crowns, public eulogies, seats of honour, positions of honour, status, inscriptions, and titles. Since Joubert argues that there are considerable overlaps and that the two are ultimately related, these similarities are not a problem for him.

Now for the differences. First, Joubert claims that patronage is about social control, but he does not define what he means by 'social control', and seems rather to merge it with the exploitation and abuse that were sometimes (perhaps even often) a part of being a client to a patron.[19] Furthermore, he presents benefaction so idyllically, imagining it seems that Seneca's selfless givers were so much the reality. It seems, in fact, that this is the primary distinction: an exchange that allows for exploitation or abuse is patronage; only selfless and truly philanthropic giving can be counted as benefaction (a position Batten takes as well).

The second problem for Joubert concerns his claim that when a benefaction has been reciprocated, the "original benefactor is placed under an obligation by the return service to react with a second service."[20] In other words, there is a constantly rotating role of benefactor and client that shifts whenever something is exchanged. This is confirmed by the general thesis of his book, that the Jerusalem church provided Paul with a benefaction by allowing him to take up his mission to the Gentiles, and that by remembering the poor and taking up the collection Paul was returning a benefaction that would then put them in his debt, owing him a benefaction. His title sums it up: *Paul the Benefactor*, despite the fact that Jerusalem was initially the benefactor to Paul. Joubert demonstrates this claim by recourse to the fact that recipients of benefactions "proudly fulfilled their obligations toward their benefactors, thus placing the latter in their debt once more."[21] This is a puzzling interpretation of something that can be understood very differently, namely that the public discharging of one's reciprocity was intended to show that giving to the person/association in question was a risk-free and worthwhile endeavour.

Honorary inscriptions set up by an association or city (the client) expressing gratitude to a benefactor most certainly *did not* place the association or city in a position of superiority to the benefactor; rather, they appeal to the *philotimia* of benefactors and patrons, their love of honour, as a form of enticement—if you give to us, you can be sure to receive plenty of honour and gratitude. Also working decidedly against Joubert on this point is that

---

[19] Joubert, "One Form of Social Exchange or Two?" 19.
[20] Joubert, *Paul as Benefactor*, 71.
[21] Joubert, *Paul as Benefactor*, 68; idem, "One Form of Social Exchange or Two?" 23.

there is no single instance (as far as I have been able to ascertain) in which a recipient of a benefaction is referred to in the vocabulary of benefaction (e.g., *euergetes*), not even in the highly idealised accounts of Seneca. What Joubert describes between Paul and Jerusalem is not benefaction, but at best gift exchange occurring within balanced reciprocity and involving rotating obligations.[22] That is to say, the bestowal of a gift places the recipient under an obligation to reciprocate. In this gift exchange, patronage and benefaction were similar. They diverge, however, when we look more closely at the nature of that which is exchanged. The recipient of a gift is obligated to return another *gift of equal or greater value*; the recipient of a benefaction or act of patronage is obligated to reciprocate by conferring honour, praise, gratitude and loyalty to a patron or benefactor. The types of exchange are similar, but differences between gift exchange and patronage and benefaction emerge when one looks at *what* is being exchanged and *who* is doing the exchanging.

Joubert is perfectly correct that patronage and benefaction are not exactly the same phenomena. The differences between them, however, are both more general and more subtle than Joubert attempts to present. Look, for instance, at the trouble Joubert has in establishing a consistent use of vocabulary when he writes, "Informally, a number of *benefactors* who did not possess the status of *patron*, nevertheless, conferred *benefactions* on communities, thus unofficially acting out the role of *patrons*."[23] In the context of a work attempting to distinguish between patronage and benefaction, this sentence sums up the difficulties of attempting to do so too absolutely.

In order to begin to understand the similarities and differences between patronage and benefaction it helps to open with the observation that patronage and benefaction are two types of general reciprocity. As Joubert rightfully points out, they are closely related but not entirely synonymous. However, as he admits on occasion, there was considerable overlap, not the least of which concerned the language used to refer to each (see below). Joubert's characteristics of Patronage and Euergetism are summarised in the following Table 1 (items marked with * indicate elements shared in common):

---

[22] I believe Batten took the same position in her paper.
[23] Joubert, *Paul as Benefactor*, 32, emphasis added.

Table 1

Patronage	Euergetism
essentially a political act, not philanthropic	not as political
about social control	generous act undertaken for collective good
exploitative	not exploitative
the exchange only emphasises the status inequality of both parties; typical patronage relationships: landlord/tenant; patrician/freedman; patron/collegia member; Rome/occupied territory; *Emperor/empire	*Emperor can be referred to as a benefactor (p. 26, n. 33)
*can be group directed or individual	*can be group directed or individual
*relations could be long term, even hereditary	*exchange can lead to a long term relationship

When we allow the common elements to cancel each other out, all that appears to distinguish patronage and euergetism is that patronage was more prone to being political, exploitative, and elitist than was euergetism. In the end, however, we find that the same person could be called a patron and a benefactor (as we shall see below), but it had more to do with the nature of the offering than with the exploitation, real or potential. That is, patronage occurred on a daily level, and tended to have to do with survival (including here career posts), while in contrast benefaction occurred sporadically and tended to have to do with luxury (games, buildings, etc.). Patronage tended to occur between individuals, and thus lent itself more to exploitation (on this Joubert and Batten are right); this is because it was easier for a patron to exploit an individual relying on his or her largesse (say in the form of a promise of a feast or by forcing a client to follow him or her around town) than it was to exploit a city or association. Nonetheless, exploitation is a secondary feature of patronage, not a defining characteristic of it. Conversely, benefactions tended to be directed at groups of people, like countries, cities, and associations.

By way of illustrating the difficulty of distinguishing patronage and benefaction too starkly based on any standard, consider the following examples. Were the gods patrons or benefactors? In some instances, what they gave to humans had to do with survival and was given to individual humans (worshippers). This would make them patrons. In some cases, however, the gods gave to "the Greeks" or to all humanity, and this would have made them benefactors. Is a god who heals a person once a benefactor, but one who establishes a long-standing relationship with that person a patron? Is a slave owner who manumits a slave, something that happens only once, a benefactor? Or if she does so only as a means of extending the service of the slave while receiving credit for manumitting a slave in her service is she a patron? Is the Emperor a patron when he provides a senatorial position and a benefactor when he funds a games? Cannot what a patron gives be called a benefaction? These questions are rhetorical; their point is to illustrate that the general tendencies of patronage and benefaction do not override the fact that they are often extraordinarily difficult to distinguish from one another.

One final comment concerning my model and my terminology in what follows is in order. Patronage and benefaction were slightly different forms of exchange that together comprised a larger social structure of exchange known to us as general reciprocity, which should not be confused with balanced reciprocity (gift exchange in which each gift in turn places the recipient under obligation). Often, however, it is difficult and awkward to decide whether the giver is in this instance a patron and in another instance a benefactor. As a result, I use the terms 'patron' and 'benefactor' carefully where the context demands it but interchangeably most of time. I use patronage when I mean to refer to daily acts that involve individual interaction and benefation to refer to items given to collectivities. The term 'client' refers to the person or group who has been placed under an obligation, whether to a patron or to a benefactor. Therefore, human individuals, associations, cities, and (less frequently) countries can be considered clients, which is fitting since each might be called a "friend" of the emperor. Although the forms of reciprocity *might* differ depending on whether the client was an individual, association, or city, the *fact* of obligation did not differ, the sanctions for failure to reciprocate were the same, and in many instances, the form of reciprocity was the same. Hence, there is no need to distinguish between types of recipient or client.[24]

---

[24] The conclusion I draw in this section is duplicated by Harrison's comparison of Roman *gratia* and benefaction of the Greek East (Harrison, *Paul's Language of Grace*, 199–210).

2.3 Human Patronage and Benefaction

2.3.1 Social Patronage

It has been said that the pivotal social value among first century Mediterranean people was honour and shame.[25] There is implicit within this fact several important characteristics about the ancient Mediterranean. The first is that life was lived publicly, that is to say, communally. Ramsay MacMullen noted long ago now, that "What most magnified honor . . . was the degree to which city life was lived publicly, in the open."[26] Honour is the "the value of a person in his or her own eyes (that is, one's claim to worth) *plus* that person's value in the eyes of his or her social group."[27] It is the peer group, or the "public court of reputation,"[28] in this world that evaluates one's worth as an individual in comparison to others. Secondly, honour was a limited good; it was in effect a commodity which people in public life sought to accumulate in order to increase their public worth (or reputation). Because honour was highly sought after, and because it was simultaneously in short supply, people competed for honour (reflected in the agonistic challenge and riposte). It must be acknowledged that not every single social interaction should be seen uncritically as a contest for honour. Other values do exist in the ancient Mediterranean, such as hospitality, but this does not lessen the importance of honour and shame themselves as cultural values. And finally, honour was both ascribed at birth (through one's family lineage, gender and ethnicity) and achieved (and lost) throughout one's lifetime. Achieved honour was the most unstable, for the honour or dishonour associated with one's family name and ethnicity generally changed very slowly, and did not tend to change much over one's own lifetime, allowing of course for the not infrequent political ruin that might be visited upon those on the wrong side of a sudden change in imperial power. Achieved honour, on the other hand,

---

[25] Bruce J. Malina, *The New Testament World* (Louisville: Westminster/John Knox Press, 1993), 28–62.
[26] Ramsay MacMullen, *Roman Social Relations, 50 B.C. to A.D. 284* (New Haven: Yale University Press, 1974), 62.
[27] Malina, *New Testament World*, 31.
[28] Julian Pitt-Rivers, "Honor and Social Status," 19–77 in *Honor and Shame: The Values of Mediterranean Society* (ed. J. G. Peristiany; Chicago: University of Chicago Press, 1966), 27.

is how people actively sought to accumulate honour, and it is this type of honour that could and did change from day to day.[29]

Patronage and benefaction worked in harmony with the values of honour and shame, for without the importance attached to accruing honour and without the hope of doing so within one's own lifetime, patronage and benefaction would not have existed in the form or to the extent it did. Consider, for example, that Dio Chrysostom connected benefactions with a hunger for honour, going so far as to claim, satirically probably, that people would endanger their well-being and survival, spending all their wealth and selling their belongings in the hope of accruing honour through grand benefactions (*1 Glor.* 2; *De lege* 7).

The complex constellation of social values and institutions continues, though it need only delay us briefly. Where honour and shame have been called the pivotal social *values* of the ancient Mediterranean, the central social institution was kinship.[30] Of course, the relationship between honour and shame and kinship was symbiotic; social roles are reflected and learned first in the context of kinship. Embedded within kinship is the institution of patronage and benefaction, taking on a form of fictive-kinship (hence the abundance of kinship terminology to refer to non-familial relationships). What we are left with is a constellation of social systems and social values, all of which are inter-related—kinship, as over-arching social structure, with the values of honour and shame informing the interaction of families and individuals, and the institution of patronage and benefaction embedded within kinship and informed by honour and shame.[31]

The act of patronage or benefaction was characterised by the provision of some good or service.[32] The patron/benefactor–client relationship was a

---

[29] Such a depiction of ancient honour and shame is, I recognise, gender-imbalanced. I am focusing on the agonistic aspect of the honour and shame system, and women did not figure prominently in (which is *not* to say they are entirely absent from) the agonistic part of this system. Women did, however, have a more active and at times central role to play in patronage and benefaction; women frequently functioned and could be publicly honoured as patrons (*IBM* IV 1032; Josephus, *A.J.* 18.181; *Vita* 16; Col 4:15).

[30] Stephan Joubert, "Managing the Household: Paul as *Paterfamilias* of the Christian Household Group in Corinth," in *Modelling Early Christianity: Social-Scientific Studies of the New Testament in its Context* (ed. P. F Esler; London: Routledge, 1995), 213–33.

[31] K. C. Hanson and D. E. Oakman, *Palestine in the Time of Jesus* (Minneapolis: Fortress Press, 1998), 15.

[32] For the classic and still important studies of Mediterranean patronage and clientage, both ancient and modern, see J. Campbell, *Honour, Family and Patronage* (Oxford: Oxford University Press, 1964); Stephen Charles Mott, "The Greek Benefactor and

vertical one between people of unequal status, one party in need of a good or service and the other with the means to provide it. The longest and most detailed treatment of ancient patronage and benefaction is Seneca's seven-volume *De beneficiis*.³³ Seneca opens with a grand statement in keeping with the rest of his treatment: "Among the many and diverse errors of those who live reckless and thoughtless lives, almost nothing that I can mention, excellent Liberalis, is more disgraceful than the fact that we do not know how either to give or to receive benefits" (*Ben.* 1.1.1). For Seneca, patronage and benefaction have cosmic importance; ingratitude is a vice that more than any other "so effectually disrupts and destroys the harmony of the human race" (*Ben.* 4.18.1), and he called benefits the "chief bond of human society" (*Ben.* 1.4.2).³⁴ Given the amount of material evidence attesting to patronage and benefaction in the ancient world, Seneca cannot be accused of wildly overstating the importance of this social institution.

Acts of patronage and benefaction could take the form of actions or concrete goods, and the staggering variety of them is a reflection of the variety of needs people had. For instance, Seneca writes "help one man with money, another with credit, another with influence, another with advice,

---

Deliverance from Moral Distress," Ph.D. diss., Harvard University, 1971; T. F. Carney, *The Economies of Antiquity* (Lawrence, Kansas: Coronado Press, 1973); J. Davis, *The People of the Mediterranean* (London: Routledge and Kegan Paul, 1977); E. Gellner and J. Waterbury (eds.), *Patrons and Clients: In Mediterranean Societies* (London: Duckworth, 1977); Saller, *Personal Patronage under the Early Empire*; S. N. Eisenstadt and L. Roniger, *Patrons, Clients and Friends* (Cambridge: Cambridge University Press, 1984); A. Wallace-Hadrill, "Patronage in Roman Society," in *Patronage in Ancient Society* (ed. A. Wallace-Hadrill; London: Routledge, 1989), 63–87. Cf. J. Hellegouarc'h, *Le vocabulaire latin des relations et des partis politiques sous la république* (Paris: Les Belles Lettres, 1963) and C. Moussy, *Gratia et sa famille* (Paris: Presses universitaires de France, 1966).

33 Though this piece of writing cannot be overlooked, it has several serious drawbacks that should not be ignored. First, Seneca, by his own admission, writes prescriptively not descriptively of patronage and clientage (*Ben.* 2.34.2). He is presenting in many instances *ideal* patron and client behaviour, not always actual behaviour. Many of his statements need to be taken with no small degree of scepticism. For instance, when Seneca claims that clients came under heavy pressure to express their reciprocity, we can believe him because of the motivating power of honour and shame. On the other hand, when he claims that reciprocity executed placed a benefactor under an obligation to benefit again, we should recognise this is an ideal for which little pressure could be brought to bear to bring about. Secondly, the considerable length of *De beneficiis* is due to its repetition, not solely to its systematic and thorough treatment of the topic.

34 In *Ep.* 81.7 Seneca relates proper execution of patronage and clientage to the value for justice.

another with sound precepts" (*Ben.* 1.2.4).³⁵ Of course, this does not exhaust the possibilities for benefactions and acts of patronage: the protection of one's reputation, removal of ignominy, saving of a life, or liberty given (*Ben.* 2.35.3), the giving of "food, financial aid, physical protection, career advancement and administrational posts, citizenship, equality in or freedom from taxation, the inviolability of person and property, support in legal cases, immunity from expenses of public service, help from the gods, and in the case of provincials, the status of *socius* or 'friend of Rome' (*proxenia*)."³⁶ Benefits would tend to fit the person. A city might be given tax-free status; an elite male might be given a high political office. But such benefactions would not serve a poor person seeking survival. This person would look for food and money. And, at the same time, a writer seeking literary patronage might not be served by any of these. Though money would allow them to focus on their trade, literary patronage might include room and board at the benefactor's home. Again, from Seneca:

> It is a benefit to bestow the gift of an estate that by reason of its fertility may lower the price of grain, it is a benefit to bestow one loaf of bread in time of famine; it is a benefit to bestow lands that have large and navigable rivers flowing through them; it is a benefit to point out a spring of water to a man when he parched with thirst and can scarcely draw breath through his dry throat. (*Ben.* 3.8.3)

It certainly cannot be said categorically that benefactions were exclusively material in nature. Plutarch once wrote that well delivered literary discourses and wisdom were better forms of benefaction than were the more typical material goods, and we shall see this in practice with Graeco-Roman philosophers, where the delivery of teachings and advice were treated as if they were benefactions, the philosophers patrons, and the disciples clients.³⁷

Being the recipient of a benefaction or an act of patronage made of one, whether individual, association, or city, a client, and this carried with it certain obligations.³⁸ Benefits were not paid back (they were not loans without interest

---

³⁵ See also Seneca, *Ben.* 1.5.3–6; 2.34.5; 3.8.3.
³⁶ For an excellent summary, see J. H. Elliott, "Patronage and Clientism in Early Christian Society: A Short Reading Guide," *Forum* 3/4 (1987): 39–48, this citation from 42–43.
³⁷ Plutarch, *E Delph.* 384E. See also Cicero, *Off.* 2.15.
³⁸ It must be emphatically stated that while the reception of a benefaction made of one a client, the reception of gratitude and honour did not turn a patron or benefactor into a client with client-like obligations. Mott ("Greek Benefactor," 67, 72) is right

or balanced reciprocity, nor loans with interest or negative reciprocity), and they were not remunerated with something of similar or greater monetary value (they were not gifts, or balanced reciprocity).[39] The primary responsibility of clients was reciprocity, demonstrated through public expressions of gratitude and other activities that would bring honour to a benefactor.[40] The publicity of the client behaviour is critical, and inextricably tied to honour and shame, for it is the public court of reputation that needs to witness the gratitude so that both client and benefactor can be given credit. Some writers even refer to the "laws" concerning reciprocity.[41]

In addition to the obvious and basic expressions of gratitude and thanksgiving, honouring activities include participating in a battle or skirmish, physical labour, appropriate compliments paid to a benefactor or patron (Seneca, *Ben.* 2.24.4), talking publicly about benefits received (*Ben.* 2.11.3; 2.23.1–2; 2.24.4), erecting a statue (*Ben.* 5.8.2), arriving at a patron's gate for the morning salute (Horace, *Sat.* 1.1.9–10; *Ep.* 2.1.103–107; Martial 10.82), and simply attending one's patron in public places (Horace, *Ep.* 1.7.9; Martial 2.18; 2.57; 6.48), such as to literary readings, court appearances, or simply following your patron around town. Escorts like this would have honoured the patron because in the eyes of the public court of reputation, the greater the retinue trailing a patron, the greater must one's honour have been.[42] Even to call someone a benefactor, and thus to draw attention to an act of generosity, was itself a way of honouring a patron, for "the very title . . . did not simply state a fact but conferred a status."[43]

---

to suggest that gratitude carried with it the hope of more benefactions in the future, so it was certainly the hope that well publicised gratitude and honour would "compel" the benefactor or patron to give again, but it is not helpful to confuse the obligations of a client (which are real) with those of a patron or benefactor (which are ideal).

[39] Pliny, *Ep.* 10.51: "I begin to realise to the full the extent of your generosity when it is thus graciously extended to my whole family: I could not venture to repay it, whatever my ability to do so might be. I can only have recourse to vows taken on your behalf and pray to the gods that I may never prove unworthy of the favours you continually bestow."

[40] Stephen Charles Mott, "The Power of Giving and Receiving: Reciprocity in Hellenistic Benevolence," in *Current Issues in Biblical and Patristic Interpretation* (ed. G. F. Hawthorne; Grand Rapids: Eerdmans, 1975), 60–72.

[41] Dio Chrysostom, *De lege* 6; Philo, *Decal.* 165–167. For more, as well as examples of ingratitude, see Mott, "Greek Benefactor," 68–71.

[42] Elliott, "Patronage and Clientism," 43.

[43] A. R. Hand, *Charities and Social Aid in Greece and Rome* (London: Thames and Hudson, 1968), 36.

Every type of source from the ancient world attests to a singular concern on the part of the client, and that is to express adequate gratitude. Seneca, so easily suspected of overstating his case so much of the time, is supported in this. Seneca, as we saw above, claims that unlike any other "crime," ingratitude "so effectually disrupts and destroys the harmony of the human race" (*Ben.* 4.18.1). Again, he claims that "Homicides, tyrants, thieves, adulterers, robbers, sacrilegious men, and traitors there always will be; but worse than all these is the crime of ingratitude" (*Ben.* 1.10.4). And yet, these seem exactly to be the sorts of sentiments that drive the need of clients to draw conspicuous attention to the fact that they have carried out their obliged gratitude. So, for instance, myriad honorary inscriptions draw attention, through their ἵνα clauses, to their public gratitude "*in order that* those who confer benefits might receive gratitude in return for love of honour, and that those who have been benefited, returning honours, might be known for gratitude before all people, never coming too late for the sake of recompense of those who wish to do good" (*SEG* XI 948).[44] The absolute necessity of gratitude is reflected even in the writings of the epistolary theorists, sources that obviously have not a pressing need to express gratitude but take such examples as axiomatic. Pseudo-Libanius, for example, offers the following in an example of a letter of reproach: "You have received many favours from us, and I am exceedingly amazed that you remember none of them, but speak badly of us. That is characteristic of a person with an ungrateful disposition. For the ungrateful forget noble men, and in addition ill-treat their benefactors as though they were enemies."[45] Finally, it is so common to read in ancient inscriptions, papyri, literary and "religious" sources the sentiment to the effect that a recipient is incapable of finding sufficient words to express the full weight of their gratitude, and that even giving their lives in return would not suffice.

The institution of patronage and clientage witnessed a third party in addition to the giver (patron or benefactor) and the recipient (client: person, group, or city)—the broker. Under some circumstances, the client dealt directly with the patron or benefactor; frequently, however, too great a distance of social status or geography separated the person in need of some good or service and the person with the ability to give it. This is most obvious

---

[44] A very small selection of possible inscriptions that say similar things include: *SEG* XXIV 1100; *IDelos* IV 1521; *IG* XII⁹ 899; *OGI* 248; *SIG*³ 721.

[45] Pseudo-Libanius, Ἐπιστολιμαῖοι Χαρακτῆρες 64. Translation is taken, with gratitude, from Harrison, *Paul's Language of Grace*, 71. One finds other examples of ancient literary theorists presupposing the centrality of reciprocal gratitude in their examples of letter types.

with respect to the Emperor, the highest ranking human benefactor or patron. Since few people could assume to approach the Emperor, one typically needed a broker to initiate the relationship, someone whose status was close enough to the client's that a client could approach the broker, and whose status was close enough to the Emperor's that the broker could approach him. Conceivably there could be a number of brokerage links on the way to someone as powerful as an Emperor. But a broker could also play a role in lower level patronal relationships, say where the client did not know the patron already.

A fine example for its popularity comes from Sophocles' *Oedipus Tyrannus*. Creon has been charged by Oedipus with treason, to which Creon asks why he would give up the fine placement of broker to the king for the lowly status of murderer: "Now all men cry me Godspeed! wish me well, | And every suitor seeks to gain my ear, | If he would hope to win a grace from thee!" (596–598). The reality of the ancient world was that everybody was a potential source of access to someone else. If one was an influence broker, one might be highly sought after to provide linkages to those with power.

A number of examples from the letters of the younger Pliny illustrate the practice of brokerage best, since he had access to the Emperor Trajan. On one occasion (*Ep.* 10.4), Pliny reveals that he has been acting as a broker between his friend Romanus (and Romanus' family) and Trajan in order to have Romanus promoted to the Senatorial order. This process had been started sometime earlier, but some confusion over the monies that were to be paid into the office had led to a delay. In one letter, Pliny writes to Trajan to assure him that all this has been fixed, and to beg him to bestow this honour upon Romanus. In another letter, Pliny asks Trajan to grant citizenship to a physician who cared for Pliny so well, as well as for two freedwomen, one of whom asked Pliny to act as broker (*Ep.* 10.5). In all these cases, Pliny entreats Trajan as a client—he flatters and honours him, and expresses his gratitude freely—but it is also clear that Pliny is acting as a patron to those whom he is serving. The broker clearly has a somewhat liminal status—he or she is both broker and patron.[46] To the client seeking something from a patron too far removed by status, the broker is a benefactor or patron because he or she

---

[46] J. F. Boissevain, *Friends of Friends: Networks, Manipulators, and Coalitions* (New York: St. Martin's Press, 1974), 147–48; Moxnes, "Patron–Client Relations and the New Community in Luke–Acts," especially 248–49; see also deSilva, "Patronage and Reciprocity," 33.

has provided a benefaction by acting as broker.[47] To the patron from whom the broker seeks a benefaction (even on behalf of another), the broker acts as a client. The broker therefore takes on the status also of patron, which then obligates the client to act appropriately towards him or her. In the example from Pliny, Trajan's granting the request to Pliny meant that both Pliny and Romanus were indebted to Trajan, and that Romanus was indebted to Pliny. This somewhat complex state of affairs is nicely expressed by Pliny, when, after securing a senatorial post for someone who passed that on to a friend, Pliny hopes that "your benefaction may be as acceptable to him as mine is to you" (*Ep.* 3.8).[48]

2.3.2 Literary Patronage

A discussion of ancient patronage and clientage is not complete without understanding the practice of literary patronage.[49] It is not that literary patronage is different from other types of patronage, and yet it offers some points of comparison with divine patronage, not the least of which is the presence of literary creation within the relationship (as in scripture). Unlike the sort of social patronage with which I have been chiefly concerned, literary patronage frequently involved people of high social standing, the wealthy and elite. Especially in late republican Rome, writers could be near social equals with their "patrons." This would mean that a writer might receive very different benefits than a non-elite client would receive in social patronage. So Pliny the Younger and Theophanes, both elites in their communities, were clearly clients of Trajan and Pompey respectively.[50] What is to be gained from looking at this practice is the understanding that though patronage and clientage took many forms, the basic rules associated with it did not change when the social standing of the players did.

The benefactions gained from a literary patron are as varied as with social patronage. First, Roman literary patronage was necessary because there was

---

[47] H. Moxnes, "Patron–Client Relations and the New Community in Luke–Acts," 248–49; see also deSilva, "Patronage and Reciprocity," 33.
[48] See Saller, *Personal Patronage under the Early Empire*, 75. For other examples of brokerage, see deSilva, "Patronage and Reciprocity," 34.
[49] Barbara K. Gold, *Literary Patronage in Greece and Rome* (Chapel Hill and London: University of North Carolina Press, 1987). See also M. Citroni, "Patronage, Literary," in *The Oxford Classical Dictionary* (ed. S. Hornblower and A. Spawforth; Oxford and London: Oxford University Press, 1996), 1124–26.
[50] For information on the social status of Theophanes, based on epigraphical material, see L. Robert, "Théophanie de Mytilène à Constantinople," CRAI (1969): 42–64.

no money to be earned from being a writer—although publication and bookselling existed by the first century B.C.E., writers did not receive money when their works were sold—and the production of writing was costly. So the first form of literary patronage was the financial support of a writer. This might take the form of financial assistance, but it also commonly entailed room and board: the writer might live in the home of his patron. Yet, since some writers were elite, and thus fully capable of funding their own efforts, there was something less tangible that the literary patron could offer a writer—access to influential audiences. Many writers craved an audience and appreciation more than financial gain, and the highly placed and well connected patron could put a writer in contact with people who appreciated writing. Maecenas, whose literary patronage was legendary even in the Renaissance, offered to Horace not only considerable financial and personal support, but membership and participation in a circle of some of the best Roman writers of his day, including Virgil and Propertius. Propertius himself praises Maecenas for gaining him the sort of audience that appreciates Callimachus, and therefore will appreciate him (3.9.43–44). Patrons also at times worked to gain their literary clients citizenship, as Cicero did for his Greek poet client Archias. Thus, we can see that literary patronage was as creative as other types of patronage, taking as many forms as there were needs to be met.

We have seen that the primary task of the client is to act in a way that will honour a patron. In some activities literary clients were no better off than their less elite counterparts—they might accompany their patron around town (Horace, *Sat.* 2.6.16ff.; Horace, *Ep.* 1.7.8–9; Martial 11.24) and on expeditions and military campaigns (as Ennius did for M. Fulvius Nobilior, Cicero, *Arch.* 11.27). There is an interesting and surprising relationship between social patronage and literary patronage. One expects that a literary client could offer to a patron or benefactor immortality by way of dedicating to him or her a single poem or poetic sequence, writing an encomium, or panegyric. Setting aside the obvious differences in terms of artistry, this was different only in degree from the common practice of inscribing stones with honorary decrees: less artful (though not necessarily so in terms of the decorations one finds on inscriptions), but no less honouring, and offering an even more enduring form of memory set in stone. Of great interest, however, is simply the fact that writing serves a common way of expressing gratitude, for attempting to make that expression more permanent. Whether literary, inscriptional, or, as we shall encounter below, religious or scriptural, writing is a primary feature of the patron or benefactor and client exchange relationship.

2.4 Divine Patronage and Benefaction

The entire system of human patronage and benefaction, from acts of benefaction on the part of patrons to the obligations of clients and the role of brokers, is mirrored in (or is a mirror of) divine patronage and benefaction.[51] Seneca moves seamlessly between discussions of human and divine beneficence because they are separate manifestations of the same phenomenon, distinguished only by who or what is being addressed (human or deity) and some of the ways that such address comes to expression. Seneca shows that the two exist on a continuum: the human practice of patronage and benefaction is a manifestation and continuation of the endless and non-judgmental generosity of the gods (*Ben.* 4.3.3). Indeed, he wishes constantly that humans would emulate the gods when it came to beneficence (*Ben.* 1.10.5; 2.1.1–4; 3.15.4; 4.26.1; 4.28; 7.30.4–5; 7.31.2–4; 7.32). What separated human and divine benefactors is that the gods were infinitely more generous; human patronage and benefaction were but a shoddy imitation of what the gods could do for people.

When Dio Chrysostom writes about humanity's first conception of God, the language and imagery he uses is of a generous benefactor conferring many things of value upon humanity (*Dei. cogn.* 21, 27–28, 32, 39). Humans addressed the gods for general and daily needs—food, protection, comfort, strength, assistance—in addition to those things which only the gods could deliver—great crops, health, and most frequently, salvation. *SEG* II 821, a second century B.C.E. aretalogy to Isis, attributes to her the institution of justice, the Greek language as well as non-Greek language for others, civic laws, tranquillity, and the practice of children honouring their parents.[52] In return, humans expressed reciprocity to their divine patrons and benefactors just as they did to their human patrons and benefactors,[53] though in some cases they did so in a slightly different manner.

That human patronage and divine patronage operate as reflections of each other can be seen in the existence of the associations of the Graeco-

---

[51] S. R. F. Price, "Gods and Emperors: The Greek Language of the Roman Imperial Cult," *JHS* 104 (1984): 79–95; Mott, "The Power of Giving and Receiving." Much of this had to do with the fact that the gods were long seen as having bestowed everything in the natural world, which of course no human could have done (Aristotle, *Eth. nic.* 1162a.6; Seneca, *Ben.* 4.5; 4.28.1; Epictetus, *Diatr.* 1.4.32; Plutarch, *Is. Os.* 351C–351D; 356A–B).

[52] See *NewDocs* 1:10–21.

[53] Martin Percival Charlesworth, "Some Observations on Ruler-Cult, especially in Rome," *HTR* 28 (1935): 5–44.

Roman era.⁵⁴ Evidence of associations, especially in the form of the inscriptions they so typically left behind, attests to a higher degree of heterogeneity and variety than previously thought. Associations were united by a something held in common. This was often a trade (e.g., bakers, merchants, purple dyers, wood cutters, etc.), though equally often there were associations of mixed or related trades (clothes washers, leather workers, linen producers, purple dyers, etc.). Associations were also formed around familial networks, and ethnicity or geographic location. Variety in the rationale behind the creation of associations is matched by variety also in their social composition. Harland finds that while *some* associations were homogeneous in terms of gender or social status, too many others reflected a fuller (even if not balanced) spectrum of society, excepting the very elites, to warrant the conclusion that social heterogeneity is a typical feature of the association. And finally, there was variety in their reasons for gathering, whether religious, funerary, or social. The most significant contribution of Harland in this regard is his observation that even within all this variety of rationales, social composition, and purpose, the activities of the associations cannot be divorced from concerns of religion or patronage, and these would often be inseparable.⁵⁵

Many inscriptions from associations acknowledge both human and divine patrons and benefactors. For example, throughout his work, Harland illus-

---

54   For fine introductions to the types and functions of associations, see Philip A. Harland, *Associations, Synagogues, and Congregations: Claiming a Place in Ancient Mediterranean Society* (Minneapolis: Fortress Press, 2003) and John S. Kloppenborg and Steven G. Wilson (eds.), *Voluntary Associations in the Graeco-Roman World* (New York: Routledge, 1996). The material in this paragraph is indebted to Harland's *Associations, Synagogues, and Congregations*, Chapter One.

55   Phil Harland responds to a prominent stream of scholarship that suggests that associations, specifically trade associations but even cultic ones as well, had little to do with religion despite their general association with a god. He shows the impressive extent to which the activities of associations were tied up in recognising and honouring their patron deities (Harland, *Associations, Synagogues, and Congregations*, 55–87). Tod went even further to claim that "it was the desire for religious fellowship and common worship that contributed to the formation of guilds within the state" (Marcus N. Tod, *Sidelights on Greek History: Three Lectures on the Light Thrown by Greek Inscriptions on the Life and Thought of the Ancient World* [Oxford: Basil Blackwell, 1932], 74). See also Philip A. Harland, "Honours and Worship: Emperors, Imperial Cults, and Associations at Ephesus (first to third centuries C.E.)," *Studies in Religion/Sciences Religieuses* 25 (1996): 319–34; B. Hudson McLean, "The Place of Cult in Voluntary Associations and Christian Churches on Delos," in *Voluntary Associations in the Graeco-Roman World* (ed. J. S. Kloppenborg and S. G. Wilson; New York: Routledge, 1996), 189.

trates the extent to which association activities, whether feasting privately or publicly "monumentalising," were concerned with honouring their human and divine patrons (the latter, of course, is *religion*).[56] Likewise, according to Horsley, *IKyme* 30 (= *NewDocs* 1:2) was established by a *thiasos* that appears to have been named after its human founder Menekleides, but it also appears to invoke the name of Dionysus, potentially its patron deity. In addition to naming patron deities, as well as naming one's association after a god, which are obvious forms of patronal acknowledgement,[57] one might claim that an inscription was done at the command of the god. So, for example, the priest Apollonios claims that he "composed this record in accordance with the ordinance of God."[58]

The gods were approached as patrons and benefactors; as much is apparent wherever we see the language of benefactions used of humans used also of the gods. To cite only one example of a great many, Aelius Aristides frequently refers to the εὐεργεσίαι of Asclepius (*Sacred Tales* 2.294.8; 4.323.14; 4.337.11; *Asclepius* 44.2; *Speech for Asclepius* 39.19) and refers to the god with the title Εὐεργέτης (*Sacred Tales* 4.329.16).[59] Like elite humans, the gods were believed to have the ability to bestow certain valued and limited goods upon those who honoured them. And honouring the gods was key, for even Euripides was compelled to acknowledge that the gods took great joy (τέρπεται) in the same honour (τιμώμενος) as did men (*Bacchae* 319–321).

In the following chapter, it shall become clearer to what extent human and divine patronage and benefaction parallel each other. Suffice to say here simply that the conduct of worshipers (in a "religious" setting) and disciples (in a philosophical setting) parallels that of clients in alarming ways. The obligation of gratitude, the practice of thanksgiving and praise, the acts of committing these to writing and to spreading the good news of a patron's

---

[56] The term "monumentalizing" is Harland's term; it brilliantly incorporates not only the activity but also *the effect* of setting up honouring statues and inscriptions (Harland, *Associations, Synagogues, and Congregations*, 17).

[57] Associations could call their patron deities 'benefactor' (*IAssos* 19, 20; *IDelos* IV 1778, 2325). They could also name their associations after their patron god: for instance, the Berytian Poseidoniastai (*IDelos* IV 1520) and the Tyrian Heraclesiastai (*IDelos* IV 1519).

[58] Sarapis in the case of *IG* XI⁴ 1299; also found with translation at Danker, *Benefactor*, 186–88.

[59] See W. Dindorf, *Aristides* (Hildesheim: Georg Olms, 1964), and in translation, C. A. Behr, *Aelius Aristides and* The Sacred Tales (Amsterdam: Adolf M. Hakkert, 1968). For other examples of the gods being approached as patrons, see *Syll*³ 365; 708.25, 30; 709.47; 731.19; 1172.9–10.

benefactions are all testimony to this parallelism between human and divine patronage and benefaction. What is more, divine and philosophical patronage also have brokers to facilitate relationships between patrons and clients— priests as in Apuleius, *Metam.* 11.25 or divine beings such as angels and demigods in Plutarch, *Is. Os.* 361C, and the philosophers themselves when they saw themselves as mediators of God's divine wisdom. This is a brief treatment, but more detail will emerge to support this portrait as the book progresses.

2.5 Divine Patronage and Benefaction in Hellenistic Judaism

It can be stated categorically from the outset that pre-common-era Palestine did not have a patron–client or a benefactor–client social structure.[60] While the Greeks and Romans had a clearly demarcated social institution of patronage and benefaction, and a fairly broad vocabulary to go with it, Israelite society lacked both. Therefore, it would be difficult to claim that Jews thought of their God as a patron or a benefactor since they lacked any social model and vocabulary which might serve as a metaphor. What they had in its stead was a system of covenantal exchange, which shared many features in common with generalised reciprocity but differed by the presence of a formalised agreement. In other words, patronage and benefaction was an informal agreement, in that it lacked formal features of agreement. The expectations and obligations between patrons/benefactors and their clients were socially enforced, but not enshrined in a formal contract.[61]

---

[60] There are a number of works that have supposed precisely either that ancient Israel *did* have a patron–client structure, or admit that it did not but think that it is still fruitful to analyse it etically as if it did. See H. Olivier, "God as Friendly Patron: Reflections on Isaiah 5:1–7," *In die Skriflig* 30 (1996): 39–58; P. Spilsbury, "God and Israel in Josephus: A Patron–Client Relationship [Ant 1–11]," in *Understanding Josephus* (ed. S. Mason; JSPSup 32; Sheffield: Sheffield Academic Press, 1998), 172–91; T. Raymond Hobbs, "Reflections on Honor, Shame, and Covenant Relations," *JBL* 116 (1997): 501–503; Ronald A. Simkins, "Patronage and the Political Economy of Monarchic Israel," *Semeia* 87 (1999): 123–44; Niels Peter Lemche, "From Patronage Society to Patronage Society," in *The Origins of the Ancient Israelite States* (ed. V. Fritz and P. R. Davies; JSOTSup 228; Sheffield: Sheffield Academic Press, 1996), 106–20; idem, "Kings and Clients: On Loyalty between the Ruler and the Ruled in Ancient 'Israel,'" *Semeia* 66 (1994): 119–32.

[61] M. Weinfeld, "*Berit*—Covenant Vs. Obligation," *Bib* 56 (1975): 120–28; George E. Mendenhall, *Law and Covenant in Israelite and the Ancient near East* (Pittsburgh: The Presbyterian Board of Colportage, 1955); Daniel J. Elazar, *Covenant and Polity in Biblical Israel: Biblical Foundations and Jewish Expressions* (London: Transaction Publishers, 1995).

All that changed, however, when Judaism encountered the linguistic and cultural influence of Hellenism.[62] It is common to acknowledge the creative effects that ensued when Jews combined Hellenistic and Jewish ways of thinking, often, for example, with reference to Wisdom Literature. This is also the case, it can be demonstrated, with respect to the sudden use of the language and imagery of patronage and benefaction by Jews to describe their interactions with God. Our best examples of this are the Septuagint, Josephus, and Philo.

2.5.1 Septuagint

The Graeco-Roman language of patronage and benefaction, epitomised in the ευεργ- and χαρ- root words, is introduced very gradually into Jewish tradition through the Septuagint. That is to say, the words most frequently appear as ways of rendering Hebrew words and ideas that originally had little to do with patronage and benefaction, and yet in their translation they started a process in which their appropriateness within a context of patronage and benefaction became apparent. There are a few instances where the words are used in such a way that does suggest a growing awareness of human and divine patronage and benefaction. A most interesting example of a Septuagint translation that incorporates the language of patronage and benefaction appears in Ps 56:3 LXX (MT 57:3): "I call out to God Most High, to God who fulfils his purpose for me (גֹּמֵר עָלָי)." The Hebrew גָּמַר is not entirely clear here, since it usually means to perfect, complete, and bring to an end. At this point, the Septuagint translator chooses εὐεργετέω, whose meaning *is* clear and quite different from גָּמַר, so that the second strophe reads "to God who benefits/ favours/does good with me." Are we to understand, that the translator thinks that God's perfecting believers is a benefaction? It is at least a possibility worth considering. Likewise, Ps 12:6 LXX represents quite a free translation of what appears in the Ps 13:6 MT: "But I trust in your faithfulness, my heart will exult in your deliverance. I will sing to the LORD, for he rewards (גָּמַל) me." The Septuagint reads, "I trusted in your compassion, my heart will rejoice in your salvation. I will sing to the Lord who benefits (εὐεργετήσαντι) me and I will praise the name of the most high Lord." Again, it hardly

---

[62] The same conclusion has been reached by Harrison in his analysis of the language of χάρις in first-century Judaism. See H. W. Attridge, *The Interpretation of Biblical History in* Antiquitates Judaicae *of Flavius Josephus* (Missoula: Scholars Press, 1976), 78ff.; Harrison, *Paul's Language of Grace*, 101–46.

requires a stretch of religious imagination that a Hellenistic Jewish translator would understand that a reward of God is quite obviously a benefaction; this at least is a fair inference based on this conscious translation decision. Finally, Ps 77:11 LXX interprets the Hebrew עֲלִילָה, normally rendered as 'deed,' with the word εὐεργεσία. Here, we find 'his benefaction' used of Israel's God.

More instructive of a growing sense of divine patronage and benefaction than translation instances are instances of that vocabulary appearing in compositional Greek. This occurs mostly in the various books of the Maccabees. For example, 2 Macc 10:38 has a very Graeco-Roman sounding: "When they had accomplished these things, with hymns and thanksgivings they blessed the Lord who benefits (εὐεργετέω) Israel and gives them the victory." It is significant that the benefaction is in this case even named—victory over enemies is a benefaction from God. Likewise, 2 Macc 6:13 calls it a benefaction when God punishes the impious rather than leaving them alone for long. The same term is used, as are the other εὐεργ- root words, with reference as well to the institution of human patronage and benefaction. 2 Macc 9:26 has Antiochus refer to his common and private εὐεργεσίαι and ask that they be remembered, and 2 Macc 4:2 refers to a man who was τὸν εὐεργέτην τῆς πόλεως—the benefactor of the city.[63] The Maccabean writings attest a growing awareness that the God of Israel benefits Jews just as the Hellenistic gods benefit their followers.

The Wisdom of Solomon also provides us with some excellent examples of a Hellenised Jewish writer finding the language of Graeco-Roman patronage and benefaction fruitful for talking about the Jewish God. The verb εὐεργετέω, to benefit or, essentially, to make a benefaction, is used in Wis 11:5 and 11:13 to describe the action of God towards the Israelites, and 11:13 goes on to clarify that the Israelites perceived their benefactions to have been the work of the Lord. Wis 16:2 reminds the reader that the Lord, whom it calls εὐεργετήσας τὸν λαόν, gave them a benefaction by preparing for them fine food for eating. The divine patron of the Israelites takes care of the people when they are in need. Wis 16:11 relates that what the Lord did for the Israelites was to have them suffer briefly so that they would not forget and become unresponsive to the benefactions of the Lord—εὐεργεσία. Wis 16:24 summarises the synkrisis (a discussion of synkrisis can be found in the following chapter) with ἡ γὰρ κτίσις σοὶ τῷ ποιήσαντι ὑπηρετοῦσα ἐπιτείνεται εἰς κόλασιν κατὰ τῶν ἀδίκων καὶ ἀνίεται εἰς εὐεργεσίαν ὑπὲρ τῶν ἐπὶ σοὶ

---

[63] See also 3 Macc 3:19; 6:24; 4 Macc 8:6, 17 for examples of human benefactors referred to.

πεποιθότων. The NRSV translates this as "For creation, serving you who made it, exerts itself to punish the unrighteous, and in kindness relaxes on behalf of those who trust in you." A translation that better emphasises the εὐεργεσία and notes that ἀνίεται εἰς εὐεργεσίαν ὑπέρ functions in parallel to ἐπιτείνεται εἰς κόλασιν κατά, would read: "creation exerts itself as punishment against the unrighteous and relaxes as a benefaction on behalf of those who trust in you." The benefaction here is that creation treated the faithful Israelites well.[64] That this language reflecting the experience of divine patronage and benefaction appears rather suddenly in the Jewish tradition through the influence of Graeco-Roman culture is significant, and it does not end with the Septuagint.

2.5.2 Flavius Josephus

A facility with the language and imagery of patronage and benefaction that increased between the translation Greek and composition Greek of the Septuagint, appears to increase another step when we encounter Jewish writers as thoroughly Hellenized as Josephus and Philo. That Josephus was well familiar with the Graeco-Roman system of patronage and clientage is well established.[65] This much is clear even at a glance, for throughout the corpus of Josephus, vocabulary based on the εὐεργ- root (εὐεργεσία, εὐεργετέω, εὐεργέτης, εὐεργετικός, εὐεργέτις) appears 111 times.[66] Frequently Josephus uses these terms with reference to the benefactions of regular people (as opposed to royalty). Thus, in re-telling the story of how Moses protected and helped the daughters of the priest of Midian at the well (Exod 2:16–20),

---

[64] Although Wis 18:2 contains the word χάρις, which is a part of the vocabulary of Graeco-Roman patronage and benefaction, it is unclear what can be made of it since the meaning of the whole verse is unclear. It appears that χάρις is the object of δέομαι, that the Egyptians were asking for a benefaction from the Israelites. The unclarity comes in assessing what that benefaction was supposed to be, since it is presumably contained in the aorist passive verb, διενεχθῆναι.

[65] Attridge, *The Interpretation of Biblical History*, 79–91; Jerome H. Neyrey, "Josephus' Vita and the Encomium: A Native Model of Personality," *JSJ* 25 (1994): 177–206; S. Schwartz, "Josephus in Galilee: Rural Patronage and Social Breakdown," in *Josephus and the History of the Greco-Roman Period: Essays in Honour of Morton Smith* (ed. F. Parente and J. Sievers; StPB 41; Leiden: E. J. Brill, 1994), 290–306; Spilsbury, "God and Israel in Josephus."

[66] Karl Heinrich Rengstorf, *A Complete Concordance to Flavius Josephus* (5 vols.; Leiden: E. J. Brill, 1973).

Josephus refers to the daughters as having been benefited (εὐεργετηθεῖσαι), has the priest commend his daughters for their regard for their benefactor (τῆς περὶ τὸν εὐεργετηκότα σπουδῆς), and has the priest point out to Moses his ability to show adequate gratitude for Moses' benefaction (*A.J.* 2.261–263). Further, Josephus relates that after several cities in the Galilee were given to him by the Emperor, they considered Josephus their "benefactor and saviour," εὐεργέτης καὶ σωτήρ (*Vita* 244 and 259) because of the services he had provided them. Finally, Josephus had a literary patron, Epaphroditus, to whom he expresses the same honour typical of the Graeco-Roman writers we saw above (*A.J.* 1.8).

Josephus also uses the language of patronage and benefaction of royalty, whether kings or pharaohs or those associated with either one. Most importantly is Josephus's relationship with Vespasian. After Josephus was captured by the general Vespasian, he asked for an audience with him during which he offered his loyalty and honoured him by "predicting" his future station as emperor (*B.J.* 3.400–403). Josephus's offer to be a client of Vespasian was more or less ignored until Vespasian became emperor, at which point he remembered Josephus's "prediction" (*B.J.* 4.622). Thus the relationship of patron and client was secured between the two men, and in fact was handed down by Vespasian to his son Titus and on to Domitian, and was characterised by the Emperors' bestowal of Roman citizenship and several parcels of land upon Josephus and by Josephus's total exoneration of the Romans of any guilt for the slaughters and horrors of the war with the Jews in his account of that war.

Another notable example of Josephus's familiarity with the practice of patronage and benefaction, notable because it is personal and because of the gender of the benefactor, comes early in Josephus's career. Here Josephus describes his relationship with the consort of Nero, Poppaea (*Vita* 16). Josephus sought and was granted an important benefaction (εὐεργεσία) from this woman, namely the liberation of the priests in Judea, in addition to other large gifts (μεγάλων δωρεῶν).[67] He describes at length the benefactions (εὐεργεσίας), almost too numerous to mention (*A.J.* 16.146–147), which Herod made towards the cities throughout Syria and Greece: many civic functions, completion of old and construction of new public works, a Pythian Temple for Rhodes, public buildings for Nicopolis, colonnades and paving for a street in Antioch of Syria, and money for the Olympic games. Josephus uses the title εὐεργέτης of such notable characters as Hyrcanus (*B.J.* 1.215), Anthony

---

[67] See also *A.J.* 18.181 for another prominent woman benefactor.

(*B.J.* 1.388), himself (*B.J.* 2.607; *Vita* 244, 259), Trajan (*B.J.* 3.459), Titus (*B.J.* 4.113), Vespasian (*B.J.* 7.71), Caesar Augustus (*A.J.* 16.98), and Herod (*A.J.* 16.212), among others.

Most notable, however, is that Josephus, like his Graeco-Roman counterparts, understands there to be a relationship between human and divine patronage and benefaction. For instance, he echoes Seneca's sense that human benefaction was a poor imitation of divine benefaction, and that to compare a human benefactor to the gods was a thing of great honour (*A.J.* 9.93). Over half of Josephus's uses of the language of benefaction have to do with relations between God and Israel. Josephus deliberately portrays the relationship between God and Israel as a relationship between patron or benefactor and client, using considerable terminology and imagery from Graeco-Roman patronage and benefaction. Throughout the *Antiquities of the Jews*, Josephus represents God's interaction with various figures in Israelite history as that of a divine patron dealing with clients. Josephus has Moses deliver a speech to the Hebrews as they are about to enter Canaan in which he reminds the Jews of God's two great benefactions to them—their freedom and the promise of land. He tells them that they have the first already, and that in order to facilitate the advent of the second, they must hold God, who is their helper and ally, in lasting honour (*A.J.* 3.300). Finally, Josephus refers to the Law not only as emanating from God, which is biblically obvious, but as a *benefaction* from God. Josephus has Moses declare that the Law was the "best of gifts" (δωρεᾶς τῶν κρειττόνων, *A.J.* 4.316), the "finest of gifts" (δώρημα κάλλιστον, *A.J.* 4.318) "which God himself presented to you" (οὓς αὐτὸς γεννήσας ὑμῖν ἔδωκε, *A.J.* 4.319).[68] Joshua's death speech invokes the hearers to recall τάς τε εὐεργεσίας τοῦ θεοῦ ἁπάσας (*A.J.* 5.115), namely their freedom from bondage to the Egyptians and their acquisition of the land of Israel. The

---

[68] Also noteworthy in this passage is that Josephus has Moses refer to himself as a broker of God, "using me as a manager and servant of those things which he wished to bestow (εὐεργετεῖν) upon our people" (*A.J.* 4.317). The citation from Josephus begs the question, if gift exchange is not patronage, then why does the language of gifts appear in these passages (and in others like them). The fact is that relationships of patronage/benefaction and clientage were frequently disguised as other types of relationships, most notably relationships of friendship and relationships of gift exchange. That benefactors frequently referred to their clients as 'friends' should be read as a convention, and not as a reflection of equal status. Likewise, the language of gifts within patronage and benefaction settings is likely little more than convention.

benefactions of God are a central theme for Josephus' recasting of Jewish history.[69]

Josephus is also consistent within the model of patronage and benefaction in portraying the faithful Jews as clients of this generous and protective divine benefactor. Again, Josephus expresses this by placing injunctions that reflect Graeco-Roman patronage and benefaction on the lips of his biblical characters. In *A.J.* 4.212, Josephus has Moses require the expression of gratitude twice daily for God's gifts (δωρεάς), and he even goes on to offer a classic description of the place of gratitude in the patronage and benefaction relationship: first, it is a natural duty, and secondly, it is meant to predispose the benefactor towards making more benefactions in the future. In another instance, Josephus redacts biblical narrative by having Abraham explain his willingness to sacrifice his son Isaac in terms of a client's obligation of reciprocity to a patron for benefactions received (*A.J.* 1.229). Similarly, *A.J.* 2.196 and 8.111 relate the need to recompense God but both texts acknowledge the uselessness of actions for doing so—praise and thanksgiving are all God accepts.[70] Finally, Josephus has the prophet Samuel chastise the Hebrews for having forgotten the divine benefactions (ἀμνημονήσειαν τῶν εὐεργεσιῶν) of their freedom and victory over the enemy (*A.J.* 6.60).

2.5.3 Philo of Alexandria

Philo is even richer and freer than Josephus in his use of the language of patronage and benefaction.[71] Harrison says of Philo that he was "intimately acquainted with the terminology and ideology of benefaction."[72] For Philo, the quintessential act of God that makes of God a benefactor is creation: "all things are a benefaction of God (χάριν ὄντα θεοῦ): earth, water, fire, sun, stars, heaven, all the plants and animals" (*Deus* 107). As it was with Josephus,

---

[69] It is worth noting, that though Josephus refers to what comes from God as benefactions, he *never* once refers to God as a εὐεργέτης; he uses the term to refer to human benefactors exclusively.

[70] For more examples of Josephus's use of patronage and clientage language to describe the relationship between God and Israel, see Spilsbury, "God and Israel in Josephus."

[71] Philo uses words of the εὐεργ- root 156 times. Peder Borgen, Kåre Fuglseth, and Roald Skarsten, *The Philo Index: A Complete Greek Word Index to the Writings of Philo of Alexandria* (Grand Rapids: Eerdmans, 2000).

[72] Harrison, *Paul's Language of Grace*, 120.

Philo's God is the supreme divine benefactor. He notes that God, aside from the benefaction of having created humans, also gave them the best of gifts (ἀρίστη δωρεῶν), namely reason (*Opif.* 77). Philo discusses at some length the χάρις of God that Noah received (*Leg.* 3.77–78). The passage is worth presenting in whole, and in a translation that shows the patronage and benefaction language:

> For if someone might ask why he [the prophet] says Noah found beneficence (χάρις) before the Lord God, having done, as far as they knew, no good deed first, we shall answer suitably that he has been shown to be of praiseworthy composition and birth, for Noah means 'rest' or 'righteous.' It is necessary, when one has ceased from unrighteousness and sin, taken up the good, and lived together with righteousness, to find a benefaction (χάρις) from God. Now to find benefaction (χάρις) is not only, as some think, equivalent to being well-pleasing, but also this: the righteous person investigating the nature of being finds this one excellent discovery that absolutely everything is a benefaction (χάρις) of God, and there is no beneficence (χάρισμα) from nature because it has no possessions since all things are in possession of God, and therefore benefaction (χάρις) is his domain alone. At any rate, to those who investigate the beginning of creation the best possible answer might be given that it is the goodness and benefaction (χάρις) of God which he bestowed (ἐχαρίσατο) upon his people. For all things which are in the world and the world itself are a gift (δωρεά) and a benefaction (εὐεργεσία) and a beneficence (χάρισμα) of God. (*Leg.* 3.77–78)

The concentration of the language of patronage and clientage in this passage makes it impossible to misread Philo.[73] Although χάρις is normally translated as 'grace,' and although the term is understood to refer to an unearned gift, the Graeco-Roman context of patronage and benefaction reveals that χάρις can be a synonym of εὐεργεσία.[74] The fact that nature is specified as having nothing to give makes clear that what is envisioned is concrete goods that are given in benefaction, not abstract grace or favour. The phrase χάρις τοῦ θεοῦ also

---

[73] See also *Mut.* 24; *Leg.* 3.76.
[74] H. S. Versnel ("Religious Mentality in Ancient Prayer," in *Faith, Hope and Worship: Aspects of Religious Mentality in the Ancient World* [ed. H. S. Versnel; Studies in Greek and Roman Religion 2; Leiden: E. J. Brill, 1982], 1–64) agrees that "the term χάρις itself can be understood as 'favor' or something close to it" (48).

supports such a translation.⁷⁵ What is clear is that Philo believes all things in the natural world, the creation of humans and of creation, and all things humans have to be benefactions of God. God is, indeed must be, the supreme benefactor because all things are God's alone; nothing else, or no one else, *has* anything to give.

If Josephus's patronage and clientage language might be described as conventional or sober, Philo's use of this language is profound, poetic, and philosophical. In *Sacr.* 60 Philo refers to receiving the marks of God's authority and benefactions (δέξηται χαρακτῆρας ἐξουσίας καὶ εὐεργεσίας αὐτοῦ). At *Plant.* 85–89 Philo goes so far as to claim that God is called "God" because of the benefactions that come from God (as opposed to "Lord" which he associates with rule, not beneficence).⁷⁶ In the same passage (*Plant.* 87) Philo also claims καθὸ δὲ εὐεργέτης θάτερον μόνον βούλεται, τὸ εὐεργετεῖν (But since he is benefactor, he wishes only the one thing, to give benefactions), and he encourages his readers that those who are single-minded in their devotion to this divine benefactor will encounter μέγιστον ἀγαθόν. At *Sacr.* 127 Philo refers to τῆς ἐλευθερίας χάριτι τοῦ εὐεργέτου, or how free with benefactions is his divine benefactor. But these examples pale in comparison to the profound evocativeness of Philo's description of God's generosity as τὸν ἀεὶ πλημμυροῦντα χείμαρρουν τῶν σῶν εὐεργεσιῶν—the eternally overflowing swollen winter river of your benefactions (*Her.* 32). The value of Philo's metaphors is unparalleled in anything we have read so far, and yet it is firmly planted within the Graeco-Roman tradition of divine patronage and benefaction.

Despite these multiple ways in which Philo depicts the Israelite God in the terms of the Graeco-Roman divine benefactor, he is at some pains to distinguish his God from other Graeco-Roman divine benefactors. Philo's divine benefactor is not like the others. Philo appeals to the reader,

> Look around you and you shall find that those who are said to bestow benefits (χαρίζεσθαι) sell rather than give, and those who seem to us to receive them in truth buy. The givers are seeking praise or honour

---

⁷⁵ See also the phrase εὐεργετεῖν χάρισι (*Opif.* 23, bis); *Leg.* 3.215, *Ebr.* 32, *Migr.* 73 also show χάρις (or χαρίζω) to be nearly synonymous with εὐεργεσία. The problem with translation is also illustrated with the term εὐεργέτης; Colson and Whitaker translate this term often as "loving kindness" (LCL). Benefactions from God were no doubt signs for Philo of God's loving kindness; however, the term is best not overly interpreted since to do so is to lose the patronage context in which the term clearly functions. Likewise, χάρις is generally over-interpreted in the course of translation and is best left in its original semantic context.

⁷⁶ See also *Sobr.* 55.

> as their exchange and look for the repayment of the benefit (χάριτος), and thus under the specious name of gift then in real truth carry out a sale, for the seller's way is to take something for what he offers. . . . But God is no seller, hawking his goods in the market, but a free giver of all things, pouring forth fountains of his free bounties (χαριτῶν) and seeking no return. For he has no needs himself and no created being is able to repay his gift. (*Cher.* 122–123)

Philo's is a polemical and theological construct, we can conclude, for two reasons. Although this sort of patronage and benefaction did exist, it was hardly the norm, and most certainly not the ideal (which at least Seneca can be said fairly to represent). Philo highlights only the most crass interpretation of the transaction. What is worse, however, is that Philo quite misrepresents his own actual position. While he may well believe that God is in need of nothing, he certainly does not believe that the God's gifts are *actually* free, as in requiring no form of reciprocity or gratitude. Indeed, Philo is as adamant as any other ancient writer that ingratitude to God is reprehensible and punishable (*Sacr.* 57–58).

While the Israelites did not have a social structure of patronage and benefaction, they did know their God to be a profoundly generous giver of all things. It seems that when some Septuagint writers, and then Josephus and Philo especially, looked to the language and imagery that the Greeks and Romans used to talk about their gods, these Jews recognised all the traits. The Graeco-Roman vocabulary then struck them as fitting, not as novel. The transition illustrated in Philo from a non-patronage to a patronage framework for talking about how God interacts with humans is seamless largely because of his innate understanding of his God.

2.6 Conclusion

In this chapter I have endeavoured to set up the broader cultural context of Paul the Hellenistic Jew. Clearly, being Jewish in no way disqualifies Paul from conceiving of his God as a divine benefactor, nor of himself or his converts as clients. This of course remains to be illustrated, as it will be amply in the following chapter, but here we can at least conclude that such a possibility is not without precedent. Greeks and Romans fashioned a society built in large part upon the unequal distribution of goods and services known as general reciprocity. This came to be applied to their conception of their

Conclusion

relationships with the gods, and in this their influence on first-century Jews was, as the writings of Philo and Josephus attest, profound. There is in the two centuries that bracket the start of the common era a pan-Mediterranean framework for understanding human–divine interaction, and this is consistently so from material as diverse as stone inscriptions, papyri of literary theory, letters and social commentary. This consistency is carried over into cultic texts, again very diverse, from Graeco-Roman to Jewish texts such as the Septuagint and the biblical interpretations of Philo and Josephus.

The significance of this should be obvious. Since the Greeks, Romans, and Jews of the first century lived in relationships of patronage and benefaction with their gods, that means that conversion in their world must have been grounded in that reality as well. If we are to understand ancient conversion, we need to begin by understanding its "religious" framework, which was indisputably that of patronage and benefaction. That work has been accomplished here. What we now need to do is narrow the focus from general cultural context to tropes and ways of talking about the interaction of human client and divine patron or benefactor. Doing so will provide us with a more concrete and precise model for understanding ancient conversion discourses, including those of Paul.

Chapter Three

The Rhetoric of Patronage and Benefaction

3.0 Introduction

Were it only on the basis of literary sources, such as Aristotle, Seneca, or Philo, that we were able to reconstruct ancient patronage and benefaction, one might fairly question whether and to what extent an elite literary ideal coincided with the lived reality. But non-literary sources, such as the inscriptions and papyri, among other ancient material realia, illustrate abundantly that patronage and benefaction were indeed a fact of daily life, well-known and widely practised. All sorts of people, from elites in positions of power to writers with talent but few resources to the poor who lived lives of subsistence, took for granted that patronage and benefaction was the foundation of their society. Patronage and benefaction were so integral that they often passed without notice or comment, in the same way that cultural institutions and values typically do. On the other hand, every society has those who reflect explicitly on the importance of local values and institutions, and in the ancient world some openly articulated that the smooth running of society was impossible without patronage and benefaction. They all had human patrons, and they prayed to divine patrons, all of whom would, ideally, support them in a startling variety of ways. That some ancient writers criticise and lampoon the motivations and inferences of patronage and benefaction does not, of course, undermine this claim. Indeed, it serves only to confirm its centrality and scope in the ancient Mediterranean. Patronage and benefaction were a part of the lived reality of daily lives of regular people, not always a positive force, but always a present one.

Not only do ancient sources reveal the central importance of patronage and benefaction, they also reveal a relatively stable set of rhetorical conventions for talking about patronage and benefaction. In other words, the practices and expectations of patronage and benefaction effected a consistent set of phrases, rhetorical tropes, and vocabulary associated with benefaction, reciprocity and honour. These conventions had to do mostly with how clients spoke and wrote about their patrons, since the greater responsibility for reciprocity resided with the client, though patrons and benefactors too did participate in a rhetoric of patronage and benefaction.

Through an analysis of a broad variety of sources, I have identified five conventions of the rhetoric of patronage and benefaction. The first convention is the call of the patron. Here we find the claim that clients were approached by the patron, as opposed to approaching the patron themselves, in order to be benefited, suggesting that clients were not solely responsible for establishing a patronal relationship. The second convention of patronage and benefaction is philosophical persuasion. Because the purpose of philosophical persuasive discourse was conversion, and because philosophical converts and disciples typically referred to their teachers and the ideas they promulgated in the language of patronage, this is an important part of the puzzle of understanding ancient conversion. The third convention of the rhetoric of patronage and benefaction includes three modes of speech that I shall cover in a single section: prayer, praise, and proselytism. A fourth convention involves a way of speaking about a patron that compares life before and after the client's encounter with the benefactions of their patron in such a way as to honour the present patron. I have come to call this convention patronal synkrisis. The final convention of the rhetoric of patronage is an overlooked element of the vocabulary of ancient patronage: the term χάρις.

These five conventions are significant for a number of reasons. First, they reveal that the rhetoric of human patronage and benefaction was more or less the same as the rhetoric of divine patronage and benefaction. This is not to say that there were no differences between the two, but simply that the forms of rhetoric within each were more similar than they were different. More importantly, that human and divine patronage and benefaction shared conventions of rhetoric suggests that they also shared a set of assumptions and expectations. Whether one was a client of a human elite, a philosopher or a god, the expectations of conduct and the rhetoric employed alongside it were largely the same. The necessary conclusion is that for all intents and purposes there are very few meaningful distinctions to be drawn between human and divine patronage and benefaction. Secondly, these conventions of the rhetoric of patronage and benefaction appear in Paul's conversion accounts with the same frequency as they appear in other conversion narratives.

It may be useful to pause here to make some clarifications about these conventions and what is significant about them for this work. First of all, these conventions do not *all* appear in every instance where patronage is described, nor in every instance where they might have served the purposes of the writer or speaker quite nicely. They do, however, all occur with sufficient consistency to establish a pattern of rhetoric within the institution and practice of patronage and benefaction. While at times two or more can occur in the same passage, it is not critical that they do so. These conventions are simply ways that clients spoke and wrote about their patrons and patronal experiences. Secondly, and by extension, these conventions do not help us to "discover" conversion narratives in the ancient world; instead, they help us to discover a patronal context for narratives that certainly have to do with conversion. In other words, it is the combination of conversion narratives and discourse with the rhetorical conventions of patronage and benefaction that is interesting, illuminating, and significant. Most significant of all is that these conventions are *also* found in Paul's conversion narratives. That is to say, that Paul uses the same rhetorical conventions to frame his conversion experience places Paul more securely in his Graeco-Roman cultural environment than a psychologising approach can. Paul's use of these conventions to frame his conversion experience tells us a great deal about how he conceived of it.

The purposes of this chapter are manifold: I wish to continue to illustrate the extent to which human and divine patronage were of a piece; secondly, I wish to illustrate that whether a person was addressing a human or a divine patron, the modes of expression were largely similar; and finally, I wish to illustrate that the rhetoric of patronage and benefaction was very often the rhetoric of religion in the ancient Mediterranean. This latter point is obviously quite important for the purposes of this book as a whole. If the rhetoric of patronage and benefaction is the rhetoric of religion, then the rhetoric of conversion narratives and discourse must be embedded in the institution of patronage and benefaction. This chapter illustrates the extent to which this was the case with many Graeco-Roman converts. The following chapter demonstrates that Paul too functioned within this same rhetoric of patronage and benefaction.

3.1 The Call of the Patron/Benefactor

3.1.1 Human Patronage and Benefaction

One might imagine that in the system of patronage and benefaction, clients approaching people (or gods) to act as their patrons/benefactors would be far more common than patrons/benefactors searching for clients. This would be a safe assumption because of the greater necessity which the poor had to survive than the elite had to accrue honour, but it is probably also the case that approaching a potential patron or benefactor was the first act of honour, which would hopefully elicit a benefit. This makes all the more remarkable occurrences of patrons and benefactors making the initial contact in seeking out potential clients. Perhaps because of what writers could offer an elite patron, we find that the call of the patron/benefactor is most prevalent within literary patronage. It was not uncommon for patrons to seek out and court literary clients.[1] While we do have evidence of writers approaching the elite for literary patronage (Theocritus, *Idyll* 16), we find more references to elites approaching writers in order to set up a relationship of patronage. Some excellent examples of this come from Cicero, especially in his speech on behalf of the poet Archias. Archias is a literary client of Cicero, and Cicero is appealing to the courts to grant citizenship to the poet. This makes Cicero a broker in this instance, since he is providing access to an institution that Archias could not have addressed with equal effect. Yet, Cicero is also Archias' patron; he is in the courts arguing on Archias' behalf.

In the process of representing Archias, Cicero reveals several interesting facts about the poet. The first is that Cicero is not Archias' only patron. Archias not only had some notable patrons before Cicero (Cicero even invokes the powerful names of the Luculli in his address), but also presently had as patrons some other powerful families. The second point of interest is that Cicero suggests that Archias was *consistently* approached by elites wanting to be his patron (*Arch.* 3.5–6; 10.26). Cicero implies that when Archias first arrived in Rome, the Luculli approached him, since even at a young age his renown as a writer preceded him. Cicero also suggests that Archias was courted and won as a laudator by Metellus Pius. In fact, Cicero suggests that Metellus was so desperate "to have his deeds immortalised" that prior to finding Archias he was interviewing far less qualified writers to serve as clients to him.

The picture presented by Cicero is that Archias was always the passive one, letting the patrons approach and court him. Barbara Gold suggests that Cicero's catalog of Archias' patrons may be more rhetorical than actual, that it may have served as part of Cicero's artifice for showing Archias as worthy of citizenship since so many leading citizens thought highly of him. Gold

---

[1] Barbara K. Gold, *Literary Patronage in Greece and Rome* (Chapel Hill and London: University of North Carolina Press, 1987). See also M. Citroni, "Patronage, Literary," in *The Oxford Classical Dictionary* (ed. S. Hornblower and A. Spawforth; Oxford and London: Oxford University Press, 1996), 1124–26; and I. Arnaoutoglou, "Associations and Patronage in Ancient Athens," *Ancient Society* 25 (1994): 1–17, see esp. p. 6.

does not, on the other hand, appear to doubt the historicity of a client like Archias being sought out by prospective patrons.[2] The fact that Cicero is able to make such a claim before the courts about Archias' passivity suggests that in the institution of patronage and clientage it was not uncommon for clients to be sought out by patrons. The same practice is even echoed in the criticism Martial makes of one of his former patrons, "when you were hunting [*captare*] me you used to send me gifts. Now that you have caught me you give me nothing" (*Ep.* 9.88).

Cicero not only describes other patrons calling clients, but participates in it himself; he claims to have tried shamelessly to win Lucceius as his own client. Likewise Virgil writes that he composed the *Georgics* at the "will" (a calling of sorts) of his patron, the legendary Maecenas (*Georg.* 3.41). Pliny writes that his collecting of his letters was prompted by Septicius (*Ep.* 1.1). These too are examples of the call of the patron, since call can be understood to be synonymous with commission. The notion that a work had been written or collected only at the request of some elite figure is likely more than simply a "modesty formula."[3] Though it may well have served that purpose, there is no reason to doubt that patrons commissioned literary works. Even if a work was not *actively* sought out by a literary patron, such a "modesty formula" would serve to invoke the honourable name of the writer's patron, as well as to give credit for the great idea to the patron as a way of honouring him or her. Later than most of our other examples, but illuminating nonetheless, is the work of fifth-century C.E. priest, poet, and statesman Sidonius. Like Pliny, with whom he reluctantly compared himself, Sidonius attributes the collection of his letters to Constantius.[4] W. B. Anderson depicts Constantius as a "friend" of Sidonius, both in the address of the letter and in the introductory essay, but he misses several items that clearly indicate that Constantius was a patron, and possibly a literary patron, to Sidonius.

Constantius was older and more politically established, and he had done a very important favour for Sidonius that would have obliged Sidonius to him. While Bishop of the see of Clermont in the last quarter of the fifth-century C.E., and with the Gauls mounting successful campaigns against the empire, Sidonius was having an increasingly difficult time motivating his people. He called in Constantius to help, and Constantius succeeded in

---

[2] Gold, *Literary Patronage*, 85.
[3] Ernst Robert Curtius, *European Literature and the Latin Middle Ages* (trans. W. R. Trask; Princeton: Princeton University Press, 1953), 85.
[4] "Friend" represents the interpretation of the Loeb translator, W. B. Anderson, since Sidonius does not actually call Constantius friend in the address.

motivating Sidonius' people to continue fighting. This most certainly would have obligated Sidonius to Constantius, and dedicating the collection of letters, which turned out to be a very popular enterprise, to Constantius would have served to honour him appropriately. In addition to that, Sidonius' language reflects just such a relationship:

> My honoured Lord, you have this long time been pressing me (and you have every claim on my attention, for you are a most competent adviser on the matters about to be discussed) to collect all the letters making any claims to taste that have flowed from my pen on different occasions as this or that affair, person, or situation called them forth, and to revise and correct the originals and combine all in a single book. (*Ep.* 1.1)

Finally, Sidonius writes, "But you see I have obeyed your command, and now submit to your scrutiny these epistles of mine. . . . For I know you are an enthusiastic friend not only to literary pursuits but to men of letters as well." It appears that a relationship of benefaction and obligation existed between these two men. The relationship of patronage was established by Constantius's favour to Sidonius, but it was solidified by Constantius's call for Sidonius to publish his works.

As I indicated above, the language of commissioning is also the language of being called. The way Horace describes the start of his relationship with Maecenas comprises our clearest such example. Horace's sixth "satire" is primarily autobiographical. In the process of satirising those who have overreached their political and social aspirations, Horace outlines how he came into his present favoured status with Maecenas. As he does this, he sidesteps the charge of zealously seeking his patron by relating how he did not choose or approach Maecenas, but rather Maecenas chose him. Starting at line 45, Horace praises Maecenas for not being disdainful of his low status, but rather overlooking the fact that Horace was the "son of a freedman father" (*Sat.* 6.45). Maecenas chose Horace for "friendship," all the more notable since Maecenas is "cautious to choose as friends only the worthy." However, much to Horace's horror, when he went to meet Maecenas, he was so nervous he could only stammer away until he withdrew. Yet, nine months later, Maecenas called again,

> and bade me to join your friends. I count it a great honour that I pleased you, who discern between fair and foul, not by a father's fame, but by blamelessness of life and heart. (*Sat.* 6.62–63)

This might be a literary device to suggest a fatedness to Horace's relationship with Maecenas; it might function as part of Horace's flattery and honouring of his patron. Even if either of these were the case, and therefore not literal, it would still be remarkable that part of the rhetoric of literary clientage is to claim to have been called by an elite patron. Having said that, there is no good reason to doubt that elite patrons sought out clients, and particularly ones with literary talents, who could offer them services they would find in few other places.

3.1.2 Divine Patronage and Benefaction

Horace's language of blamelessness echoes the language and concerns of clients to divine patrons/benefactors, who were also reputed on occasion to inaugurate benefit relationships with humans. The most prominent example of a call of a divine patron/benefactor is from Aristides' lengthy first person account of his experience of favour under the healing God Asclepius. In Aristides' lengthy *Sacred Tales*, we find the call of the patron in two ways. The first quite resembles the call of the literary patron, since Aristides claims that the frequent request of Asclepius was the catalyst for him to put in writing the many benefactions he received from the god. Secondly, Aristides admits that on several occasions he was summoned directly by the healing god. To be clear, Asclepius did not initiate the relationship with Aristides; it was Aristides who in desperation and feeling neglected by Sarapis turned to Asclepius for help (we have here then an obvious conversion account coupled with the feature of the rhetoric of patronage and benefaction). However, eight months after Asclepius had started appearing to Aristides (thus in the summer of 145 C.E.), Aristides claims to have been called (κλῆσις) by Asclepius to his Temple in Pergamum: μετὰ ταῦτα κλῆσις καὶ ἄφιξις Σμύρνης εἰς Πέργαμον μετὰ τῆς ἀγαθῆς τύχης (*Sacred Tales* 2.292.14).

The call of Asclepius is a familiar refrain of Aristides, for again, in 148 C.E., he claims to have received another call (κλῆσις) from Asclepius to Pergamum: μετὰ ταῦτα ἔφεσις, κλῆσις ἡγεμόνος, κλῆσις τοῦ σωτῆρος εἰς Πέργαμον (4.345.14). Aristides in fact receives the call from two sources to come to Pergamum, one from the Governor and the other from his saviour Asclepius. Finally, he recalls that in 153 C.E. Asclepius again called him into Pergamum: κἀν τούτῳ ἐκάλει ὁ θεὸς πάλιν εἰς Πέργαμον (4.341.3). That Aristides uses the imperfect ἐκάλει here is fitting since it reflects grammatically what the texts portray narratively, namely that calls from Asclepius for Aristides to come to the Temple were on-going throughout Aristides' relationship with his divine patron.

It is important to note too, however, that the call of the divine patron/benefactor could occur simply in the event of a divine revelation. For instance, Asclepius, so known for calling Aristides to be healed, is said to have simply appeared to others, thus indicating to them that they were invited to be healed.[5] *IG* XIV 966 is an inscription with four healing accounts inscribed upon it. It is unclear whether we are dealing with a conversion narrative here. It would be if we knew that the healed entered into a client relationship with Asclepius, but this may well not have been the case. What is important is simply the trope of the "call" of the patron who initiates a relationship with the sick. Mind you, in the four healing narratives that appear in this inscription, the person healed is not called *per se*, but rather it is *revealed* to them where they are to go and what they are to do in order to receive the benefaction of healing from the god. These narratives illustrate that the vocabulary of 'call' does not have to be present for a divine patronal calling to have occurred. The revelation that these men received offering instructions that would lead to a healing is the call of the divine patron to enter into a relationship of clientage inaugurated by the benefaction of healing.

Here I have suggested that the rhetorical convention of the patronal call is found in a number of texts that depict healing as a benefaction. Would it have been possible to have such healings without patronage? I would argue no. Recalling the model of exchange I established in Chapter Two, it is not possible to think of the healing as a gift in the technical sense of the word. That is, a technical "gift" implies equality of status between giver and recipient, and the balanced exchange of goods. The very scenario of a god healing a human sets it well outside the bounds of gift exchange, since the human cannot repay the god in a balanced way. The status inequality and the necessity of the human worshipper to pay in kind places the relationship in the bounds of general reciprocity—the person healed is the recipient of a divine benefaction and thus is expected to (and generally does) behave as a client ought to. This can be confusing to the modern observer, however, since the ancients used the vocabulary of "gift" (δῶρον, δωρεάν, etc.) often in their depictions of patronage and benefaction. For example, on benefactions Seneca writes that "It is a benefit to bestow the gift of an estate that by reason of its fertility may lower the price of grain" (*Ben.* 3.8.3). This tells us that the ancients had a fluid vocabulary, but their conduct tells us they did not confuse the two categories of exchange. In other words, their use of "gift"

---

[5] *IG* XIV 966 = *SIG* 1173; translated in Danker, *Benefactor*, 194.

vocabulary with respect to the gods or to the emperor was not interpreted as a claim of equal status or ability to repay in a balanced manner. In fact, it is stated categorically that even in those instances where the recipient had the ability to balance the scales, an act of benefaction precluded him from doing so—it was wrong to repay a benefaction, but necessary to repay a gift.

Let us return to more examples of the call of the divine patron/benefactor, these ones found in a second-century C.E. papyrus found at Oxyrhynchus. The writer relates that whenever he tried to show his gratitude, which he attempted to do in various ways, Asclepius made clear that there was only one thing he wanted—a written account of his healings.

> But when he said repeatedly that he cared not for these but for what had been previously promised, I was at a loss, and with difficulty, since I disparaged it, felt the divine obligation of the composition.[6]

As with many of the examples cited earlier, we have here an example of literary patronage that is divine in nature.

The *idea* or image of a god calling or commissioning a human and establishing a relationship of unequal status (generalised exchange) can be found in cultures without the patronage system, for example ancient Israelite society. As we saw above, there was no system of patronage and benefaction in Palestine, but the elements of the Jewish understanding of God's interaction with humanity would have sounded familiar to Graeco-Roman ears, and certain Jews found the Graeco-Roman framework of divine patronage and benefaction a fruitful way of talking about their own God. The call of the divine patron/benefactor might have been one such element that sounded familiar to either listener. Jewish identity has long been based on the understanding that the Jews were chosen by God. Looking back at their narratives from within a Graeco-Roman cultural system, they (Philo and Josephus most readily) understood God as the divine patron who initiated contact with many of the key figures in Jewish history. For example, God chose Noah, Noah did not approach or choose God.

The formula that is used, and which I shall cover in greater detail in the last section of this chapter, is that Noah "found favour in the eyes of the LORD" (Gen 6:8). The word 'favour' represents the Hebrew חֵן, which the Septuagint

---

[6] *P.Oxy.* 1381, lines 145–167. The translation is from Edelstein and Edelstein, *Asclepius*, 175.

will almost always translate as χάρις. Likewise, God called Abram, offering him a benefaction from the outset (to be father of a great nation), and he appeared to him frequently. Finally, there is Moses, who is called and who ends up brokering a relationship between the LORD and the Israelites. In this vein, the call of the Hebrew prophets would have been understood by Hellenised Jews not as a call that inaugurated a new patronal relationship, but rather one that *altered* the patronal relationship. The calls of Samuel, Isaiah, Jeremiah, Ezekiel, Jonah (notwithstanding his initial hesitance!), Hosea and Amos by God inaugurated their respective roles as prophets, that is to say as brokers, of God, but of course they are already members of the covenant community.[7] Again, these interpretations of the relationship would have been foreign to the Israelites who composed the Hebrew Bible, but were much more natural an interpretation for the Hellenised Jews of the first-centuries B.C.E. and C.E.

3.2 Persuasion and Philosophical Conversion

Philosophical persuasion was about converting the ignorant: one either persuaded them that they were in need of salvation, or persuaded them that one particular philosophical outlook could provide them with that. The rhetoric of patronage and benefaction also included the work of the philosophers, and the language of conversion drew from this body of imagery. In order to illustrate this, however, it is likely necessary to show that philosophy too worked within the institution of patronage and benefaction. This claim is, in fact, easily illustrated. Ancient people clearly thought the gods gave them *things*, that is many things in tangible form (crops, health, protection, children, wealth), though of course the gods gave things less tangible as well (salvation, peace of mind). These are enumerated in abundance throughout the ancient world. What philosophers gave was never as tangible as what the gods gave, and thus many might miss the similarities.[8]

---

[7] 1 Sam 3:2–4:1; Isa 6:6–8; Jer 1:4–19; Ezek 2:1–3:11; Jonah 1:1–3; Hos 1:2; Amos 7:15.
[8] H. Gregory Snyder, *Teachers and Texts in the Ancient World: Philosophers, Jews and Christians* (London: Routledge, 2000), refers to philosophical, Jewish, and Christian teachers as "text brokers" (since they offer something that many people in antiquity would not have had access to, namely textual culture) throughout his work (see his index for occurrences of the term).

3.2.1 Philosophy and Religion

First a warning: we are accustomed as modern observers to distinguish between religion and philosophy, but such a distinction shares little in common with "religion" and philosophy in the ancient world.[9] It is not that the two were interchangeable in the ancient world, but they were far more intimately related than they are at present. This view is shared by the majority of historians of religion who include a section on philosophy in their comprehensive studies of Graeco-Roman *religion*.[10] Though risky, we might take Trypho's initial question to Justin as an expression of this reality: "Is not all philosophy concerned with God?" (*Dial.* 1.3), and the Stoic Cleanthes' hymn to Zeus below.[11] Philosophy was a feature of ancient cultic life, and the acknowledgement of the gods was far from absent in the pursuit of philosophical knowledge.

There are, however, a number of unique features associated with philosophy that are not associated with ancient cult. Foremost among these is that philosophy required and invited a considerable degree of exclusive loyalty. One generally did not follow the teachings of more than one philosopher at a time because their teachings could be quite at odds with one another. In those instances where there appears to be overlap, say in the combination of Stoic and Aristotelian ideas, the disciple might point out that the Stoic ideas ultimately have Aristotelian roots, thus solving the problem, as did the second century Academic Antiochus of Ascalon (whom we shall encounter in detail in Chapter Five). This leads to another unique feature of philosophy—teachings about the structure and nature of the world, the origins of life and death, suffering, etc. were integral to philosophy. Because these things were so much the domain of philosophy, the embrace of a philosophy tended to be life-transforming, though of course so too could an encounter with Isis or Asclepius be life-transforming. Still, cultic association only

---

[9] L. Alexander, "Paul and the Hellenistic Schools: The Evidence of Galen," in *Paul in his Hellenistic Context* (ed. T. Engberg-Pedersen; Minneapolis: Fortress Press, 1995), 60–83, esp. 62.

[10] See Édouard des Places, *La Religion Grecque: Dieux, cultes, rites et sentiment religieux dans la Grèce antique* (Paris: Éditions A. et J. Picard et Cie, 1969); W. Burkert, *Greek Religion* (trans. John Raffan; Cambridge: Harvard University Press, 1985); and Hans-Josef Klauck, *The Religious Context of Early Christianity: A Guide to Graeco-Roman Religions* (trans. Brian McNeil; Edinburgh: T&T Clark, 2000).

[11] The text used here and below is that of J. C. M. van Winden, *An Early Christian Philosopher: Justin Martyr's Dialogue with Trypho, Chapters One to Nine* (Philosophia Patrum 1; Leiden: E. J. Brill, 1971), and the citation is a paraphrase of the series of questions Trypho asks Justin in 1.3.

occasionally involved injunctions on how to conduct oneself, on orthodox opinion or world-view. Philosophy taught one how to understand the gods, how to be fearless of death, how to behave towards others. These differences, however, should not lead us to see greater differentiation between the two than is warranted from an ancient perspective. A number of critical observations reflect the common ground between cult and philosophy, both in terms of modern associations concerning religion, but also and more importantly with respect to patronage and benefaction in the context of ancient "religion."

The relationship between philosophy and "religion" in the ancient world was both closer and more complex than the relationship between the two in the modern world. As modern Western readers we naturally think of "religion" as having to do with the relationship between the gods (or the divine) and human beings and of philosophy as knowledge derived from outside of a religious context or influence. But ancient philosophy was commonly concerned with knowing about the gods and about the relationship between the gods and the world (even if the result of philosophical reflection was to reject the role or interest of the gods in human affairs altogether). Take for instance, the Stoic Cleanthes' hymn to Zeus. The prayer is addressed to the divine but spoken by the philosopher.

> Most exalted of the immortals . . . always ruling all,
> Zeus, prime mover of nature, you who govern all things according to law,
> all hail! For it is fitting for all mortals to call on you
> . . .
> Therefore I will praise you and always sing of your power.[12]

It is at the end of this philosopher's prayer that we discover the connection between ancient philosophy and the ancient framework of patronage and clientage:

> Let us find knowledge, the basis of your righteous governance of all things, so that we may be honoured and pay you honour in return, by praising your works without cease, as is fitting for a mortal. For there is no greater gift of honour for mortals or for gods than to praise the universal law, as is right.[13]

---

[12] I.537, lines 1–7, *SVF*. The translation is that of Klauck, *Religious Context*, 351–52.
[13] I.537, lines 34–38, *SVF*.

It almost appears as if Cleanthes is asking to become a broker between Zeus and humanity. He asks to be given knowledge so that he can be honoured by impressed humans, and in keeping with the role of the broker, Cleanthes' benefiting humans in this way would result in greater honour being directed towards the divine patron (lines 35–36). And of course, as a broker of divinely inspired knowledge, Cleanthes knows he will be a patron to people, for as broker he will be offering an important benefaction to them—access to a knowledge they would not otherwise have found.

Another important connection between the philosophers and the gods is that both offered benefactions to people. The philosopher is often described in terms echoing the divine patron/benefactor; a philosopher bestows wisdom and insight, teaches people to understand the world as it really is. This state is often described as salvation, being saved from the misery of enslavement to ignorance, corruption, or intemperance. The philosophers were benefactors to any who would hear them and incorporate their words into their actions. Their teachings were believed to offer some tangible good to those who followed in their footsteps. Only this can explain how it is that Epictetus can describe his predecessor, the great Stoic teacher Chrysippus as a "great benefactor," μεγάλου εὐεργέτου (*Diatr.* 1.4.29). In another notable text, philosophy itself, as opposed to the philosopher, is addressed as a patron.

> O philosophy, guide of life, O explorer of virtue and expeller of vice. Without you what could have become not only of me but of the life of man altogether? You have given birth to cities, you have called scattered human beings into the bond of social life, you have united them first of all in joint habitations, next in wedlock, then in the ties of common literature and speech, you have discovered law, you have been the teacher of morality and order: to you I fly for refuge, from you I look for aid, to you I entrust myself, as once in ample measure, so now wholly and entirely. . . . You have freely granted us peacefulness of life and destroyed the dread of death.[14]

This passage not only reflects the notion of philosophy and the philosopher as a benefactor of humanity, but it also reflects the all important praise of the client. This text is, in effect, a hymn of praise to philosophy on the part of the client, proclaiming the benefactions that philosophy has bestowed upon humanity, honouring philosophy by crediting it with many fantastic

---

[14] Cicero, *Tusc.* 5.5 (King, LCL, with modifications).

discoveries and by claiming loyalty to and dependence upon it. Philosophy and cult did different things in the ancient world, but this much is clear: both operated within the same cultural framework that structured many forms of interaction in terms of the patron-client relationship.

One aspect that can be associated with philosophers over other human or divine patrons is the role of rhetoric in what they do. After all, philosophers were involved in something that few human or divine patrons were, namely persuasion. Persuasion is the primary rhetorical goal of the philosopher. Of the three classes of rhetoric, deliberative, demonstrative, and judicial, philosophical persuasion occurs mostly within deliberative rhetoric, and within that class protreptic figures most prominently.[15] The writings and public discourses of the Hellenistic philosophers were designed not simply to expound ideas for their own sake, but to persuade people to see the world as they saw it. According to Schenkeveld, protreptic above other styles of rhetoric was "concerned with converting a person to the study of philosophy."[16] What is more, every philosophical school appears to have produced protreptic texts; it was not the occasional practice of a few philosophers.[17]

3.2.2 Philosophy and Persuasive Rhetoric

The importance, of course, of attracting one to the "study of philosophy" is in persuading them of the truth of one's position, not simply in persuading them to study it for the sake of study. What philosophers were most frequently involved in persuading others of was the necessity to secure their own happiness, the health of their souls, salvation from ignorance, and the like. In this way then, the philosopher offered benefactions to people in the form of teachings that would save them, but this of course required more work (hence the use of rhetoric) than was typical among patrons or benefactors — one did not usually have to convince a client to accept a benefaction. It is also

---

[15] M. D. Jordan, "Ancient Philosophic Protreptic and the Problem of Persuasive Genres," *Rhetorica* 4 (1986): 309–33; Dirk M. Schenkeveld, "Philosophical Prose," in *Handbook of Classical Rhetoric in the Hellenistic Period, 330 B.C.–A.D. 400* (ed. S. E. Porter; Leiden: E. J. Brill, 1997), 195–264. Both of these writers also refer to the use of diatribe in persuasion. Schenkeveld suggests that protreptic and diatribe coincided with the basic needs of philosophical schools: to convert or attract others (protreptic), and then to teach or correct them (diatribe). Jordan makes the same point though by a different means ("Ancient Philosophic Protreptic," 313).

[16] Schenkeveld, "Philosophical Prose," 204, 205.

[17] Jordan, "Ancient Philosophic Protreptic," 310–14.

worth pointing out that protreptic was not simply about recruiting devoted students, though this was often the result; protreptic was also about changing the behaviour of the listener, that is with conversion.

When considering the relationship between philosophy and rhetoric, several things must be commented upon. First, there was a long-standing debate among philosophers as to the validity and attractiveness of using rhetoric.[18] Some philosophers (Theophrastus, Demetrius of Phaleron, Zeno, Philodemus) embraced the practice of rhetoric in the delivery of their speeches, while others eschewed rhetoric as morally fatuous (Critolaus, Epicurus), though admittedly there were also those who only rejected rhetoric in certain instances while embracing it in others (Plato, Aristotle, Isocrates, Philo of Larissa, Cicero).[19] For many ancient writers, the practice of rhetoric without substance (which was best provided by philosophy) was very nearly offensive. Yet the goal of those who rejected the formal reliance on rhetoric was no different from those who embraced it: both sought to persuade. Thus we must conclude that even the rejection of flowery rhetoric is a rhetorical approach in and of itself because the speaker's goal is no less to persuade. Second, there is by far no consensus among ancient writers on what constitutes good or effective rhetoric. Some rhetorical features were utterly rejected by writers while those same features are used and praised by others. The implication of this is that we must not be too rigid in our expectations of or standards for what comprises (effective) rhetoric. Wuellner rightly emphasises that rhetoric was not only practised in the academy, but ever more so in the marketplace.[20] Rhetoric is everywhere, and as such it will not always be practised in a polished or attractive fashion. What is more, rhetoric is especially present where persuasion is the goal of discourse. We must be careful not to equate the absence of a consistent or polished rhetorical style with an absence of *persuasive* intent.[21] Rhetoric cannot be measured by its

---

[18] R. Dean Anderson, *Ancient Rhetorical Theory and Paul* (rev. ed.; CBET 18; Kampen: Kok Pharos, 1996), 62–66.

[19] See Schenkeveld, "Philosophical Prose," 197–202.

[20] Wilhelm Wuellner, "Biblical Exegesis in the Light of the History and Historicity of Rhetoric and the Nature of the Rhetoric of Religion," in *Rhetoric and the New Testament: Essays from the 1992 Heidelberg Conference* (ed. S. E. Porter and T. H. Olbricht; JSOTSup 90; Sheffield: Sheffield Academic Press, 1993), 492–513; see esp. p. 500.

[21] Carol Poster, "The Affections of the Soul: *Pathos*, Protreptic, and Preaching in Hellenistic Thought," in *Paul ands*(ed. T. H. Olbricht and J. L. Sumney; Atlanta: Society of Biblical Literature, 2001), 23–37.

polish or level of sophistication but by its intention to persuade, and its effectiveness should be measured by its ability to persuade.

We need not look in detail at the rhetorical structure of protreptic, which Schenkeveld presents more thoroughly than I need to here; it will be useful, however, to look at some exemplary texts in order to see the relationship of philosophy, protreptic, and conversion. Originally, protreptic carried the simple sense of persuasion, and only later came to be more closely associated with *philosophical* persuasion. The point of protreptic is not only to convince but to move to action. That action, obviously, is conversion, μετάνοια and ἐπιστρέφω as we find it occasionally in the language of the philosophers.[22] Plato's *Euthydemus* shows Socrates seeking to move Clinias, and of course the reader, "to love wisdom (φιλοσοφεῖν) and practice virtue" (275A). Aristotle's *Protreptikos* seeks to move the reader to practice prudence (φρόνησις). Seneca's 90th moral epistle ("On the Part Played by Philosophy in the Progress of Man") invokes the reader to embrace philosophy in order to understand the origin of human mental faculties.[23] Why do these writers attempt to induce such action on the part of the reader and hearer? In order to bring happiness into the reader's life. Of course, happiness is not so much to be understood as a simple emotional state but rather as a state in which the human lives well with what she or he has, within his or her means, and true to the nature of the world. Hence, claims to happiness that did not exhibit these qualities would not have been accepted as true happiness. Aristotle goes so far as to suggest that to choose philosophy is to avoid the choice of death; philosophy offers life itself, since its absence in life makes life worse than death (*Protreptikos* 108–110). For Seneca, philosophy is both benefactor, in that it benefits people, and a benefaction, in that it was given by the gods. Seneca opens his protreptic epistle with the observation that "life is the benefit (*munus*) of the immortal gods but living well of philosophy." Thus, he suggests, it would be natural to feel a greater debt to philosophy because of its benefactions (*beneficium*) than even to the gods were it not for the fact the philosophy also derived from the gods (90.1).

---

[22] For example ἐπιστρέφω in Plato, *Resp.* 7.518 (the Parable of the Cave); μετάνοια in Cebes, *Tabula* 10.

[23] While these are but three examples of protreptic, nothing would be gained by presenting a longer or more detailed list. There are important differences between the protreptics of various writers, but none of these differences concerns us, since what does not differ is the desire on the part of the writer to persuade. See Jordan ("Ancient Philosophic Protreptic") and Schenkeveld ("Philosophical Prose") for other important examples of protreptic.

3.2.3 The Call of the Philosopher-Patron

One final feature uniting philosophy with patronage and benefaction is the call of the philosopher-patron. The call of the patron/benefactor reviewed in the previous pages, and associated there with literary and sometimes divine patronage, is present in philosophical patronage as well. Diogenes Laertius tells the story of the initial encounter between Socrates and Xenophon, in which Socrates first asks Xenophon where he can buy food, then asks him "where do men become good and honourable" (*Lives* 2.48). Of course, the second question quite catches Xenophon off guard, and Socrates strikes while the proverbial iron is hot: "Follow me," Socrates invites Xenophon (Socrates says simply, ἕπου), from which point Xenophon becomes a pupil (ἀκροατής) of Socrates. Vernon Robbins writes that "the dynamics of summons and response accompanied the social identity of a teacher from the fifth century B.C.E. onwards in Graeco-Roman literature and culture."[24] In this sense, philosophical instruction and some forms of patronage and benefaction both involved the motif of the patronal call.

What has teaching to do with patronage and benefaction? Teachers (of anything, of course, but here primarily teachers of philosophy) provided benefactions to their pupils in the form of what they taught. Xenophon talks about Socrates as one whose teachings and actions are a benefit to people. He writes on two occasions: "Socrates spent his life in lavishing his gifts and rendering the greatest services to all who cared to receive them. For he always made his associates better men before he parted with them" (*Mem.* 1.2.61), and "In order to support my opinion that he benefited (ὠφελεῖν) his companions, alike by actions that revealed his own character and by his conversation, I will set down what I recollect of these" (*Mem.* 1.3.1). Xenophon closes his defence of Socrates by pointing out that Socrates "conferred the greatest benefits on all who dealt with him (ὠφελεῖν δὲ τὰ μέγιστα τοὺς χρωμένους αὐτῷ)" (*Mem.* 4.8.11).

Teachers or philosophers surrounded with students eager to learn were clearly successful, and thus honourable in the eyes of the public court of reputation. The philosopher who called people did not do so solely for the benefit of the student; this was a happy result of the search for a honouring retinue. The student's response to the call is the acceptance of the responsibilities that come to one who receives benefactions. Witness Alcibiades's

---

[24] Vernon K. Robbins, *Jesus the Teacher: A Socio-Rhetorical Interpretation of Mark* (Philadelphia: Fortress Press, 1984), 88. He cites as paradigmatic examples Socrates's calls of Theaetetus (Plato, *Theaet.* 144D) and Charmides (Plato, *Charm.* 155A).

response and proclamation of loyalty to Socrates: "From this day onward it must be the case that I am your attendant, and that you must always have me in attendance on you" (Ps-Plato, *Alc. maj.* 135D). Disciples and clients were closely related: they were both the recipients of some benefaction, and they both laboured to honour their benefactors, whether human, god, or philosopher.

Commenting on Kennedy's claim that "all religious systems are rhetorical," Wuellner suggests that what this means is that all religious systems are "purposeful."[25] The rhetoric of philosophical patronage/benefaction is intended to persuade others to adopt a certain perspective. In this way, then, we can say that philosophy is a part of the Graeco-Roman "religious" system since it was so often interpreted by ancient participants as functioning within the same rubric as religion, namely that of patronage and benefaction. The rhetorical skill no less than the ideas expressed by philosophers were intended to benefit the listener; even the sorts of aggressive and inflammatory outbursts characteristic of Cynic philosophers were not said simply for the sake of their shock-value, but were intended to shock people out of their enslavement to social conventions and guide them into the discovery of true happiness. Philosophy aimed to convert listeners, to benefit them by means of a philosopher's teachings in a way that would save them from ignorance and other long-term ills. That the rhetoric of patronage and benefaction figures so largely in philosophical conversion is another important element of our analysis of ancient conversion.

3.3 Prayer, Praise, and Proselytism

3.3.1 Prayer and Praise

It is by way of the many public expressions of gratitude and praise that have survived in inscriptions and other writings that we know both what we do of ancient patronage and benefaction and that it was so present a practice in the Graeco-Roman world. As a convention of the rhetoric of patronage and benefaction prayer, praise, and proselytism was designed to accomplish three things: to give thanks to a patron, to praise a patron, and to secure future benefactions.

---

[25] Wuellner, "Biblical Exegesis," 502.

Prayer could take the form either of prayers of gratitude or prayers of supplication, and perhaps counter-intuitively both honoured a patron equally. Prayer is the term assigned to communication between a human client and a divine patron, though it differs little in substance and form from communication between human clients and their human patrons and benefactors.[26] Seneca sees the practice of prayer as proof of divine benefactions, though he clearly has in mind prayers of thanksgiving. He writes that anyone who claims that the gods give nothing or are uninterested in human affairs fails to "hearken to the voices of those who pray and of those who all around him, lifting their hands to heaven, offering vows for blessing public and private" (*Ben.* 4.3.2).[27] Concerning various benefits, Epictetus asks "Would we not thank God for this?"[28] In his *Isis and Osiris*, Plutarch emphatically calls for people to honour the gods for what they have given humanity: "and if we revere and honour what is orderly and good and beneficial as the work of Isis and as the image and reflection and reason of Osiris, we shall not be wrong" (377A), and "even so these men of old did not refrain from calling by the names of the gods the gifts and creations of the god, honouring and venerating them because of the need which they had for them" (379D).[29] It must be made clear, however, that thanksgiving directed at human or divine patrons is not about being polite or courteous but about honouring patrons and benefactors. Giving thanks acknowledges the

---

[26] For example, Odysseus prays to Nausicaa for the benefaction of safe passage, promising to offer prayers to her though she is not a god (Homer, *Od.* 8.464ff.). See also M. P. Charlesworth, "Observations on Ruler-Cult," 8–20; H. S. Versnel, "Religious Mentality in Ancient Prayer," in *Faith, Hope and Worship: Aspects of Religious Mentality in the Ancient World* (ed. H. S. Versnel; Studies in Greek and Roman Religion 2; Leiden: E. J. Brill, 1982), 1–64.

[27] See also *P.Fay.* 124.16; *P.Giss.* 1.17.6; *P.Hib.* 1.79.6; *P.Oxy.* 963.6; *P.Petr.* 1.29.2; *PSI* 1.94.6.

[28] See also Epictetus, *Diatr.* 1.10.3; 2.23.5; 4.1.91–98; 4.4.7; 4.5.9; 4.7.9. Interestingly, the rhetoric of thanks-giving also took non-verbal forms. The establishing of shrines and altars in acknowledgement of benefits received from the gods was a form of thanksgiving, that clearly honours the gods (*Diatr.* 1.4.32). Likewise sacrifice was an expression of gratitude, a request for future benefactions, and a way of honouring the gods. See W. Pötscher, *Theophrastos 'Peri Eusebeias': Griechischer Text, herausgegeben, übersetzt und eingeleitet* (Leiden: E. J. Brill, 1964), frg. 12; F. T. van Straten, "Gifts for the Gods," in *Faith, Hope and Worship: Aspects of Religious Mentality in the Ancient World* (ed. H. S. Versnel; Studies in Greek and Roman Religion 2; Leiden: E. J. Brill, 1982), 67ff.; S. R. F. Price, "Between Man and God: Sacrifice in the Roman Imperial Cult," *JRS* 70 (1980): 28–43; Versnel, "Religious Mentality," 55.

[29] See also Gen 32:11; Num 14:19; Jonah 4:2.

benefactions given, allowing others to witness them as well, and can be attended by titles and descriptions of the gods that honour them.

Even prayers of supplication, however, honour a patron, for they say a great deal about the potential generosity of the patron by implying that the patron has the ability to give what is being asked. An excellent New Testament example of this is the Lord's Prayer. There are two interesting features about the Lord's Prayer. First, both synoptic versions are petitions for benefactions directed at the undisputed divine patron of Israel, and both open with the title "Father" (πατήρ). This is not a prayer of thanksgiving, but a prayer of supplication, yet it is clearly designed to honour God. This is done first in the title πατήρ.

Pater, despite the obvious etymological relationship, is not a synonym for patron, though it is significant that the Latin title *patronus* is derived from the same word; one should not think that every occurrence of the word πατήρ refers to a patron, but in certain instances to draw a connection is necessary. There are a number of instances, usually where the usage is metaphorical and not literally familial, that the title is part of the nomenclature of patronage and benefaction. In other words, patronage language should not be mistaken for kinship language, but kinship language can often be the language of patronage and benefaction.[30] The patron-benefactor and client relationship is expressed in categories of fictive-kinship. Father language is used in this way for Emperors who are called *"pater patriae"* (Caesar and the Emperors), but is also used of other rulers, lesser notables (Cicero according to Pliny the Elder, *Nat.* 7.117), and the gods.

In both Latin and Greek literature, "Father" is a title equal in honour to saviour, founder, benefactor, or god. Benefactors, whether Emperors or divine patrons or simply local large holders, could be called "Father" because of the care they distributed to those around them. Dio Chrysostom calls Zeus "Father" of the world repeatedly and relates the title to the beneficent act of creation (2 *Regn.* 75; 4 *Regn.* 22; *Borysth.* 35–36, 60). That Jesus calls his god "Father" might appear interesting to some because of the implication of sonship, but in the context of Graeco-Roman patronage and clientage it is parallel to similarly metaphorical titles of human and divine patrons. It is, at the very least, fitting that Jesus should be depicted calling the supreme patron and "ruler" of Israel "Father."

---

[30] See T. R. Stevenson, "The Ideal Benefactor and the Father Analogy in Greek and Roman Thought," *CQ* 42 (1992): 421–36; idem, "Social and Psychological Interpretations of Graeco-Roman Religion: Some Thoughts on the Ideal Benefactor," *Antichthon* 30 (1996): 1–18.

Prayer and praise might be seen most often together in the form of hymns. In the following example, a client in a voluntary association is credited with composing a hymn to the divine patron of the club, Isis. We read that "Maiistas composed this hymn for the temple on this subject: 'Innumerable and wonderful are your deeds, O Glorious Sarapis, with miracles being celebrated as far as the fortified cities of Egypt which is beloved of the gods, and others celebrated all over Greece, and they also praise your consort Isis.'"[31] Hymns also figure prominently throughout Aristides' *Sacred Tales* (e.g., 4.322.1–2; 4.330.13–16). In every case, Aristides is explicit that the hymns are designed to be honouring, and that they represent the least he can do as a grateful client. Yet Aristides goes a step beyond composing hymns; he composed several lengthy orations in which Asclepius is either the topic of honour (as well as things related to Asclepius, such as the well in the Pergamum temple) or the primary character within them.[32] Regardless of the source or subject of a hymn or speech, the composition itself and the effort of composition is an act of client gratitude and honour, but the quality of the words serves to double the honouring effect.[33]

That Luke thought of the Jesus movement in terms of patronage and benefaction, with God as patron and Jesus as broker, has been established by Frederick Danker.[34] Here I shall focus on Luke's infancy narratives, where we see Luke's penchant for composing hymns of praise to the divine patron/benefactor. The intent of hymns is to honour God by illustrating all the good God does, with the hope that the benefactions from God will continue. Philo, for instance, argues that gratitude to God is expressed best through eloquent speech and song (*Plant.* 125–131). Luke has composed (or less likely has inherited) three hymns of praise. In Luke 2:28–32, a stranger named Simeon is pictured taking the infant Jesus into his arms and praising God, attributing

---

[31] *IG* XI[4] 1299.29–36. The translation is from McLean, "Place of Cult," 206.

[32] In fact, Aristides composed orations to several other of his divine patrons as well: Sarapis, Athena, Dionysus, Zeus, and Poseidon. He even claims that his speeches are the single best way he can conceive of to honour the gods: *Speech for Asclepius* (Λαλία εἰς ᾿Ασκληπιόν) 37.1–7; 40.1–2.

[33] See also two hymns to Asclepius, composed five centuries apart, which honour the god in much the same way: Edelstein and Edelstein § 592 and *IG* II[2] 4473. See also J. M. Bremer, "Greek Hymns," in *In Faith, Hope and Worship: Aspects of Religious Mentality in the Ancient World* (ed. H. S. Versnel; Studies in Greek and Roman Religion 2; Leiden: E. J. Brill, 1982).

[34] F. W. Danker, *Luke* (Philadelphia: Fortress Press, 1976). See also H. Moxnes, "Patron–Client Relations and the New Community in Luke–Acts," in *The Social World of Luke–Acts: Models for Interpretation* (ed. J. H. Neyrey; Peabody: Hendrickson, 1991), 241–68.

to God the sending of a light to the Gentiles. The benefaction is Jesus, and the recipient of the praise and thanksgiving is the divine benefactor, God. Secondly, in Luke 1:67–79, Zechariah praises God at the birth of John the Baptist for supporting the Israelites, and thanks God for sending a saviour to rescue them from their enemies. Zechariah proclaims God's affection and protection of Israel, in effect broadcasting the benefactions of God. But one Lukan hymn stands above these, the one traditionally known as the Magnificat, Mary's hymn to God (Luke 1:46–55). In the hymn, Luke has Mary honour God with the common Graeco-Roman honorific, Σωτήρ; she proclaims God's affection for Israel, protecting them and raising them to positions of status. She proclaims that God has done many great things for her, acknowledging that God is her divine patron. In moving language, Mary praises and thanks God, ascribing to God the honour that was the client's to ascribe, and doing so in a public and vociferous way. Given these things, one wonders, when Luke has Gabriel call Mary κεχαριτωμένη, usually translated as "favoured one" (Luke 1:28), might "benefacted one" be closer to how Luke envisions his God's dealings with humanity? Luke would surely consider it a benefaction to Mary that she was chosen to carry a messiah.

3.3.2 Patronal Proselytism

Clients of divine patrons had another interesting way of showing honour and gratitude: they could try to convince other people of the worthiness and generosity of their divine patrons. In other words, spreading the good news of a divine patron's wonderful deeds, and thus attracting clients and increasing the number of worshippers, in effect 'patron evangelisation,' served to honour the god. Consider, for example, Philo's claim that God was to be properly honoured by recounting God's benefactions in prose or poetic eulogies and eloquent speeches and songs (Philo, *Plant.* 126–131). This borders, no doubt, on praise, but its purpose was perhaps to attract admirers: why else invoke lists of deeds done?

In the case of human patrons, the intent might be to bring clients to the patron, since the number of clients one had was a reflection of one's honourable status, or it might simply be to get people talking about this patron. In the case of divine and philosophical patrons, reciprocity appears to have been concerned frequently with bringing in new worshippers, adherents, or students/disciples. Persuading people to worship your god in the hope of tapping into the divine benefactions that one had received was analogous to the groups of clients that would follow a human patron around town. Such a retinue reflected well upon the human patron, and so too would the honour of the divine patron increase with the increased number and visibility of devotees.³⁵ Imagine the public effect of the parade in honour of Isis at the end of Apuleius' *Metamorphoses*, in which Lucius manages to find the roses he has been seeking and is restored to his human form. All those people participating in the parade, all of them claiming in some way to have benefited from their association with Isis as their divine patron, would have increased the honour of that god in the eyes of the public court of reputation, and would have attracted additional worshipers/clients, perhaps from among the curious standing at the side of the road. Lucius does not narrate that there were any conversions unless they are to be included among those who raised their hands: "the people [at the side] began to marvel, and the religious honoured the goddess for so evident a miracle. . . whereby they lifted their hands to heaven and with one voice rendered testimony of so great a benefaction (*beneficium*) which I received from the goddess" (*Metam.* 13). Following Lucius' metamorphosis, the priest tells him about the "yoke of ministry," presumably counselling him to prepare to spread the good news of his salvation at the hands of Isis (*Metam.* 15).

Aristides relates the practice of telling others of the great things his patron had done for him, and of their effect:

> And there is no city, nor individual, not even of those who ended up as leaders, who even after a brief encounter with us did not celebrate by extending his support in his own way, not that my own words brought this about, but because you are my lord.³⁶

These words echo Paul's words at 1 Cor 15:10 (which I shall cover in greater detail in the following chapter) where Paul is boasting about his success and then pauses to claim that it is not really his doing but that of the χάρις of God.³⁷ Such sentiment attempts to divert credit to the divine patron, and thus serves to honour him or her. Of course, it is not only these words but the voluminousness of Aristides' writings themselves in honour of Asclepius that

---

35 It is most interesting that the impulse to proselytise as a means of patron-honouring conduct never seems to result in the command to those proselytised to proselytise themselves, neither in the examples of the Graeco-Roman cult nor in Paul.
36 *Speech for Asclepius* 40.6–8.
37 Consider also Danker's reconstruction of an inscribed letter from King Nebuchadnezzar to his people in which it is purported that he intends "to show you and your wise men that this god [the God of Israel] exists, and great are his marvelous works" (Danker, *Benefactor*, 173–75).

show him to be an evangeliser and proselytiser for the god.[38] Such writings relate what the god has done for his clients, and thus the implication is that he could do the same for other clients. Aristides appears to have been quite pleased when people responded positively to his message, and though he claims it was not really his own doing, but rather that of the god working through him, the man was a trained rhetor. What else, for example, could have been the point of singing the praises of Asclepius to the ends of the Roman empire if not to increase the reputation, and thus the honour, of the divine patron/benefactor?[39] He no doubt took great pride in effecting a kindly disposition among people for his patron Asclepius.

It is worth noting that votive (or ex-voto) offerings can be seen to work in a similar way in the context of divine patronage and clientage. Votive offerings honoured the divine in two ways. On the one hand, they were the result of contractual obligations; the client or worshiper promised to honour the god if the god made a certain benefaction.[40] For example, "Aristoklea of Kitium, in fulfilment of a vow, dedicated [this altar] to Aphrodite Ourania" (*IG* II² 4636); "Marcus Salvius Douiscus [dedicated this] to Apollo who hears prayers" (*IBM* IV 1034).[41] The vow would have been something to the effect of a promissory note in exchange for a benefaction. These people, then, set up these public endorsements, inscribing their debt and gratitude as a means of proclaiming and honouring the generosity of their gods. On the other hand, votive offerings were honouring because of what was represented pictorially on the inscriptions—honouring acts such as people praying and sacrificing to the gods; some votive offerings also depict images of the gods; and by inscribing one's name in the offering a claim of loyalty is made. Votive offerings were meant to serve the interests of both the client and the divine patron: they serve the client in that they show that the duty of reciprocity has been discharged;[42] they give the client the opportunity to ask for future benefactions

---

[38] I leave aside the question of whether Jewish hymns to God were meant to attract new believers in this manner, but it is worth noting that discussions of this issue should begin to take this data into account.

[39] Edelstein and Edelstein § 596.

[40] For more on this see, Bradley McLean, *An Introduction to Greek Epigraphy of the Hellenistic and Roman Periods From Alexander the Great Down to the Reign of Constantine (323 B.C. – A.D. 337)* (Ann Arbor: University of Michigan Press, 2002), 246–59.

[41] Translations of these inscriptions are from McLean, *Greek Epigraphy*, 212–13.

[42] This is especially the case in an epigram from Callimachus. Having paid his debt, the inscriber claims that if Asclepius were to forget and try to claim it a second time, the tablet would prove his innocence. See van Straten, "Gifts for the Gods," 71.

and in a more permanent medium than the usual way (prayer); and they serve the god by honouring him or her with both titles and by depicting in pictures the god actually *being* honoured.

The gospel of Mark presents an interesting example of this sort of patronal proselytisation. Those who receive the benefaction of healing from Jesus are often said to spread the news of the affair, and they are said to do so exuberantly. Of course, adding to the enigma of Mark's Messianic Secret is that they do this, for the most part, in defiance of Jesus' direct requests that they remain silent. Their proselytism takes the form of testimony concerning the benefactions received and of the generosity of the divine patron/benefactor in question and the broker. It begins very early in Mark (1:45), where a person has been healed and he proclaims it freely and begins to spread the account (λόγος). This man was the perfect client, for the story relates that Jesus' fame spread so quickly that after this healing he had to stay out in the country. The theme continues in the very next pericope; when Jesus finally ventures into town a huge crowd has gathered outside his door (Mark 2:2), and again later, there are so many people crowding him on the sea shore that he has to get into a boat to address them (Mark 3:9). It is not clear from the Markan narrative that Jesus is entirely pleased with this turn of events, but such a possibility does not occur to those who were healed; they naturally take up the role of the client to a divine patron or benefactor, and honour him or her by going about bragging about the benefactions received, with the result that people were attracted to the movement. Mark's recording that Jesus could not enter a city, or could not leave his house, or had to speak to crowds from a boat would have alerted ancient readers to the great honour of this man as a healer.

Our discussion of the philosopher as patron/benefactor above touched on the rhetorical practice of protreptic—the custom of persuading people to incorporate the teachings of one's preferred philosophy. In his brief study of proselytism in the Graeco-Roman world, Martin Goodman claims that philosophical protreptic and anything appearing to be zeal for converting on the part of the Cynic and Epicureans, was merely part of an educational mission (the desire simply to educate others about what one believes but not convert them) and not as proselytising mission (the intent to actually have outsiders hold the same views as insiders[43]). Goodman places both cultic and philosophical groups in the same camp when he claims of each that "No pagan seriously dreamed of bringing all humankind to give worship in one body to

---

[43] Martin Goodman, *Mission and Conversion: Proselytizing in the Religious History of the Roman Empire* (Oxford: Clarendon Press, 1994), 14.

one deity,"[44] and "it seems unlikely that adherents of any of the distinctive philosophies of the early Roman empire converts to their own self-defined groups."[45] But Goodman stacks the deck against finding evidence of interest in conversion by the strict standards he places on the phenomenon. He illustrates that few people in the ancient world express an interest in converting "*all* outsiders"[46] (in addition to the sheer impracticality of it) and that converting others does not appear to have been a "religious duty."[47] These are easily granted, but there are other more flexible options. An interest or openness to conversion did not have to be universal or to seek to convert every living soul in order to have been present at a lower level of magnitude. Do we have any evidence to suggest that it even occurred to these people that *all* humans could potentially join, and thus that this was a legitimate concern? Likewise, it does not have to have been a duty to still have been an option to some people.

I am finding through my work that a number of conventions exist for talking about one's generous patron or benefactor, but these conventions exist as *options*, none of which are *all* practised by the same person. Patronal proselytism is an option, not a duty, but that cannot be read as evidence of a lack of interest in bringing some followers into the fold. Goodman seems to undervalue the intensity of Cynic παρρησία, as well as of the point of protreptic in general when he claims that these were concerned with nothing more than education of the masses. In fact, what most impairs Goodman's claim, at least with respect to the Cynics, is that the Cynics claimed to have been sent by God as messengers to humanity. It is patently unlikely that Cynics thought they were sent solely to educate and not rather to reform (which *is* philosophical conversion). Nock states, quite accurately I believe, that the prime interest of philosophy after Socrates was the "desire to free humanity from error and lead it into truth."[48] And, concerning cultic proselytism, is it likely that Apuleius' Lucius is depicted telling the tale of his metamorphosis by Isis merely as entertainment? After all, the man is a devotee of Isis when he tells the fantastic story.

Prayer, praise, and patronal proselytism, though each distinct, are clearly all part of a single pattern of behaviour that sought to request benefactions, express gratitude, honour the god, and secure future benefactions. These

---

[44] Goodman, *Mission and Conversion*, 32.
[45] Goodman, *Mission and Conversion*, 36.
[46] Goodman, *Mission and Conversion*, 23, emphasis original.
[47] Goodman, *Mission and Conversion*, 24.
[48] Arthur D. Nock, *Conversion: The Old and the New in Religion from Alexander the Great to Augustine of Hippo* (London: Oxford University Press, 1933), 165.

were in fact the primary means by which a client could exercise his or her reciprocity towards a generous patron or benefactor. Whether human or divine, the patron/benefactor were honoured in similar ways.[49] The expression of gratitude is not simply about being polite and grateful, but about being *publicly* grateful. Inscriptions were even more effective than public prayer because of their permanence, but clients soon discovered that bringing in other clients (patronal proselytisation), and thus accruing greater honour for the patron, also had a permanence. In the context of cult and philosophy, assuring the growth of cultic loyalty or the teachings of a philosopher by taking the message or the good news to other people served to honour the patron, as we ourselves can attest, well into the future.

3.4 Patronal Synkrisis

We have noted how many opportunities there were for clients to honour or express gratitude to their patrons that were verbal in nature—hymns, confessions, panegyric, etc. That these all have to do with appropriate client conduct has, as we have seen, been noted by some. What has not been noted before is the frequent presence of a particular rhetorical trope, synkrisis, in the context of verbal expressions of gratitude and honour directed at a patron or benefactor. Synkrisis occurs as a part of patron-oriented rhetoric often and deliberately enough that it warrants its own sub-category, which I have come to call patronal synkrisis.[50]

Synkrisis is a particularly simple rhetoric trope—comparison. Aristotle refers to comparing a person with others when there is not enough to say about one of them alone (*Rhet.* 1368a, 19–23). The same simple trope occurs in Latin as well (*comparatio*); Quintilian describes more or less the same practice of comparing the merits of two characters (*Inst.* 2.4.21). The two most commonly cited illustrations of synkrisis come from two Greek writers. The first is Isocrates, who wrote a lengthy encomium for Evagoras. Evagoras lived 435–374/373 B.C.E.,

---

[49] H. S. Versnel attributes this to the political and cultural change that led people to associate human and divine benefactors in the same language ("Religious Projection: A Hellenistic Instance," in *Religious Transformations and Socio-Political Change: Eastern Europe and Latin America* [ed. L. H. Martin; Religion and Society 33; Berlin/New York: Mouton de Gruyter, 1993], 25–39).

[50] The term "patronal synkrisis" does not reflect that synkriseis of this type were not also directed at benefactors, for we shall find quickly that they are; "patronal synkrisis" is simply a clear and more usable form of "synkrisis directed at both patrons and benefactors."

during which time he was a general and governor of Cyprus. Isocrates, a onetime teacher of rhetoric, wrote three orations as rhetorical exercises, one of which covered the life of Evagoras, and was written eight years after that man's death.[51] Isocrates compares Evagoras with the greatly admired Cyrus, but claims that Evagoras was an even more impressive ruler. Despite Cyrus's greatness, "no one, whether mortal, demigod, or immortal, will be found to have obtained his throne more nobly, more splendidly, or more piously" (*Evag.* 39).

A second very common illustration of classic synkrisis comes from Plutarch, whose *Parallel Lives* involves the pointed comparison of numerous great men throughout history. Each of the comparisons is loose and implied, but following nineteen of these twenty-two pairs there is a more explicit "synkrisis" in which Plutarch compares the two people he had up to that point been comparing only indirectly. In each case, the title reads the same: δεῖνος καὶ δεῖνος σύγκρισις. Despite the fact that there are numerous occurrences of synkrisis in ancient writing, there is no systematic or detailed definition for it, neither in ancient nor modern critical writing. It appears that the translation 'comparison' is understood to be self-explanatory. Timothy Seid, noting this same deficiency, has attempted recently to rectify this lack of a full definition.[52] Seid offers the following:

> Synkrisis is the comparison of two subjects of similar quality and is characterized by the comparative exchanges (often with the μέν . . . δέ construction) which praise (or censure) one subject by drawing parallels to a model subject often using the common topics of encomium in order to persuade the audience to modify their character and behavior accordingly.[53]

Seid's definition reflects well the examples of the synkrisis cited above, and thus it is fitting that he situates synkrisis exclusively within the demonstrative or epideictic type of oratory, for the uses of synkrisis by Isocrates and Plutarch

---

[51] G. L. Cawkwell, "Isocrates," in *The Oxford Classical Dictionary* (ed. S. Hornblower and A. Spawforth; Oxford: Oxford University Press, 1996), 769–71.

[52] Timothy W. Seid, "Synkrisis in Hebrews 7: The Rhetorical Structure and Strategy," in *The Rhetorical Interpretation of Scripture: Essays from the 1996 Malibu Conference* (ed. S. E. Porter and D. L. Stamps; JSNTSup 180; Sheffield: Sheffield Academic Press, 1999), 322–47.

[53] Seid, "Synkrisis," 325. Seid's definition is similar to but fuller than that of Heinrich Lausberg, *Handbook of Literary Rhetoric: A Foundation for Literary Study* (trans. M. T. Bliss, A. Jansen and D. E. Orton; ed. D. E. Orton and R. Dean Anderson; Leiden: E. J. Brill, 1998), 495. See also R. Dean Anderson, *Glossary of Greek Rhetorical Terms* (CBET 24; Leuven: Peeters, 2000), 110–11.

support this. Isocrates wrote encomiastically, and Plutarch's own stated aim was not to write histories, but to epitomise and teach virtue using the lives of great men as illustration. Both are typical uses and examples of epideictic rhetoric. But this definition of synkrisis overlooks a considerable number of comparisons that are very different in nature and intent from those of Isocrates and Plutarch. Synkrisis is used not only to compare two people, but also two states of life. Frequently synkrisis involves the comparison of life before and after some significant event, usually an event that is interpreted by the writer to be a benefaction from a patron or benefactor. Thus, synkrisis occurs very often in the description of a relationship between two people.

Isocrates and Plutarch wrote of their subjects long after they were dead; there is no indication that there was any relationship between these writers and their subjects. Frequently, however, synkrisis is found in writings in which there is an explicit relationship between the writer and the subject, that of patronage or benefaction and clientage. Patronal synkrisis, as I would like to call it, does not differ formally from classic synkrisis; the form of synkrisis is always simply the comparison of two things. Patronal synkrisis differs, however, in its function and in its intent. The function of synkrisis when it occurs in a setting of patronage and clientage is to honour the patron on behalf of an interested party, the client; it is a part of a client's expression of gratitude for benefactions received. The comparison being drawn is always intended to honour the patron. Most commonly this is done not by comparing two people, in the fashion of either Isocrates or Plutarch, but by comparing the "before-and-after" state of the client. This is the language of transformation and includes the claim that a patron's benefactions have changed the client's life. By comparing one's life before and after benefactions, a client honours and expresses gratitude to the patron. Occasionally, however, this is done by comparing the treatment that a client has received from a patron to the treatment experienced by that client's enemies. Nonetheless, the function of this second type of patronal synkrisis is still to honour the patron and to express gratitude for their present favoured status. That clients frequently used synkrisis in their expressions of honour and gratitude, in their public broadcasts of the benefactions they received, is a fact deserving close attention.

3.4.1 Human Patronage and Benefaction

Among the many things written by Pliny the Younger, his *Panegyricus* stands out as a model for Latin panegyric. Pliny wrote the *Panegyricus* for the emperor Trajan who had acted generously with Pliny many times. Thus, there is an immediate difference to be noted in the function of the synkrisis as it occurs in this writing for instance and in the writings of Isocrates and Plutarch. The point is not to claim that Pliny uses synkrisis *throughout* his writings, but rather to note how he uses it differently than writers like Plutarch. The *Panegyricus* was presented to Trajan; it was given to honour not only a living character, but one who served as a patron/benefactor to Pliny (among other people, of course). Pliny is not merely showing his rhetorical skill by using synkrisis to portray his subject favourably; he is addressing a patron who happens to be the most powerful of human patrons/benefactors.

Since this synkrisis operates within the system of patronage and clientage, it is incumbent upon us to see how it functions differently for Pliny than the trope appears to have for Isocrates or Plutarch. The panegyric is built upon the comparison between the paltry emperors, who misgoverned the empire prior to Trajan, and Trajan, who introduced a new model of rule (*Pan.* 5.6–8).[54] At the close of the panegyric, Pliny writes in a personal voice, "in bad times I was one who lived with grief and fear, and can be counted among the serene and happy now that better days have come" (*Pan.* 95.4). Note the change in the quality of life that Pliny attributes to the ascension of Trajan to power. Pliny had just been granted consulship by Trajan (c. 100 C.E.), so he had already been the recipient of Trajan's benefactions when he wrote his *Panegyricus*. In addition, the letters between Trajan and Pliny that are collected in book 10 begin about 98 C.E., two years before Pliny's consulship, and these too illustrate the close relationship that Pliny had with Trajan. Pliny's synkrisis of his life before and after Trajan grants to Trajan responsibility for what is good, even what is better, in Pliny's life. This convention of the rhetoric of patronage/benefaction allows Pliny to honour Trajan; since it is delivered publicly, it encourages others to honour him as well. And like all patron-oriented rhetoric, it hopes to secure a continuing relationship and further benefactions.

Even Martial, whose writings make him appear quite bitter about the patron-client relationship, writes of Caesar that "no epochs can be thought superior to our times" (*Ep.* 5.19). In this epigram, he compares the very favourable acts of patronage that the emperor has done for the empire to the generally sorry state of patronage and clientage in society in general. He honours the patron/benefactor of the empire by asking,

---

54 This glorification of the present is all the more noteworthy because it contradicts a far more common tendency in both ancient and modern cultures: that of glorifying the past with such terms as "the golden years" and "the good old days."

> When could men watch triumphs better deserved? When did the gods of the Palatine merit more? Under what leader was Mars' Rome more beautiful and great? Under what prince did liberty so flourish? (*Ep.* 5.19)

Later Martial writes:

> It used to be a game to betray the sacred marriage and a game to castrate males. You forbid both, Caesar, and come to the aid of future generations; for by your order their birth is made safe. Under your rule no man shall be either eunuch or adulterer. Formerly, even a eunuch (alas for our morals!) was an adulterer. (*Ep.* 6.2)

In both of these examples of patronal synkrisis Martial compares the imperfections and limitations of past ages and rulers' works within the sphere of patronage and reciprocity. Martial honours Caesar in an appropriate and public manner by drawing the comparison which demands a positive assessment of Caesar's accomplishments and benefactions to humanity. That Caesar is not Martial's own personal patron, as was the case with Trajan and Pliny, is not significant. The benefactions to which Martial refers are extended to the entire empire; Martial writes as a member of that empire, and thus as a recipient of benefactions no less than if he were a personal client of the emperor. The Emperor is patron of the empire and those in it, not only of close personal clients. Patronal synkrisis is an appropriate trope to use then in even this case.

Cicero provides us with another example of patronal synkrisis. Cicero was a Roman elite of the first-century B.C.E. He held many prestigious offices and positions and, as his many letters reveal, had many patrons among the most elite. In the middle of his life, however, a political catastrophe took place and Cicero, unwilling to barter away his independence, was exiled in 58 B.C.E. Though the exile lasted approximately one year, it is an event Cicero appears uninterested in describing in any detail. It is all the more remarkable that when Cicero does mention this period of his life, he consistently does so with reference to his present restored status and with reference to the patron who was able to effect such a restoration on his behalf. In December of 54, Cicero wrote to Lentulus Spinther, "thanks to your public endeavours, dear sir, I conceived myself as restored, not only to my family and friends, but to my country" (*Fam.* 20.4). Later in the same long letter, Cicero refers to how Lentulus raised him "from the dust," implying, as was typical to the feeling of exile, that he was as good as dead without access to his honourable land

and citizenship. Not surprisingly, Cicero compares and contrasts his past position of dishonour and exile with his present state of honour, prestige, and privilege, and equally clearly he attributes this state to the benefaction of Lentulus Spinther, to whom Cicero confesses he is unable to express adequate gratitude for the magnitude of the benefaction he received (*Fam.* 20.1).

Cicero also traces the credit for his restoration back to the emperor, in this case Pompey. In a letter addressed to Appius Pulcher, Cicero attributes his restoration to Pompey, writing "If services count, it was through him that I consider I regained country, children, citizenship, rank, my very being" (*Fam.* 73.10). Perhaps this suggests that Lentulus Spinther was a broker of Pompey, and that the benefaction of restoration ultimately derived from Pompey. Regardless, as we have seen, the broker and patron are both rightful recipients of praise and honour. With the benefactions of these two men, Lentulus Spinther and Pompey the Great, Cicero was saved from his dishonourable state and restored to positions of honour and prestige. His frequent comparisons between these two states are short on details but consistent in their attribution of his present excellent position to the benefactions of his patrons. Cicero's patronal synkrisis is a common feature of the patron or benefactor and client relationship, and of the expression of reciprocity required of client conduct.

One does not need to argue that patronal synkrisis was the *only* way a client might express his or her debt of gratitude to a patron, nor that its use was ubiquitous; clearly there were other ways of expressing praise and gratitude, and synkrisis does not occur in *every* place it could potentially have been put to good use. One needs only to note that patronal synkrisis is a sufficiently common rhetorical trope available to a grateful client, and, most importantly, that it functions seamlessly in the reciprocity of a client towards a patron or benefactor. It appears that a comparison of a client's past with the better present to the credit of the benefactor would not have been surprising for a human patron to encounter, and the same can be said for encounters between human clients and their divine benefactors.

3.4.2 Divine Patronage and Benefaction

On the level of divine patronage and clientage, the *Metamorphoses* of Apuleius presents a example of such a comparison between an old and new life in reciprocity for a divine benefaction. The *Metamorphoses* is the first-person narration of Lucius, who accidentally turns himself into an ass when he and a Thessalian lover carelessly experiment with magic. The story follows

Lucius' misadventures and hardships on his ill-fated journey to escape from his predicament. Finally, after many failed attempts to reverse his condition, and as he prays to an unknown female figure on the water outside of Corinth, it is Isis who offers to restore Lucius. Her benefaction to Lucius is salvation from his present wretched state, and Lucius' response, appropriately, is loyalty and devotion (not to mention the very act of telling the story to curious passers-by!). Lucius strives with great zeal to become initiated into her sacred mystery, and indeed moves through several levels of the mystery. His final position as a devotee to Isis is contrasted both indirectly and directly to his previous life. The entire story functions as an indirect synkrisis. Lucius' final state as a man who has made the right decisions is presented both in contrast to his cursed existence as an ass, but also to his existence as the foolish man who played with magic, who perhaps was a con-man (the narrative is unclear as to whether or not Lucius had a legitimate letter of recommendation to ingratiate him to the household of Milo), and who was attracted to, perhaps governed by, the sensual pleasures of sex, eating meat, and drinking alcohol. Lucius the devotee of Isis is a different man, and the narrative here is clear: he is a better and more content man than the Lucius prior to and certainly during his metamorphosis. That the entire book is a synkrisis is what stands behind Lucius' brief statement at 11.19, "And so I dutifully spoke to each of them and rapidly described both my former sufferings and my present joys."

Lucius credits Isis with his restoration, as if there was any other option, and this is made explicit in his final speech to her, a lengthy and endearing testament of his gratitude and loyalty to the goddess. Lucius does not express this patronal synkrisis to Isis, but he does, in a fashion typical and consistent with client reciprocity, lament his inability to offer sufficient gratitude: "The fullness of my voice is inadequate to express what I feel about your majesty; a thousand mouths with as many tongues would not be enough, nor even an endless flow of inexhaustible speech" (11.5). The benefaction of Isis to Lucius is his restoration to human form, the restoration from a wretched state to a perfect present.

A segment of the population where we might most predictably expect to find people who have arrived at a better state of being from a previously inferior one are the sick who were healed. It is almost too obvious that the testimonies of Asclepius will provide us with many examples of patronal synkrisis having to do with healing. There are so many first- and third-person accounts from people claiming to have been made healthy by Asclepius, the patron god of medicine. Aristides' orations and *Sacred Tales* (1–5) are in and of themselves a series of synkriseis, for they tell over and over how Asclepius assuaged some ailment or another of Aristides. Yet humorously, Aristides is *not* the best example of patronal synkrisis since he was perpetually ill! Many other texts of Edelstein's and Edelstein's collection of Asclepeia attest to the healing success of the God by outlining their previous state of misery and attributing the current state of wholeness to Asclepius. One adherent relates an evening spent in incubation in the Temple of Asclepius where he was being consumed by a violent fever. His mother was with him, and watched as the God approached her son. As the fever broke, and the son awoke, he told her that everything she had seen he too had seen in a dream. He was cured of the fever and went off, as a good client ought to, proclaiming the benefactions of Asclepius.[55] Another person recorded in an inscription how he suffered from dyspepsia. He spent the better part of two weeks in the Temple during which time Asclepius gave him many directions for a cure. In the end he claims that, "Knowing beneficence (χάρις) and becoming healthy, I was released."[56] Finally, an inscription from Crete relates much the same story of how Asclepius took an active role in effecting a cure to an incessant cough.[57]

These healing testimonies, and for that matter the other examples of patronal synkrisis cited earlier in this section, highlight clients' experiences of the benefactions and effectiveness of their patrons; they also illustrate that patrons could effect positive change in a client's life. But what we most need to see in them is that synkrisis was a common rhetorical convention available to clients seeking to honour their patrons and benefactors for benefactions received. Synkrisis was a part of the typical client behaviour that involves advertising the deeds and generosity of one's patron. Synkrisis was a way of showing the good things a patron, human or divine, had done for a client and simultaneously emphasising the positive impact of this on the life of the client.

3.4.3 Philosophical Patronage and Benefaction

Given that philosophic patronage, like some forms of divine patronage, was credited with changing one's life, it is not surprising to find that synkrisis is also a feature of the disciple's expression of gratitude and honour towards the

---

[55] Edelstein and Edelstein, § 331.
[56] *IG* IV² 126; Edelstein and Edelstein § 432.
[57] *IKret* I 17; Edelstein and Edelstein § 439.

philosophic patron. For example, in a work entitled *Nigrinus*, Lucian of Samosata presents a dialogue between two people, one of whom has returned from a conversation with the philosopher Nigrinus in Rome. In this dialogue, speaker B recalls that he has been converted to see the world as the Platonic Nigrinus sees it, namely as overrun with loathsome people everywhere, particularly the haughty elite and the shallow clients who pander to them and perpetuate their fatuous behaviour. The role of speaker A is primarily to give speaker B the opportunity to relate the teachings of Nigrinus, and speaker B relies on a passionate synkrisis in order to draw the listener in, both the reader of the work and speaker A within the work.

Speaker B is clearly agitated, and tells his dialogue partner that "I have come back to you transformed by the wayside into a happy and blissful man—in the language of the stage, 'thrice blessed'" (*Nigr.* 1). More to the point, speaker B relates, "Don't you think it wonderful, in the name of Zeus, that once a slave I am now free! 'once poor now rich indeed'; once witless and befogged, now saner?" (*Nigr.* 1). As in every other example of patronal synkrisis we have seen, speaker B is comparing his past, which almost embarrasses him, with a present almost equally embarrassing for its riches. He has been transformed from a poor witless slave to a rich, sane and free man. It is unnecessary for this past state of denigration to have been actual; the comparison being drawn is still meaningful in that it honours the benefactor, even if it was nothing more than a perception based on a present state of favour. Likewise speaker B's altered status from slave to free and from poor to rich is probably not literal, but it does nonetheless speak to a real sense of benefactions and of improved status due to the efforts his philosopher-patron. The past misery and present status do not have to be real for the gratitude the synkrisis expresses to carry its intended weight.

It is worth noting that speaker B appears to embody precisely the sort of philosophic conversion that Nock attributed to the ancient philosophies: traumatic, emotional, intellectual, and resulting in a uniform loyalty. Steve Mason refers to the synkrisis of this work, but finds it not in speaker B's comparison of life pre- and post-encounter, but in Nigrinus' didactic comparison between typical Roman life and the better philosophical life.[58] Because of the broader sweep of his focus, Mason (in addition to others) overlooks the

---

[58] Steve Mason, "*PHILOSOPHIAI*: Graeco-Roman, Judean and Christian," in *Voluntary Associations in the Graeco-Roman World* (ed. J. S. Kloppenborg and S. G. Wilson; New York: Routledge, 1996), 31–58.

role of Nigrinus in speaker B's conversion, or the patronal synkrisis.[59] Speaker B relates that he went to pay his respects to this Nigrinus, of whom we know nothing except that he was a Platonic philosopher whom Lucian respected. Immediately the relationship is set up as one of unequal status, at least as it concerns philosophical prestige. In the end, Nigrinus gives speaker B the benefaction of salvation, of seeing correctly. In fact, in one of Lucian's less subtle moments, he has speaker B cured of the very ailment that brought him to Rome in the first place—his faulty vision! The benefactions to speaker B then are clear and as the one who bestowed them upon him Nigrinus becomes his philosophical patron, father, or benefactor. Finally, since Lucian is a satirist of most things Roman, the dialogue ends with the very same transformed speaker B suggesting that he, and speaker A whom he inadvertently converted by relating the story, ought to return to Nigrinus for a cure to their new-found disease. Note, however, that despite the satire and social critique involved, Nigrinus is still the benefactor, who, in this case, it is suggested, will be able to reverse the effects of his first benefaction.

Another of Lucian's works worth noting is *The Double Indictment*. In it we find a rare example of a patron, in this case the Academy, showing the good things that came from the client's relationship with "her." The setting is a court case in which the Academy defends herself against the charge, brought by Intemperance, that it kidnapped Polemo and brainwashed him so that he would forget what Intemperance had taught him. Clearly, Intemperance cannot imagine how anyone would leave it willingly, but the defence of the Academy is that Polemo did exactly that. Constantly in a haze of drunkenness, he disgraced his ancestors and his city by carousing in the market in midday. But one day when the doors of the Academy remained open, Polemo passed and heard the strains of articulate thought on virtue and temperance. After listening to what the Academy had to offer, Polemo chose to abandon Intemperance. Academy claims that "he joined me, not because he was summoned nor forced, as this person says, but he has come because things are better here." It was for what Polemo could get from the Academy as a patron, the better and greater benefactions, that he left Intemperance.[60] Later the Academy closes her defence with the following rendition of events:

---

[59] Hubert Cancik, "Lucian on Conversion: Remarks on Lucian's Dialogue *Nigrinos*," in *Ancient and Modern Perspectives on the Bible and Culture: Essays in Honor of Hans Dieter Betz* (ed. A. Yarbro Collins; Atlanta: Scholars Press, 1998), 26–48.

[60] See also Diogenes Laertius, *Lives* 4.16.

> Gentlemen of the jury, taking this man, a laughingstock, unable to make a sound or stand his ground because of the power of unmixed drink, I turned and sobered him, producing an orderly and temperate man out of a slave; he is of great value to the Greeks. And both he and his relatives know the gratitude (χάριν οἶδεν) that is warranted to me for these things. (17)

We have here a catalogue of the benefactions the Academy granted to Polemo, a synkrisis of his state before and after his falling under the patronage of the Academy, and the claim that Polemo and those around him recognize the benefactions he has received, and are showing gratitude. It is highly significant because of its rarity that this speech has been delivered by the patron in the relationship, and not (though apparently not disagreeable to) the client.

A papyrus fragment, probably from Menander, puts in the starkest terms we have seen yet an example of a speaker who sees his life before his conversion as some sort of death whereas what follows is life. In this fragment, the words ἀρίστων φιλόσοφος μαθήματα appear at the bottom of the fragment, making it appear that the speaker was referring to an encounter with a philosopher, who in bestowing right teaching gave this speaker the gift of life itself. The fragment reads:

> Believe this of me, O men, my whole life until now has been death rather than life. All was shadow: the beautiful, the holy, the good was evil; such was the ancient darkness of my understanding that it seems all these things were hidden and veiled from me. But now, since I have come inside, just as one who lies down in an Asclepion and is saved, I have been restored to the end of time: I walk about, I talk, I comprehend. The sun, so great and fine, O men, I have discovered as if for the first time; I now see you, the sky, the acropolis, the theater in the clear light of day.[61]

What makes the philosopher a patron is that something is being given to someone in need, there is a beneficiary, and there is an expression of gratitude, at least in these examples, in the form on a patronal synkrisis of life before and after the fateful encounter with the patron. The philosopher teacher was a benefactor too, and his followers fell into the client mold.

---

[61] Menander fragment found in D. L. Page, *Select Papyri: Literary Papyri, Poetry*, vol. 3 (Cambridge: Harvard University Press, 1970), 247.

For a final example of Graeco-Roman patronal synkrisis, let us return to Seneca's 90th moral epistle. Recall that at the start of this protreptic Seneca claims that philosophy is a patron who gives benefactions (*munus*), the most important of which is "living well." That philosophy is a patron/benefactor is reflected as well in the patronal synkrisis that closes the letter. Seneca attributes to philosophy human wisdom. He does not claim that people before philosophy lacked all reason, but that they had imperfect reason (*Ep.* 90.24); Seneca differentiates between ingenuity and wisdom (*Ep.* 90.12), and between man and wise-man (*Ep.* 90.24). Seneca, in fact, attributes a great deal to humanity before the benefaction of philosophy, but their feats count for little because of the state of human wisdom since then: "No matter how excellent and guileless was the life of the men of that age, they were not wise men; for that title is reserved for the highest achievement" (*Ep.* 90.44). Lastly, Seneca writes, "even in the best of men, before you refine them by instruction, there is but the stuff of virtue, not virtue itself" (*Ep.* 90.46). Seneca's comparison of humanity's state before and after philosophy taught them how to pursue virtue, and his claim that humanity is so much better off because of it, honours philosophy itself as a benefaction (and a benefaction also of the gods).[62] That philosophy is treated as a patron yet is neither human nor god, and thus at least understood to have a physical form, is all the more revealing of the role of synkrisis. That is, there is nothing to be gained, no benefactions to be curried, by way of patron-oriented rhetoric directed at philosophy, yet Seneca nonetheless feels that philosophy is to be honoured and thanked for its improvements of humanity.

3.4.4 Patronal Synkrisis in the Septuagint, Philo, and Titus

As we saw above, the Wisdom of Solomon reflects a knowledge and use of the Graeco-Roman framework of patronage and benefaction to talk about the Jewish God. This is confirmed in the presence of an extended series of synkriseis in the book that serves, I think, as a patronal synkrisis, honouring the divine patron/benefactor of Israelite history. The second half of the Wisdom of Solomon is structured around a series of seven patronal synkriseis, comparisons that highlight the benefactions of the divine patron/benefactor. In the first synkrisis (11:1–14), for instance, Sophia acts as a benefactor when she gives the Israelites water on their journey through the wilderness

---

[62] Note that his endorsement of philosophy is not universal; he excludes Epicureanism in *Ep.* 90.35.

(Wis 11:4). What is being compared in this synkrisis is the extent to which the Egyptians suffered while the Israelites benefited from the same works of the Lord. The synkrisis here is of the treatment of the Israelites and the treatment of the Egyptians by God; the Israelites received a benefaction in the form of their enemy's defeat. That this synkrisis has everything to do with divine patronage is confirmed by the use of εὐεργετέω twice in this passage (Wis 11:5 and 11:13) to describe the action of God towards the Israelites. The second synkrisis, Wis 16:1–4, compares the hunger of the Egyptians with the feeding of the Israelites by the Lord, εὐεργετήσας τὸν λαόν. The third synkrisis, Wis 16:5–14, compares the suffering of the Egyptians under the rage of wild animals with the mild suffering of the Israelites that had a positive purpose (Wis 16:11 —εὐεργεσία).

The fourth synkrisis, Wis 16:15–29, compares the plight of the Egyptians who were struck with rain, hail and relentless storms with that of the Israelites who were fed manna and cared well for. As I said above, a translation of Wis 16:24 that stresses the benefaction received would read that creation "exerts itself as punishment against the unrighteous and relaxes as a benefaction on behalf of those who trust in you." The benefaction in this synkrisis is precisely that creation treated the faithful Israelites far better than it treated the unrighteous Egyptians. The fifth and most elaborate synkrisis, Wis 17:1–18:4, compares lightness and darkness associated with the Israelites and the Egyptians respectively. Specifically, it characterises the Egyptians living in perpetual intellectual and spiritual darkness. But for the Israelites, characterised as the holy ones of God, "there was very great light," and they suffer nothing. The comparison of how God deals with those who are loyal and how God deals with the enemies of the loyal ones emphasises the power and generosity of the Israelite God as a divine benefactor from an Hellenistic perspective.

The final two synkriseis are relatively simple. The sixth synkrisis, Wis 18:5–25, records that the first-borns of the Egyptians were destroyed while the Hebrews offered sacrifices and thus were protected and gloried. The seventh and final synkrisis, Wis 19:1–12, coincides with the end of the Exodus: the Hebrews pass safely through the water, but the pursuing Egyptians are drowned by it. Each of these seven synkriseis is built around the experience of the Hebrew exodus from Egypt, but is written from the perspective of the Hellenised Jew familiar with the conventions of Graeco-Roman divine discourse. Hence, God is depicted in the imagery and some of the technical language of the patron/benefactor who ushered the Jews out of slavery and protected them and cared for them during their time in the desert. There is an implied patronal synkrisis here, of course, as the Jews, once in misery and slavery, having lived in harsh conditions and without their freedom, owe to their divine patron their present freedom and their occupation of a homeland. These synkriseis function to remind the Israelites of what their divine patron has done for them, lest they forget to show appropriate gratitude (Wis 16:11), and by presupposing their present freedom, they honour that patron by proclaiming those good works and by comparing the benefits they enjoyed with the suffering of their former oppressors. In the Wisdom of Solomon, then, we have an excellent example of the sense of religious patronage and clientage from a Hellenistic Jewish writer. Of course, this writer was not alone among Hellenised Jews and the early Jesus movement in having this sensibility.

There are two examples of synkrisis that illustrate the relationship between synkrisis and conversion. The first instance comes from Philo, and the second from Titus, both of which serve to unite the topics of conversion, philosophy, and patronage, topics that will loom larger in the coming chapters.[63] In *De virtutibus*, Philo describes *metanoia*, a term that is generally understood to refer to repentance (changing of mind) but is closely associated with ancient conversion narratives (e.g., Cebes, *Tabula* 10), as involving a shift from, among other things, ignorance to knowledge, from senselessness to good sense, from timidity to boldness (*Virt.* 180). Those who follow and thus honour God (ἐπηλύται), whom we have seen Philo depict in strongly patronal imagery and language, take on many excellent virtues, including temperateness, modesty, kindness, humanity, seriousness, and high-mindedness, while those who reject God become unjust, shameless, quarrelsome, perjurers, etc. (*Virt.* 182). This example of patronal synkrisis is not delivered in order to honour God directly, though one could argue that there is indirect honour ascribed to God through Philo's description. Rather, what is curious about this passage is that Philo is describing what happens in conversion in the terminology of synkrisis, the comparison of a past poor state and an excellent present state.

The pseudepigraphal letter to Titus contains a synkrisis that is full of philosophical language, especially Tit 3:3–7, and all within the context of conversion. Here the writer starts out "For we were once (ἦμεν γάρ ποτε) foolish, disobedient, led astray, slaves to various passions and pleasures, passing our days in malice and envy, despicable, hating one another" (Tit 3:3). But this state changed, the writer continues, "when (ὅτε δέ) the goodness

---

[63] This is the point made well by Stephen Charles Mott, "Greek Ethics and Christian Conversion: The Philonic Background of Titus II 10–14 and III 3–7," *NovT* 20 (1978): 22–48.

and loving kindness of God our saviour appeared" (Tit 3:4). This salvation, as with all sources of salvations, was a benefaction, in this case the benefaction (χάρις) of Jesus Christ (Tit 3:7). This is also made clear in Tit 2:11, in which salvation is referred to as ἡ χάρις τοῦ θεοῦ. Of course salvation is a benefaction.

Given what we now know of patronal synkrisis, it becomes possible even to identify the trope where all the parts may not be present. For example, in one of the many aretalogies to Isis, *SEG* II 821, Isis is credited with, among other things, the institution of law and justice, the Greek language as well as non-Greek language for others, and civic laws.[64] These benefactions in particular are laid out in such a way that the reader is compelled to consider what life would have been like before the arrival of such benefactions. Justice, language, and laws, it could be argued, are what allow societies to function, for without them there would be no justice, no communication, no order. This Isis aretalogy claims directly that Isis gave both communication and order to the people, that she gave them life (salvation: line 11). Even though we lack here the balanced 'before and after' portrait of other patronal synkriseis we have seen, the 'before' part is certainly implied in the grand or foundational nature of the benefactions that are attributed to Isis.[65]

Synkrisis is a broader rhetorical trope than the examples I have chosen as illustrations would suggest. I have narrowed the focus in order to illustrate that synkrisis can function in ways that the classical definition of synkrisis neither recognises nor even really allows. In other words, not every occurrence of synkrisis is a sign that a client is honouring a patron. But synkrisis in the context of patronage and clientage, whether human or divine, whether concrete (as with humans and ostensibly with gods) or abstract (as with philosophy personified), occurs frequently enough that it needs to be recognised as a type of synkrisis. When synkrisis occurs in the context of patronage and clientage, it takes on a function beyond one that is merely didactic; it is not simply a rhetorical exercise. Patronal synkrisis focuses on the client, specifically on the state of the client, and functions to honour the patron or benefactor by crediting him/her/or it with the present state of

---

[64] *SEG* II 821 can be found, with translations, at Horsely (ed.), *NewDocs* 1:11–12, and Danker, *Benefactor*, 180–81.

[65] The same can be concluded of another Isis aretalogy, this one expressed in the first person, in which Isis claims to have separated heaven from earth, set the paths of the moon and sun, given laws, established the order of procreation, taught humanity reverence for the gods, and so on it goes. The implication is clearly that the world must have been no place for living before Isis so dramatically benefacted it (inscription can be found at Danker, *Benefactor*, 197–99).

happiness, bliss, or favour. Patronal synkrisis offers the client a powerful option for patron-oriented rhetoric, and is a prominent element of many conversion narratives.

3.5 The Χάρις of the Patron/Benefactor

Our final convention of the rhetoric of patronage and benefaction is the use of a term that has only recently been given its full due as part of the language of patronage and benefaction, namely χάρις. There are several article length attempts that have been immensely helpful in drawing scholarly attention to the relationship between χάρις and patronage and benefaction,[66] but none will likely have as much influence as the very recent and thoroughly researched book by Harrison on the topic, *Paul's Language of Grace in its Graeco-Roman Context*. This book became available while I was working through the final revisions of the present work; I was delighted to find that Harrison independently comes to many of the same conclusions that I do, not least because his work is far more thorough than mine could be in a section of this length.

3.5.1 Meanings of χάρις

The term χάρις functions in four semantic contexts, the first three of which, as we shall see below, are closely related — beautiful, beneficence or kindness, a concrete gift or benefaction, and gratitude. I have intentionally avoided using the term most frequently used to render the Greek χάρις, namely 'grace,' in this list of meanings for reasons that will be explained more fully shortly; 'grace' carries very strong Christian overtones in a post-reformation

---

[66] Bruce J. Malina, "What is Prayer?" *TBT* 18 (1980): 214–20; Frederick W. Danker, *Benefactor: Epigraphic Study of a Graeco-Roman Semantic Field* (St. Louis: Clayton Publishing House, 1982); J. H. Elliott, "Patronage and Clientism in Early Christian Society: A Short Reading Guide," *Forum* 3 (1987): 39–48; Bruce J. Malina, "Patron and Client: The Analogy Behind Synoptic Theology," *Forum* 4 (1988): 2–32; H. Moxnes, "Patron-Client Relations and the New Community in Luke-Acts," in *The Social World of Luke-Acts: Models for Interpretation* (ed. J. H. Neyrey; Peabody: Hendrickson, 1991), 241–68; J. K. Chow, *Patronage and Power: A Study of Social Networks in Corinth* (Sheffield: Sheffield Academic Press, 1992); R. A. Horsley (ed.), *Paul and Empire: Religion and Power in Roman Imperial Society* (Harrisburg: Trinity Press International, 1997); David A. deSilva, "Patronage and Reciprocity: The Context of Grace in the New Testament," *ATJ* 31 (1999): 32–84.

culture. In this section I shall lay out the basic meanings of χάρις, present and critique three influential studies of the term, illustrate the extent to which χάρις was a part of the social system of patronage and benefaction, then show how this context is presupposed by some first-century Jewish and Jewish-Christian writers—Philo, James, and Paul.

The first three uses and meanings of χάρις exist on a continuum where the first is the most abstract, the second a little more concrete, and the third the most concrete. The most abstract meaning of χάρις represents the aesthetically pleasing quality of an object or words. This is often translated as 'beautiful,' and is used of jewelry, portraits, speeches, or the movement of (graceful) people. So, for instance, in the *Iliad*, the jewelry that Athene wears can be called χάρις, presumably carrying the meaning of 'beautiful' (14.183). The *Odyssey* describes the power of moving speech as beautiful (8.175), as most likely does Luke when he represents the crowd's awe at how Jesus spoke in his inaugural ministry (Luke 4:22).[67] Some translations follow too closely the more common translation, adapting it to describe Jesus' words as "gracious," though this is quite a confusing reading since it is unclear to what 'gracious' refers. Conversely, more free translations such as *Today's English Version* and *New Testament in Modern English* render χάρις as 'eloquent' and 'beautiful' respectively, moving further from traditional attempts to associate the quality of Jesus' speech with the Christian theological category of Grace.

The term χάρις carries a second meaning that is slightly less abstract in its meaning, this time in reference to that quality of a person that makes them likely to be generous—beneficence, or a beneficent disposition towards others. Thucydides relates that Demosthenes consented to the Messenian plan to attack the Aetolians in order to please, or to show a beneficent attitude, towards the Messenians (Thucydides, *Peloponnesian War* 3.95.1). Likewise, Hesiod "prophesies" that "there will be no χάρις for those who keep to their oaths or who are just and good" (Hesiod, *Op.* 190). This use of the term χάρις is most likely what stands behind the Septuagint phrase εὑρίσκειν [usually in the aorist] χάριν ἐναντίον τοῦ θεοῦ or κυρίου. That is, when people were blessed with courage or the ability to impress others, especially it seems when their survival depended upon it, the Septuagint expressed this in terms of having come into contact with the beneficence of the Israelite God. There are

---

67   Interestingly, Louw and Nida list four meanings of χάρις: a) kindness, b) gift, c) thanks, and d) goodwill. Yet in their *Lexical Semantics of the Greek New Testament* (Atlanta: Scholars Press, 1992), they correctly list this term as having an additional meaning, namely "attractive in form" (67).

instances of this meaning also in the New Testament. For example, Acts 20:24 relates a speech by Paul on his humility and courage in which he claims his mission is to "testify to the good news of the beneficence of God." Luke does appear here to be talking about a certain quality of God, but there is also an ambiguity that arises in this and the preceding examples. It is difficult to discern whether "the beneficence of God" is a generous disposition towards others or rather whether it is meant to be understood as a concrete act of generosity—a benefaction.[68]

The reason for this potential confusion (at least when it comes to a strict translation of the term in different settings) is that the third and most concrete level of meaning for χάρις is quite closely related to the second. It is quite a short step from exhibiting a quality of generosity to being generous, and undoubtedly the only way one could have exhibited such a quality is if one had in fact already been generous in the past. But there is another way in which exhibiting a beneficent attitude might qualify as a concrete benefaction resulting in a client relationship. For instance, when Demosthenes accepted the plan of the Messenians to attack the Aetolians he gave a benefaction to them. The correct response on their part would have been gratitude. Hesiod may well have meant that those who are good citizens would receive not only goodwill, but also something concrete for their actions, favours.[69]

Χάρις with the meaning of concrete benefaction is far more common a usage than χάρις as a generous disposition (these two occur far more frequently than χάρις as beautiful). Let me offer only a few illustrations here, since it is this meaning of χάρις that is most closely associated with the institution of patronage and benefaction and that will therefore be discussed in greater depth below. A χάρις could be something concrete given to benefit someone. So, for instance, incessant storms meant that there were no favourable seas or winds to benefit Agamemnon in Euripides' *Iphigenia in Tauris* (line 14). Herodotus records that Pausanias requested that the Athenians send him their archers as a χάρις to him (*Hist.* 9.60.3). Often the term χάρις can be translated as 'favour,' meaning that there is no concrete benefaction named, but rather what is referred to is that *something* was given. In this sense, χάρις seems to function as the indefinite version of εὐεργεσία. In this instance 'favour' might be a better option than 'benefaction,' but we should not

---

[68] Nida and Louw, *Lexical Semantics*, 68.
[69] Evelyn-White (LCL translation of Hesiod's *Homeric Hymns and Homerica*) offers "there will be no favour for. . .," while LSJ offers this passage as an instance in which "goodwill" is meant for χάρις.

confuse favour with kindness (in terms of a personal quality). To show favour is more than simply to show kindness; it is also and more importantly to bestow *something*. It should also not be confused with the modern sense of favour which does not by necessity inaugurate a relationship of dependence, though it may well result in expectations of reciprocity along the lines of gift exchange—a favour in the modern sense is a gift that is reciprocated with another favour of equal value, but not a benefaction. In terms of translating the term, however, in a way that is sensitive both to its semantic context and the prevailing cultural context of general reciprocity, benefaction is to be preferred over gift, even though 'gift' will often appear to make sense. Again, here one must be aware of the social status of those involved in the exchange, aware of the nature of the goods or services exchanged, and aware of the nature of the relationship that ensues as a result of the exchange. Language, of course, functions in semantic contexts, and it is those that we must consider when translating language.[70] The categories of gift and benefaction exchange are best not confused.

The fourth use of χάρις is different from the first three, and yet it is clearly related: it carries the meaning of gratitude. This meaning occurs often in instances where χάρις is followed by the dative, requiring a reading of "χάρις to . . ." as well as in instances where it is clear that it is not a benefaction that is being bestowed, but the response to one that is being recorded.[71] Gratitude appears sometimes in set phrases, such as "to acknowledge (ὁμολογέω) gratitude" (*P.Grenf.* 92.9 and *P.Lips.* I 34.21 of a human patron and *P.Oxy.* 939.6 of the Christian God). Sometimes the phrase is "to know gratitude" as in *P.Oxy.* 1021.17–18 (εἰδέναι χάριτας)[72] and *P.Oxy.* 963 (χάριν . . . οἶδα). The phrase εἰδέναι χάριτας might have initially meant literally, "to know or

---

[70] It is at this point that I must lodge my sole complaint concerning the otherwise excellent work of James Harrison, *Paul's Language of Grace in its Graeco-Roman Context*. It is unclear whether the problem is one Harrison more or less inherited by using the translations of others, or whether the translation decisions were his own, but Harrison translates with a number of different and not necessarily synonymous terms. This would have been unavoidable and understandable had the context demanded it, but I was rarely able to see how this was the case. Terms Harrison uses to translate χάρις throughout his work include: gift, favour, benefits, boons, grace.
[71] See Joseph William Hewitt, "The Terminology of 'Gratitude' in Greek," *CP* 22 [1927]: 142–61; John William Franzmann, "The Early Development of the Greek Concept of 'Charis'" (Ph.D. diss., University of Wisconsin, 1972), 1–24; J. H. Quincy, "Greek Expressions of Thanks," *JHS* 86 (1966): 133–58.
[72] See also Thucydides, *Peloponnesian War* 6.12; Theognis 1319; Herodotus, *Hist.* 4.136 for the use of the same phrase.

acknowledge a benefaction," and it may have developed from there into an expression of gratitude.[73] This is possible because the first step in the expression of gratitude was the acknowledgement that a benefaction had been conferred and received. This could account for why the failure to acknowledge or recognise one's benefactor was associated with ingratitude by Seneca. Regardless, there is clearly a common component between χάρις as favour/benefaction and χάρις as gratitude, that is the social context of patronage and benefaction.[74] Another common phrase in which χάρις means gratitude appears as "returning great gratitude (χάριτας) to benefactors (εὐεργετοῦσιν)," as is found in numerous inscriptions.[75] Paul uses the term χάρις in expressions of gratitude frequently as well: Rom 6:17; 7:25; 1 Cor 15:57; 2 Cor 2:14, usually in the form χάρις τῷ θεῷ.

3.5.2 Moffatt, Manson, and Conzelmann on χάρις

There have been a number of attempts to understand the concept of grace from a biblical perspective, and those of Moffatt and Manson warrant a close look at this point.[76] Both Moffatt and Manson understand grace to be something that is given and that is not earned by the receiver. The emphasis is clearly on the will and generosity of the giver. This is not so far removed from the use of χάρις in the ancient Mediterranean, but these authors work under the assumption that χάρις in the New Testament is used differently, or infused with a new importance. As a result, they overly theologise Paul's use of the term, reading too great a *theological* significance into the term. For example, Moffatt writes of the New Testament understanding of grace that

---

[73] Hewitt, "The Terminology of 'Gratitude'," 143–144, 149.

[74] The phrase "common component" is offered by Louw as a means of avoiding claims concerning general or primary meanings from which others are derived: "What is often regarded, or sensed, as something binding meanings together, is not a 'general' meaning, but a *common component*" (Johannes P. Louw, *Semantics of New Testament Greek* [Philadelphia: Fortress Press, 1982], 33, emphasis original). The common component binding together the three meanings of χάρις as beneficence, favour or benefaction, and gratitude is the arena of patronage and benefaction.

[75] *Syll*[3] 162.18–19; 226.15; 282.26–27; 285.22–23; 356.25–27; 374.50–51; 391.13; 485.27; 613.36–37; 615.10; 645.79–80; 709.45; 1098.54–55. *Syll*[3] 731.18 uses the same phrase with respect to the gods.

[76] James Moffatt, *Grace in the New Testament* (New York: Ray Long and R. R. Smith, 1932); William Manson, "Grace in the New Testament," in *The Doctrine of Grace* (ed. W. T. Whitley; London: SCM Press, 1932), 33–60.

"When sin or evil is omitted from the view of the world, the content of 'grace' as presented in the gospel is missed, no matter how belief in a friendly spirit or causal Reality within the universe may be stated in terms of grace."[77] James Barr criticised the same tendency to overly theologise early Christian language in Kittel's *Theologisches Wörterbuch zum Neuen Testament* (*TDNT* in English), many entries of which also attempted to read "the maximum possible theological content into a linguistic choice."[78] Part of what lies behind this weakness of *TWNT*, and also of Moffatt, is the confusion between a word and a concept. In *TWNT*, the entry on ἁμαρτία becomes an essay on Sin, and the entry on μῦθος an essay on Myth and Religion. Likewise, Moffatt is undertaking, ultimately, a study of the concept of "Grace" in the New Testament, and not of the Greek word χάρις and his analysis of χάρις starts from there.

Moffatt does not overlook or ignore the cultural importance of the term χάρις, but he tries too hard to show that Paul meant to do something new, even radical, with the term.[79] Moffatt rightly says that Paul found χάρις ready at hand in the local language, but he qualifies this by claiming that he filled it "with fresh content."[80] To this Barr might have responded that the "semantic value of words in their contexts" is lost when too great an emphasis is placed on the theological content and intent of the words. This occurs also when one attempts too strongly to show that New Testament usage of a term is special and separate from Graeco-Roman usage. These words of Barr were not, of course, directed at Moffatt, but they respond to similar problems in the work of others. Barr would write that the

> attempt to relate the individual word directly to the theological thought leads to the distortion of the semantic contribution made by

---

[77] Moffatt, *Grace*, 6.
[78] James Barr, *The Semantics of Biblical Language* (Oxford: Oxford University Press, 1961), 129.
[79] Likewise, D. J. Doughty, "The Priority of ΧΑΡΙΣ: An Investigation of the Theological Language of Paul," *NTS* 19 (1973): 163–80, recognises as I do that for Paul χάρις is very closely related to salvation, and thus forms the backbone of Paul's theological understanding. But he feels that Paul uses χάρις in an entirely different way than the well established cultural context of the term most obviously suggests. There is no reason, if salvation were a major χάρις from God, that the term would necessarily mean anything different at all for Paul. For a thorough treatment of the relationship between χάρις and salvation in the philosophical tradition and in the New Testament, see Mott, "Greek Ethics and Christian Conversion," 32–44.
[80] Moffatt, *Grace*, 99. Likewise, Manson ("Grace," 34) claims that the Christian usage of χάρις "involved a high enoblement and extension of the Greek word."

words in contexts; the value of the context comes to be seen as something contributed by the word, and then it is read into the word as its contribution where the context is in fact different. Thus the word becomes overloaded with interpretive suggestion.[81]

More troublesome is that Moffatt seems to look at the term χάρις from a position that is informed and shaped by a fully developed Christian theology of grace. For example, he suggests that there were aspects of Greek usage that were *unfit* for Paul to use. He argues, for example, that the common Septuagint usage of χάρις in the phrase "to find favour with/in the eyes of/before the Lord/God" would not have been proper for Paul to use. Moffatt suggests that Paul avoided this usage because of the implication that humans could earn or seek out God's favour. While it is true that Paul never reproduces this Hebraism (though interestingly Luke does), it is difficult to claim that Paul *consciously* avoided it. Further, the theological use of a term does not set its proper usage thereby in a theological context. To borrow Barr's example, that Muslims call Allah "Great" does not mean that the word 'great' should only be used of Allah, or that it is used improperly if used of anything other than God.[82] Barr says it best when he warns that "The attempt to interweave theological and linguistic arguments only produces an ignoring or a wrong assessment of linguistic facts."[83] As we shall see below, the context in which this term frequently operates is the setting of patronage and benefaction, and it may well be that Paul does not take over every aspect of its common usage. It may also be the case that Paul objected to certain implications of the common use of the term, but one must start by acknowledging the assumptions held in common before one can make a fair assessment of what was (significantly) different.

The most suggestive contribution of Manson's study is his serious treatment of ancient Imperial inscriptions, which allows him to place χάρις in a cultural context lacking in Moffatt's study. These inscriptions show that χάρις "constantly designates the imperial favor as shown in some deed of gift or benefaction."[84] Based on this, Moffatt concludes that "'Grace' on Christian lips will be primarily the 'gift' or 'benefaction' of God to man, the generous favor by which the Supreme Being makes men recipients of His salvation."[85]

---

[81] Barr, *Semantics*, 233–34.
[82] Barr, *Semantics*, 162.
[83] Barr, *Semantics*, 194.
[84] Manson, "Grace," 38.
[85] Manson, "Grace," 39.

Unfortunately, after establishing so well the semantic context of this term, his discussion of Paul's use of χάρις is limited to theological interpretation; he associates grace variously with love, mercy, and self-giving.

The entry of Conzelmann in *TDNT* is also one of the most cited sources for biblical explanations of "grace." Conzelmann suggests that χάρις was a widely used term for things pleasant. This might entail sweet sounding songs or articulate rhetoricians, but it also included concrete pleasantries such as gifts, benefactions and patronage appointments, and not surprisingly, it also represented the appropriate response to such signs of goodwill, gratitude, since gratitude was also something one *gave*. Conzelmann distinguishes starkly between these various features of χάρις and while in some ways this is helpful, one needs to see that all the various nuances of χάρις share the same central motif—that of a good (thing) in movement from one person to another (or others). Therefore, while χάρις is many things, it is first and foremost a part of the language of patronage and benefaction; χάρις is not a synonym for *gift* but for benefaction or favour. In fact, while Conzelmann identifies only a few occurrences in which χάρις means benefaction, throughout his discussion the theme of benefaction sits prominently, though in the background. This is no less true in his detailed treatment of Paul's use of the term vis-a-vis salvation (pp. 383–96), since salvation as Paul presents it is nothing if not a benefaction (as undeserved and appreciated as any other of this magnitude) from that best of divine benefactors, Paul's God.

3.5.3 Χάρις and Patronage and Benefaction

All these treatments share the understanding that New Testament χάρις can be analysed separately from its Graeco-Roman context. They assume New Testament χάρις is imbued with a special meaning that on the one hand shows New Testament writers were doing something completely novel with the term, and on the other hand, used it in such a way that would have appeared almost foreign to Graeco-Roman hearers. It is this notion that I want to challenge here.[86] It may well be that Paul was doing something

---

[86] This also seems to be the case even with Louw and Nida's *Greek-English Lexicon of the New Testament Based on Semantic Domains*, despite their indebtedness to Barr. For example, they establish the semantic domains of the εὐεργ- root words despite the fact that εὐεργέτης and εὐεργετέω appear one time each and εὐεργεσία appears twice in the whole New Testament! As a result perhaps, they place εὐεργετέω and εὐεργεσία into the domain of Moral and Ethical Qualities (Sub-domain Goodness). A broader focus on the Graeco-Roman usage, of which the New Testament *must* be viewed to be a part of, would surely have placed these terms in the domain of

slightly different with the term, though I have not seen this adequately illustrated. Rather, the way the term χάρις is used suggests very pointedly that Paul and other Graeco-Roman writers shared a great deal in common. In what follows I shall focus on the meaning of χάρις as benefaction or favour, as opposed to gratitude. Although χάρις as gratitude also operates within the sphere of Graeco-Roman patronage and benefaction, its meaning as benefaction or favour is more germane to our topic of divine patronage/benefaction and the language people used to talk about it.

The term χάρις occurs in numerous settings, in addition to those cited above, in which it clearly means benefaction or favour, and refers to the conferral or reception of something concrete. For example, *P.Grenf.* 68 is a deed of gift (ἀπόκτησις) in which a fourth of the writer's business is to be given to Aurelius Petechon. It opens, "I agree to give to you as a benefaction (χαρίζεσ[θαι] σοί) by way of an unrevokable and unrepentant benefaction (χάριτι ἀναφαιρέτῳ καὶ ἀμετανοήτῳ) . . . ." Later the writer refers to the benefaction as ἡ δὲ χάρις αὕτη ἁπλῆ. The arena of patronage between kings and client states, as recorded in a number of instances by the historians Polybius, Diodorus Siculus, and Dionysius of Halicarnassus, also attests to the use of χάρις in terms of benefaction. The most revealing example concerns a meeting between the Roman consul Atilius Regulus (3rd century B.C.E.) and the recently defeated Carthaginians. Polybius relates that because Regulus thought of himself as complete master over the Carthaginians, he thought they should accept every concession he offered as a gift or ἐν χάριτι, that is as a benefaction. Of course, knowing full well the implications of accepting this, namely that they would be admitting to their position as inferior and reliant, they refused even to listen to what he had to offer (*Hist.* 1.31.6). Likewise, Polybius refers to the obligations of one Nicander to the house of Macedon because Philip had restored him to his previous status (*Hist.* 20.11.10). Polybius calls this restoration a benefaction (χάρις). And we know that client kings were offered lands and the revenues they might gain from them by their patron-kings; several times these are called benefactions: Polybius, *Hist.* 30.31.7; Dionysius of Halicarnassus, *Ant. rom.* 5.21.3.[87] Diodorus Siculus uses the term χάρις, on the one hand, to refer to a local praetor's willingness to

---

Possess, Transfer, Exchange, the same domain as χάρις[b] (gift), χαρίζομαι[a] (give generously) and χαρίζομαι[c] (cancel debt). The bottom line: a broader cultural and contextual focus would have shown Louw and Nida that the χαρ- and εὐεργ- root words are closely related semantically.

[87] D. C. Braund, *Rome and the Friendly King: The Character of the Client Kingship* (London: Croom Helm, 1984).

accept the appeals of local nobles (36.3.3), and to Nature's seeming benefactions made in terms of food, vessels, homes, and ships (3.21.5).

The χαρ- terminology functions here in the same way we would expect of εὐεργ-terminology, namely as the vocabulary of patronal exchange. This is most evident in places where χαρ- and εὐεργ- root words operate side-by-side, as they do in *Syll³* 587. This inscription is a public decree from Peparethus: "In order both that the gratitude (εὐχάριστος) of our people might be apparent and that the apportioning of honours to good men and their benefactions (χάριτας) might be worthy of the good things (εὐεργέτημα) that have happened among us, the people and the council of Peparethus praise. . . ." Significant for the same reason is a reference to Dionysus by Diodorus Siculus: "They say the god [Dionysus] came into the inhabited world bringing the regions into a cultivated state by way of cuttings, and making benefactions (εὐεργετοῦντα) to the people with great and valuable benefactions (χάρισι) for all time" (3.73.6; see also 1.70.6). The χάρις here could mean 'favours,' but the context suggests something more concrete than that. The two terms appear together also in a passage from Polybius (*Hist.* 21.19.10), where Polybius records a speech of King Eumenes of Pergamum (d. 158 B.C.E.), Rome's important ally against Antiochus, to the senate in which he warns of the self-serving Rhodians (*Hist.* 21.18–19). Rhodes, Polybius records, was conspiring to give the illusion to the people of Asia Minor that they had set them free, and several cities of Asia Minor felt indebted to Rhodes for "the greatest of benefactions" (namely their freedom), when in fact Rhodes was subservient to Rome. Then Polybius has Eumenes beg the senate to be suspicious of the Rhodians in case they disturb the balance of power and inadvertently favour (εὐεργετέω) their enemies. It appears from these examples that the εὐεργ- and χαρ- words were in many instances more or less synonymous, functioning perhaps as a hendiadys.

The term χάρις appears also as a term of benefaction or favour from the gods. For example, an Egyptian papyrus decree honouring the Emperor (*BGU* I 19.21) refers to benefactions of the Emperor with the phrase προσφυγεῖν τῇ χάριτι τοῦ θεοῦ ἐπιφανεστάτου Αὐτοκράτορος (to flee into the refuge of the benefactions of the God manifest Emperor). Somewhat less helpfully, but revealing nonetheless, a papyrus fragment *BGU* IV 1085.5, a royal decree, refers to τὴν χάριν τοῦ θεοῦ. When χάρις refers to a benefaction of the gods, its meaning is in no way different from when it refers to a benefaction of humans. In other words, its usage in a setting of divine patronage and benefaction should not elicit unwarranted claims that its use is different from a "secular" usage. What is more, χάρις and εὐεργεσία are more or less synonymous.

As a Hellenised Jew operating within the framework and armed with vocabulary of Graeco-Roman patronage and benefaction, Philo was able to look back on his scripture, and on the abundant imagery there of God as a generous giver, and very easily harmonise what he saw there with his new semantic framework.[88] Above we encountered a long citation from Philo that illustrated his recasting of his Jewish experience of God into a Graeco-Roman framework (*Leg.* 3.77–78). Without quoting the lengthy passage in full, it is useful to return to the prevalence of χαρ- root words and also of the association of εὐεργ- and χαρ- root words. Philo refers to the beneficence (χάρις) found before God, and shortly to the fact that everything is a benefaction (χάρις) from God. Finally, Philo writes "For all things which are in the world and the world itself are a gift (δωρεά) and a benefaction (εὐεργεσία) and a beneficence (χάρισμα) of God."[89] In another instance, Philo talks about the rewards that come to the good from God: "These are the blessings invoked upon good people and those who keep the law by their deeds, which blessings will be accomplished as a benefaction (χάρις) of the generous (φιλοδώρου) God" (*Praem.* 126). The χαρ- root words operating alongside the εὐεργ- root words illustrates that for Philo as for many other Graeco-Roman writers, χάρις etc. was a part of the semantic range used within the practice of patronage and benefaction.

What works in a Jewish and Graeco-Roman setting should be assumed to work in an early Christian setting as well.[90] The letter of James stresses the need for loyalty to the divine patron. Jas 4:1–6 criticises those who are in any way loyal to the world, and calls them instead to be "friends" to God, "friend" being a typical expression of clienthood.[91] This passage addresses the need of people in general, inviting them to ask for what they need from their

---

[88] Myriad texts from Philo suggest that he found it quite easy to apply the fully developed vocabulary of Graeco-Roman patronage and clientage to the Jewish image of God. See Mott, "The Power of Giving and Receiving," 64–66, esp. for Philonic examples.

[89] See also *Mut.* 24; *Leg.* 3.76; the phrase εὐεργετεῖν χάρισι in *Opif.* 23, *bis*; *Leg.* 3.215, *Ebr.* 32, *Migr.* 73 also show χάρις (or χαρίζω) to be nearly synonymous with εὐεργεσία.

[90] F. W. Danker, *Benefactor: Epigraphic Study of a Graeco-Roman Semantic Field* (St. Louis: Clayton Publishing House, 1982); R. P. Saller, *Personal Patronage under the Early Empire* (New York: Cambridge University Press, 1982); J. Ober, *Mass and Elite in Democratic Athens* (Princeton: Princeton University Press, 1989); I. Arnaoutoglou, "Associations and Patronage in Ancient Athens," *Ancient Society* 25 (1994): 5–17; deSilva, "Patronage and Reciprocity"; BDAG.

[91] K. C. Hanson and D. E. Oakman, *Palestine in the Time of Jesus* (Minneapolis: Fortress Press, 1998), 71.

divine patron, but to do so in an appropriate manner (Jas 4:3). The passage closes with the promise that God μείζονα δὲ δίδωσιν χάριν. What is presupposed behind this saying is not a post-reformation theology of grace, but the first-century system of patronage and benefaction. The translation "gives all the more grace" reflects the former, while the translation "gives a greater benefaction" is a reflection of the latter. That the benefaction is named immediately following indicates that we are not dealing with an abstract category of moral behaviour, but the bestowal of something concrete: the opposition of the proud is a benefaction to the poor. The readers and hearers of James can take heart that this divine patron will make their lives better.

Within the New Testament, the term χάρις is most prevalent in the writings of Paul, appearing some 66 times. The term χάρις is used by Paul in three different ways (Table 1).[92]

Table 1

Beneficence (33x)	Benefaction (25x)	Gratitude (8x)
Rom 1:7; 4:16; 5:15, 20, 21; 6:1, 14, 15; 11:5, 6 (3x); 16:20;	Rom 1:5 (vision/apostleship); 3:24 (justification); 4:4 (not wages); 5:2 (peace), 15 (justification), 17 (righteousness); 12:3 (vision/apostleship), 6 (gifts); 15:15 (vision/apostleship);	Rom 6:17; 7:25;
1 Cor 1:3; 16:23;	1 Cor 3:10 (vision/apostleship); 15:10 (3x; vision/apostleship); 16:3 (collection);	1 Cor 1:4; 10:30; 15:57;
2 Cor 1:2; 4:15; 6:1; 9:14; 12:9; 13:13;	2 Cor 1:12 (holiness and godly sincerity), 15 (letter and Paul's presence); 8:1 (joy, liberality), 4 (participation in collection), 6 (collection), 7 (collection), 9 (richness), 19 (collection); 9:8 (everything);	2 Cor 2:14; 8:16; 9:15
Gal 1:3, 6; 2:21; 5:4; 6:18;	Gal 1:15 (vision); 2:9 (vision/apostleship)	
Phil 1:2, 7; 4:23;		
1 Thess 1:1; 5:28;		
Phlm 2, 25		

---

[92] In the following table, beneficence represents the quality of a person that leads to a benefaction, but since one is not named in the passage, 'beneficence' is probably a better translation than 'benefaction.' On the other hand, where something is named, 'benefaction' is used. In both cases, one would fairly translate χάρις as 'beneficence' and 'benefaction' or 'favour' respectively.

The term is used in the rest of the New Testament in similar ways, of course, but there are some noteworthy differences. First, it is used also to denote the pleasing quality of speech and of people, and χάρις as a concrete benefaction is used elsewhere far less frequently than it is in Paul's letters. The term χάρις is used in the rest of the New Testament in the following ways (Table 2):

Table 2

Beneficence (57x)	Benefaction (16x)	Gratitude (5x)	Pleasing Quality (11x)
Luke 1:30; 2:40 John 1:14, 16 (2x), 17		Luke 17:19	Luke 2:52; 4:22; 6:32, 33, 34
Acts 6:8; 11:23; 13:43; 14:26; 15:11, 40; 20:24, 32	Acts 4:33 (needs were met); 14:3 (signs, wonders); 18:27 (ability to believe); 24:27 (Paul jailed); 25:3 (person sent to Jerusalem), 9 (Paul tried)		Acts 2:47; 7:10, 46
Eph 1:2, 6; 2:5, 7; 3:2, 7; 6:24	Eph 1:7 (redemption); 2:8 (salvation); 3:8 (Paul's ministry); 4:7 (gifts), 29 (pleasing speech)		
Col 1:2, 6; 4:18		Col 3:16	Col 4:16
2 Thess 1:2, 12; 2:16; 3:18			
1 Tim 1:2, 14; 6:21		1Tim 1:12	
2 Tim 1:2; 2:1; 4:22	2 Tim 1:9 (Christ)	2 Tim 1:3	
Tit 1:4; 2:11; 3:7, 15			
Heb 2:9; 4:16; 10:29; 12:15; 13:9, 25	Heb 4:16 (various)	Heb 12:28	
	Jas 4:6 (2x; opposition of enemy)		
			1 Pet 2:19, 20
1 Pet 1:2, 10, 13; 4:10; 5:5, 10, 12	1 Pet 3:7 (life)		
2 Pet 1:2; 3:18			
2 John 1:3			
Jude 4			
Rev 1:4, 22:21			

In a discussion of this nature, one must acknowledge that Paul does not use the εὐεργ- root words even once. Surely, it is often felt, this must be a significant omission. Often it is assumed that by rejecting εὐεργ- terminology altogether Paul is rejecting the ideology of divine patronage and benefaction. Such cannot possibly have been the case, however. What we have seen in this chapter and what we will see in the next chapter make it impossible to sustain such a claim. Paul has definitely *not* rejected the framework of patronage and benefaction, or as Harrison calls it "benefaction ideology,"[93] in talking about his God; he has simply replaced the εὐεργ- root words with an equally explicit range of patronage and benefaction words, those of the χάρ- root: χάρις, χαρίζομαι, χάρισμα. At best we are left to speculate why he chose one range of words over the other, but one is not free to suggest that he was unfamiliar with or unapproving of the language of patronage and benefaction, much less that he avoided using them to describe his relationship with his God. Let us look carefully at some of the places where Paul uses the term χάρις to denote a concrete benefaction, and thus where we should reason that the term 'benefaction' would be a reasonable translation of χάρις.

Paul refers both to human as well as divine benefactions with the term χάρις. Among divine benefactions he counts justification (Rom 3:24), peace (Rom 5:2), righteousness (Rom 5:17), holiness and godly sincerity (2 Cor 1:12), joy and liberality (2 Cor 8:1), and richness (2 Cor 8:9). He refers, as we shall see in greater detail in the following chapter, to his vision of Christ, or to his apostolic office (the question of which it is will also be answered in the next chapter) as a divine benefaction (Rom 1:5; 12:3; 15:15; 1 Cor 3:10; 15:10; Gal 1:15; 2:9). But he also refers to human benefactions, most notably in the form of his collection for Jerusalem (2 Cor 8:4, 6, 7 and 19). Relationships of exchange presuppose a quid pro quo, so people are frequently compelled to ask what is the quid pro quo in the relationship of exchange between a believer and God according to Paul. As always, and as expected, that quid pro quo comes in the form of gratitude and praise, and Paul says so explicitly when talking about God's beneficence. At 2 Cor 4:15 he writes, τὰ γὰρ πάντα δι' ὑμᾶς, ἵνα ἡ χάρις πλεονάσασα διὰ τῶν πλειόνων τὴν εὐχαριστίαν περισσεύσῃ εἰς τὴν δόξαν τοῦ θεοῦ—"for everything is for your sake, in order that when the beneficence [of God] extends to more and more, thanksgiving might abound for the glory of God." The ἵνα phrase really says it all: beneficence

---

[93] Harrison, *Paul's Language of Grace, passim.*

comes in order that thanksgiving might increase and that happens so that God might gain all the more honour (δόξα).[94]

It is worth looking at Harrison's comments on Paul's presentation of God as a divine benefactor in relation to the language of χάρις. Harrison establishes that χάρις was part of the lexicon of patronage and benefaction throughout the Graeco-Roman world—it appears in myriad types of sources over a long span of centuries, and consistently expresses that a benefaction or favour has been received. The bulk of Harrison's book is indispensable. When he comes to his treatment of Paul's use of the term, however, he seems to change tactics, and in so doing, falls into the same trap James Barr accused the writers of *TWNT* of falling into. Barr argued that *TWNT* entries were not treatments of the words themselves, but treatments of the concepts associated with them. Harrison's treatment of χάρις in Paul focuses on Romans because, and this is the telling part, it is the "most systematic exposition of divine χάρις."[95] This perhaps explains why others of Paul's letters are not considered equally revealing, not the least of which could have been 2 Corinthians in which the term appears more often than in Romans, or 1 Corinthians in which the term is closely affiliated with Paul's references to his vision of Christ. Equally problematic, and quite puzzling, is Harrison's use of Ephesians as the only other "Pauline" source he considers carefully when discussing divine benefactions.

Harrison argues quite rightly that Paul's depiction of God as a benefactor would have struck the readers of Romans, who were still living in the age of Augustus, the greatest of all saviours and benefactors, as familiar in many ways. Harrison points out a number of ways, however, in which Paul's claims would have been slightly novel, though these would only have served to emphasise the divine beneficence of God, not underplay it. For instance, in Romans, Paul claims that God has been dishonoured because of being improperly worshipped. Yet, despite having been dishonoured by humanity, God still gave humanity the greatest of benefactions—a bridge by which salvation could be extended to all (Christ). Harrison argues that this would have struck Graeco-Roman listeners as very novel and probably striking.[96] In the end, Harrison places Paul's use of χάρις well within the realm of Graeco-

---

[94] Terms like εὐχαριστέω and εὐχαριστία also function explicitly in a system of patronage and benefaction. In sixteen of twenty-two occurrences of these words, Paul uses them to thank his God as divine patron and benefactor: Rom 1:8, 21; 14:6; 1 Cor 1:4, 14; 14:18; 2 Cor 4:15; 9:11, 12; Phil 1:3; 4:6; 1 Thess 1:2; 2:3; 3:9; 5:18; Phlm 4.

[95] Harrison, *Paul's Language of Grace*, 212.

[96] Harrison, *Paul's Language of Grace*, 223.

The Χάρις of the Patron/Benefactor   147

Roman usage, allowing Paul to have adapted it slightly to fit his message, but insisting that it was intended to communicate to Graeco-Roman audiences in their own language and vocabulary, and that they would have understood it as familiar.

Finally, let us consider the Pauline phrase "By the χάρις given to me" (Rom 12:3; 15:15; 1 Cor 3:10; and Gal 2:9[97]). The ease with which scholars translate the term χάρις is part of the problem with the interpretation of those phrases, for it lends to the illusion that its meaning is self-evident.[98] Scholarship is nearly unanimous in translating χάρις as 'grace'—hence, in this phrase, "by the grace given to me." Unfortunately, a term like 'grace' is so loaded with modern theological implications and post-reformation overtones that unless modern theological application is the goal, such a translation risks being thoroughly meaningless.[99] This is not because a translation of 'grace' lacks any sense of meaning altogether, for indeed, such a term is interpretively fertile. Typically, 'grace' is understood as a quality (anthropomorphically, it even seems to become a *personality* trait) of God, serving to illustrate God's unwarranted generosity. The situation is further complicated when "grace" is made synonymous with "mercy" as a characteristic of God. This is not entirely groundless, since God is frequently depicted as being merciful when generously loving the undeserving; nonetheless, it is helpful to remember that separate terms existed for mercy and grace, and that they are not synonymous. A *theological* understanding of 'grace,' therefore, appears to occupy a position somewhere between an emotion, like love, and a character trait, like generosity and mercy.[100] Yet the term χάρις, as we have seen, frequently refers to a concrete item of benefaction or patronage. Paul's use of this phrasing should invite readers to ask, far more often than they have, *which* benefaction is he referring to here? Paul claims that a benefaction has

---

[97] 1 Cor 3:10 Κατὰ τὴν χάριν τοῦ θεοῦ τὴν δοθεῖσάν μοι; Gal 2:9 τὴν χάριν τὴν δοθεῖσάν μοι; Rom 12:3 διὰ τῆς χάριτος τῆς δοθείσης μοι; Rom 15:15 διὰ τὴν χάριν τὴν δοθεῖσάν μοι. In addition, 1 Cor 15:10 very closely approximates the sense of these other passages, but will be discussed in Chapter 4.1.

[98] Another instance of the word reveals this very point. In his commentary on Galatians 1:15, Martyn barrels straight over the term χάρις as if its meaning and significance is totally self-evident, using phrases like "God's grace," and "God's elective grace" as if these actually help clarify what χάρις means when Paul uses it (J. Louis Martyn, *Galatians* [AB 33A; New York: Doubleday, 1997], 157). In fact they only invite the question all the more.

[99] Max Turner, "Modern Linguistics and the New Testament," in *Hearing the New Testament* (ed. J. B. Green; Grand Rapids: Eerdmans, 1995), 146–74, esp. 165.

[100] See, for example, M. S. Miller and J. L. Miller, *Harper's Bible Dictionary* (New York: Harper and Row, 1973), 236–37.

been given to him, and in the context it appears either to have been his vision of Christ or his apostolic office. In the following chapter I shall work towards suggesting an answer to this question.

In the meantime, we can conclude this section by admitting that χάρις (used as benefaction) is not the most common word Graeco-Roman writers had to talk about the benefactions their human and divine patrons and benefactors bestowed upon them. But that is not the more salient point. More critical is that it frequently *was* used in precisely this context. In short,

> χάρις[b] is an ordinary secular word meaning 'gift (thing given).' We must avoid reading other senses of χάρις into it, just as we must avoid collapsing contextual assertions about the things called χάρις[b] into the sense of the lexeme itself.[101]

Indeed, one might be fairly tempted to press Danker's claim a little further to suggest that within the setting of patronage and benefaction our term χάρις is *at least* a "t.t. [technical term] in the reciprocity-oriented world dominated by Hellenic influence."[102] χάρις may never have attained the status of the technical vocabulary of patronage and benefaction, as did the εὐεργ- root words, but it is no less a part of the rhetoric of patronage and benefaction.

3.6 Conclusion

All Greek and Roman cities had patron deities. As a rule, Greek and Roman cultic practices—offerings, sacrifices, vows, prayers, hymns, incantations, erecting temples, statues and inscriptions—were each of them designed to acknowledge, to express gratitude towards, and to honour the gods, as well as to secure the future favour of the gods. The very foundation of Graeco-Roman cult and philosophy was the understanding that the gods and the philosophers could be approached for benefactions: protection or restoration of health, protection on a journey, protection from foreign military incursion, rich crops and healthy children, philosophical insight, prophetic and ethical knowledge, salvation, freedom from suffering and help during hardship. The gods were ascribed responsibility for setting up justice and language, two features of the Graeco-Roman world that distinguished it from οἱ βάρβαροι. Not only were the gods understood to be patrons and benefactors, but humans

---

[101] Turner, "Modern Linguistics," 157.
[102] BDAG, 1079.

participating in this religious system reflect all the expected behaviour of clients in a relationship with a patron or benefactor. While loyalty to a human or divine patron was rarely exclusive in the ancient world, all measures had to be taken to ensure one did not find one's patrons had become enemies. For this reason, perhaps, exclusive loyalty was more a feature of Graeco-Roman philosophical life than it was of Graeco-Roman cultic life (which we shall see in Chapter Five). Whether we are speaking of the Graeco-Roman gods or philosophers, the structure that governs, predicts, and explains the conduct of the various players is that of general reciprocity, namely in the form of patronage and benefaction. In so many instances, and often with an air of deliberateness, the rhetoric of patronage and benefaction is given permanence in stone, though of course all our material evidence attests to a certain permanence. Imagine the sense of satisfaction on the part of a writer or inscriber at knowing that two millennia or more later his or her attempts to honour a patron or benefactor are still being read, and thus the hallowed names of patrons or benefactors still invoked.

Greek language and imagery concerning the Gods equipped Hellenised Jews with the same perspective on the gods as benefactors and worshippers as clients, and likewise with the writers of the Jesus movement. These features of the rhetoric of patronage and benefaction are common to a fairly broad spectrum of Mediterranean cultic and philosophical traditions. Hellenised Jews, early Christians, and those whose gods were among the Graeco-Roman pantheon, used a number of conventions to describe their relationships, their encounters, their gratitude, and their debts to the gods. Consistent with some forms of human patronage, some refer to having been called by their divine patron or benefactor, either into a new or into a renewed relationship. Many references to philosophers, to philosophy itself, and within philosophical treatises, rely on the language and imagery of patronage and benefaction, most probably because of how appropriate an analogy it seemed to frame the philosopher a patron. As patron, the philosopher benefits people with helpful teaching designed to improve the quality of their lives. Followers, disciples, or students increase the honour and status of philosophers and teachers in the public court of reputation by being their students, by asking easy questions in public, and by living in accordance with the relevant philosophical expectations. In every case, clients or worshipers respond to benefactions with a patron-oriented rhetoric in the form of prayers (or gratitude or supplication), praise (which is always honouring and public), and proselytism (spreading the good news of a patron's benefactions in order to attract others into the patron's retinue, thus increasing the honour of the human or divine benefactor). Another option available to clients was to compare their life in the present under a new patron or benefactor with their life prior to encountering their new patron or benefactor. The comparison is always the same, in that the advent of the new patron has brought nothing but good to the client's life. The comparison, which I called patronal synkrisis, honours the patron by attributing to him or her honourable intentions and abilities in addition to the obviously honourable concrete benefactions. And finally, as a foundation for understanding Paul, the term χάρις must be firmly set in a context of ancient patronage and benefaction. Whether it is used in reference to human or divine patronage or benefaction, the meaning of the word is not altered; neither will it be when it is used by Paul.

We are now ready to turn to an analysis of Paul's "conversion" passages, in which these examples of the rhetoric of patronage and benefaction figure largely, and with the same frequency as they do in non-Christian texts. That is to say, these conventions did not appear all together in single texts, nor did they each appear individually in every single text; neither do they in Paul's conversion narratives. Nonetheless, they appear frequently and fittingly in many contexts of patronage and benefaction. That Paul participates in this same rhetoric of patronage and benefaction invites us to understand his conversion in the light cast by the details of this chapter. What is gained most by focusing on the rhetoric of patronage and benefaction is that we are able to move away from claims that are impossible to support, namely claims of personal (and especially psychological) experience on Paul's part. A psychological approach almost demands such speculation, since it is inherently introspective, but this speculation is even more problematic when directed at ancient personalities than it is when directed at modern ones. A focus on rhetoric means we are focusing on what they say, not what they felt or what they experienced. Thus the subject of our study is far more concrete than a psychological approach allows. Yet, having said that, there must be something of a relationship between how one *expresses* something and how one *understands* it. That is to say, the rhetoric of patronage cannot be completely rhetorical, all but divorced from an ancient understanding and, if I may, experience of conversion in that context.

Chapter Four

The Rhetoric of Patronage and Benefaction in Paul's Conversion Passages

4.0 Introduction

If ancient people understood their relationships with their gods on the model of patronage and benefaction, and so much evidence in the writing of the ancient world suggests that they did, then we should expect to find this in the writing of Paul as well. It is not enough to say, "The Christians and Jews were different." Of course they were, as were each of the Graeco-Roman cults and philosophies different from each other. But the evidence suggests that despite some theological innovations, which we would be surprised *not* to find, people in the first century, whether Jewish or Christian, a follower of Isis or a disciple of a philosophy, framed with their experiences and discourse in the language of patronage and benefaction. Indeed, in Chapters Two and Three we saw numerous Pauline depictions of God as patron, of the benefactions of God, and of worshipers as clients. In this chapter, however, I wish to look more closely at those passages that are unanimously accepted as Pauline conversion passages in order to see what they reveal about Paul's understanding of his conversion experience.

Commentary on Paul's conversion is ostensibly based upon five passages: 1 Cor 9:1, 16–17; 15:8–10; Gal 1:11–17; and Phil 3:4b–11.[1] Although it is rarely acknowledged, the popular and scholarly understanding of Paul's conversion tends not to be based on these passages alone, but is often either implicitly based upon, or strongly supplemented by, Lukan biographical details from the Acts of the Apostles. Luke, of course, presents Paul's conversion in three different places and each in a different context (Acts 9:3–9; 22:6–11; 26:12–18).

---

[1] Seyoon Kim, *The Origin of Paul's Gospel* (Grand Rapids: Eerdmans, 1981), 3–31, believes that Paul's conversion is referred to in many additional places as well: Rom 10:2–4; 12:3; 15:15; 1 Cor 3:10; 2 Cor 3:4–4:6; 5:16; Gal 3:9; Eph 3:1–13; Col 1:23–29; as well as in the opening verses of Romans, 1 and 2 Corinthians, and Galatians. While this is possible, it is the five passages listed above that are universally cited as evidence of Paul's conversion, and not any of these additional passages cited by Kim.

I am not interested in the differences of detail between these three accounts, though that issue remains a curiosity that has not been explained satisfactorily.

Luke's influence on the majority of works dealing with or referring to Paul's conversion is tangible. The simplest and ultimately least significant level of Lukan influence is evident when a commentator situates any of the Pauline conversion references on the Lukan road to Damascus, one of the few details about which the Lukan passages are unanimous, despite the fact that there is no such reference in the Pauline passages. For example, Paul's allusion to his vision of Jesus at 1 Cor 9:1 and 15:8 tends to be placed in the concrete and historical setting of the road to Damascus.[2] Yet all that can be securely inferred from these passages is that this vision of Jesus happened in the past, and that Paul's apostolic claim is somehow associated with it. Likewise, Gal 1:11–17 is associated with Acts' Damascus Road account.[3] But neither here is Paul so explicit or clear. To the credit of the scholars who so situate *this* particular passage, Paul does refer in the context of this passage to the city of Damascus, specifically to "returning" (ὑπέστρεψα) to Damascus (Gal 1:17). But to suggest that this is a sign that the conversion happened on the way to Damascus

---

[2] Kim, *Paul's Gospel*, 7–11; A. Robertson and A. Plummer, *A Critical and Exegetical Commentary on the First Epistle of St. Paul to the Corinthians* (Edinburgh: T&T Clark, 1911), 177, 340; C. K. Barrett, *A Commentary on the First Epistle to the Corinthians* (New York: Harper and Row, 1968); J. Murphy-O'Connor, *1 Corinthians* (Wilmington: Michael Glazier, 1979), 85, 139; F. F. Bruce, *1 and 2 Corinthians* (Grand Rapids: Eerdmans, 1980); Gordon D. Fee, *The First Epistle to the Corinthians* (Grand Rapids: Eerdmans, 1987), 732. Cf. H. Conzelmann, *1 Corinthians* (trans. J. W. Leitch; Philadelphia: Fortress Press, 1975), 152, 259; Richard B. Hays, *First Corinthians* (Louisville: John Knox Press, 1997), 149, 259; R. H. Horsley, *1 Corinthians* (ANTC; Nashville: Abingdon Press, 1998), 198.

[3] Joseph B. Lightfoot, *Epistle to the Galatians* (London: MacMillan and Co, 1856), 82; E. de Witt Burton, *A Critical and Exegetical Commentary on the Epistle to the Galatians* (Edinburgh: T&T Clark, 1921), 49–51; R. Y. K. Fung, *The Epistle to the Galatians* (trans. H. Zylstra; Grand Rapids: Eerdmans, 1953), 62–66; D. Guthrie, *Galatians* (London: Nelson, 1969), 67; J. Bligh, *Galatians: A Discussion of Paul's Epistle* (London: St Paul Publications, 1969), 95; C. B. Cousar, *Galatians* (IBC; Atlanta: John Knox Press, 1982), 30–31; F. F. Bruce, *The Epistle to the Galatians: A Commentary on the Greek Text* (Grand Rapids: Eerdmans, 1982), 92–93; Kim, *Paul's Gospel*, 6, 31; C. K. Barrett, *Paul: An Introduction to his Thought* (Louisville: Westminster/John Knox Press, 1994), 10; Jerome Murphy-O'Connor, *Paul: A Critical Life* (New York: Oxford University Press, 1996), 79. By contrast, Hans Dieter Betz, *Galatians: A Commentary on Paul's Letter to the Churches in Galatia* (Hermeneia; Philadelphia: Fortress Press, 1979), 71; G. Ebeling, *The Truth of the Gospel: An Exposition of Galatians* (trans. D. Green; Philadelphia: Fortress Press, 1985), 64; and N. H. Taylor, "Paul's Apostolic Authority: Autobiographical Reconstruction in Gal 1:11–2:14," *JTSA* 83 (1993): 65–77, are reluctant to locate this reference on the road to Damascus.

Introduction 153

is to assume that very little time elapsed between the conversion and the "return to Damascus," something which is not strongly supported by the evidence. Finally, Phil 3:4b–11 too is placed on the road to Damascus.[4] In each of these instances, the majority of scholars "find" references to the Damascus road, presumably by reading between the lines, though in actuality such details are attained by only reading Acts in concert with the Pauline references.

The second measure of Lukan influence is more complicated, more subtle, and more methodologically significant than the first. The Lukan depiction of Paul's conversion is *not* psychological—that much needs to be said from the outset. Rather, the Lukan accounts portray alleged *physiological* effects in the encounter between Jesus and Paul, such as voices, lights, falling to the ground, and blindness. Despite the fact that Luke records these only as physiological experiences, that is somatic and tangible, the modern psychological framework has led many scholars to read these not as physiological but as psychological experiences. The flashing lights and the blindness become internal experiential (or perhaps metaphorical) evidence of Paul's cataclysmic emotional trauma, and thus Luke becomes the foundation for describing Paul's psychological experience. For example, Beker writes, "Acts is more interested in a psychological description of its hero Paul."[5]

What we have here then is a methodological miscue that is twice removed from its subject—it is not only a matter of using Luke to read Paul (which would be one methodological miscue), but of using psychology to read Luke and from there to read Paul. It can only be by interpreting Luke's physiological descriptions from within a modernistic psychological perspective in order to get to Paul that we so frequently find Paul's conversion described as "the most shattering experience of his life,"[6] "wrenching and decisive,"[7] "an entire

---

[4] Bruce, *Galatians*, 92–93; Gordon D. Fee, *Paul's Letter to the Philippians* (Grand Rapids: Eerdmans, 1995), 346; M. R. Vincent, *A Critical and Exegetical Commentary on the Epistles to the Philippians and to Philemon* (Edinburgh: T&T Clark, 1897), 108; F. B. Craddock, *Philippians* (IBC; Atlanta: John Knox Press, 1985), 55–58; Markus N. A. Bockmuehl, *A Commentary on the Epistle to the Philippians* (London: A&C Black, 1997), 221; and P. T. O'Brien, *The Epistle to the Philippians* (Grand Rapids: Eerdmans, 1991), 401.

[5] J. C. Beker, *Paul the Apostle: The Triumph of God in Life and Thought* (Philadelphia: Fortress Press, 1980), 4. See also Johannes Munck, *Paul and the Salvation of Mankind* (trans. F. Clarke; Atlanta: John Knox Press, 1977), 13.

[6] Murphy-O'Connor, *Paul*, 71. Later, Murphy-O'Connor says "Paul's world was turned upside down" (*Paul*, 78). Kim claims that it "brought about a complete change in Paul's life" (*Paul's Gospel*, 56).

[7] Alan F. Segal, *Paul the Convert: The Apostolate and Apostasy of Saul the Pharisee* (New Haven: Yale University Press, 1990), 6.

transformation,"[8] and a "swift and abnormal change."[9] Abraham Malherbe suggests that Paul might recall his own conversion as a "dislocation" creating "confusion, bewilderment, dejection, and even despair."[10] These scholars do not cite Acts when making these statements. It is possible that Paul's statements concerning his past harassment of the Jesus movement also figure into such reconstructions of Paul's experience, but even those are supplemented by a Lukan dramatic framework that Paul's letters do not echo.

There are two immediate problems with these descriptions of Paul's experience. The first is that this language of emotional tumult is, as we saw in the first chapter, characteristic of the psychological approach to understanding and analysing conversion. The second is that it champions Luke's testimony concerning Paul over Paul's own testimony. What is worse, Paul himself never associates any such physiological effects, if you follow Luke strictly, or psychological/emotional trauma, if you follow those who interpret Luke badly. Paul's conversion passages are profoundly bereft of any such data. Further, no one who follows this line of interpretation (of Paul through Luke) ever seems to wonder how Luke came to know so accurately first, what happened inside of Paul's head, and secondly, what Paul himself shows no evidence of ever having known. We should be deeply sceptical about Luke's *interpretation*, here in the form of somatic embellishment, of Paul's conversion experience and suspicious of his motivation. Failure to do so represents one way in which many scholars have failed to follow what is Knox's otherwise universally accepted principle of never letting Acts overrule Paul's testimony. We should be no less sceptical of those who interpret Paul through the lens of modern Western psychology, and who then proceed as if Luke provides corroboration of Paul's psychologically traumatic conversion. In other words, the influence of Acts on modern treatments of Paul's conversion can also be measured in how modern readers mistake Luke's details as psychological, and thus *think* they are corroborating Luke's testimony by "finding" the psychological in Paul's own words.

If, as so many scholars have established, Luke's account of the conversion, not to mention of his biography of Paul in general, is an *interpretive* and not a simple historical exercise, then we must actually succeed in rejecting Luke's influence on our understanding of Paul's conversion. We must assume that

---

[8] A. Deissmann, *Paul: A Study in Social and Religious History* (trans. W. E. Wilson; New York: Harper and Brothers, 1957), 128. Similarly, Burton calls it a "revolutionary revision" (*Galatians*, 56).

[9] Robertson and Plummer, *First Epistle of St. Paul to the Corinthians*, 339.

[10] A. J. Malherbe, *Paul and the Thessalonians* (Philadelphia: Fortress Press, 1987), 45.

Paul has not simply been silent or coy on those sorts of details that Luke has; rather, we must assume that what Paul has shared with his readers represents his own and his full understanding of the event. This is not to say that Paul, or any other convert for that matter, did not also re-interpret the past through the conversion event, but even if this is the case to an alarming degree, there is still something valuable to be gained by accepting the first hand "interpretation" of Paul over the second hand interpretation of Luke. In the end we cannot measure the extent of Paul's interpretation and selective memory, if you will, and thus are more or less obliged to start with the experience as he presents and perhaps interprets it. We might not have access to Paul's actual feelings or experience, but we do have access to how he expresses his understanding of his interactions with his God. Treating seriously Paul's attempts to understand and express his experience is every bit as valuable as knowing his actual experience. How Paul talks about his conversion and religious experience tells us a great deal about Paul that we do not discover if we rely so heavily on Luke's or on modernistic perspectives. And what we do find is that Paul appears to conceive of these things in the same framework as that of his Graeco-Roman and Hellenised Jewish peers.

In what follows, I shall look at each of Paul's conversion passages to see what they reveal about how he expressed and understood his conversion experience and his relationship with his God. In each of the following sections we shall look at the conversion passage in full, identify Paul's rhetoric of patronage and benefaction as outlined in the previous chapter, highlight the ways in which the context of patronage and benefaction illuminates other aspects of the passages in new ways, and finally, show what has been gained by such a reading over and against representative commentaries.

4.1 First Corinthians 9:1, 16–17; 15:8–10

Three times in 1 Corinthians Paul is said to refer to his conversion, and each time he does so it seems with increasing detail. This increasing detail reaches a peak in 1 Cor 15:8–10, a text that becomes the cornerstone for understanding Paul's conversion within the context of the rhetoric of patronage and benefaction. This passage is the single richest statement Paul makes concerning his experience of his God and of his conversion. First, however, let us look at each passage in full. 1 Cor 9:1 reads[11]:

---

[11] The order in which the Pauline conversion passages are treated here is strictly canonical (from 1 Corinthians to Philippians). It does not represent a statement

Οὐκ εἰμὶ ἐλεύθερος; οὐκ εἰμὶ ἀπόστολος; οὐχὶ Ἰησοῦν τὸν κύριον ἡμῶν ἑώρακα; οὐ τὸ ἔργον μου ὑμεῖς ἐστε ἐν κυρίῳ;

1 Cor 9:16–17 reads:

ἐὰν γὰρ εὐαγγελίζωμαι, οὐκ ἔστιν μοι καύχημα· ἀνάγκη γάρ μοι ἐπίκειται· οὐαὶ γάρ μοί ἐστιν ἐὰν μὴ εὐαγγελίσωμαι. εἰ γὰρ ἑκὼν τοῦτο πράσσω, μισθὸν ἔχω· εἰ δὲ ἄκων, οἰκονομίαν πεπίστευμαι.

Finally, 1 Cor 15:8–10 reads:

ἔσχατον δὲ πάντων ὡσπερεὶ τῷ ἐκτρώματι ὤφθη κἀμοί. Ἐγὼ γάρ εἰμι ὁ ἐλάχιστος τῶν ἀποστόλων ὃς οὐκ εἰμὶ ἱκανὸς καλεῖσθαι ἀπόστολος, διότι ἐδίωξα τὴν ἐκκλησίαν τοῦ θεοῦ· χάριτι δὲ θεοῦ εἰμι ὅ εἰμι, καὶ ἡ χάρις αὐτοῦ ἡ εἰς ἐμὲ οὐ κενὴ ἐγενήθη, ἀλλὰ περισσότερον αὐτῶν πάντων ἐκοπίασα, οὐκ ἐγὼ δὲ ἀλλὰ ἡ χάρις τοῦ θεοῦ σὺν ἐμοί.

The single most important feature of these passages, and one we see repeated elsewhere, is Paul's reference to his vision of Christ. In 9:1 Paul claims he saw Christ and in 15:8 that Christ appeared to him. A second feature that stands out in these passages is that Paul establishes some sort of relationship between this vision and his status as apostle. This relationship has long puzzled scholars, and we shall wade into it briefly shortly. Finally, it is clear that the event is, or at the very least Paul believes it to have been, an external event, not an experience limited to the confines of his mind. Let us look at Paul's reception of the vision.

Our starting point for understanding the context of Paul's having received a vision from a god needs to be the divine appearances we encountered in the previous chapter, not as some might suggest, with Paul's moment of internal spiritual awakening or psychological breakthrough. Divine visitations were part of ancient cultic belief and life. Isis appeared to Lucius, Asclepius appeared numerous times to Aristides and is known for appearing to others in order to heal them. In each case we saw that the appearances of the gods to these people were tied to benefactions, yet we should understand that the vision itself was also a benefaction. Such people were the recipients of dual benefactions: Isis did not only appear to Lucius and then disappear; she appeared *and* offered him a solution to his predicament. So is it with Asclepius to Aristides. *P.Oxy.* 11.1381 preserves a story of an ill man who was

---

about chronological priority, development of Paul's thought, or the degree of importance to Paul.

being watched over by his mother. The man relates that the god appeared to him in his sleep (though it turns out the mother saw it as well) to grant him a cure to his ailments. In response, the man "praised his [the god's] benefactions." It is likely that reading the plural here as reference to two benefactions—one in the form of the vision and the other in the form of the cure—is reading too much into the plural, though it must be considered. Given general human responses to visions from the divine, one fairly assumes they would think of that as a benefaction from a god. An appearance alone would count for less had it not also been attended by a cure, but the appearance is a central feature of the event.

Gods never seem to appear and then simply disappear—they appear *and* they offer or do something: a message, a cure, an insight. Perhaps due to the distant nature of the gods, their appearances to humans were always cause for celebration, as well as for awe, for praise, and for honouring the divine. A vision from the God was a benefaction even though it was attended by other benefactions, and the response it elicits from the recipient is consistent with client behaviour. I think it can be said that there is no such thing as an innocuous revelation of a god—each one is a divine benefaction and puts the recipient into the place of a client to that god.

Paul's reference to having received a vision of Jesus from God is to be understood in this context. The appearance of God to Paul was a benefaction to him. Nowhere does Paul state this more clearly than in 1 Cor 15:10a: χάριτι δὲ θεοῦ εἰμι ὅ εἰμι. As we saw in the previous chapter, χάρις is a part of the technical language of ancient patronage and benefaction. We also saw that we should not assume that Paul used this term in a novel way, for his usage of it, read in an ancient context and not in a post-reformation one, suggests otherwise. Taking this observation seriously then, we might translate χάρις in 1 Cor 15:10 in the following way: "By a benefaction of God I am what I am, and his benefaction to me was not in vain." Paul cannot be clearer; he was the recipient of a benefaction from God that changed him, and given the proximity of his allusion to it (1 Cor 15:8), this benefaction must have been the appearance of Jesus to him.[12] Of course, "grace" is usually meant to convey

---

[12] Of course, there is one primary difference between Christ on the one hand and Isis and Asclepius on the other. Asclepius and Isis are both divine patrons, whereas Jesus, as we saw above, is a broker. Paul never refers to Jesus in the language of a patron, but only ever as a broker, though as Chapter Three showed the role of brokerage brought many of the same benefits as that of patronage and benefaction. A broker provides a benefaction and thus is part patron and part client; we have seen Jesus depicted as a broker in the previous chapter, and the depiction there is consistent with the general pattern of Graeco-Roman human and divine brokerage.

the generosity of God as a loving giver, in which sense it is synonymous with "benefaction," but the term "grace" does not reflect as strongly the social context of χάρις; "benefaction" might appear less theologically appealing, but it also seems so much more evocative.

Paul's claim that the vision was a benefaction is consistent with other examples we saw in the previous chapter. Just as Isis' appearance to Lucius on the beach, and just as Asclepius' appearances to Aristides, were clearly benefactions to those people, so too must Christ's appearance to Paul have been a benefaction. In each of these cases, Isis, Asclepius and Christ is established as a divine patron in the relationship through their appearance to a human. Isis gave Lucius the key to his escape from his present shape; Asclepius called Aristides to Pergamum to be healed. What Jesus gave to Paul is uncertain, but it clearly had an effect on him. Paul underwent a change from self-professed pursuer of the Jesus movement to witness on behalf of it. While we should be wary of reading too much of Luke into Paul's allusions to his having troubled the movement, that he did move from opponent to supporter of the *ekklēsiai* of God is indisputable. We shall return to the topic of Paul's persecution of the Jesus movement below.

That the vision of Jesus was a benefaction to Paul is evident also from the effects of that vision: Paul's behaviour reflects that of proper and honouring client conduct. Paul's mission to the Gentiles represents his client reciprocity for the benefaction he received from his god. This will be suggested again below in a discussion of Patronage and Apostleship, but it is featured in this passage as well. In 1 Cor 9:1 Paul draws attention to the fact that the Corinthian *ekklēsia* was the result of his labour (οὐ τὸ ἔργον μου ὑμεῖς ἐστε ἐν κυρίῳ;). In 1 Cor 15:10, he writes "his benefaction to me was not in vain, but rather I toiled more than all of them," that is more than the previous apostles, though he adds the disclaimer that it was not actually his own doing but, significantly, ἡ χάρις τοῦ θεοῦ σὺν ἐμοί. These verses are particularly rich in the language of patronage and benefaction, and the fact that Paul repeatedly emphasises that he worked hard to establish these churches should be read in terms of client reciprocity. His communities are the outcome of his concerted effort to honour and express his reciprocity to his divine patron, God. This behaviour is meaningful and predictable when seen in the context of ancient Mediterranean patronage and benefaction. In response to the benefaction and brokerage of Christ's appearance that re-defined the relationship

---

But that Jesus is broker and not patron does not lessen the need for honoring address or reciprocity of conduct to be directed to him by the recipients of his services/benefactions.

of patronage and benefaction between Paul and God, Paul can be seen acting in the same way that countless nameless clients of Asclepius did, that Aristides did for the same patron, or that Lucian depicts his Speaker B doing in his *Nigrinus*: they are broadcasting the benefits that are to be gained from approaching and honouring a certain divine patron in a certain way. Paul's mission *in toto*, that is the fact that he went out spreading the gospel and founding communities of believers, that he did so at considerable personal cost and risk, and that even from a distance he cared for his communities, represents his client-reciprocity for the benefactions he received from his divine patron through the broker Jesus. It also functions as part of Paul's patron-oriented rhetoric, namely the tendency to proselytise to others concerning the superiority of one's patrons and his or her benefactions. Other clients of divine patrons would go about publicly broadcasting the unparalleled generosity and assistance of their respective patrons, and they did so with the express purpose of attracting loyal clients and/or bringing increased honour to their divine patrons; Paul did likewise through his work among the Gentiles.

If one is provoked, even at this point, to ask why Paul would have done such a thing, he himself gives us his answer in predictable language in 1 Cor 9:16: ἐὰν γὰρ εὐαγγελίζωμαι, οὐκ ἔστιν μοι καύχημα· ἀνάγκη γάρ μοι ἐπίκειται· οὐαὶ γάρ μοί ἐστιν ἐὰν μὴ εὐαγγελίσωμαι. Paul admits that his mission does not really give him grounds for boasting, because he did not have much of an option (ἀνάγκη γάρ μοι ἐπίκειται). The fact is that client reciprocity was an obligation, something that a client knew was expected and that failure to reciprocate adequately would threaten to dishonour a patron and benefactor. We have seen more or less the same admission from others in a client relationship. Some writers express this bitterly (e.g., Martial resents having to follow patrons around town), but more, as on inscriptions, we see it with the sense of urgency on the part of the *demos* and *boule* to make perfectly clear to the reading public that they have discharged their obligation to reciprocate by proclaiming the generosity of their patron or benefactor. What is more, Paul's language of having had an obligation laid upon him is echoed most closely in Seneca's *De beneficiis*. What the Loeb edition of Seneca consistently translates as "to place under an obligation" is actually two different and equally important words. The most common word Seneca uses with this meaning is *obliger* (*Ben.* 2.11.5; 2.17.7; 2.30.2; 3.8.2; 5.7.2). This word comes closest to approximating Paul's phrase and the Loeb translation "to place under an obligation." Yet this word also carries with it a moral element; the obligation to reciprocate in response to benefactions received could take on a nearly moral imperative, something that we should not be in the least surprised to see Seneca of all people express. The second word Seneca uses with this meaning, though not as frequently, is *debeo* (*Ben.* 2.19.2; 6.4.1). *Debeo* is a particularly evocative word in the context of patronage and benefaction since it implies that there is debt on the part of the client, but duty is also an element of this word. Yet, the debt referred to is not of the monetary variety, but is rather a debt of gratitude and reciprocity, as Seneca makes abundantly clear. Of course, in the context of patronage and benefaction, this is no less weighty or serious a debt than a financial one would have been.

That Paul claims he was placed under an obligation is not a surprising or special admission in the context of ancient patronage and benefaction. As the recipient of a divine benefaction, in the first instance in the form of his vision, Paul would have been obligated to reciprocate. Paul was, as he says of himself, compelled to honour the new requirements of his patron/benefactor and client relationship. 1 Cor 9:17 reflects that Paul knows what happens when a client fails to honour a patron adequately, namely destruction (οὐαί) if he does not spread the good news (ἐὰν μὴ εὐαγγελίσωμαι) of the patron's benefactions. Obligation within the context of patronage and benefaction is felt both as a desire to live up to one's moral duty to express gratitude and honour to a patron or benefactor, and as a practical need to ensure future benefactions and thus survival. These expressions by Paul are his rhetoric of patronage and benefaction, indicating both that he knows what is expected of him, and no less that he has taken pains to ensure he has worked clearly towards that.

The final feature that needs to be discussed with respect to the Corinthian conversion passages and the context of patronage and benefaction is Paul's use of the term οἰκονομία that appears in 1 Cor 9:17, here too keeping in mind that the ancient rhetoric of patronage and benefaction brings Paul's language into sharper relief. Οἰκονομία refers most commonly to the management of a household or family, which is not in the least incompatible with the general terminology Paul uses of his churches.[13] Οἰκονομία has literal meanings in addition to what *BAGD* refer to as "figurative" meanings, by which they mean those having to do with cultic settings.[14] Such a distinction, however, is unnecessary, since the two meanings are in fact the same, differing only in whether the office is divinely or humanly commissioned.[15] Paul is not a head-

---

[13] Plato, *Apol.* 36b; *Resp.* 498a; Xenophon, *Oec.* 1.1; Josephus, *A. J.* 2.89; 12.200; Luke 12:42; 16:1–8.

[14] *OGI* 50.12 and 51.26 refer to the office of οἰκονόμος in religious associations.

[15] John Reumann, "'Stewards of God'—Pre-Christian Religious Application of *Oikonomos* in Greek," *JBL* 77 (1958): 339–49, shows that the office of *oikonomos* was

of-the-household figure, primarily because of how Paul claims he came to hold this position—he was commissioned for it (πεπίστευμαι). Paul is not the natural *paterfamilias*; he is the appointed "supervisor" of a (very extended) household or estate.[16] It is this feature that makes the office of οἰκονόμος a part of the system of ancient patronage and benefaction.

To be promoted to, or simply to hold the office of, manager of the estate would be an honour and a benefaction from one's owner or employer, since it would involve some degree of honour and would imply a degree of trust. While Martin shows that οἰκονόμος may have belonged to the language and institution of slavery, the obligations that attend the giving of benefactions suggest that too much should not be made of Paul's apparent unwillingness (ἄκων).[17] It is not clear that Paul was unwilling; what Paul expresses is his understanding that clients were obliged or, better, obligated towards reciprocity, an obligation that was powerful, public, and socially enforceable. Finally, we should not assume that the office of οἰκονόμος to which Paul refers was different from his office as apostle, but that the two were interrelated.

Before we turn to our discussion of patronage and apostleship, let us take a minute to compare what we have gained here to what is presented in commentaries on these passages. To summarise briefly what we have established by placing these passages in their social context of patronage and benefaction, here is what we know: Paul received and alludes frequently to a vision of Christ; consistent with other ancients, such a visitation of the divine should be seen as a divine benefaction, and Paul's own language reflects that he does see it this way (using χάρις repeatedly to refer to it); also reflective of the fact that Paul understood this vision to be a divine benefaction is the extent to which he credits its having changed him; and finally, his concern to show his effort expended in building up the Gentile *ekklēsiai*, his statement that he was

---

very much associated with cultic functions, both when the *oikonomos* was an official of the state, but especially significantly when the *oikonomos* was a private individual operating within a religious association. He lists such individuals from inscriptions of a wide geographical provenance: Ephesus, Priene, Magnesia, Ptolemaic Egypt. He also finds the terms definitely associated with mystery religions, Sarapis and Hermes-Trismegistus in particular.

[16] *P.Tebt.* 24.62 27.21 (114 B.C.E.) shows that by the second century B.C.E., οἰκονόμος was an office. See also *Zenon Papyri in the University of Michigan Collection* (ed. C. C. Edgar; Ann Arbor: University of Michigan, 1931).

[17] Dale B. Martin, *Slavery as Salvation: The Metaphor of Slavery in Pauline Christianity* (New Haven: Yale University Press, 1990), 72–77. Martin, *Slavery*, 22–42 shows that the slave–master relationship follows the same pattern as the patron/benefactor and client relationship. See also J. D. Crossan, *The Historical Jesus* (San Francisco: Harper Collins, 1991), 43–71.

compelled to do so, reflect a man working (for the most part quite willingly) under the social expectations of client reciprocity.

Of the four questions Paul asks in 1 Cor 9:1, commentators typically focus on the second, Paul's apostleship, on the third only as an explanation of the whence of the second, and on the fourth as proof, again, of the second. They read these questions as having everything to do with Paul's apostleship, even when that does not mean Paul is defending his use of the title.[18] Of course there is a relationship between Paul's apostleship and the vision, but no one attempts to get behind that relationship, preferring instead simply to draw the reader's attention to the fact that one exists.[19] But given that Paul understood his God to be a divine patron, what then is the significance of details such as these? What was the vision to Paul? What did his apostleship and his work towards it represent? Regardless of whether or not Paul is under attack, there is something more that lies behind Paul's allusions to these facts. Aside from the potentially ecclesial setting (Paul in conflict with other churches and other apostles), what do these questions tell us about Paul's experience or of his image of his God?

The focus of commentators with respect to 1 Cor 9:16–17 is on Paul's use of the word ἀνάγκη. Almost universally Paul's alleged unwillingness is emphasised. Hays reads Paul's language as that of the slave who has been ordered to work by his owner.[20] But this was also the language of ambassadors, whom we should not assume were typically unwilling (this will be developed below shortly). If the apostleship was a call to honour, a claim to represent someone with power, then it is incumbent upon us to see also that Paul has been honoured to do what he is doing. His commission does not then represent a summons, but an opportunity and a status up-grade.

Another way commentators understand Paul being compelled to action is not quite as literal, but borders on the psychological. Fee, for example, sees Paul's compulsion as a "divine destiny," preaching is something he *must* do because he is driven from a desire within. Fee is like the others in that he sees this as a sign of Paul's involuntary preaching, but he sees it as completely internally driven, that Paul was so moved by the love and presence of God

---

[18] Anthony C. Thiselton, *The First Epistle to the Corinthians* (NIGTC; Grand Rapids: Eerdmans, 2000), 666–68; *contra* Fee, *First Epistle to the Corinthians*.

[19] Conzelmann, *1 Corinthians*, 151–52; Raymond F. Collins, *First Corinthians* (SP 7; Collegeville, Minn.: Liturgical Press, 1999), 335.

[20] Hays, *First Corinthians*, 153. See also Thiselton, *First Epistle to the Corinthians*, 695–97; Collins, *First Corinthians*, 347–49.

that he could do nothing except burst forth in preaching!²¹ Fee's interpretation fits perfectly within the modern theological category of "vocation," called both by inner compulsion and ostensibly by God to do the work of the church. Absent however, is any social context for this language; Paul's language here echoes that of the client obligation found throughout antique patronage and benefaction.

The third of our Corinthian texts is perhaps the most fraught with difficulty for commentators because of the prevalence of the word χάρις within it. The overwhelming tendency is for this word to be understood as an element of Christian theological expression. For example, Thiselton completes his exclusively theological treatment of χάρις by claiming that "cost in Christian work, far from suggesting the absence of God's grace, presupposes the gift of such grace to prosecute the work through all obstacles."²² God's grace, at least in this context, is the gift of energy and fortitude to Paul; this suggests that the χάρις to which Paul refers came after Paul was apostle, while doing his work for the Lord, whereas Paul's use of it (in 1 Cor 15:8–10) in such close literary proximity to the vision he received, suggests powerfully to the contrary. Thiselton's interpretation implies that Paul was no longer a persecutor when this benefaction came, which raises a number of questions: if Paul *was already* doing such good work, why was he undeserving of it? If Paul did not deserve the benefaction he received, then does that not suggest that the benefaction he is referring to is the benefaction he received in his revelation of Jesus? Thiselton's over-theologising of χάρις seems to paint him into an exegetical corner.

Fee understands χάρις as 'forgiveness', since God's "grace" to Paul was in not striking him down as a persecutor of God's *ekklēsia*. It was this act of God that, according to Fee, made Paul realise that just as God had been with him so God was with all people, forgiving them despite their sins. It is a promising feature of Fee's commentary that χάρις is seen as an undeserved and unearned gift from God, as is Paul's apostleship, but discussion of this ends before it really gets started. Paul's apostleship may well have been a gift, or more technically, a benefaction, of God, though later I will take a different position. Either way, the apostleship as a *gift* does not justify Paul's behaviour as a *client*. The apostleship would have to be a benefaction in order to explain Paul's conduct. It is not that Fee does not understand the category of grace; it is rather that he over-theologises it by focussing on the undeserved nature

---

21 Fee, *First Epistle to the Corinthians*, 418–20; see also Collins, *First Corinthians*, 347–49.
22 Thiselton, *First Epistle to the Corinthians*, 1212.

of it (which leads him then to focus on sin and justification) rather than on the relationship between giver and recipient that the exchange inaugurates—namely patron/benefactor and client—and the obligations and expectations that attend such a relationship.

What characterises a theological understanding of grace is the presence of and emphasis on sin. It is not enough that χάρις is a gift from God that was unrequested; grace has to be something that comes to one in spite of the fact that one is a sinner, and thus to one who was offensive to God. Theological χάρις thus carries with it the implication of justification, of forgiveness for and from sins. Such a theological aspect may well be part of Paul's understanding of χάρις, though this aspect likely has more to do with the result of centuries of Christian handling of the term; still, such an approach only gets at part of the implication of χάρις, why it was a meaningful term for Paul to have taken over from his culture, and what associations it would have carried for the hearers of Paul's letters. What we need to do is situate this language not in post-reformation theology with its fully developed theology of grace, but in first-century expressions about human-divine relationships.

4.1.1 Patronage and Apostleship

The Corinthian conversion passages indicate that there is some sort of relationship between the vision or revelation of Christ and the office of apostleship that Paul came to hold. At the basic level of causality, which will detain us only very briefly, there are two positions that scholars hold concerning whether Paul received the office and title of apostle at, during, or by way of the vision, or whether Paul arrived at it later as some sort of intellectual or faithful development out of that vision. F. F. Bruce and Seyoon Kim represent the former of these two options, claiming, for instance, that

> Some verbal communication, beyond the heavenly vision itself, is implied in Paul's statement that 'he who had set me apart before I was born, and had called me by his grace, was pleased to reveal his Son in me, *in order that I might preach him among the Gentiles*' (Galatians 1:15f.) . . . He speaks as if the call and commission were part of the one conversion experience.[23]

---

[23] F. F. Bruce, *Paul: Apostle of the Heart Set Free* (Grand Rapids: Eerdmans, 1977), 75, emphasis original.

Indeed, Paul does speak *as if* this were the case, yet most scholars are less willing to take Paul's words here at face value. Instead, most contend that there was a period of learning and interpretation that led Paul eventually to formulate his mission to the Gentiles.[24] Hurtado observes that "it may be more logical to assume that some sort of prophet-like sense of being divinely commissioned to the gentiles came to him and that subsequently and as a consequence and corollary of that eschatological commission, Paul developed his emphasis on salvation through Christ without observance of Torah."[25]

Donaldson too fits into this latter group of scholars, though his own approach is worth detailing. Donaldson holds that the apostolic mission and the call are not one and the same event or phenomenon, but that the mission was derived from certain convictions Paul held prior to his conversion. Paul's mission is the result of combining his current "new assessment of Jesus" and his previous interest in the Gentiles. Paul previously believed that Gentiles had a part in an Israel-centred salvation. Yet, as Donaldson points out, this alone does not account for Paul's undertaking the mission, since the author of *2 Baruch* also held opinions similar to Paul's concerning Gentile participation in salvation and the imminence of the end times, yet did not attempt any such mission to convert them. Donaldson continues with the observation that what would account for the difference between Paul and the author of *2 Baruch* would be if Paul had been involved in "preaching circumcision" to the Gentiles prior to his conversion.[26] Donaldson works this out in greater detail later (pp. 273–92) where he argues that Paul may have had previous interests in the reception and instruction of Gentile converts, but need not have been involved in a wholesale outreach to them.[27]

Donaldson's explanation is plausible, though there is little explicit material or literary evidence to support the existence of such a mission. There is another direction, however, by which we can come at this question, namely patronage and benefaction. What light can patronage and benefaction shed

---

[24] See Terence L. Donaldson, *Paul and the Gentiles: Remapping the Apostle's Convictional World* (Minneapolis: Fortress Press, 1997), 360 n. 3, for examples.

[25] Larry W. Hurtado, "Convert, Apostate, or Apostle to the Nations: The 'Conversion' of Paul in Recent Scholarship," *Studies in Religion/Sciences Religieuses* 22 (1993): 277.

[26] See Donaldson, *Paul and the Gentiles*, 258.

[27] Donaldson is not willing to go as far as Segal in imagining some members and groups within formative Judaism to have been involved in pointed and organized missions to convert the Gentiles (Segal, *Paul the Convert*, Chapter Three). For a powerfully voiced argument to the contrary see Martin Goodman, *Mission and Conversion: Proselytizing in the Religious History of the Roman Empire* (Oxford: Clarendon Press, 1994).

on the issue of whence Paul derived his mission to the Gentiles? Can the mission be understood within the context of ancient patronage and benefaction? As a feature of patronage and benefaction, the most immediately obvious option would be that Paul's apostleship was a benefaction that he received from God at his encounter. In this scenario, Paul's status and title would have been conferred on him as a divine benefaction, most likely at the time of the vision or revelation (though it could conceivably have occurred during a subsequent revelation).[28] That apostleship was something to be conferred on people is, as we shall see shortly, consistent with the ancient data.

Apostleship, not surprisingly, has been the focus of many studies.[29] At its simplest the term, and indeed title, "apostle" pertains to anyone (or anything) sent out with an appointed task.[30] Both the verb and the substantive are used in a variety of settings. The word ἀπόστολος is used to refer to ships or naval fleets that are sent out (Demosthenes, *Cor.* 18.80, 107), as well as to men sent on a mission (Herodotus 1.21; Dionysius Halicarnassus, *Ant. Rom.* 9.59; Luke 19:14) and to commanders of expeditions. What is striking, and surely to be overruled, is Rengstorf's claim that ἀπόστολος in a Hellenistic setting lacked any sense of authorisation, in contrast he points to the way in which it is used by Paul.[31] Even a ship is authorised by the state, in that an attack on the ship

---

[28] The specific timing of this scenario (though not the language of benefaction), namely that the vision and commission were one in the same event, is represented most notably by Kim (*Origins*) and Bruce (*Paul*). See also Seyoon Kim, "'The grace that was given to me . . .': Paul and the Grace of his Apostleship," in *Die Hoffnung festhalten* (ed. G. Maier; Neuhausen-Stuttgart: Hänssler-Verlag, 1978), 50–59.

[29] K. H. Rengstorf, " ἀποστέλλω/ἀπόστολος," *TDNT* 1:398–447; idem, *Apostleship* (trans. J. R. Coates; London: Adam and Charles Black, 1952); Walter Schmithals, *The Office of Apostle in the Early Church* (trans. J. E. Steely; Nashville: Abingdon Press, 1969); C. K. Barrett, *The Signs of an Apostle* (London: Epworth Press, 1970); J. Andrew Kirk, "Apostleship Since Rengstorf: Towards a Synthesis," *NTS* 21 (1975): 249–64; Ronald F. Hock, *The Social Context of Paul's Ministry: Tentmaking and Apostleship* (Philadelphia: Fortress Press, 1980); Bruce, *Galatians*; Andrew C. Clark, "Apostleship: Evidence from the New Testament and Early Christian Literature," *VE* 19 (1989): 49–82; Jerry L. Sumney, "Paul's 'Weakness': An Integral Part of his Conception of Apostleship," *JSNT* 52 (1993): 71–91; Calvin Roetzel, *Paul: The Man and the Myth* (Minneapolis: Fortress Press, 1999).

[30] Leif E. Vaage, *Galilean Upstarts: Jesus' First Followers According to Q* (Valley Forge: Trinity Press International, 1994), 19. Rengstorf ("ἀπόστολος," *TDNT* 1:437), Burton (*Galatians*, 363–84), and J. B. Lightfoot (*Galatians*, 92) all find little in common between general Hellenistic and New Testament usage of ἀπόστολος because they imbue the word with too great a theological force and lose sight of the simplicity of its meaning in its broader social context.

[31] Rengstorf, *Apostleship*, 1. The criticisms of Barr (James Barr, *The Semantics of Biblical Language* [Oxford: Oxford University Press, 1961]) introduced in the previous

would be considered as an attack upon the state that sent it out. So too with respect to people sent out; these people are sent out, obviously, by someone more powerful than they and as the representative of that powerful person.[32] Several of the Zenon papyri from the Michigan Collection in particular refer to people sent out (ἀποστέλλω) in order to implement a wish of someone with power (23.4; 78.1; 98.4).[33] In Longus' romance *Daphnis and Chloe*, the patron Dionysophanes sends several slaves to prepare for his visit to his estate. They each carry instructions for the steward of the estate, and in this manner represent the interests and authority of their patron. People who are sent out are not likely to be confused with the one who sent them, but they certainly stand in their place; one who is sent *is the sender* by proxy, he or she stands in for the sender *in absentia*. I am thus inclined to follow Vaage's response to Rengstorf that "In every case, to say that one was 'sent' responded to concerns about authority and authorization."[34]

Also of considerable interest is the fact that *apostoloi* could be derived not only from human authority but also from divine authority. By the first and second centuries C.E., the verb is commonly associated with "religious" commissioning that comes from God. Epictetus describes the true Cynic as ἄγγελος ἀπὸ τοῦ Διὸς ἀπέσταλται (*Diatr.* 3.22.23), and goes on to say that they were sent in order to show people the error of their ways with respect to right and wrong. Epictetus uses the same language at *Diatr.* 3.23.46, namely that God (ὁ θεός) sent a man to be an example to people of how it is possible to live the peaceful life.[35] Further, it is profoundly noteworthy that within the context of Epictetus describing the Cynic as having been sent by God, not called an apostle *per se*, but sent (ἀπέσταλκεν) nonetheless, he has the Cynic apostle ask, οὐκ εἰμὶ ἐλεύθερος? Gordon Fee has suggested that the parallel of this question to 1 Cor 9:1 is "purely coincidental," but given that both

---

chapter with respect to building walls around New Testament and Graeco-Roman usage is surely appropriate here as well.

[32] Of course, context is important too. Not every occurrence of ἀποστέλλω is about authority or status; some uses are quite mundane, appearing to be synonyms of πέμπω and στέλλω (*pace* Rengstorf, "ἀποστέλλω," 398). Epictetus, who as we shall see shortly uses the term in both ways, uses the verb of children who are sent out to their school-teacher (*Diatr.* 3.22.74). Also, some of the Oxyrhynchus papyri evidence a highly specialized meaning of "bill of lading" or invoice (*P.Oxy.* 9.1197.13). The context can tell us when ἀποστέλλω or ἀπόστολος involves sending and authority.

[33] ἀποστέλλω in the gospels reflects this same sense. Jesus sends out the disciples (Matt 10:16//Luke 10:3), and angels and prophets are sent out by God (Matt 13:41; 23:34).

[34] Vaage, *Galilean Upstarts*, 22.

[35] See also Epictetus, *Diatr.* 4.8.31.

questions are associated with apostleship makes this claim quite questionable.[36] Harrison on the other hand makes no effort to diminish the significance of the parallels, which as he shows are considerably greater in number than those few shown here, implying that they are in his opinion hardly coincidental.[37] It is not that Paul takes over the language uncritically, nor that he always means the same thing when he does. But he frequently does take over the language, it is sometimes used in the same manner (legitimation, for example), and Harrison never neglects to ask what the Graeco-Roman reader would have thought about Paul's language, regardless of how Paul may have meant it.

It is this context of divine commissioning then that seems most to approximate the apostolic status of Paul and others in the New Testament of whom the noun and verb are used. Paul's claim to have been sent by God with a mission to carry a message finds sufficient context in a Cynic/Stoic environment to make it meaningful.

While it does not appear that *apostolos* was a part of the vocabulary of patronage and benefaction, it involves no stretch of the imagination to envisage a patron (or patron deity) sending out a client for some official purpose.[38] Even the circumstance of a slave owner sending out slaves, as that portrayed in Longus or in the synoptic Parable of the Tenants (Mark 12:1–12; Matt 21:33–46; Luke 20:9–19), while not patronage explicitly, may well have involved freedmen as clients. Nonetheless, I am not arguing that Paul's apostleship was a benefaction given at the moment of his divine revelation, but rather that the option is consistent with Pauline data, with how some interpreters of Paul have understood the timing of the two phenomena, and with ancient usage of the term.

As satisfactory as this option might be, it is not the only one afforded to us by the context of patronage and benefaction. A second option, and one that coincides with the majority of scholars who allow for a period of germination between revelation and mission, is that Paul came to the idea of his mission to the Gentiles as a form of client reciprocity in recognition of the benefactions given to him and to humanity by his divine patron/benefactor. If Paul

---

[36] Fee, *Corinthians*, 394. This brings up an interesting question which might profitably be pursued elsewhere: what is the relationship between apostleship and freedom? Why would both Paul and Epictetus invoke the combination?

[37] James R. Harrison, *Paul's Language of Grace in its Graeco-Roman Context* (WUNT 2.172; Tübingen: Mohr Siebeck, 2003), 273–74.

[38] On this, however, see the recent article by Guido O. Kirner, "Apostolat und Patronage (I): Methodischer Teil und Forschungsdiskussion," *ZAC* 6 (2002): 3–37.

understood the revelation of Christ to him by God as a divine benefaction, and there are strong reasons to think he did, then we need to start looking for what necessarily follows from that, namely at Paul's expressions of reciprocity. Paul refers to being compelled to preach the gospel, and having had an obligation laid upon him. As we saw this is not the language of slavery, but of the well-known obligations of the client. Not unlike others in the ancient world, even if Paul's response was a touch more extensive than most (allowing for the understatement), Paul's response was *to tell others* of the generosity and benefactions to be gained through association with this particular divine patron.[39] No doubt, Paul initiated conversations with potential converts by describing some of the benefactions that might be gained from allegiance with this new patron, not the least of which must surely have been salvation. In this scenario, Paul undertook a mission to the Gentiles to spread the good news of benefactions in order to attract them to the new movement, and by doing so to increase the honour of God as the divine patron. The mission then was how Paul came to express his client reciprocity for the magnitude of the benefactions he himself had received.

Of course, this scenario is not free of its own problems. First of all, it does not account for why Paul chose to approach the Gentiles and not other Jews (either as well or exclusively). Any answers to that question remain highly speculative or hidden entirely. Secondly, one could object to this scenario by invoking the testimony of Gal 1:16, in which Paul claims that Christ was revealed in him ἵνα—the all important purpose clause—he might preach him to the Gentiles. Obviously a reading that has Paul arrive at the mission to the Gentiles at a later date, a position most scholars appear to hold, must read Paul's claim at Gal 1:15–16 as typical of a convert's retrospective interpretation of their conversion experience. It is not a perfect solution, granted. For example, it is striking that despite interpreting the origin of his mission to the Gentiles here, he has not done so in the language of patronage and benefaction that he uses elsewhere. He has not, for instance, suggested or even really implied that his mission was part of his client obligation. We may never, unfortunately, uncover what precisely the relationship was between Paul's conversion experience and his mission to the Gentiles. Every suggestion, it seems, can be supported and contradicted by equally relevant Pauline data.

---

[39] For an analogy of extreme reciprocity in return for an extreme benefaction, we might consider the establishment of the Ruler-Cult, which Mott explains gave honors to human rulers/benefactors that were normally reserved for the gods in recognition of the "magnitude of the benefactor's deed" (Mott, "Greek Benefactor," 158–60).

4.2 Galatians 1:11–17

From the three passages in First Corinthians we get a glimpse of how Paul viewed, or at the very least, how he expressed his understanding of, his conversion experience. Paul was the recipient of a benefaction from God in the form of a vision of God's broker Jesus. The title and office of apostle was either a benefaction from God the divine patron received with the call, or it was Paul's way of responding to the benefaction of the call, but either way it seems impossible to separate the apostleship from divine patronage and benefaction. In the Corinthian passages there is also evident a concern on Paul's part to show he has reciprocated as best he could the benefactions that were done to him by undertaking a passionate, motivated, and extensive mission to the Gentiles. His language of obligation and his use of χάρις function clearly as a part of Paul's rhetoric of patronage and benefaction. This portrait is complemented and confirmed by the others of Paul's conversion passages.

Gal 1:11–17 is another passage that is consistently referred to for evidence of Paul's conversion. As I did with the Corinthian passages, let me present the text in its entirety and then illustrate some of the ways in which Paul's rhetoric of patronage figures within it, and then compare our reading with typical commentary treatments.

> ¹¹Γνωρίζω γὰρ ὑμῖν, ἀδελφοί, τὸ εὐαγγέλιον τὸ εὐαγγελισθὲν ὑπ' ἐμοῦ ὅτι οὐκ ἔστιν κατὰ ἄνθρωπον· ¹²οὐδὲ γὰρ ἐγὼ παρὰ ἀνθρώπου παρέλαβον αὐτὸ οὔτε ἐδιδάχθην ἀλλὰ δι' ἀποκαλύψεως Ἰησοῦ Χριστοῦ. ¹³Ἠκούσατε γὰρ τὴν ἐμὴν ἀναστροφήν ποτε ἐν τῷ Ἰουδαϊσμῷ, ὅτι καθ' ὑπερβολὴν ἐδίωκον τὴν ἐκκλησίαν τοῦ θεοῦ καὶ ἐπόρθουν αὐτήν, ¹⁴καὶ προέκοπτον ἐν τῷ Ἰουδαϊσμῷ ὑπὲρ πολλοὺς συνηλικιώτας ἐν τῷ γένει μου, περισσοτέρως ζηλωτὴς ὑπάρχων τῶν πατρικῶν μου παραδόσεων. ¹⁵ὅτε δὲ εὐδόκησεν [ὁ θεὸς] ὁ ἀφορίσας με ἐκ κοιλίας μητρός μου καὶ καλέσας διὰ τῆς χάριτος αὐτοῦ ¹⁶ἀποκαλύψαι τὸν υἱὸν αὐτοῦ ἐν ἐμοί, ἵνα εὐαγγελίζωμαι αὐτὸν ἐν τοῖς ἔθνεσιν, εὐθέως οὐ προσανεθέμην σαρκὶ καὶ αἵματι ¹⁷οὐδὲ ἀνῆλθον εἰς Ἱεροσόλυμα πρὸς τοὺς πρὸ ἐμοῦ ἀποστόλους, ἀλλὰ ἀπῆλθον εἰς Ἀραβίαν καὶ πάλιν ὑπέστρεψα εἰς Δαμασκόν.

A number of features in this passage warrant only cursory comment. The first is Paul's defensiveness; he appears at some pains to emphasise that what he teaches the Galatians (τὸ εὐαγγέλιον τὸ εὐαγγελισθὲν ὑπ' ἐμοῦ) is not a human creation, nor was it the result of his having been taught it; he returns at the end of the passage to reiterate the point that he never went to Jerusalem for his gospel. The gospel was not his own, and it was not taught to him by anyone; rather, it was revealed to him δι' ἀποκαλύψεως Ἰησοῦ Χριστοῦ. Several features in particular echo and confirm aspects established in our analysis of the Corinthian conversion passages. The first is that at the root of Paul's conversion experience lies a vision. In 1 Corinthians Paul refers to "having seen" the Lord (1 Cor 9:1 and 15:8); here he refers to an ἀποκάλυψις of Jesus Christ. Surely the revelation here recalls the visions in 1 Corinthians and refer to one and the same event of seeing. The second aspect confirmed here is that Paul considered this vision to have been a divine benefaction. In this passage the benefaction of the vision is mentioned explicitly at Gal 1:15, in which Paul claims to have been called διὰ τῆς χάριτος αὐτοῦ. We shall return shortly and in detail to the notion of being called by a patron, but for now it is enough to notice that the benefaction referred to here can only be the revelation named earlier in the passage, a fact confirmed by our reading of the Corinthian conversion passages.

The Galatians passage is framed by Paul's defensiveness concerning the source of his teachings, but verses 13–16 in the middle contain a modest synkrisis. My comments here will be brief, since I will return to discuss this particular synkrisis later in this chapter when I deal with a longer synkrisis in greater detail. Gal 1:13–14 represents the first part of the synkrisis. Paul, implying the audience is already familiar with his story, illustrates his time before he was a member of this new movement. He harassed the church, and he excelled beyond his peers in zealousness for the traditions of his Judaism. Verses 15–16a represent the second part of the synkrisis, which as we will see later, naturally focuses on Paul's present. Paul credits his God with making the first contact (another point to which we shall return shortly).[40] He writes that he was called (καλέσας) διὰ τῆς χάριτος αὐτοῦ. The sentence as a whole emphasises that the benefaction was the vision that Paul had of Christ: "But when it pleased [God,] who had set me apart from my mother's womb and who had called me through his benefaction, to reveal his son in me . . ." (Gal 1:15–16). Here we find Paul's clearest acknowledgement yet that God *was* the actual benefactor and Jesus "only" the broker. Paul was summoned through a common act of benefaction: the appearance of a divine being.

---

[40] That God is explicitly (rather than implicitly) the instigator in Gal 1:15 depends on how one interprets the rather evenly weighted manuscript evidence: ὁ θεός ℵ D Ψ 33 M sy^h cop; *omit*) 𝔓^46 B F G 0150 *pc* vg it^mss sy^p. The indecisiveness of this manuscript evidence is marked by the square brackets around the text.

What has perhaps most encouraged commentators to stress the cataclysmic in Paul's conversion experience is the fact that Paul, by his own admission here (as well as Gal 1:23–24) and in 1 Corinthians, went from agitator to supporter of the earliest Jesus movement. Of course, most commentators make the degree of difference between these two positions greater than this description implies by having Paul change from ruthless blood-letter to selflessly persecuted apostle. The greater the extent of Paul's passion the more commentators are given license to emphasise how emotionally cataclysmic Paul's conversion must have been. A closer look at the Pauline passages that reflect some form of persecution results in other possibilities, however. At 1 Cor 15:9 Paul claims to have been a "pursuer" of the churches of God (ἐδίωξα), and he quotes others as saying the same thing in Gal 1:23 (διώκων) about him. Διώκω in these passages is usually translated as "persecutor," though of course there is a spectrum of behaviour that could constitute persecution, ranging from social harassment to violence potentially resulting in death. But that διώκω is not synonymous with murder is suggested by two passages: *Barn.* 5:11 modifies διώκω with ἐν θανάτῳ, and Matt 23:34 claims that διώκω is what the people did to the prophets when they were *not* killing and crucifying them (ἀποκτενεῖτε καὶ σταυρώσετε).

It is the typical reading of Gal 1:13 that invites translators to read maximum violence into Paul's use of the term διώκω. Most translators read καθ' ὑπερβολὴν ἐδίωκον τὴν ἐκκλησίαν τοῦ θεοῦ καὶ ἐπόρθουν αὐτήν as "I was violently persecuting the church of God and was trying to destroy it (NRSV)." Martyn, for instance, thinks that Paul *literally* tried to destroy the church.[41] This reading of Gal 1:13 has plenty of lexical support. The phrase καθ' ὑπερβολήν is well known to function as an intensifier, and Paul is familiar with this usage. At Rom 7:13, for instance, he refers to behaviour that is "exceedingly sinful" or "sinful beyond measure" (καθ' ὑπερβολὴν ἁμαρτωλός). In two other Pauline uses of this phrase, however, it does not appear to work as an intensifier, but rather as a marker of exaggeration or of the conscious use of hyperbole. Lauri Thurén has argued that exaggeration is a common feature of Paul's writing, and discusses in detail several examples of Paul's rhetorical use of hyperbole.[42] Further, he shows that the phrase καθ' ὑπερβολήν frequent-

---

[41] J. Louis Martyn, *Galatians* (AB 33A; New York: Doubleday, 1997), 154, 161–63.
[42] Lauri Thurén, *Derhetorizing Paul: A Dynamic Perspective on Pauline Theology and the Law* (Harrisburg, Pa.: Trinity Press International, 2002). He lists, for example, 1 Thess 1:2, 3, 8; 2:8, 9; 3:10; 1 Cor 1:4, 5, 7; 2:2, 3; 4:8–13; 6:12; 11:2 (pp. 29–35).

ly functions as a marker of hyperbole, that is rhetorical intensification.[43] This observation helps make better sense of Paul in *some* places. For example, it seems unlikely that at 2 Cor 1:8 Paul was so "utterly, unbearably crushed that [he] despaired of life itself" (NRSV). Was Paul so badly beaten or tortured in Asia that he hoped for death? It seems a lot to ask. What seems more likely is that Paul was "persecuted" to the same extent as he persecuted the early Jesus movement, namely that he harassed them and then was harassed in turn, that he frustrated their efforts to proselytise, and at most practised minimal violence against them. This would be reflected then in a translation that reads, "speaking in hyperbole, we were weighed down so beyond our power that we despaired even our lives." Such a translation is suggested and supported by 1 Cor 12:31, which introduces the profoundly hyperbolic hymn of 1 Corinthians 13. Paul's questions at the start of the chapter are certainly hyperbolic when he suggests that faith can move mountains, or that one with the profoundest faith and selflessness gains nothing at all without love. In this case, καθ' ὑπερβολήν modifies δείκνυμι instead of ὁδός, an option represented also by Witherington. The introduction to the hymn then would read, "I will display a way, by means of hyperbole,"[44] or "And now I will show you a way with some exaggeration."[45]

We return, then, to Gal 1:13 in which it is certainly possible to argue that in keeping with one of Paul's uses of the phrase καθ' ὑπερβολήν he means to say here that, "speaking by way of hyperbole, I *persecuted* the church and *was destroying it*"; as in the example from 1 Cor 12:58, the hyperbole modifies the verbs (as marked).[46] This reading is more in concert with the generally more subdued tenor of διώκω (especially in comparison to words like ἀποκτείνω, συντρίβω, πορθέω, and διαφθείρω) which Paul uses more often to describe his previous behaviour towards the movement he came to represent. It is, however, in sharp contrast to Luke's description (Acts 8:3; 9:1; 22:4; 26:10–

---

[43] See his article, "'By Means of Hyperbole' (1 Cor 12:31b)," in *Paul and Pathos* (ed. Th. H. Olbricht and J. L. Sumney; Atlanta: Society of Biblical Literature, 2001), 97–113, esp. pp. 99–100 for many classical literary examples and examples from rhetorical handbooks.

[44] So Ben Witherington, *Conflict and Community in Corinth: A Socio-Rhetorical Commentary on 1 and 2 Corinthians* (Grand Rapids: Eerdmans, 1995), 266–67.

[45] So Thurén, "'By Means of Hyperbole'," 101.

[46] Interestingly, Thurén appears to have mixed feelings about this option. In his article, "'By Means of Hyperbole'," he lists Gal 1:13 as an example of καθ' ὑπερβολήν functioning as an intensifier (p. 98), but in his book, *Derhetorizing Paul*, he lists it as an example of Paul speaking in hyperbole (p. 71).

11).⁴⁷ I would suggest that it is the Lukan depiction of Paul's persecutorial activities and the bloody violence depicted *there* that provides the foundation of translations of Gal 1:13 that have Paul literally trying to destroy the church.⁴⁸ It is not that διώκω or πορθέω are meant here or are generally to be read as metaphorical—it is the presence of καθ' ὑπερβολήν as a possible marker of hyperbole that recommends such a reading.

The language one adopts to describe Paul's conduct—whether persecutor or murderer—is important because it plays a role in how people imagine Paul's conversion. Even allowing for a lesser degree of violence perpetrated by Paul against the Jesus movement, it is still fair to ask whether a change from agitator to missionary does in fact not suggest the sort of dramatic and emotionally cataclysmic conversion that people typically ascribe to Paul. We cannot comment on Paul's emotional state, but nor need we assume (in the absence of hard data) that such must have been the case. This is because we can talk about another feature of this move that can be quantified, namely Paul's loyalty to his patron God, a topic we will take up in the following chapter. Paul's behaviour both before and after his conversion was (or he likely understood it to be) honouring of and loyal to his divine patron. Paul's guarding of the Torah from misuse by apostates and blasphemers, assuming that is the origin of his harassment of the Jesus movement, would have been intended to honour his divine patron. As we shall see in the next chapter, punishing disloyalty is an expression of loyalty. Clearly, Paul would not have harassed the early Jesus movement had he thought such actions would dishonour his patron. What the conversion represents is Paul's reception of the news or the realisation that his divine patron was, in fact, *not* honoured by his behaviour. Paul, as any conscientious client would have done, altered his behaviour upon making the discovery that what he thought expressed loyalty and honour in fact reflected the opposite. Thus, the vision of Jesus would have represented for Paul the point at which he learned that, since Jesus was a broker of Paul's divine patron, then he must have been wrong about him all along. This is, interestingly, somewhat consistent with Acts, but it is a conclusion we can draw when we read Paul's words within the context of divine

---

47 See Ernst Haenchen, *The Acts of the Apostles* (trans. B. Noble et al.; Philadelphia: Westminster Press, 1971), 295, for a list of those who have disputed the strict accuracy of Luke's account of Paul's persecuting activities.

48 So Arland J. Hultgren, "Paul's Pre-Christian Persecutions of the Church: Their Purpose, Locale, and Nature," *JBL* 95 (1976): 108. Hultgren rejects that Paul was a violent persecutor of the church and suggests instead that καθ' ὑπερβολήν refers to the quality of Paul's zeal.

patronage and benefaction. Paul's conversion experience itself, and especially the way in which he expresses it, has to do with his behaviour as a client trying to act appropriately and loyally to bring honour to his divine patron. Both before and after, Paul sought to honour his divine patron, but continuing to do so required some adjustments to his patterns and expressions of loyalty.

The most important feature of this Galatians conversion passage, especially because it occurs in a conversion passage, is Paul's reference to having been called (καλέσας) by God (Gal 1:15). Recall the claim of having been called or commissioned is part of the rhetoric of patronage and benefaction, as we saw in Chapter Three. There we saw Horace called by a patron, Maecenas, and more *à propos* to Paul's experience, Aristides called (κλῆσις) by Asclepius numerous times (2.292.14; 4.345.14). Of course, it is not only in this Galatians conversion passage that Paul emphasises the fact that he too was called by his patron. Paul's letter-openings in Romans and in his first letter to the Corinthians both claim that he was called to be an apostle (κλητὸς ἀπόστολος). The openings of 2 Corinthians and Galatians possibly imply this same call by saying that the apostleship was God's will (θέλημα) in the first instance and by saying that Paul is apostle through (the actions) of the broker Jesus, though of course later in Galatians this is made explicit (1:15).[49] The claim that Paul was called has several important parallels. For one, Jesus and God are depicted frequently as calling people. Paul refers to the Roman Christians as having been called by Jesus (Rom 1:6–7). Rom 8:18–30; 9:24; 1 Cor 1:9 (among many others) mention people who had been called by God. In 1 Corinthians, after Paul says that he was called to be an apostle he says that the Corinthians were called to be saints (1 Cor 1:2). These and other passages show that the divine patron or benefactor of the Christians was the sort of patron who called people, including Paul, to be clients. One can imagine that this might have been an attractive feature of Pauline Christianity. While there are sufficient examples of patrons seeking out clients to refer to it as a type of patron behaviour, the fact is it was not the prototypical conduct of a patron. A divine patron with such a reputation for actively seeking to benefit clients might have attracted many people to the Jesus movement. Thus, this is a feature of Paul's honouring portrayal of his divine patron, just as Horace's pointing out his call by Maecenas says something very positive about Maecenas as a patron. Paul's rhetoric of patronage and benefaction, as with all such rhetoric, means to bring honour to his (divine) patron.

---

[49] Interestingly, the Philippians and Philemon letter-openings both lack any of this sort of terminology, opting instead for the titles servant and prisoner respectively.

The second parallel to this language in Paul is, obviously, the language of the prophets. While this has been looked at many times before, it may be worth visiting again with a context of divine patronage and benefaction in mind. The calls of Samuel, Isaiah, Jeremiah, Ezekiel, Jonah by God inaugurated their respective roles as prophets of God.[50] The two prophets that seem most to provide Paul with his prophetic model are Isaiah and Jeremiah, since both claim to have been called before they were born and while in their mother's wombs (Isa 49:1; Jer 1:5), which Paul's language in Galatians can only be meant to echo. The question arises then: was Paul invoking the Graeco-Roman example of the call of the generous divine patron-benefactor, or was he invoking the well-known example of the call of the Hebrew prophets?

When Krister Stendahl tackled this question, he did so within the context of arguing whether it was appropriate to refer to Paul as "converted," since the term so typically presupposes someone having left one religion to join another. Stendahl of course argued that Paul's own language closely resembled that of the Hebrew prophets; thus, he argued, it was not fair to claim that Paul converted (understood in the sense of leaving a previous religion). Donaldson accurately represents the consensus when he suggests that Stendahl's definition of conversion was too narrow, and that "properly understood [the term] can be appropriately applied to Paul."[51] What Donaldson is referring to is that if conversion is understood to occur within religions and not only across them, then the term conversion does not have to imply that Paul *left* Judaism.

As we saw in the previous chapter, however, Hellenistic Jews appear to have taken over quite comfortably the notion of God as a divine patron or benefactor, and of their own conduct as mirroring that of a client. The call of the prophets, then, was likely another feature of their traditional religion that they easily reinterpreted in a Graeco-Roman context of patronage and benefaction. That is, the controversy to which Stendahl responded is potentially side-stepped in two ways. On the one hand, within a context of divine patronage and benefaction, the distinction between 'called' and 'converted' is not valid. It is no longer a question of whether Paul was called *or* converted because as a client of a divine patron, Paul can be both called and *thus* converted. Secondly, it is not a question of whether the Jewish or the Graeco-Roman influence figures more prominently in Paul's use of the call motif. In

---

[50] 1 Sam 3:2–4:1; Isa 6:6–8; Jer 1:4–19; Ezek 2:1–3:11; Jonah 1:1–3.

[51] Terence L. Donaldson, *Paul and the Gentiles: Remapping the Apostle's Convictional World* (Minneapolis: Fortress Press, 1997), 17.

Paul's context of thorough enculturation, there is no reason, especially in this instance, why the influence cannot be Jewish *and* Graeco-Roman.

The call of Paul by his divine patron-benefactor through the divine broker Jesus leads to his conversion, in that it leads him to alter behaviour he had thought was honouring of God, as well as alter his understanding of certain issues having to do with the relationship of God with non-Jews.[52] Paul's call leads him into a new understanding of loyalty to his patron; conversion and loyalty are here bound up together. Paul's having been called does not mean he was not converted, because in the system of patronage and benefaction, being called by a patron, whether human or divine, generally leads to a new expression of loyalty and client status, hence a new understanding of conversion. In another important way, then, we see that Paul's language of call that established his new perspective and his new way of acting towards the followers of Christ confirms and augments what we would expect to see within a structure of religious patronage and benefaction.

As we did with the Corinthian passages, let us compare what we see in this passage from a perspective of patronage and benefaction with what commentaries tend to offer. To summarise first of all, as with the Corinthian passages, we see here again Paul's reference to the revelation of Christ, and again we see this very closely aligned with his reference to the benefactions of God (Gal 1:15). We see also the synkrisis of Paul's life before and after his conversion, but have delayed commenting on it until the following section. Perhaps not surprisingly, commentaries focus on the aspect of this passage having to do with Paul's call. Martyn, for instance, points out that it was God who did the revealing of Jesus to Paul, but there is no connection of this observation to the fact that Paul alludes to this event as a benefaction from God.[53] Likewise, with the language of call, Martyn finds parallels only within the Jewish prophetic tradition, which there certainly are, but overlooks revealing parallels of the divine call among Graeco-Roman religions and within the practice of literary patronage.[54] Overall, the notion that Paul understands his God to be a patron, and what the implications might be for understanding Paul is not an option in most commentaries, Martyn's included. But it is hardly fair to single out Martyn. R. Y. K. Fung emphasises the call of God as the revelation, and also the obedient response of Paul to that call. But there is little explanation of what this response represents. Fung implies that the

---

[52] See Segal, *Paul the Convert*, Chapter Four; and Daniel Boyarin, *A Radical Jew: Paul and the Politics of Identity* (Berkeley: University of California Press, 1994).
[53] Martyn, *Galatians*, 144.
[54] Martyn, *Galatians*, 156–57.

correct response is obedience, but does not explain *why* that is the case.⁵⁵ It is probably the case that one who has been called by a God, who has received a revelation, *will* respond with obedience, but there are reasons for this that deserve explanation. Sam Williams emphasises that Paul received something from God, but there is no discussion of what it meant or entailed to receive something from a god.⁵⁶ What, for instance, would that have required of Paul? As with the others, this is understood in pious Christian terms — Paul could have done nothing but respond obediently and faithfully to God for the simple reason that "*this* is the Christian God." The language of divine call and reception of divine benefactions becomes far more meaningful when it is recalled that Paul not only had an obvious context, but that that context was wider than Judaism alone, for it too had a context — the religions of the Graeco-Roman world. So many commentaries are mostly descriptive: they describe what Paul says in other words, but they do not attempt to get behind Paul's words or enter into the socio-cultural context that gave meaning to those words.

Commentaries, it seems, tend to be written from within the context of a fully developed Christian theology and faith. Paul is presented as even understanding that he is involved in *Christian* theology. For example, all of Fung's descriptive categories are theological and specifically Christian theology at that — revelation, grace, etc.⁵⁷ Paul becomes the adept and first handler of these profoundly important Christian theological terms. It appears not to be a concern that Paul probably understood these things differently from modern commentators, that reception of divine gifts, grace, and one's response might have been understood differently by Paul than by later Christians. From the perspective offered here, Paul ceases to be an early Christian theologian with a very nearly fully developed Christian theology behind or within him, but rather a man who received a benefaction from his divine patron, and who was thus required to respond in an appropriate way. Most importantly, Paul ceases to be *sui generis*, for there are parallels from all over the Mediterranean for people receiving divine benefactions and their resulting actions and rhetoric. Paul is not the unique first Christian theologian but the typical (in most ways) recipient of a divine benefaction. Why did Paul persecute the church? Zeal is not enough of an answer — whence and why this zeal?⁵⁸ Why does Paul continually mention "receiving" the revelation of Christ from God?

---

55 Fung, *Galatians*, 62–66.
56 Sam K. Williams, *Galatians* (ANTC 9; Nashville: Abingdon Press, 1997).
57 Grace: p. 39; revelation: pp. 53–54.
58 On the whence and why of zeal, especially in the context of patronage and benefaction, see below page 247.

Descriptive answers, which amount to little more than "Because that is the way it happened," are insufficient. Paul's language and rhetoric of patronage and benefaction has to be seen *and* weighed; it cannot simply be brushed over as pious Christian language.

4.3 Philippians 3:4b–11

The last of the passages typically cited for evidence of Paul's conversion experience is Phil 3:4b–11. The Greek of this passage reads:

> ⁴ᵇκαίπερ ἐγὼ ἔχων πεποίθησιν καὶ ἐν σαρκί. εἴ τις δοκεῖ ἄλλος πεποιθέναι ἐν σαρκί, ἐγὼ μᾶλλον· ⁵περιτομῇ ὀκταήμερος, ἐκ γένους Ἰσραήλ, φυλῆς Βενιαμίν, Ἑβραῖος ἐξ Ἑβραίων, κατὰ νόμον Φαρισαῖος, ⁶κατὰ ζῆλος διώκων τὴν ἐκκλησίαν, κατὰ δικαιοσύνην τὴν ἐν νόμῳ γενόμενος ἄμεμπτος. ⁷[ἀλλὰ] ἅτινα ἦν μοι κέρδη, ταῦτα ἥγημαι διὰ τὸν Χριστὸν ζημίαν. ⁸ἀλλὰ μενοῦνγε καὶ ἡγοῦμαι πάντα ζημίαν εἶναι διὰ τὸ ὑπερέχον τῆς γνώσεως Χριστοῦ Ἰησοῦ τοῦ κυρίου μου, δι' ὃν τὰ πάντα ἐζημιώθην, καὶ ἡγοῦμαι σκύβαλα, ἵνα Χριστὸν κερδήσω ⁹καὶ εὑρεθῶ ἐν αὐτῷ, μὴ ἔχων ἐμὴν δικαιοσύνην τὴν ἐκ νόμου ἀλλὰ τὴν διὰ πίστεως Χριστοῦ, τὴν ἐκ θεοῦ δικαιοσύνην ἐπὶ τῇ πίστει, ¹⁰τοῦ γνῶναι αὐτὸν καὶ τὴν δύναμιν τῆς ἀναστάσεως αὐτοῦ καὶ [τὴν] κοινωνίαν [τῶν] παθημάτων αὐτοῦ, συμμορφιζόμενος τῷ θανάτῳ αὐτοῦ, ¹¹εἴ πως καταντήσω εἰς τὴν ἐξανάστασιν τὴν ἐκ νεκρῶν.

As a conversion passage, Phil 3:4b–11 stands apart from the others. It lacks, for instance, any reference to a vision or to a revelation of Jesus; it does not contain anything that could be construed as a benefaction, nor obviously the term χάρις itself. There is in fact very little in this passage to suggest it as a conversion narrative. Yet commentators agree that this is one of Paul's conversion narratives. This is likely due to the presence of the one feature that really does make this passage a conversion narrative, and that allows it to share something with other ancient conversion narratives—the comparison of Paul's life past and present. In a traditional understanding of conversion, Paul's reference to κέρδος and σκύβαλον represented confirmation that Paul left Judaism behind him. The new perspective on Paul, on the other hand, reads these words as rhetorical in effect, meant to compare only the relative merits of Paul's life in Judaism and his life in Christ.[59] There is indeed

---

[59] See, for instance, Bockmuehl, *Philippians*, 208.

something rhetorical happening in this passage; it is precisely that feature that, in a context of patronage and benefaction, so clearly and predictably marks this passage as an ancient conversion narrative, namely the rhetorical comparison of a present depicted in a strongly positive way with a past that is depicted in a (at times strongly) negative way. As we saw in the previous chapter, patronal synkrisis is commonly found in narrative descriptions, often though not inevitably in the first person, of gratitude and loyalty to a new patron or patronal relationship.

The comparison involved in patronal synkrisis does not have to be literal in order for it to be meaningful and effective, but neither should one assume that patronal synkrisis is always simply rhetorical. It is possible that Paul's synkrisis here that seeks to honour his patron and his new broker does represent a sincere opinion of Paul. One must be careful, however, if one intends to read this passage as literal, not to read it as Paul's definitive statement on his relationship to his past. Paul is fantastically inconsistent on this question, so the most that can be said is that, if read literally, this statement represents *one* of Paul's positions concerning his past. Nevertheless, given the manner in which Paul expresses it, and the examples of patronal synkrisis I have seen, I am more inclined to suggest that Paul's comparison in this passage is rhetorical and not literal.

Also significant to the question of whether we are to take Paul's synkrisis literally is the rhetorical context of this passage within the letter. Paul seems to refer, throughout the letter, to four different groups of opponents: those who proclaim Christ for questionable motives (1:15–17); those who appear to be intimidating the Philippians (1:28); those who are enemies of the "cross of Christ" (3:18); and those whom we tend to call Judaizers (3:2). Our passage is set against this lastly named group of opponents, and thus we should expect bombast of this sort from Paul, spoken in the sharpest possible terms and less likely for that reason to be literal.

One important feature of Paul's patronal synkrisis in Philippians is that, with the exception of Paul's use of the terms κέρδος and σκύβαλον, Paul describes his previous life with great pride. Paul's patronal synkrisis starts with a catalogue of what made Paul an excellent Jew—circumcised on the eighth day, an Israelite, a Benjaminite, a Pharisee, indeed a Hebrew among Hebrews. Paul uses these terms to establish his honourable status, his pedigree, especially among those fellow Jews who trouble him. Paul's status as a member of the people of Israel conveys a sense of *"belonging* to God's ancient people."[60] As

---

[60] Fee, *Philippians*, 307.

a Benjaminite, Paul claims a status that proselytes could never have: family status. Paul was a member of the family line that boasted Saul, the first Israelite king, as well the tribe blessed by Moses (Deut 33:12). By narrowing the focus further, Paul claims that he was not only descended from a prestigious line by birth but joined and followed the Pharisees by choice. Claiming Pharisaical associations is a claim of purity, of adherence to the *mitzvot* of the Torah, and of honourable conduct before God. According to Fee, Paul's reference to Pharisaism provides the framework for the zeal referred to in the phrases that follow.[61] Regardless, Paul expresses equal pride in harassment of the early Jesus movement. Finally of pride to Paul was his blamelessness (again the language of blamelessness to illustrate proper client conduct appears) under the law. As commentators since Stendahl have observed, these are categories of great pride for Paul, and they are the undoing of any depiction of Paul that has him *escape* Judaism on grounds of guilt or some personal identity crisis.

It is not, however, a typical feature of patronal synkrisis for clients to refer to their past with such glowing praise; its presence here is thus very significant. Normally the convert's past is described in pejorative terms. As we saw in the previous chapter, patronal synkrisis draws attention to the correction of past ails such as exile, ignorance, and illness. These were (or at least were meant to be understood as) literal ailments that were made better by the benefactions of the current patron. Other synkriseis were more vague about the details of the past life, but ended by describing it as death, something that Paul does more or less within his synkrisis. Yet, that Paul talks about his Jewish past as something in which he had great pride simply raises the stakes. How difficult, after all, is it to improve upon illness or exile? But to improve upon an excellent past that in comparison to one's present is actually (or appears to be) worthless (or worse than worthless) must be all the more powerful a synkrisis. If patronal synkrisis was meant to honour the patron by attributing to him or her a tremendous improvement in life by comparing the good one has received to the ill one knew previously, then Paul's synkrisis in Philippians does this all the more so. And as we shall see in the following chapter, that Paul does not change patrons precisely, but rather undergoes a change in the patronal relationship, alters little the rhetoric or reality of the change.

Phil 3:7 marks the break in this synkrisis. Paul claims that all he had attained in the past, though commendable and distinguished, can now only

---

[61] Fee, *Philippians*, 308.

be considered ζημία—loss, as opposed to gain. He goes on to clarify that he actually considers all things (πάντα) as ζημία, implying that there is only one thing of value left to him. And again he takes the clarification a step further in emphasis, declaring that all that he has lost from his past he now regards as "shit" (σκύβαλα). Herein lies the power of Paul's patronal synkrisis: Paul's past was excellent; it was a source of pride for him. Yet, in comparison with Paul's awesome present status, even something as excellent as that appears so profoundly diminished as to call it σκύβαλον. Further, there are two contrasts at work in this patronal synkrisis. In the first, Paul contrasts righteousness that can come from the law (Phil 3:6, 9) with righteousness that comes solely through faith in Christ (Phil 3:9). In the second and more powerful synkrisis Paul compares his past and his present where the present is excellent because of the benefactions of his patron.

Let us return to look at the synkrisis that appears in Gal 1:11–17. Paul's synkrisis there is less elaborate than the one in Philippians, and the two differ also in terms of intensity. If the more positive terms with which Paul refers to his past in Philippians serve to intensify the honouring aspect of the synkrisis in that letter, the Galatians synkrisis lacks this. In Philippians, Paul speaks with pride about his Jewish gains; he seeks to trump those who would try to out-do his Jewish credentials. In Galatians, however, the referent is different. Paul is in the process not of showing how great he was, but the source of the gospel he preaches. Paul starts by suggesting that they might have heard about his previous life while in Judaism, then refers them to his past as a pursuer of them. It is not with pride here that Paul refers back to his past role. Conversely, verse 14 has Paul claim to have excelled beyond his peers and compatriots in his zeal for the traditions of their forefathers, a sentiment that echoes some of the pride Paul expresses in Philippians. Nevertheless, given how Paul has set up the synkrisis in verse 13, the zeal referred to in verse 14 recalls the zeal in his acts of harassment, suggesting that Paul is drawing a negative comparison here with his past, not the positive comparison initiated in Philippians 3. It was from this place that Paul relates he was called by the benefaction of God through the revelation that changed his sense and his expression of loyalty. This comparison of negative past with positive present is, as we saw previously, more typical of patronal synkriseis than that found in Philippians. As a result, however, the comparison in Galatians is less intense.

It speaks volumes about the relationship between patronal synkrisis and the ancient conversion narrative that Paul uses the rhetorical trope in the conversion narratives of two separate (and very different) letters. Likewise, it shows a degree of comfort with the trope that Paul manipulates the intensity of his synkrisis, yet in each case maintains his appropriate expression of honour and loyalty. For all that Phil 3:4b–11 lacks in other features of Paul's conversion narratives, it fits very comfortably within ancient conversion narratives.

Finally, as we did with the previous passages, let us look at what has been gained in our understanding of the Phil 3:4b–11 conversion passage by comparing what commentators have had to say about it. To sum up, Paul's conversion narrative in this passage does really only one thing: it presents Paul's more intense and lengthy patronal synkrisis. There is little else in this passage to suggest conversion; however, the presence of the patronal synkrisis in such a consistent way with others seen in the previous chapter indicates clearly that we have here a conversion narrative. Further, we recognise that synkrisis is a common element of the rhetoric of patronage and benefaction that is designed to honour the patron. In this case, the fact that Paul speaks with pride concerning his past, only subsequently to reduce all he had gained to σκύβαλα, serves all the more to bring honour to God who was part of both of Paul's lives, pre- and post-conversion.

Like other commentators, Bockmuehl focuses on the gain/loss language, and observes that it is the language of the accountant. At Paul's conversion, according to Bockmuehl, his previous balance sheet became quite alarming.[62] Be that as it may, Bockmuehl does not discuss why the language of the accountant is actually quite appropriate for a person in this context to use of their divine patrons. Many commentators, perhaps wanting to save Paul from offending a more spiritual sense of piety, claim that Paul's language of gains and losses is metaphorical. For example, Fee reads the gain/loss language as strictly theological; Paul regards all past gains as loss and all present gains as true gain because of the surpassing power of knowing Christ. But what is that to Paul if not a benefaction that he has received from God? Modern religious piety tends not to think about God as a patron, and certainly does not think of worshipers as clients adhering to patrons because of what can be gained from doing so—exactly in the language of the balance sheet. And it is in this sense then that most people want to understand Paul, as if he shared this modern sense of piety. But the language Paul and his peers use suggests

---

[62] Bockmuehl, *Philippians*, 204. Bockmuehl describes Paul as one who made business investments earlier in his life that though they were valuable once their value dropped later. Because of Christ, Bockmuehl argues, Paul realized that the value of his previous investments had dropped considerably.

otherwise. This language should not be read as a sign that the ancients lacked *piety*, but it does force us to reevaluate in what ancient piety consists.

The gods as patrons in the ancient world was an issue definitely about more than faith in the gods; it had to do with what one could hope to gain from them, what were the benefactions that one could hope to encounter.[63] Piety is not simply action driven by a faithful perspective, as we might be prone to think of it, but may actually have had more to do with the right action, believing or not. The client's correct behaviour is to express gratitude and praise towards a patron for benefactions received, whether or not those benefactions were even particularly worthy. In an externally-lived honour and shame culture, what one believes on the inside matters far less than what one's actions express. An example of this can be found in one of Cicero's letters to his friends; he uses the word *piety* to illustrate the proper relationship of client to patron (*Fam.* 20.1). Paul's piety may very well and rightly consist in an awareness of what he has gained under his present relationship with his God over what he had previously; the literal language of the balance sheet is no less pious in an ancient setting than the metaphorical use of such imagery is in a modern setting.

For Martin, this language (coupled with the use of σκύβαλον) suggests that Paul treats his past with disgust, that he rejects it wholly, but he does not ask why Paul speaks this way.[64] So many commentaries are directed at what Paul says and what he meant, but are short on explanations that seek to get behind those words. They comment on what he says as if he was up to nothing more than simply expressing himself. This is not to say that in everything Paul writes he has a hidden agenda or motives, but language can often have a function and life beyond its face value, and we might think this especially when someone is operating within a genre of persuasion. Paul is not simply observing that his present status leads him to reject his past; he is up to something. In this case, his synkrisis of his quite honourable past is meant to reflect quite positively on his even more honourable present.

The best treatment of this passage is that by Carolyn Osiek for its use of social scientific criticism, and even the combination of that with rhetoric.[65]

---

[63] F. W. Beare, *A Commentary on the Epistle to the Philippians* (BNTC; London: A.&C. Black, 1959), 110–11, goes quite out of his way, it appears, to clarify that Paul is not speaking literally in his usage of the language of assets and liabilities, but strictly metaphorically.

[64] Ralph P. Martin, *Philippians* (London: Oliphants, 1976), 129.

[65] Carolyn Osiek, *Philippians, Philemon* (ANTC; Nashville: Abingdon Press, 2000), 86–96.

Firstly, Osiek ties this passage to Paul's honour. She is hesitant to claim too much knowledge about Paul's conversion, and even appears uncomfortable to use that term at all. She does not say whether this conversion happened suddenly on the road to Damascus, or gradually over time; she claims only what can be supported by Paul's letters, namely that he believed that he had seen the Lord, that God had revealed Christ to and in him. The language of gain and loss, the comparison of Paul's past with his present Osiek reads as Paul's language of the ledger, or business language. But Osiek does not mention that the language of gain in terms of the balance sheet is also the language of patronage and benefaction, at least it is most forcefully when the balance sheet is out of balance. Witness Juvenal's critique of patrons who do not give to their clients what they have coming to them:

> First of all be sure of this, that when bidden to dinner, you receive payment in full for all your services. A meal is the return which your grand friendship yields you. . . So if after a couple of months it is his pleasure to invite his forgotten client, lest the third place on the lowest couch should be unoccupied, and he says to you, "Come dine with me" . . . . And what a dinner after all. You are given wine that fresh-clipped cotton would refuse to suck up. . . . Why, the water you clients drink is not the same! . . . See now that huge lobster being served to me lord, all garnished with asparagus . . . . Before you is placed on a tiny plate a shrimp hemmed in by half an egg—a fit banquet for the dead. (*Sat.* 5.80–85)

Ancient patronage was certainly *not* only about the balance sheet, but that the balance sheet might become a cause for concern is clear and natural in a relationship that was ostensibly about reciprocity *and* exchange. Recall for instance the 'balance sheet' conversions of Polemo in Lucian's *Double Indictment*, and Aristides' in how he left Sarapis in favour of Asclepius because of what he was *not* getting from Sarapis.

Although Osiek notes that there is a rhetorical element to Paul's language of loss and gain, she claims that it was not only rhetorical but also reflective of his own personal experience. Osiek, however, does not notice that the primary rhetorical trope within this passage is synkrisis, the comparison of Paul's past and present.[66] She recognises the fact that Paul credits God with what happened to him, but she misses that this too is the language of patronage

---

[66] Likewise, Fee talks about some rhetorical aspects of this section of the letter, visible "in a variety of literary devices" (*Philippians*, 311–12), but synkrisis is not one of them. He expends most of his effort highlighting structural elements such as chiasm.

and benefaction. Consequently, she misses the combination of these two elements, Paul's patronal synkrisis that honours God his patron even as parts of it comprise his own claim to honour. Osiek provides the start of an excellent model that other commentaries would be served well to imitate by recognising the socio-rhetorical function behind the mere face value of Paul's words.

4.4 Paul and the Patronage of Philosophy

All the elements of the rhetoric of patronage and benefaction that were outlined in the previous chapter have been seen to be present in Paul's conversion passage, with the exception of one: the philosopher as patron. In this section, I would like to look at the similarities between Paul and philosophers, though before doing so I must make clear what I hope to gain by doing so. As we saw previously, much of the rhetoric of philosophy operates within the same framework of religious patronage and benefaction along with the Graeco-Roman cults. That is, philosophers were seen to bestow benefactions in the form, most commonly, of teachings designed to bring salvation from slavery to ignorance and from suffering. Some of the rhetoric of patronage and benefaction is no different (or only slightly different allowing for the different scenarios) between cult and philosophy. It will be useful to look at the ways in which Paul resembles the philosophers as patrons of a certain teaching or view of life, or even as brokers bringing teachings that are actually derived from the gods. My point will not be to argue that Paul was himself a philosopher, or that the Jesus movement is understood best as a philosophy. Rather, it will be to invite the reader to consider the similarities between Paul and the philosophers of the day, similarities that we ought to assume were noticed by those who encountered Paul. Paul may well have been mistaken for a philosopher at times, and if this is the case, then we would do well to understand some of the implications of this for our understanding of patronage and conversion, perhaps less with regards to Paul than with regards to his converts.

Parallels between Paul and the Graeco-Roman philosophers have long been pointed out and their significance debated.[67] It has been argued many

---

[67] J. N. Sevenster, *Paul and Seneca* (NovTSup 4; Leiden: E. J. Brill, 1961); N. W. DeWitt, *St. Paul and Epicurus* (Toronto: The Ryerson Press, 1954); Robert L. Wilken, "Collegia, Philosophical Schools and Theology," in *The Catacombs and the Colosseum: The Roman Empire as the Setting of Primitive Christianity* (ed. S. Benko and J. J. O'Rourke; London and Valley Forge: Oliphants, 1972), 268–91; H. C. Kee, "Pauline Eschatology: Relationships with Apocalyptic and Stoic Thought," in *Glaube und Eschatologie: Festschrift für Werner Georg Kümmel zum 80. Geburtstag* (ed. E. Grässer

times that Paul was influenced by Stoic thought.⁶⁸ For instance, it is argued that the lengthy catalogue of virtues and vices found at Gal 5:16–23 has close parallels in Stoic writing (Seneca, *Ep.* 10.2–4); such catalogues are all the more revealing of some connection between Paul and Stoicism since, according to Longenecker, their use cannot be traced to Paul's Jewish roots.⁶⁹ Vocabulary that was commonplace in the ancient world but was nonetheless also typically Stoic can be found in Phil 4:8–9, 11 and 1 Cor 8:6.⁷⁰ The strongest parallel between Paul and Stoic influence, according to Richard Gibson, is found in Rom 1:18–32. Gibson writes,

> In analysing human rebellion, Paul employs a series of characteristically Stoic phrases. The antithesis between immortal and mortal (*aphthartos, phthartos*) in 1:23 is 'probably drawn ultimately from Stoic philosophy.' There is no genuine Hebrew antecedent for the concept of 'what is contrary to nature (*physis*)' (1:26). It is a common enough

---

and O. Merk; Tübingen: J. C. B. Mohr [Paul Siebeck], 1985), 135–58; Abraham J. Malherbe, *Paul and the Thessalonians: The Philosophic Tradition of Pastoral Care* (Philadelphia: Fortress Press, 1987); idem, *Paul and the Popular Philosophers* (Minneapolis: Fortress Press, 1989); John W. Martens, "Romans 2:14–16: A Stoic Reading," *NTS* 40 (1994): 55–67; Nigel M. Watson, "'The Philosopher Should Bathe and Brush his Teeth'—Congruence Between Word and Deed in Graeco-Roman Philosophy and Paul's Letters to the Corinthians," *ABR* 42 (1994): 1–16; Bruce W. Winter, "Is Paul Among the Sophists?" *RTR* 53 (1994): 28–38; David E. Aune, "Human Nature and Ethics in Hellenistic Philosophical Traditions and Paul: Some Issues and Problems," in *Paul in his Hellenistic Context* (ed. T. Engberg-Pedersen; Minneapolis: Fortress Press, 1995), 291–312; Clarence E. Glad, *Paul and Philodemus: Adaptability in Epicurean and Early Christian Psychagogy* (NovTSup 81; Leiden: E. J. Brill, 1995); Bruce W. Winter, "'The Seasons' of this Life and Eschatology in 1 Corinthians 7:29–31," in *Eschatology in Bible & Theology: Evangelical Essays at the Dawn of a New Millennium* (ed. K. E. Brower and M. W. Elliott; Downers Grove, Ill.: InterVarsity Press, 1997), 323–34; idem, *Philo and Paul Among the Sophists* (Cambridge: Cambridge University Press, 1997); Graham Tomlin, "Christians and Epicureans in 1 Corinthians," *JSNT* 68 (1997): 51–72; Karin Lehmeier, "Gemeinschaft nach dem oikos-Modell: Philodem und Paulus im Vergleich," in *Text und Geschichte: Facetten theologischen Arbeitens aus dem Freundes- und Schülerkreis* (ed. S. Maser and E. Schlarb; Marburg: N. G. Elwert, 1999), 107–21; Peter G. Bolt, "The Philosopher in the Hands of an Angry God," in *The Gospel to the Nations: Perspectives on Paul's Mission* (ed. P. Bolt and M. Thompson; Downers Grove, Ill.: InterVarsity Press, 2000), 327–43; Richard J. Gibson, "Paul and the Evangelization of the Stoics," in *The Gospel to the Nations*, 309–26.

68 See Gibson, "Paul and the Evangelization of the Stoics," 313–18, for a recent survey of the issues.
69 Richard N. Longenecker, *Galatians* (WBC 41; Waco: Word, 1990), 250–52.
70 See Gibson, "Paul and the Evangelization of the Stoics," 314–15 for discussion of the parallels.

Greek idea, but Paul could hardly have been unaware of the crucial role it played in Stoic and Cynic accounts of virtue.[71]

It would be better of course if some of Paul's vocabulary were *exclusively* Stoic, but we are not trying to argue that Paul was himself a Stoic, nor even that he was conscious of his intellectual debt to them; parallels such as those identified by Gibson are sufficient to make the argument that Paul's *audiences* may have recognised the Stoic parallels to what he was saying and writing, and thus may themselves have made assumptions between the action he was asking for from them and what philosophers typically asked of them— namely philosophical conversion.

Abraham Malherbe has found extensive parallels between Paul and the Cynics. Malherbe argues that Paul was well acquainted with, spoke in the language, and used the imagery and argumentation of the popular Cynic philosophers of his day. For example, he traces the military imagery in 2 Cor 10:3–6 to two threads of Cynic self presentation. One tradition, he suggests, started by Antisthenes, used Odysseus, commonly criticised for his duplicity and guile, as a sort of proto-cynic (but was also used extensively by Stoics). Antisthenes presents the rational faculties as the wise man's fortifications (as did the Stoics, Epictetus, and Seneca after him).[72] In another interesting example, Malherbe argues that the "apology" of 1 Thess 2:1–12 sounds much like a popular philosopher attempting to distinguish him- or herself from less savoury or virtuous "philosophers," though he rules out the notion that Paul was in fact confused for one himself and thus rejects that the apology may have been real.[73]

Paul's usage of the peristasis catalogue is another feature of his writing that finds a distinct parallel among the writings of, in particular, Cynic and Stoic philosophers.[74] J. T. Fitzgerald looks at the numerous types of peristasis catalogues and concludes that Paul's are most analogous to those of the wise man, and especially of the Stoic sage. Philosophers understood hardship in a number of ways. Some saw them as tests from God designed to make them stronger; others saw them as in no way associated with the divine, but rather

---

71   Gibson, "Paul and the Evangelization of the Stoics," 316. Within the quote he cites J. D. G. Dunn, *Romans* (2 vols.; WBC 38; Waco: Word, 1988), 1:62. For Stoic and Cynic parallels, see Seneca, *Ep.* 39.6; Diogenes Laertius 7.87–89; Stobaeus, *Ecl.* 2.7.6; Cicero, *Fin.* 3.31; Epictetus, *Diatr.* 2.6.9.
72   Malherbe, *Paul and the Popular Philosophers*, 91–119.
73   I, and others, have disagreed. See Zeba Antonin Crook, "Paul's Praise and Riposte of the Thessalonians," *BTB* 27 (1997): 153–63.
74   J. T. Fitzgerald, *Cracks in an Earthen Vessel* (SBLDS 99; Atlanta: Scholars Press, 1988).

understood them to be chance events. Yet, unanimously, all agreed that hardships were never to destabilise the sage. Indeed the sage is marked by tranquillity in the face of vicissitudes and hardship. Again, Fitzgerald does not claim that the catalogues make Paul a Stoic sage. He suggests, and shows, that the model of the peristasis catalogue has a cultural foundation, and thus understanding Paul's use of such catalogues within that context is fruitful.

Many have taken issue with the drawing of such parallels between Paul and the philosophers of his day. Most go out of their way to argue that Paul is simply borrowing the language of the philosophers, but is not involved in anything other than the complete alteration of the meaning of such language. For example, of Cynic terminology in Philippians, O'Brien claims that Paul is not appealing "to some pagan religious ideal, much less to some wholesale acceptance of the norms and values of the world."[75] Likewise, Fee implies that comparing Paul's use of some terms to Cynic usage of them is fruitless, because Paul so profoundly changed (does he mean *Christianised*?) their meaning that they are, in effect, no longer the same term.[76] The scholars are right to object to calling Paul a Cynic, or some other popular philosopher, yet these examples show a profound discomfort with much less than even that: many will not accept even the likely hypothesis that Paul could have been influenced by popular philosophical ideas or language or that he might have found a certain compatibility with the philosophers in some ways. What is more, the opinions of O'Brien and Fee seem to presuppose another position few (explicitly) argue: that Paul was a Christian, evidenced by the fact that he borrowed terms from the culture but used them in a completely novel way. It does invite the question: how can someone who uses familiar terminology in a completely radical way expect to be understood by her or his audience? The position almost seems to presuppose that Paul was writing for audiences well into the future of the world and not for audiences anchored in their own time and cultural milieu.

It is one thing to object to a claim that was himself a card-carrying member of some popular philosophy (an argument that few would dare attempt anyway), but those who work so hard to deny even signs of possible influence usually miss the more salient point. Paul made frequent use of popular philosophical terminology and analogies that he did not derive from his Jewish heritage. He used philosophical and rhetorical tropes like peristasis catalogues in similar ways to the suffering sages who prove their virtue as people and philosophers. It seems almost certain that to the audiences of Graeco-Romans

---

[75] O'Brien, *Philippians*, 503.
[76] Fee, *First Epistle to the Corinthians*, 155.

certainly familiar with these popular philosophers, Paul would have appeared to them to be a philosopher with a different (but not entirely novel) message and method. The fact that it was not entirely novel is suggested by the number of parallels between Seneca and Paul. Later Christians we know thought Seneca was one of them; it stands to reason that first century Stoics could have thought Paul was one of *them*.[77] In fact, 1 Thess 2:1–12 appears to make this all but certain—the Thessalonians mistook Paul for the worst of the itinerant philosophers, or at the very least criticised Paul with the same sorts of accusations. This important point bears repeating: if later Christians mistook Seneca for a Christian, then it is possible that Graeco-Roman audiences could have mistaken Paul for an itinerant philosopher, or at least saw parallels between him and these people.

Along these same lines, Loveday Alexander has shown the extent to which the early Christian *ekklēsiai* mirrored the Hellenistic philosophical schools.[78] Indeed, she points out how Galen treated "both Judaism and Christianity as defective philosophies" and goes on to show that Galen might have had good cause to think of Paul's work along the same lines as the Hellenistic philosophical schools.[79] Perhaps most interesting for our purposes is her extension of David Sedley's observation concerning philosophical loyalty (which we will engage with greater detail in the following chapter). Philosophical schools, especially but, Sedley argues, not limited to the Epicureans, were well known for their near "religious" veneration of their long dead teachers. Sedley claims that "what gives philosophical movements their identity is less a disinterested quest for the truth than a virtually religious commitment to the authority of a founder figure."[80] This has obvious parallels with the Jesus movement that Paul worked to spread, but Alexander extends the parallel. She argues that while Paul would not have been teaching in "public" spheres, which Stanley Stowers has shown was allowed only for people of a certain status, teaching in "private" spheres does not imply that it happened behind closed doors.[81] Rather, people might still happen upon a

---

[77] Sevenster, *Paul and Seneca*, 10–14; Gibson, "Paul and the Evangelization of the Stoics," 311–12.

[78] L. Alexander, "Paul and the Hellenistic Schools: The Evidence of Galen," in *Paul in his Hellenistic Context*, 60–83.

[79] Alexander, "Paul and the Hellenistic Schools," 64.

[80] D. Sedley, "Philosophical Allegiance in the Greco-Roman World," in *Philosophia Togata: Essays on Philosophy and Roman Society* (ed. M. Griffin and J. Barnes; Oxford: Clarendon, 1989), 97.

[81] Stanley K. Stowers, "Social Status, Public Speaking and Private Teaching," *NovT* 26 (1984): 59–82.

"lesson," Pauline or Sophistic, taking place ostensibly in "private." Alexander suggests that one would find at such a lesson "an inner ring" of students or disciples who would not question their teacher in front of others who were present, and behind them those who happened upon the meeting and were either uncommitted or committed to another teacher and thus prone to hostility. She goes on to observe that one of the possible results of such an encounter, in addition to simply listening in or heckling, might have been conversion, "that is, a passerby may be attracted by the teacher and ask to be enrolled in the inner circle of disciples."[82] In the next chapter, we shall see more fully the relationship between patronage, loyalty and conversion. That is, in cases like this, conversion was marked by an expression or a change in loyalty. What is interesting here, and what will be developed in the following chapter, is the combination of honouring or pious behaviour towards the teacher/patron (disciples will not question him in public), and the idea that conversion is closely tied to loyalty and patronal affiliation. We may surmise that conversion in these cases did involve μετάνοια, changing of one's perspective, but first and foremost it involved recognising that the philosopher had benefactions to offer, and then taking on the role and expectations of a client.

The very phenomenon of conversion is another way in which the early Jesus movement has been compared with philosophical schools, going all way back of course to Nock's understanding of conversion and picked up by Malherbe.[83] Of course the overlap between the philosophies and the Jesus movement had to do with the emotional turmoil associated with each type of conversion. Yet, as we have already seen they also held in common a number of other features, all linked by the overarching institution of ancient Mediterranean patronage and benefaction. Conversion to Christianity, like conversion to a philosophy, involved *metanoia*; it also involved the bestowal

---

[82] Alexander, "Paul and the Hellenistic Schools," 76.
[83] Arthur D. Nock, *Conversion: The Old and the New in Religion from Alexander the Great to Augustine of Hippo* (London: Oxford University Press, 1933), chapter 11; Abraham J. Malherbe, "Conversion to Paul's Gospel," in *The Early Church and Its Context: Essays in Honor of Everett Ferguson* (ed. A. J. Malherbe et al.; NovTSup 90; Leiden: E. J. Brill, 1998), 230–44. For the relationship between philosophical and early Christian conversion, see also Mark D. Jordan, "Philosophic 'Conversion' and Christian Conversion: A Gloss on Professor MacMullen," *SecCent* 5 (1985–86): 90–96. P. S. MacDonald, "Philosophical Conversion," *Philosophy and Theology* 10 (1997): 303–27; Werner Jaeger, *Early Christianity and Greek Paideia* (Carl Newell Jackson Lectures; Cambridge: Harvard University Press, 1961); Everett Ferguson, *Backgrounds to Early Christianity* (2nd ed.; Grand Rapids: Eerdmans, 1993); Johannes Weiss, *Earliest Christianity: A History of the Period A. D. 30–150* (trans. F. C. Grant; New York: Harper and Row, 1959).

of teachings, a world-view, answers to questions concerning the origins and future of the universe. But most like philosophical conversion, conversion to the Jesus movement required exclusive loyalty, and its followers were disciples, students, or clients of the movement, expressing gratitude for what they had received.

This relationship between philosophy and conversion is carried on in the later Christian writer Justin. Justin was an educated Greek man who, after investigating several philosophies, settled on Christianity as his favourite philosophy. The way Justin portrays his conversion and the language he uses is found throughout many non-Christian accounts of philosophical conversion, but as Wilken says, this only serves to emphasise that he "wished to present his conversion to Christianity as a conversion to philosophy."[84]

If Paul had appeared to many like a philosopher, then we encounter another way in which he would have functioned within the framework of ancient patronage and benefaction. We saw, in the previous chapter, that part of the rhetoric of patronage and benefaction included that of the philosophers, whose teachings were benefactions in that they were designed to benefit listeners and those who embraced the teachings. In his travelling and teaching, in his attempts to benefit humanity with a share in the divine benefactions to which he was himself party, Paul would have looked every bit the part of the philosopher patron. This is the more interesting feature of the numerous parallels between Paul and the popular philosophers. It does not require us to conclude that Paul was a philosopher, or even that he consciously modelled himself on popular Hellenistic philosophers. It does, however, require us to acknowledge that Paul may have appeared to many to have been such a familiar figure, and even that such associations may have worked to his advantage more often than not.

4.5 Conclusion

By placing Paul in a context that is more his than ours, he ceases to be a man without precedent and peer. It seems too many commentators want Paul to be fully Christian as opposed to Jewish, even while they pay lip service to his Jewishness; but even more offensive it seems is any suggestion of Graeco-

---

[84] Robert L. Wilken, "Collegia, Philosophical Schools and Theology," 272. Christianity was not only hailed as a philosophy but also attacked as one by Galen, another Greek educated man who, unlike Justin, did not choose Christianity.

Roman influences. They also want him to be Christian as opposed to Hellenistic, implying that his Hellenism did not extend past his use of the Greek language. In the end, though, too often Paul ends up sounding modern, Christian, and quite unlike either a first-century Jew or Graeco-Roman. When we allow Paul to be a man and product of his culture, he ceases to be that all-important and paradigm-setting first Christian convert. Instead he becomes another example in a Mediterranean pattern of religion, or at the very least he fits into a Mediterranean pattern of the rhetoric of religion and patronage–benefaction.

Many have lamented that Paul says very little about his conversion experience. Paul's apparent lack of detail has resulted in three interpretive practices. In the first, scholars justify their reliance on Acts for biographical details in order to satisfy their own need for such details. In the second, Paul's lack of detail invites them or allows them to import their psychological cognitive framework in order to bring detail into the picture. Finally, Paul's lack of detail is read as unwillingness to be forthcoming concerning his experience of his conversion. Commentators often go on to say that since such an event must have been so important to Paul, his lack of detail must have been a conscious attempt to undervalue the experience, perhaps motivated by embarrassment or humility. But the fact is that Paul offers plenty of detail concerning his experience and understanding of his conversion. The explanatory model within which he operates is, like it was for so many of his ancient peers and predecessors, that of ancient religious patronage and benefaction. What so strongly recommends ancient religious patronage and benefaction as the best model for understanding ancient conversion, including Paul's, is precisely the manner in which it illuminates details that are already present in the text but have been unnoticed or misidentified for lack of the appropriate questions. That is, like the Oracle of Delphi, the text can only answer the questions it is asked. The model is also recommended by the way it provides such a full picture of Paul's life, both before and after his encounter with Jesus. It turns out that Paul's letters have not been so bereft of detail concerning his understanding of his conversion experience after all. Let me illustrate.

In the event of Paul's conversion, Paul's patron, obviously, did not change. God remained Paul's divine patron throughout his life. This is another way of saying that Paul died a Jew. As a Hellenised Jew, Paul would have understood that the God of the Jews was a profoundly generous divine benefactor. This god gave Paul's people (and Paul) a perpetual covenant, and God gave the Torah and the *mitzvot* as a means of allowing the Jews to identify themselves as members of the covenant community.⁸⁵ This God also benefacted humanity through creation. Benefactions that came from God in the form of protection and deliverance from enemies, as well as agricultural fecundity, were commemorated weekly and annually through scenes and events in which Jews thanked and honoured their divine benefactor. Pious Jews could not have been charged with neglecting their obligations to honour their divine patron, for they had many ways, some corporate and some personal, of bringing honour onto and expressing gratitude towards their divine patron. In Paul's case, this was to remain blameless under the Torah, and to harass those he felt dishonoured God or God's benefactions, in this case it appears the earliest Jesus movement. Perhaps Paul felt that people who went out of their way to alter the teachings of the Torah, assuming this was the case with the earliest Jesus movement, were an affront to God. One might justifiably speculate that the later Sicarii and the Zealots were also working to protect the honour of God, either against the Roman occupiers or the Jewish elite who were collaborating with them. At least, we know that such motivation would have been consistent with the cultural centrality of honour and patronage and benefaction. Thus, the wrong actions of people would dishonour God who had given them so much and whom dishonouring would insult.

While Paul's conversion did not involve a change in patron, it clearly involved a change of another type. When Paul discusses his life ἐν τῷ Ἰουδαϊσμῷ, he never explicitly mentions a broker, but one could argue, given the role he is credited with playing in the delivery of the Torah, that Moses was the broker between a Jewish client and her divine patron God. At the very least, Paul's broker changed from Moses (or possibly simply Torah) to Jesus.⁸⁶ The alternative to this portrait is that a broker was introduced into the relationship between God and Jewish believer where one had not existed before. Arguing that Moses or the Torah was a broker between God and believer cannot be undertaken too forcefully, since neither is ever referred to

---

85   So E. P. Sanders, *Paul and Palestinian Judaism: A Comparison of Patterns of Religion* (Philadelphia: Fortress Press, 1977).

86   Though he does not use the language of patronage and benefaction, I submit that throughout his *Paul and the Gentiles*, Donaldson's description of Paul's "reconfiguration" of convictions (as opposed to 'conversion') is consistent with what I am suggesting. Donaldson argues that Paul shifted "from a Torah-centered proselytism to a Christ-centered one" (242), uses phrases like "adherence to Christ, rather than to Torah" (296), and refers to Paul's "shift from Torah to Christ" (298). Donaldson's portrait of Paul is supported by the context and data of ancient patronage and benefaction.

with such terminology. In this work, however, I have not claimed that Second Temple Judaism had or knew a fully developed system of patronage and benefaction, but only that in many respects their portraits of their God and of their own conduct closely resembles that of people who did have a fully developed system of human and divine patronage and benefaction. More to the point, it is not until Hellenistic Jews began producing writings that we begin to see the explicit vocabulary and imagery of patronage and benefaction use of their relationship with their god. The result is a sort of pan-Mediterranean framework for understanding and expressing the relationships between humans and their gods. The primary difference appears to lie in the extent to which this framework was explicitly coded in their language.

Either way, whether or not one can claim that the Torah was Paul's previous broker, Paul claims that Jesus appeared to him, and he indicates that his conversion was the point at which he came to the realisation that behaviour he had always thought was honouring to his divine patron, namely harassing members of the *ekklēsia*, never had been. For some time now, Paul had been actively dishonouring God, it appeared to him, by harassing the Jesus movement. The way in which Paul expresses his understanding of this event is not lacking in detail. God remained Paul's divine patron unchanged. Throughout Paul's letters and the New Testament, Jesus is depicted solely as God's divine broker and thus is the agent through whom salvation was now to be attained. Since he was the deliverer of salvation, such a grand benefaction in the eyes of all Mediterranean people, the honour that had to be directed at Jesus was great, and because of this it became ever greater throughout the centuries and people mistook the role of the broker for that of the patron.

Paul came to express this vision of Jesus to him, and the initiation of an altered patronal relationship, as a benefaction from God. It was his Greek language and culture that gave him the vocabulary and the fully formed institution of patronage and benefaction (both religious and human) as the framework of his rhetoric. The vision was by far the most important benefaction Paul had received from his divine benefactor, though certainly only one of many to which Paul alludes to having received both before and after his conversion. The gratitude that Paul had originally directed only at God was now to be directed at God *and*, appropriately, at God's broker Jesus. Both are honoured and are the recipients of Paul's words and actions of praise, gratitude, and loyalty. Significantly, however, in the letters of Paul, Jesus as broker is always subordinate to God as divine patron. The confusion of the two for one is a later theological development that, from the perspective of patronage and benefaction, would have appeared foreign to Paul. Paul is consistent on this: Jesus *must* be honoured—as God's broker his benefactions are utterly indispensable to Paul—but he is the broker and not therefore to be confused with the divine patron. Indeed, such a confusion would have been quite insulting to the patron. Imagine somebody worshipping the priest (or broker) of Asclepius rather than Asclepius and what this would have communicated to the god.

In so consistently associating the mission to the gentiles with the benefaction of the vision, Paul shows that his mission (and therefore his status as apostle) is to be understood within that category of client behaviour that seeks to gain converts and proselytes. Of course, new converts, resembling a larger retinue for a human patron, brings increased honour to any god. This is not unique behaviour to Paul, even if one wished to argue that Paul took it to a new level of intensity. The magnitude of Paul's response may simply reflect his perception of the magnitude of the benefaction he received. Paul frequently emphasises the effort he made in this regard; it is not inappropriate for a client to ensure there is no misunderstanding concerning the fulfilment of his or her obligations. Also, Paul's patronal synkriseis are designed to honour the patron and broker for the good effect of their benefactions. So much Paul does and writes is designed to bring increased honour to his divine patron, whether by his own actions or through the actions of others. And finally, so many of Paul's actions among his Graeco-Roman peers would have appeared of a piece with the Hellenistic philosophers of his day.

For Paul, as for his ancient peers and predecessors, the language of cult and philosophy and thus the language of conversion is the language of ancient human and divine patronage and benefaction. There is no other way to account for the prevalence of such language in so much "religious" narrative from the ancient world other than to conclude that the language of "religion" was the language of patronage and benefaction. Throughout Paul's conversion narratives, just as throughout his letters in general, there is consistent and abundant detail in the language of divine patronage and benefaction concerning his conversion and his relationship with his God. What most recommends this model for understanding religion and religious experience in the ancient Mediterranean, from the religions of the Greeks and Romans to those of the Jews and Christians, is that it explains so much and does so in their own language. There is much to be said for describing and analysing Paul's conversion with language and analogies that Paul himself would have recognised. The same cannot be claimed for psychological explanations and analogical descriptions of ancient religion or of Paul's conversion. Paul uses the language of patronage and benefaction in his theological thinking and in his biographical narratives, such as his conversion passages. Seeing this allows us to understand Paul and his religious experiences very nearly through his own eyes, not through Luke's eyes, nor through the "corrective lenses" of modern individualistic and psychologically framed spectacles.

Chapter Five

Patronage and Benefaction, Loyalty, and Conversion

5.0 Introduction

I have, thus far, attempted to establish and draw connections between a number of related phenomena in the ancient world. The first is that the widespread *fact* of patronage and benefaction in the real world was wholly matched by the equally widespread *perception* of patronage and benefaction between humans and their gods. The second is that the language of conversion in the ancient world was composed of the rhetoric of patronage and benefaction shared with its human counterpart. These are both important because of what they tell us about the ancient understanding of interaction with the gods and with their philosophers—in effect, ancient religion.

First and foremost, patronage was a concrete relationship that was defined by the exchange of goods and reciprocity between two (sometimes among three) entities. Patronage, as we saw, is not primarily an emotional or psychological category. It is revealing then that Paul too relies on the rhetoric of patronage when he talks about his conversion and his relationship with his God. Based on this cultural construct, Paul's conversion experience is about the ensuing relationship primarily and not primarily about his emotional or psychological state. From what we know about the construction of identity in the ancient world, it is safe to conclude that Paul's conversion would not have been an *essentially* internalised and introspective experience. To put it another way, while it is hard to believe that some degree of introspection would be wholly absent from Paul's conversion experience (and, for the record, I am not making any such claim), what seems likely is that this feature was not the primary or defining characteristic of that experience, and hence would have been quite different from its modern counterpart.

If ancient conversion occurred within the conceptual, linguistic, and experiential framework of patronage and benefaction, then ancient conversion must have been, in essence, some change in a patronal relationship. Yet, there is something quite unsatisfactory about a definition of religious or philosophical conversion that makes it nothing more than a business transaction (which we might characterise as sterile or commercial). It is abundantly clear that ancient conversion, even while it was cast in the framework of patronage and benefaction, did involve more than the accounting balance sheet of revenues and expenditures.

There was indeed a dynamism to ancient conversion, though our access to it is not through psychology or presuppositions of emotional universalism but through an understanding of the role of loyalty in the relationship between the patron or benefactor and her or his client. Understanding how loyalty was expressed and how loyalty changed will complement our understanding of ancient conversion considerably, for it will show that there was something at stake in ancient conversion. The important place of loyalty in the patron-benefactor and client relationship reveals that the change from one patron or benefactor to another, in whatever context, involved more than a simple and unencumbered change in recipients and benefactors. A change within patronage relationships carried consequences, it communicated socially meaningful messages that would have been embedded in honour and public reputation. Loyalty allows for the possibility of an emotional component to enter into the model of ancient conversion, but it is most helpful because it does not rely on emotion for its central or defining characteristic.

In this chapter I discuss the nature of loyalty, establishing that, according to the ancient sources and illustrations, loyalty was a set of behaviours, it was not a feeling. The important distinction here is that loyalty was not an internal state of mind as much as it was an external set of actions. From there I treat three types of loyalty that arise in relationship to three different relationships: Imperial, manumission, and philosophical loyalty. Each of these is useful in terms of our present topic of conversion for a number of reasons.

Imperial loyalty, that is loyalty to the Emperor on the part of allied client-kings, is the best place to start in order to establish the critical relationship between patronage or benefaction and the phenomenon of loyalty. It will not, however, help us to understand loyalty and conversion, since I have not been able to find examples of client-kings changing patrons. And yet, there are other gains to be had by looking at this kind of loyalty. There is a clear relationship between the language of kingship and the language of divinity and therefore of conversion. In other words, kings existed on a continuum that included the gods as holders of honour and power and as benefactors of humanity. Loyalty to the emperor and loyalty to one's divine patrons were cut from the same cloth, and the political realm provided the ancients with many useful analogies for casting their relationship with the gods.

Treating manumission loyalty will enable us to establish several important aspects of loyalty and conversion in a context of patronage and benefaction. Firstly, it shows the central place that loyalty occupied within the patron-benefactor and client relationship. Where loyalty was clearly a concern in all forms of patronage and benefaction, in settings of manumission attempts were made to even legislate loyalty. Further, few forms of patronage and benefaction appear to have bred such anger at signs of disloyalty as did manumission relationships. Manumission loyalty also offers us insights into how ancient conversion might look in a context of patronage and benefaction, for slaves did not change patrons when they attained their freedom, but rather underwent a considerable change *within* the patronal relationship. That is, their patron often remained the same, but the relationship between them changed. Features of manumission loyalty, such as the changing of one's name as a way of signifying one's attachment to the patron (as well as a way of advertising the generous benefaction of the patron) also find immediate parallels in some forms of cultic conversion.

Philosophical loyalty also offers important insight into the relationship between loyalty, patronage and benefaction, and conversion. Philosophical conversion can involve the wholesale change of patrons, but it can also commonly involve what appears to have been a change in the patronal relationship, a change of patrons but done while remaining loyal to the philosophical movement as a whole. Further, philosophical loyalty illustrates very well the dynamics of disloyalty and its relationship to conversion. Together, these three types of loyalty in patronage settings illustrate that loyalty was a tremendously important feature of patron-benefactor and client interaction, and if we are to understand conversion within this framework, then we need to understand the role that loyalty plays within it.

5.1 The Nature of Loyalty

In order to talk about the nature of loyalty, the best place to start is with an analysis of the word that comes closest to representing the meaning "loyalty" in the Roman world, the Latin term *fides*. The general institution of patronage and benefaction was, as we have seen throughout this work, common in various forms throughout much of the ancient Mediterranean. It was also, however, worked out with a far greater degree of clarity and detail by the

Romans than it was by any other group. The Greeks certainly had as full an understanding of the rules and expectations of patronage, as did Jewish writers near the turn of the common era who had been strongly Hellenised, but it was the Romans who spent the greater effort explaining the "rules." As a result, it is the Romans who have the greater range of vocabulary for the different features of the institution, and who provide us with the abundance of sources. Starting with the Roman sources provides us with a context for understanding our Greek sources and vocabulary better. So, I shall start with *fides* and then look to the Greek near-equivalent πίστις.

Fides is an extraordinarily rich word, reflecting profoundly diverse meanings and functioning in diverse contexts. Sixteenth-century writers, who tended to be well-versed in classical literature and were themselves immersed in a culture of patronage and benefaction, were well aware of the diversity of meanings for *fides*. One in particular writes:

> That which in Latin is called *Fides* is a part of justice and may diversely be interpretted, and yet finally it tendeth to one purpose in effect. Sometime it may be called faith, sometime credence, other whiles trust. Also in a French term it is named loyalty. And to the imitation of Latin it is often called fidelity. All which words, if they be entirely and (as I might say) exactly understood, shall appear to a studious reader to signify one virtue or quality, although they seem to have some diversity. As believing the precepts and promise of God it is called faith. In contracts between man and man it is commonly called credence. Between persons of equal estate or condition it is named trust. From the subject or servant to his sovereign or master it is properly named fidelity, and in a French term loyalty.[1]

What is interesting about this sixteenth-century quote is that though Elyot was an English speaker, and thus struggling with the same language gap as us, he was reading the language of *fides* as one who was, unlike us, firmly embedded in a context of patronage and benefaction. It is perhaps what allows him to associate *fides* with loyalty more readily than we might tend towards.

---

[1] Sir Thomas Elyot, *The Book Named the Governor*, originally published in 1531 (ed. S. E. Lehmberg; London: Dent, 1962), 172.

Modern scholarly work on *fides*, as the following notes will reveal, has remained centred in Europe (as opposed to North America) largely. In keeping with the title of his book, *Le vocabulaire latin des relations et des partis politiques sous la république*, Hellegouarc'h places *fides* mostly in the context of political life, but it is still worth looking at his general definition of the term. He writes that *fides* is

> the bond (*le lien*) that unites those, whoever they might be, who struggle for the same political goal. It expresses above all the relationship (*le rapport*) that develops between a client and his patron.[2]

Hellegouarc'h shows that *fides* is part of the many domains of political life in the Roman Empire, including friendship, love, obedience, power, fellowship, benevolence, patronage and tutelage. He focuses, however, on the *fides* of the patron and of the client, emphasising that *fides* is supposed to be characteristic of both parties in such a relationship. Yet he shows too that it is critical not to confuse the *fides* of the patron with the *fides* of the client, for while the terminology is the same, the different positions of power make for a very different meaning. He observes that "the difference of obligations leads to a different nuance in the appropriate meaning of the word."[3] The difference in power between the patron and client means that the obligation of *fides* on the part of each in the relationship carries a very different weight. Hellegouarc'h claims that *fides* on the part of the patron (that is directed at the client) is mostly associated with protection, and with a sense with credit (since it is a short step from "the capacity for protection" to "protection"; hence, credit for some benefaction before it is carried out).[4] On the other hand, he claims that *fides* of the client (that is directed at the patron) refers most commonly to *loyauté*, but he warns that when it comes to the patron "le mot latin n'a pas dans ce domains la même extension que le terme abstrait du français" (nor, of course, of the English word 'loyalty').[5] Nonetheless, *fides* on the part of the patron is an ideal, something that is hoped for, and the absence or neglect of which cannot be regulated against or much resisted. The most a neglected

---

[2] J. Hellegouarc'h, *Le vocabulaire latin des relations et des partis politiques sous la république* (Paris: Les Belles Lettres, 1963), 23.
[3] Hellegouarc'h, *Le vocabulaire*, 32.
[4] Hellegouarc'h, *Le vocabulaire*, 31.
[5] Hellegouarc'h, *Le vocabulaire*, 30.

client can do is complain, or write satires if they are so lucky, neither of which really amounts to any substantial action at all.[6]

The *fides* of the client on the other hand carries a weightier obligation because of the place of need which the client inhabits and because of the place of power that the patron inhabits. The patron can demand *fides*, directly or indirectly, from the client, but the client can demand nothing from the patron. The place of the client in the patron-benefactor and client relationship compels *fides*, or as Freyburger has concluded, the client had a certain *obligation of loyalty* towards the patron that the patron lacks towards the client.[7] For this reason, we should think of client and patron *fides* as nearly completely different phenomena, the one real and concrete, the other ideal and abstract.

As a result, we should expect client *fides* to look very different from patronal *fides*. *Fides*, according to Hellegouarc'h, of a client is "the act of having confidence which results in the support of the client."[8] Here Hellegouarc'h points to the words of Cicero, "fides est firma opinio" (*Part. or.* 9), in the sense that *fides* is the steadfast and, it goes without saying, the positive opinion that the client holds of the patron. Hellegouarc'h calls this aspect of client *fides* the reciprocal side of protection as patronal *fides*; both are active forms of *fides* and both represent what is needed most by both parties—the client needs above all the security offered by a patron and a patron needs above all the honour and personal high status offered by having clients. Freyburger emphasises the relationship aspect of *fides* in his definitions, in that he holds *fides* to entail two component parts—'bonne foi' and 'loyauté.' 'Bonne foi,' he explains, is "l'intention droite" and 'loyauté' is "le respect d'un engagement."[9]

There lies in the background of these various definitions and discussions of loyalty an important feature that warrants being made explicit. Loyalty was not an internal quality but rather an external action (or set of actions). This will be amply confirmed by the ancient sources. That loyalty was not an internal quality is really suggested by two features of it. First, while we have some examples in which loyal behaviour is accompanied by emotional attachment, there are too many other examples in which loyalty and possibly

---

[6] R. Heinze, "Fides," *Hermes* 64 (1929): 151. While ancient critical authors risked punishment (like exile—Ovid) for their writings, there is no evidence to suggest that Horace, Juvenal, or Martial were punished for dishonouring people more powerful than them, suggesting in turn that their satires must not have been terribly effective.

[7] G. Freyburger, *Fides: Étude sémantique et religieuse depuis les origines jusqu'à l'époque augustéenne* (Paris: Les Belles Lettres, 1986), 153.

[8] Hellegouarc'h, *Le vocabulaire*, 32.

[9] Freyburger, *Fides*, 49.

hostility co-exist. That is to say, we will see instances where one might be considered loyal despite having *feelings* of hostility towards the client or benefactor, and never is there any suggestion that there was a problem with this. Secondly, we know of attempts to *legislate* 'loyalty' (in the case of freedperson loyalty, as we shall see below), which suggests that the conduct of loyalty was what they were after, and not the feeling of loyalty. Surely such legislators did not expect that they could legislate feelings or internal emotional states; it is most likely they expected only to legislate actions or behaviour. Feelings of affection were clearly not necessary conditions for the existence of loyalty; the necessary conditions existed solely in the appropriate actions expressing loyalty. The result of the following examples suggests that we should understand loyalty as an action, and not even as action that reflects internal emotions, since it is clear that we cannot take the presence of those emotions for granted.[10]

Let us consider a number of examples of loyalty (and some of disloyalty) in order to illustrate these two points. Seneca (*Ben.* 3.25) tells the story of a slave who, when his master had been called to fight in the civil war, hid his master away and presumed his identity to those who arrived at the house to conscript him. Seneca is highly impressed that the slave was willing to die in the war to save his master from that fate; he characterises it as "*rara . . . fides*," or "a rare show of loyalty." He also goes on to commend the slave to his reader for coveting "death as a reward for loyalty." We should not imagine that the relationship between slave and master here was devoid of emotion, say sincere feelings of respect and affection. Nonetheless, we must not lose sight of the fact that what marks loyalty in this story is the action and we actually have no idea what the slave *felt* about his master.[11]

The Roman historian Sallust describes an interesting case of loyalty in his *Bellum jugurthinum*. He writes about Nabdalsa who received a letter outlining a plot to overthrow the king Jugurtha (*Bell. Jug.* 71). However, we are told, Nabdalsa fell asleep promptly with the letter on the pillow above his head because he had just exercised and was tired. When Nabdalsa's Numidian

---

[10] A helpful distinction might be found in romantic love, which one might argue also requires a relationship or behaviour in order to be manifest. Yet, in contrast to loyalty, we would reject something as authentic romantic love if we learned that loving *actions* were accompanied by *feelings* of animosity or hostility. This is because romantic love *is* primarily an emotion that can find external expression, whereas loyalty is primarily an external expression (an action) that can sometimes include authentic *feelings* of affection. Simply put, the one is an emotion while the other is an action.

[11] Freyburger, *Fides*, 51.

secretary, whom Sallust describes as very loyal (*fidus*), heard a letter had arrived, he went into Nabdalsa's sleeping quarters and, as was his custom and in keeping with his loyalty, retrieved the letter so that he could anticipate what services might be required of him. But discovering the plot in the letter, he departed immediately to notify the king. Of course, when Nabdalsa awoke to find the letter missing, he knew immediately what had happened. He tried to overtake the secretary on the way to the king, but eventually went directly to the king to explain that he himself had every intention of letting the king know of the arrival of this letter. Interestingly, Nabdalsa describes his secretary to the king as *perfidia clientis*, charging him, of all things, with being disloyal. Such a charge would serve as a claim that the secretary's action was an illustration not so much of his loyalty to the crown, but as disloyalty to his master for not having the confidence that his master would act appropriately. Yet clearly, the secretary had to make a choice on discovery of the plot: to be loyal to Nabdalsa, or to be loyal to the king and doubt his master. The story illustrates the complex web of loyalties that can arise—it goes without saying that the secretary must be loyal to his master since he works for him, and loyal to the King, since he is a citizen of the city. And of course, Nabdalsa needs also to be loyal to the king for this same reason: Sallust claims that Nabdalsa wept before the king and drew attention to his own status (*amicitia*) as the king's long-loyal client and promised his loyal service, or literally, acts of loyalty (*fideliter acta*).

Note that the many examples of loyalty on the parts of clients in this story are measured by the actions associated with each of them. The secretary loyally informs the king of the plot, which is itself a clear act of disloyalty to the master; the secretary is charged with disloyalty for acting against Nabdalsa, but in doing so his actions have been loyal to the king; Nabdalsa fears being seen as disloyal for acting against the king; and he promises to be loyal by acting only in the interests of the king in general and into the future. Of course the King was not the direct patron of the secretary, yet nonetheless, the King is patron and benefactor of all—one does not need to be a direct client of the king in order to be charged with disloyalty (i.e., sedition).

In the other of his history books, *De Catilinae coniuratione* (19), Sallust describes the mysterious death of Piso, a Roman general, at the hands of his own cavalry. Martial law always has demanded and expected loyalty to one's commanding officers, as the serious ramifications of being charged with insubordination or mutiny suggest. Obviously, questions of loyalty abound in a case like this, and Sallust does not claim to be able to answer any of them. One explanation he offers though is that perhaps the cavalry could not endure the command of the nasty or corrupt Piso. This of course would be, as it still is, a serious breach of loyalty, though as Sallust presents the character of Piso, he implies a considerable amount of empathy for the actions of the soldiers. The other possible explanation Sallust offers is that perhaps the cavalry were the loyal clients (*fidos clientis*) not of Piso of course but of Pompey, Piso's enemy.[12] In this case, the actions of the cavalry would have been actions of loyalty to Pompey. There is no way of knowing which of Sallust's suggestions is the more likely; my point here is not to weigh in on either side of the issue, nor certainly to suggest that loyalty is easily counted on or always where you expect it, but rather to show that *fides* is measured by one's actions. Regardless of whether the soldiers were loyal clients of Pompey, they clearly decided they were *not* loyal to Piso, as their actions towards him amply attest.

One of Terence's plays (*Andria*) opens with a conversation between Simo and his freedman Sosia (a relationship, as we shall see below, that was of patron and client). At the request for his ear, Sosia assumes he is about to be asked to cook something (29–30), the skill that probably won the man his manumission. But it is not this particular quality of Sosia that Simo seeks in this instance, but rather something he claims he has long known to be present in his freedman, namely his *fides* (33). What will be the evidence of Sosia's *fides*? A sham wedding is being organised so that Simo can trap and rebuke his son (who has secretly impregnated a woman of lower status), and Simo wishes Sosia to support the plan (and thus the patron) by observing the son's movements and not letting him realise anything is afoot (155–169). Again, *fides* is a quality of the client, but it is measured solely in terms of its manifestation in action that supports the patron. For Sosia to let Simo's son know what was about to happen would be to show disloyalty to his patron, and it would make of the son his patron.

These examples support Hellegouarc'h's claim that *fides* is not an internal disposition (he uses the more problematic term 'moral') resident in one regardless of whether it is ever manifested in actual behaviour, but rather that it is a social quality. Yet these examples also show that neither was *fides* an emotional quality. Here Cicero weighs in again. We encountered above his definition of *fides* as "firma opinio" but delayed reading on in the text at that point. Cicero is in the process of contrasting *fides* and *motus* (emotion). He

---

[12] Stephan Joubert claims that "unpropertied citizens . . . viewed their military commanders as patrons and showed 'clientele allegiance' to them" (Stephan Joubert, *Paul as Benefactor* [WUNT 2.124; Tübingen: J. C. B. Mohr (Paul Siebeck), 2000], 25–26), but offers no examples.

writes, fides "is a firmly established opinion, while emotion is the excitement of the mind to either pleasure or annoyance or fear or desire" (*Part. or.* 9).[13] This illustrates that loyalty (*fides*) resides in the *relationship* of two people, mainly client and patron or benefactor; it is evidenced only in the way that such a relationship is expressed and not in any resident *feelings* or emotional states. That is, loyalty is found in the positive actions that a client takes to protect his patron from enemies, that he takes to increase the honour and public reputation of his patron, and that he takes simply to reflect well on his patron. Loyalty may in some instances involve elements of emotion, but as Hellegouarc'h says, "l'action de *fides* n'est pas limitée au domaine intérieur; le mot definit aussi relations. . . ."[14] This thought is echoed also by Fabre. Speaking about *fides* in the patron–freedman relationship, Fabre puts it best when he says that "elle [*fides*] n'est pas liée à une certaine sentimentalité ou limitée au domaine de l'affection pure." In fact, to focus too much on the emotional aspects of *fides* conceals the very "réalités matérielles" of *fides*.[15]

Another example of how *fides* cannot be assumed to be an emotional category comes to us from a section of one of Plautus' plays. In his *Miles gloriosus* (or, *The Braggart Warrior*) a slave grabs a young girl whom he is willing to release only on the condition that she be loyal to him (that is, that he can count on her to do what he wants of her). The slave might demand the loyalty of the girl (we are not told her status), but in such circumstances he surely does not expect *affection* from her. In other words, it is remarkable that had she agreed to be loyal to him, he likely would have believed her, yet surely he would not have thought she liked him (or some other category of emotional affection). Her *fides* would not have been measured by way of her feelings or affection for the slave, but only by way of her actions towards him. Had she done his will, regardless of her predictable animosity towards him, she would have been perceived as loyal. As it happens, as soon as the slave lets her go, she goes her own way and makes clear she will not be loyal to him. Her sign of "disloyalty" (only from the perspective of the slave of course) is that he cannot count on her to support him, since clearly her feelings towards him did not likely change from one moment to the next—in each she would have been equally ill-disposed against him. Loyalty, or *fides*, is not about the feeling of warmth, affection, or friendship; it is the expression of the bond through the appropriate and honouring actions of the client. We

---

[13] The translation is that of H. Rackham in the Loeb Classical Library series.
[14] Hellegouarc'h, *Le vocabulaire*, 35.
[15] Georges Fabre, *Libertus: Recherches sur les Rapports Patron–Affranchi à la fin de la République Romaine* (Rome: École Française de Rome, 1981), 228.

can easily imagine other scenarios where loyalty might co-exist with feelings of animosity—a client of an exploitative patron, a slave of a harsh master, etc.

While Greek lacks a single term for loyalty like the Latin enjoys with *fides*, it certainly could not be claimed that the lack of such a term in Greek represents the lack of a concern or understanding of loyalty in Greek culture. What Latin has in the form of a single word that so frequently translates as loyalty, Greek has in a number of words that can be used to express loyalty. For example, εὐσέβεια was used to express loyalty to the Emperors (Claudius in *P.Lond.* 3.1178.14; Nero in *SIG*² 814.2), a usage that is particularly meaningful in the context of the Emperor cults and how one expresses *piety* towards a patron.[16] Sophocles uses two different words that both carry the meaning of loyalty. First he refers to those who were in no way one's 'loyals' (i.e., friends[17]) with the term δίκαιος (*Ant.* 292), and then he refers to loyalty to the divine law with the term εὐνομία (*Ajax* 713; *P. Agon.* 6).[18] Homer speaks of a servant who is loyal to his master's house with the term ἐρίηρος (*Od.* 1.346). One must grant, however, that loyalty is not the usual meaning of these terms.

Loyalty is far more commonly an element, on the other hand, of the words πιστός and πίστις. The πιστ- root words reflect a remarkably broad range of meanings. In the field of New Testament studies, we are most accustomed to them referring to 'faith,' but we should remain open to the likelihood that the πιστ- root words carry connotations that the English 'faith' alone might not.[19]

---

[16] That piety has to do with patronage and loyalty is suggested by several very different texts: Cicero claims that piety to the gods is equal parts gratitude and reverence (*Planc.* 80); Plutarch associates impiety with atheism (*Superst.* 169f–170a); see also *IG* II² 1297.16; 1283.27; 1327.28. See also the entry on *pietas* in C. T. Lewis and C. Short, *A Latin Dictionary* (Oxford: Clarendon Press, 1962), which shows the strong relationship between piety and appropriate actions towards patrons and benefactors, including an association with loyalty.

[17] The context is a discussion of men who were rebelling against an edict of Creon. "Friends" for δίκαιος is the suggested translation of Elizabeth Wykoff in *Greek Tragedies*, vol. 1 (ed. D. G. Greene and R. Lattimore; Chicago: University of Chicago Press, 1960).

[18] See also Dio Chrysostom's *First Discourse on Kingship* (*1 Regn.*) in which he uses the term εὔνους (of good mind) in the sense of loyalty, illustrated in the Loeb translation of J. W. Cahoon.

[19] On this point, see Paul Ellingworth, "More About Faith: Synopsis of a Discussion between Daniel D. Arichea and Eugene Botha," *TBT* 38 (1987): 330–32; Bruce J. Malina and Jerome H. Neyrey, *Portraits of Paul: An Archaeology of Ancient Personality* (Louisville: Westminster John Knox Press, 1996), 167–68. Louw and Nida's lexicon based on semantic domains follows the same course as with χάρις (see Chapter Three, p. 139, note 86). They offer for the various πιστ- root words a very closely

These words can connote, in addition to faith in the cultic/religious sense, faithfulness, steadfastness, trustworthiness in the sense of loyalty between parties. There are places in the New Testament where πίστις can mean nothing other than 'faith' in the way it has been traditionally interpreted, say, when people are said to become "obedient to the faith" (Acts 6:7). Yet there are also a number of places where πίστις makes equal or better sense as loyalty. Even in instances where these words cannot be directly translated as loyalty/loyal, they frequently reflect conduct that is consistent with such meanings.[20]

That πιστός and πίστις function as Greek parallels for the Latin *fidelis* and *fides* is suggested most strenuously by the testimony of the Vulgate. In every single instance the Vulgate translates πιστός as *fidelis* and πίστις as *fides*. Can we then assume that πίστις carried some of the same connotations as *fides* in order to recommend such a translation? There are indications in the Greek use of πιστός and πίστις that such an association with *fides* in the sense of loyalty was indeed warranted. Most of the evidence marshalled in this section is designed to illustrate not that πίστις meant loyalty but that at times loyalty was the dominant characteristic that πίστις was describing. So, for example, Demosthenes describes the Greeks as πιστῶς towards their fellow Greeks, which has been translated as "faithful," though 'loyal' avoids the confusing association between 'faith' and 'faithful' (3 *Olynth.* 3.26).[21] The third-century B.C.E. tactician Aeneas, when writing about how to guard a city during a festival (22.15–18), suggests that only the wealthy and most honoured citizens (ἐντιμοτάτους) should be sentinels, since they would have the most to lose by

---

related semantic range—trust, belief, religious belief. It may be the case that *in the New Testament*, πίστις has mostly to do with faith, but there are also occasions when fencing off New Testament vocabulary from uses common in Hellenistic usage is misleading.

[20] In *Oedipus Tyrannus*, for instance, Sophocles talks about consulting the god to learn desirable courses of action (lines 1438–1439, 1442–1443), and in one instance embellishes upon this with the word πίστις to say "Now even you will trust the god." Even while the context suggests a meaning of "you will trust" over "you will be loyal towards," trust in and faithfulness to the god is quite consistent with the conditions of loyalty. Dennis R. Lindsay reads this as evidence of an early Greek usage of πίστις as religious faith, but note also, in keeping with the nature of loyalty, that this πίστις is measured by the actions of Oedipus: faith in a god is measured by one's willingness to consult their oracles and to trust/believe in what they read (*Josephus and Faith: Πίστις and Πιστεύειν as Faith Terminology in the Writings of Flavius Josephus and in the New Testament* [AGJU 19; Leiden: E. J. Brill, 1993]). Along these same lines, see other examples Lindsay offers of this in *Josephus and Faith*, 11–13.

[21] For instance, in Demosthenes, *Works* (trans. J. H. Vince; LCL; Cambridge: Harvard University Press, 1962).

becoming distracted by pleasures (22.15). Next he suggests that especially during feasts, those who are viewed with suspicion (ὕποπτος) by their peers and thought to be disloyal (ἄπιστος) should be sent out to enjoy the festival (22.16). It is not only distraction (say, by the festival) that Aeneas is worried about, for he goes on to say that if such people are sent to celebrate they will think they are being rewarded but will be unable to plot anything (πράσσω). The distraction of pleasure Aeneas referred to above might have more to do with the pleasure of wealth (through bribery) than the distraction of celebrating crowds. What is more, the benefit of this move is that it will enable one to replace unreliable men with men who are more loyal (πιστοτέρως) than these (22.17) without raising suspicion.[22]

The πιστ- root words clearly share a considerable area of overlap with *fides* as loyalty as opposed to the traditional translation as 'faith.' Dio Chrysostom describes that a king's ability to maintain stability and control is less the result of his wealth and his armies but rather has everything to do with the loyalty of his friends—ὡς τῇ πίστει τῶν φίλων (3 *Regn*. 86). And again from Dio Chrysostom, a king cannot depend on laws for stability, but rather upon loyalty—πίστις (3 *Regn*. 88). Finally, a first-century stele has a slave owner bury and grieve his aged slave whom he describes as "faithful" or "loyal" with the word πιστόν.[23]

The relationship between πίστις and loyalty in a cultic context is reflected in Sir 15:15. In the context of relating those benefactions that God has given to humans, the author relates that humans thereby have a choice to act either with loyalty or with disloyalty towards the divine patron: "If you wish, you can abide by the commandments, and to act πίστιν is a matter of choice." Most translate πίστιν ποιῆσαι here as "to act faithfully," but the reference to action, to keeping God's commandments, to avoiding those things that God considers abominations (15:12–13) all make this consistent with the actions of loyalty. At the very least, this is completely consistent with loyalty as we have seen it operating already in numerous other places. Consider the benefactions that for Philo derive from ἡ πρὸς θεὸν πίστις: "consolation of life, fulfilment of bright hopes, dearth of ills, harvest of goods, rejection of misery, knowledge of piety, inheritance of happiness" (*Abr*. 268).[24] The context is one of divine patronage and benefaction; 'loyalty to God' best captures the sense of the phrase. Loyalty to a patron or benefactor results (ideally) in benefactions

---

[22] See also Xenophon, *Hell*. 2.4.30.
[23] *SEG* XXVIII 1033; also *NewDocs* 3.10.
[24] The language of πίστις πρός as 'loyalty to' is found also in Thucydides 4.51 and Lysias, *Speeches* 19.32.

being bestowed. As strict monotheists, it was (exclusive) loyalty to God that set the Jews apart from their Mediterranean peers and that led to many problems in their encounters with Hellenistic culture. It was not only faith in the one God that Jews maintained, but also loyalty to that God alone, a loyalty that would be undermined by the acknowledgement of other Gods. All this and more is contained in the word πίστις.

New Testament usage of πίστις/πιστός also reflects a shared domain with loyalty; the root sometimes indicates as much 'faith' as it does 'loyalty.' That loyalty is frequently an element of the πιστ- root words is evident from the context of the term. As I said above, sometimes the context suggests no other option than 'faith,' usually in the claims that the Jesus movement was making of Jesus. Other places allow for another nuance, however. For example, 3 John 5 reads Ἀγαπητέ, πιστὸν ποιεῖς ὃ ἐὰν ἐργάσῃ εἰς τοὺς ἀδελφοὺς καὶ τοῦτο ξένους—which most certainly could be translated "Friends, you act loyally whenever you work for the brothers and sisters and especially foreigners."[25] A number of times in the New Testament, servants are referred to with the term πιστός, clearly in the sense of 'loyal,' 'faithful,' or 'trustworthy,' not in the sense of believing or having faith (Matt 24:45//Luke 12:42; Matt 25:21, 23//Luke 19:17; 1 Cor 4:2). And note also, πιστός is measured by the actions taken, not by the feelings felt. The servants who are called 'loyal' in the Parable of the Talents are those who wisely invest the money they were given to hold on to by their owner. Even the slave who failed to do this because he *feared* his master is not called ἄπιστος, but rather wicked and lazy; the emphasis is on what the servants did, not only on what they felt.

William Barclay's translation of the New Testament takes this distinction between faith and loyalty the farthest, and the results can be quite illuminating. This is particularly the case in 1 Tim 6:9–10. Here the author is discussing what appears to be divided loyalties—God on the one hand and wealth on the other. One cannot be devoted to both wealth and God. This is reiterated in 1 Tim 6:11, where loyalty is listed among the characteristics of the person of God. A similar point about divided loyalties is made in 2 Timothy, this time between God and youthful passions (2 Tim 2:22). Barclay is right to stress the loyalty aspect to these uses of πίστις/πιστός because what is being described has to do with the relationship that is enacted between humans and God and not so much with what is believed or thought. This much can also be said of the role of πίστις/πιστός in Revelation, every occurrence of which

---

[25] Pheme Perkins reads πιστός in this way (*The Johannine Epistles* [Wilmington: Michael Glazier, 1979]), 93. See also William Barclay, *The New Testament: A New Translation* (2 vols.; London: Collins, 1968).

Barclay translates as loyalty. Rev 2:13, for instance, Barclay translates very evocatively as "And yet I also know that you never lose your grip on me, and that you did not deny your loyalty to me even in the time of Antipas, who was so steadfast in declaring his loyalty to me that he was put to death among you." It is loyalty to Christ that resulted in the persecution of Christians at the hands of the Romans. Like many Jews before them, some Christians were unwilling to divide their loyalties between Roman leaders and God.[26]

Faith and loyalty are as intertwined in Paul's letters as they are anywhere.[27] Paul is preaching to Gentiles who are accustomed to expressing loyalty to numerous gods and human patrons. Yet, while his monotheism—loyalty to one god alone (and done in a particular way at that)—is not totally foreign to them, neither does it come easily. Paul praises the Thessalonian believers for taking that first step towards exclusive loyalty, turning away from idols to serve a true and living god. It is in this setting that Paul relates how in every place their loyalty to God (ἡ πίστις ὑμῶν ἡ πρὸς τὸν θεόν) has become known. He praises them also for remaining loyal to that God, and to the things that he told them (1 Thess 4:1), though this is expressed without the explicitness of the term πίστις. Paul was not so lucky with his Galatian converts, who appeared to have been disloyal to his teachings and were being swayed by the teachings of another (Gal 1:6–7). Might it be because of this that at Gal 5:22 Paul stresses loyalty as one of the fruits of the spirit?[28] That πίστις can be related to loyalty for Paul is reflected in a subjective genitive reading of the πίστις Χριστοῦ phrase—the faithfulness (loyalty) of Christ to God's plans for him.[29] According to this way of thinking, that Christ remained

---

[26] For other illustrative examples of how Barclay sees loyalty rather than faith at play in the terms πίστις/πιστός, see Matt 23:23; Acts 16:15; 2 Thess 1:4; Eph 1:1; 6:21; Col 1:2, 4, 7; Heb 10:38; 13:7; Rev 2:19; 13:10; 14:12. See also Donald S. Deer, "Whose Faith/Loyalty in Revelation 2.13 and 14.12?" BT 38 (1987): 328–30.

[27] Πίστις is a favourite Pauline word, appearing 89 times in his letters.

[28] So Barclay, *The New Testament*.

[29] G. Hebert, "'Faithfulness' and 'Faith'," *Theology* 58 (1955): 373–79; G. M. Taylor, "The Function of ΠΙΣΤΙΣ ΧΡΙΣΤΟΥ in Galatians," *JBL* 85 (1966): 58–76; George Howard, "Notes and Observations on the Faith of Christ," *HTR* 60 (1967): 459–84; J. J. O'Rourke, "*Pistis* in Romans," *CBQ* 35 (1973): 188–94; George Howard, "The 'Faith of Christ'," *ExpTim* 85 (1974): 212–15; A. J. Hultgren, "The *Pistis Christou* Formulation in Paul," *NovT* 22 (1980): 248–63; L. T. Johnson, "Rom 3:21–26 and the Faith of Jesus," *CBQ* 44 (1982): 77–90; Richard B. Hays, *The Faith of Jesus Christ: An Investigation of the Narrative Substructure of Galatians 3:1–4:11* (Chico: Scholars Press, 1983); M. D. Hooker, "ΠΙΣΤΙΣ ΧΡΙΣΤΟΥ," *NTS* 35 (1989): 321–42; B. W. Longenecker, "ΠΙΣΤΙΣ in Romans 3:25: The Neglected Evidence for the 'Faithfulness of Christ'," *NTS* 39 (1993): 478–80; R. Barry Matlock, "Detheologizing the ΠΙΣΤΙΣ ΧΡΙΣΤΟΥ

loyal to God despite having to face death is for Paul what made salvation for the Gentiles possible.[30]

The intent here is most certainly not to suggest that πίστις has been wrongly translated as 'faith' nor that it should always be rendered as 'loyalty.' The fact is that Greek does not appear to have had a single word for loyalty, but rather a range of words, all of which normally carry other meanings but which in places connote loyalty—δίκαιος, εὐσέβεια, and the πιστ- root words, in addition to ἐρίηρος and εὐνομία. This is suggested both, as we have seen, by the context in which the words sometimes occur, and by the fact that, in the New Testament at least, the πιστ- root words came to be translated with *fides*, which was even more explicitly a term of loyalty.[31] In the case of Paul, however, we should not see this as much of a limiting factor, nor likely even for the rest of the New Testament; it goes without saying that a monotheist like Paul can be characterised, among other things, by a strong sense of loyalty to a single god, even if he did not have a single term to express it. Loyalty, as we are about to see, was a central part of the relationship between patron-benefactor and client, and certainly for this reason would have been a central feature of Paul's relationship with his God. This would be fully consonant with the entire cultic system in which Paul operated—loyalty (though not always exclusive loyalty) was, as we shall see below, a virtue of the system of patronage and benefaction on every level.

The most important feature of loyalty in the ancient world is that while it can be understood to have had an emotional component in certain circumstances, emotion itself was peripheral to the *definition* of loyalty. We know this because loyalty can be adequately and duly expressed even if feelings of hostility lie beneath the surface. Loyalty is not a state of mind nor an emotional state (as faith likely is primarily): loyalty is an action within a relationship with another person or persons. This is what makes it an excellent bridge for connecting conversion in the ancient world to human and divine patronage and benefaction.[32]

Debate: Cautionary Remarks from a Lexical Semantic Perspective," *NovT* 42 (2000): 1–23.

[30] Barclay uses loyalty or fidelity also at Rom 1:8; 3:3.

[31] This is not the case, however, with the verbal form πιστεύω, which the Vulgate translates with the verb *credo* rather than *fido*.

[32] It is worth noting, and clarifying, that loyalty is not the exclusive domain of patronage and benefaction. Loyalty appears no less in covenantal, kinship, and marriage relationships, and numerous other contexts. Nonetheless, loyalty is necessarily a part of the patronage and benefaction system, though it is not exclusive to it.

5.2 Loyalty and Patronage and Benefaction

By focusing on explicit references to loyalty marked by the presence of the vocabulary of *fides*/πίστις, as we have just done, we are able to identify loyalty even where the vocabulary might not be present. That is to say, although the examples cited above (in order to build a definition of *fides*/πίστις) all used the appropriate terms, it is certainly not the case that loyalty can only be identified where terms for it are found. This is because loyalty is an action of the client that reflects well upon or supports the patron. Said another way, where we find clients present at their patron's literary readings or filling the courts for their speeches, where we find them at the gate in the morning, where we find them setting up inscriptions of praise and gratitude, where we find them telling others of what they have gained through the benefactions of their patron, there is where we find loyalty. As we saw above, *fides* can be understood as an expectation of both clients and their patrons or benefactors,[33] but it would be an error to assume that patronal and client loyalty are similar things. Because my focus throughout this work has been on the client-side of patronage and benefaction, especially in terms of the rhetoric of patronage, that focus will continue throughout the following sections of this chapter.

In previous chapters, we have looked at how a client was expected to act towards a patron or benefactor. This had mostly to do with increasing the honour of one's patron. Loyalty, I would suggest, is what stands behind all this appropriate client conduct. That is, the different ways in which a client honours a patron are where we find (client) loyalty expressed in the ancient world. It is loyalty to the patron that results in a client honouring and expressing public gratitude to a patron. In the case of ancient patronage and benefaction, we should keep any definition of loyalty very broad. For instance, we might be inclined to think of loyalty as implying exclusivity (say, in the case of monotheism), but within ancient patronage and benefaction it was possible in some settings to have multiple patrons, though so too was it possible to be loyal to one patron alone. We must not think that exclusivity is the central feature of ancient loyalty to a patron, but rather is an occasional feature, present but not central.[34] If we attempt to define loyalty based on the

---

[33] N. P. Lemche, "Kings and Clients: On Loyalty Between the Ruler and the Ruled in Ancient 'Israel'," *Semeia* 66 (1994): 122.

[34] Philip Harland offers an example of a voluntary association that restricted participation in other mysteries (*ISardH* 4), but he recognises that these examples are not widely attested (Philip Harland, *Associations, Synagogues, and Congregations:*

pattern of behaviour we have come to expect of a client, a general definition appears: loyalty can be exclusive, but it is mostly a positive action directed towards one's patron(s). Client loyalty is about being committed to actions and conduct that increase the honour of one's patron.

That these things are each reflections of loyalty is especially evident when we consider how the opposite behaviour, disloyalty, is expressed. Clients who attempt to sue their patrons in civil court, who mock their patron's deeds, who come to support the affairs of their patron's enemies, who fail or refuse to express public gratitude or to acknowledge their patron in public, and the like, participate in clear acts of disloyalty to the patron. A lack of gratitude could be interpreted as an unwillingness to admit to someone being your patron or benefactor. Thus, ingratitude, which Seneca so despises, would be despicable because it represented a lack of loyalty to one's patron or benefactor, part of which involved the public acclamation of those who gave generously.[35] Loyalty then can but need not be exclusive but it must always result in appropriate and honouring actions. Disloyalty is most easily illustrated in examples of philosophical patronage that we shall encounter later in this chapter.

In the following sections, I shall focus on client loyalty within three types of patronage: the loyalty of client-kings and client-cities to the Emperor, the loyalty of former slaves to their patrons (manumission loyalty), and the loyalty of students of philosophy to their philosopher-patrons (philosophical loyalty). Within these types of patronage we frequently find loyalty most explicitly expressed, though as we shall see, this explicitness does not result in a fixed vocabulary of loyalty. What we find here is a consistently expressed desire to show loyalty, and a consistent attempt on the part of a client to be loyal. While loyalty, defined as the positive predisposition resulting in appropriate conduct towards one's patron, is an expectation of *all* patron-benefactor and client relationships, there are some types of patronage for which loyalty is a more explicit element of the relationship than in others, such as imperial, manumission, and philosophical loyalty. What is more, in these types of patronage, the loyalty we see more closely approximates the sort of loyalty we see between human clients and their divine patrons or benefactors. Thus, seeing this sort of loyalty at work will help complement

---

Claiming a Place in Ancient Mediterranean Society [Minneapolis: Fortress Press, 2003], chapter 2).

[35] On ingratitude as a serious offence, see Stephen Charles Mott, "The Power of Giving and Receiving: Reciprocity in Hellenistic Benevolence," in *Current Issues in Biblical and Patristic Interpretation* (ed. G. F. Hawthorne; Grand Rapids: Eerdmans, 1975), 62.

our understanding of ancient conversion in a setting of divine patronage and benefaction.

5.2.1 Imperial Loyalty

To say that politics, by which I mean the influence of people in positions of power within states as well as relations between states, in the ancient world was immersed in patronage practices implies, from a modern perspective, that this was an unfortunate state of affairs, that somehow things had spiralled out of control. Few things could be less true. Patronage was the fuel that allowed the political engine of the Roman empire to run as efficiently as it did given its size.[36] In this section I am less concerned with the fact of political and imperial patronage than I am with locating loyalty within the system of statehood.

Evidence of the central importance of loyalty in political exchange in the Roman empire and principate is abundant. As Saller shows, every political office in Rome was filled at the pleasure either of the Emperor or those the Emperor had chosen to make such decisions (acting as brokers and/or patrons-benefactors in their own right). Such an act would either inaugurate new or strengthen existing ties and obligations between political patrons and clients.[37] These obligations of reciprocity comprised many things, the foundation of which in every instance can and should be understood to have been loyalty to the Emperor. The confession of Tacitus at the start of his history covering the last thirty years or so of the first century C.E. offers a glimpse of one of the ways in which loyalty was expected and expressed. Tacitus confesses that when he writes about Galba, Otho and Vitellius, the first three Emperors covered by his work, he is able to write about them impartially because he was never the recipient of a benefaction from them. Presumably this means we ought to be slightly suspicious of his treatments of Vespasian, Titus, and Domitian, from whom we know Tacitus did receive benefactions in the form of his political appointments. The fact of these benefactions likely means we cannot count on Tacitus to speak impartially but rather loyally of his political patrons (if the two should happen to be different in certain

---

[36] Ronald Syme, *The Roman Revolution* (Oxford: The Clarendon Press, 1939); G. Alföldy, *The Social History of Rome* (trans. D. Braund and F. Pollock; London: Routledge, 1988); A. Wallace-Hadrill, "Patronage in Roman Society," in *Patronage in Ancient Society* (ed. A. Wallace-Hadrill; London: Routledge, 1989), 71–78.

[37] R. P. Saller, *Personal Patronage under the Early Empire* (New York: Cambridge University Press, 1982), 42–53.

instances). Tacitus refers to his expression of loyalty in the form of the avoidance of criticism and by doing his best not to embarrass his (former) patrons. As we shall see below, client-kings bequeathing their kingdoms to the Emperor is a measure of loyalty, but so too was it common for Roman political beneficiaries to express loyalty to the Emperor through their wills. In fact, Dio himself interprets one such example where Tiberius is named in a will as an attempt on the part of the client to prove his loyalty (Dio 58.4.5). As Saller writes, "First and foremost, this *gratia* [of the client] was expected to take the form of loyalty," a theme to which he returns time and again.[38]

It is not the case, nor am I claiming or assuming it to be, that loyalty in political patronage is synonymous with exclusivity.[39] As Saller shows, in a response to criticisms of his work, there is simply so much evidence that shows that even within political patronage clients might have multiple patrons.[40] I have suggested previously, however, that though this may well have been the case, it would have been incumbent upon a client to ensure his various patrons did not become enemies of one another. Clients with multiple patrons could easily find themselves caught in the middle of shifting political fortunes. They could also, however, make decisions themselves concerning where to place their loyalty that would backfire on them, as was the case with the ill-fated T. Labienus.[41] Labienus was a military man, serving in Gaul under Caesar (58–51 B.C.E.). Yet, at some point Labienus abandoned Caesar for Pompey. Syme rules out that this move was motivated by political principle, by military calculation, or by an over-reaching and politically gauche Labienus. Rather, he finds a better explanation in the personal realm, namely loyalty. While Pompey was away from Rome (in the 60s B.C.E.), he had tribunes, Syme suggests, working in Rome to further his ambitions there. Record of Labienus turns up among these men allied to Pompey (Celer and Nepos). Syme establishes that prior to Labienus's service under Caesar in the Gallic war a bond had likely been established between Labienus and Pompey though not through these tribunes. Labienus gained the military experience that recommended him to Caesar, and Syme estimates that this happened

---

[38] Saller, *Personal Patronage*, 70.
[39] On the other hand, J. Rich claims that "if Rome was the patron [of a foreign kingdom or state] there could be no other" (J. Rich, "Patronage and Interstate Relations in the Roman Republic," in *Patronage in Ancient Society*, 117–35, this quote on p. 127).
[40] R. Saller, "Patronage and Friendship in Early Imperial Rome: Drawing the Distinction," in *Patronage in Ancient Society*, 49–62.
[41] Ronald Syme, "The Allegiance of Labienus," *JRS* 28 (1938): 113–25.

while Labienus was under the command of Pompey in Spain or in the East. Syme then suggests that since Caesar was a neophyte in the realm of military command, the seasoned and competent soldiers were supplied from Pompey's ranks. By the middle of the century, however, Caesar and Pompey were no longer working together; Caesar's political gains have been made at the expense of Pompey, and so Labienus's loyalty to the latter became an issue of contention. Compelled then to choose between Caesar and Pompey, Labienus remained loyal to his initial relationship with and obligations to Pompey. Not surprisingly, this was not acceptable to Caesar. Labienus's loyalty to Pompey, when Pompey became an enemy of Caesar, resulted in the death of Labienus. Syme rightly concludes that the story confirms "the fundamental importance in Roman political life of patronage and ties of personal allegiance, of *fides* and *amicitia*."[42] Political developments were, of course, beyond the control of Labienus and were unpredictable, but this did not exonerate those caught suddenly on the wrong side of a political dispute or shift.

Loyalty between the players of political patronage at the level of individuals and individual offices *within* Rome was mirrored also in the relationships between the city (or more properly the Emperor) and outlying kingdoms and provinces.[43] It is frequently attested that Rome's practice of leaving the foreign ruling infrastructures intact but ensuring the placement of rulers loyal to Rome was a primary reason for the longevity of the Roman empire.[44] Establishing loyal client-kings kept the Romans from having to rule first-hand in lands that were distant, and in some cases geographically

---

[42] Syme, "Allegiance of Labienus," 125.

[43] Niels Peter Lemche argues that Rome was not the 'inventor' of patronage, nor of the practice of establishing client-kings as allies. As early as the second millennium B.C.E., the practice was used successfully by Hittite overlords with their Syrian and Asia Minor vassals (in the form of treaties). Indeed, according to Lemche, vassals to the Hittites were required to appear before their overlord once a year to swear their loyalty, in addition to performing certain ceremonies that expressed as much, though in a less explicit sense (Lemche, "Kings and Clients," 127). The same arrangements existed between Assyria and its client states, and Egypt and its client states, Syria and Palestine. This is echoed also by D. C. Braund (*Rome and the Friendly King: The Character of the Client Kingship* [London: Croom Helm, 1984], 181), who refers in addition to client kingship in the Chinese, Persian, Byzantine, and Islamic empires, and suggests the modern world has a parallel in the form of 'satellite states.' Unfortunately, Lemche, more so than Braund, confuses patronal exchange with covenantal exchange. The two were of course similar, but they were not synonymous types of exchange or relationship.

[44] Clifford Ando, *Imperial Ideology and Provincial Loyalty in the Roman Empire* (Berkeley: University of California Press, 2000); Braund, *Rome and the Friendly King*.

inaccessible. The term 'client-king' is not attested in ancient writing, since the term 'client' would unnecessarily bring dishonour to a foreign king. Thus the client-king was more commonly referred to as 'friend' and 'ally.'[45] It is clear nonetheless, however, that these foreign kings were clients and Rome was their patron. The term, therefore, while modern is fitting.

The exchanges involved in client kingship and Roman patronage were mutually beneficial. Indeed, the whole arrangement, in order to benefit Rome at all, required the willing, even the enthusiastic, participation of these client-kings. Both parties could expect to gain from the relationship. These kings (and their nations by proxy) expected from Rome, first and foremost, fair treatment and protection from enemies. They expected not to be taxed by Rome. In fact, more than this, Rome was known to give benefactions of cash and land to client-kings. For example, Augustus gave to Herod the Great a portion of the revenues deriving from the copper mines in Cyprus. Such monetary benefactions were typically far more modest than this example suggests. Often, benefactions to client-kings from Rome involved tracts of land and smaller one-time payments of cash.[46] In terms of protection, Rome was expected to help its client-kings from potential and actual aggressors. This is an interesting expectation because in fact, it was not in Rome's best interests to have its frontier provinces reduced, or to have the fall of such states gain momentum and roll on towards Rome. Thus, it was as much in Rome's interests as it was in the interests of the client-kings to have a stable frontier. The fact is, however, that Rome rarely had to come to the aid of its client-kings militarily. It is likely, as suggested by David Braund, that the mere presence of Roman armies in the rough vicinity of a client-king's land would serve to dissuade the movement of enemy troops towards a client kingdom.[47] It is also likely that would-be aggressors understood allegiance with Rome to involve the prospect that Rome would not let military action against its client states go unpunished, and thus were naturally dissuaded

---

[45] As Badian shows, however, these expectations of loyalty and respect towards Rome were not limited to states bound to Rome by treaty, but also to states that were not so bound. He found the analogy of patron–client to be most fruitful for understanding the relationship between Rome and neighbouring states. See E. Badian, *Foreign Clientelae (264–70 B.C.)* (Oxford: Oxford University Press, 1958); Rich, "Patronage and Interstate Relations," 126.

[46] Braund, *Rome and the Friendly King*, 183. See also P. Richardson, *Herod: King of the Jews and Friend of the Romans* (Columbia: University of South Carolina Press, 1996), 22–34, 90–102, 144–45.

[47] D. C. Braund, "Client Kings," in *Oxford Classical Dictionary* (ed. S. Hornblower and A. Spawforth; Oxford: Oxford University Press, 1996), 348–49.

from such attacks on these grounds. Nonetheless, Rome did on occasion move to protect its client-kings. This and the mere promise of protection counted as benefactions (say, in the form of peace of mind) from Rome to its clients. Also, these kings were frequently accorded Roman citizenship, clearly designed to create consent in a relationship that could otherwise be rife with tension and resentment. What client-kings gained from their relationship with Rome was thus considerable.

What Rome gained from these relationships is also considerable, and likely accounts for the impressive number of its client states. From such relationships Rome gained the administration of outlying areas at someone else's expense. Although these client-kings typically did not pay tributes to Rome, Rome did benefit from access to their reservoirs of wealth and natural resources.[48] But of course, the primary expectation that Rome had, and that stands behind any positive element of the relationship, was loyalty. The primary characteristic of the client-king was loyalty to Rome, and the primary characteristic of loyalty was, not surprisingly, marked by actions (or the absence of actions): peaceful coexistence, absence of hostility, a willingness to follow Rome's commands.

A number of interesting expressions of loyalty from client-kings towards Rome are preserved in the historical record. Many such expressions appear to have to do with proclaiming, that is making obvious and open, the client-king's relationship with Rome. In other words, to make any attempt to hide the fact of one's relationship with Rome would be read as a first act of disloyalty to Rome. It goes without saying that the simplest and most direct way of expressing loyalty to Rome was to do so verbally or in writing. Of course, we have no transcripts of verbal exchanges from the time attesting to this, but we do have transcripts of another sort—inscriptions. We have a number of Bosporan inscriptions that make the close relationship between client ruler and Rome explicit.[49] Also, as we shall see below, client-kings were known to have set up their wills, in which they might have bequeathed their land to Rome or to Roman guardianship, inscribed in public places (*SEG* IX 7). T. B. Mitford discusses an inscription in which the government of Cyprus made an oath of allegiance before its local deities. In it they swore, among other things, to regard with loyalty (εὐνοήσειν) Tiberius Caesar Augustus and his house.[50] That this sort of oath of loyalty was not without precedent

---

[48] Braund, *Rome and the Friendly King*, 184.
[49] Braund, *Rome and the Friendly King*, 120–21 (note 92), lists *CIRB* (*IBosp*) 38; 1046; and 978.
[50] T. B. Mitford, "A Cypriot Oath of Allegiance to Tiberius," *JRS* 50 (1960): 74–79.

Mitford shows by referring to another inscription in which the elite of Paphlagonia gathered to swear loyalty to Rome when they became a Roman province in 3 B.C.E. (*IGRR* 3.137).

A relationship of patronage with Rome was also commonly advertised and expressed by changing one's name, or taking on the names of prominent Roman citizens. The titulature of client-kings often explicitly names the Emperor, especially for example in 'names' such as Φιλορωμαῖος, which begins appearing early in the first century B.C.E. and was followed by the appearance of Φιλόκαισαρ, and Φιλοσέβαστος.[51] These honorary titles appear on coins at times as well. Herod of Chalcis, a client-king of Claudius, issued coins that carried the title Φιλοκλαύδιος and one Mannus VIII of Osrhoene, who was restored to his kingship by Rome, issued coins carrying the title Φιλορωμαῖος.[52] Coinage carrying images of or dedications to Rome were a very direct way of illustrating a close relationship. Braund observes that "Royal coinage under the Principate regularly bore the imperial head and other types recalling Rome."[53] These were relatively simple and inexpensive ways of expressing loyalty to Rome. Not all options were as readily available as these were.

Building monuments and buildings in honour of and naming them after the Roman emperor was another way of expressing loyalty to Rome, and would have been quite impressive were it not for the fact that this paled in comparison to building and naming entire cities after the emperors. Nonetheless, the latter option, to be treated shortly, was available only to the wealthiest of client-kings. For the remainder, they made do with building and honouring monuments and buildings to their patron emperors, though neither were these insignificant. Thus, not only was Caesarea Maritima named in honour of Augustus, but its magnificent harbour too — Augustan Harbour. And overlooking this Harbour sat a temple of Rome and Augustus, and within this temple could be found impressive statues of each.[54] It might not be overstating it to suggest that Caesarea Maritima in its entirety was an expression of loyalty and proclamation of the benefactions associated with the Roman emperor.

---

[51] Braund, *Rome and the Friendly King*, 105. See also B. H. McLean, *An Introduction to Greek Epigraphy of the Hellenistic and Roman Periods from Alexander the Great down to the Reign of Constantine (323 B.C. – A.D. 337)* (Ann Arbor: University of Michigan Press, 2002), 229–32.

[52] Braund, *Rome and the Friendly King*, 105 and 107 respectively.

[53] Braund, *Rome and the Friendly King*, 115.

[54] Braund, *Rome and the Friendly King*, 109.

As an expression of a client-king's gratitude and loyalty, Caesarea Maritima was, despite its impressive nature, neither unique nor unprecedented. It fits within a pattern of client-king loyalty that Suetonius called *Caesareas urbes*, namely, the practice of client-kings naming cities after their Roman patrons or that patron's family members, when he relates that each of the client-kings under Augustus named one of their cities Caesarea (*Aug.* 60). Caesarea Maritima was only one of many other Caesareas; others were so named by the likes of Archelaus I of Cappadocia, Juba II of Mauretania, Polemo I in the Bosporos, and Philip the tetrarch.[55] Also under Augustus, cities named in his honour include several by the name of Sebaste, a Juliopolis, and an Autocratoris.[56] And obviously this practice was not limited to honouring Caesar Augustus, since another city name that should stand out for New Testament scholars is Tiberias, built by Herod's immediate successor Antipas on the shores of Lake Gennesaret (Sea of Galilee) between roughly 17–22 C.E. Unlike many of the previous examples, which were cities *renamed* (that is expanded upon existing cities) in honour of an Emperor, Tiberias was built from the ground up. Clearly to name a city, especially but not even a major city, after a person would have the same effect, though multiplied, as offering a benefactor a crown on an inscription. Braund writes,

> Within the kingdom, these cities stood as vast monuments to the king's connections with Rome and the emperor in particular. At the same time, as great foundations, they were also monuments to the ruler's kingship, in the Hellenistic tradition. These cities were invariably important entities in their particular areas and some, especially the ports, were key centres in the Mediterranean world as a whole.[57]

Every time the city was named or spoken of, the patron's name would be invoked and the relationship of patronage, loyalty, and reciprocity would be brought to light. Regardless of the potential negative effects this might have had, the name of cities was an especially grandiose way of expressing loyalty and gratitude to Roman emperors/patrons.[58]

---

[55] Braund, *Rome and the Friendly King*, 108.
[56] There are many more examples provided by Braund, *Rome and the Friendly King*, 108.
[57] Braund, *Rome and the Friendly King*, 109.
[58] In circles resentful of Roman presence and influence, these city names would have been bitter reminders of the unwelcome presence and cultural and political hegemony of Rome. A number of recent works chart the profoundly negative social and economic impact of the founding of Tiberias to account for feelings (and

Naming yourself, your cities, your buildings, and, so to speak, your coins, after the Emperor and his family is an expression of client loyalty that speaks to a close relationship between the two parties. Another manner of expressing this came in the manner of reception of Roman dignitaries visiting states of client-kings. These were, in a word, lavish. As Braund writes, "The wise king was a lavish host when Romans came to visit him."[59] Braund draws our attention to an Egyptian papyrus that lays out the painstaking details undertaken to welcome and receive not even the Emperor, but a 'mere' senator on his visit to an Arsinoite nome in 112 B.C.E.[60] Likewise, Josephus relates that when Octavian passed through Herod's kingdom after the battle of Actium, Herod received him with much ado. Herod gave gifts to the soldiers, cash to Octavian, and fed them all in luxury. Indeed, Josephus suggests that the extent of Herod's warm reception of Octavian resulted in the expansion of Herod's kingdom.[61] The expression of loyalty and honouring of the patron resulted, as is always the hope, in increased benefactions. One might be tempted to see these sorts of exchange as the exchange of gifts between equals, but it ought to be borne in mind that client-kings, though kings, under Rome were not truly sovereign but rather ruled but by the grace (read: benefaction) of Rome. These were not relationships among equals, and thus gift exchange is not an appropriate model for understanding such exchanges.

A final way in which loyalty towards Rome was expressed was through royal wills.[62] It was not uncommon for client monarchs to leave their kingdoms to Rome, or to place their young heirs under the guardianship of Rome. Braund claims that the earliest example of a client-king leaving his territory to Rome comes from the royal will (publicly inscribed in 155 B.C.E.: *SEG* IX 7) of Ptolemy VIII Euergetes II 'Physcon.'[63] While this will was never enacted because Physcon produced heirs before he actually died, the will of a client-king of Pergamum, one Attalus III (170–133 B.C.E.), was executed by

---

experience) of social upheaval (William E. Arnal, *Jesus and the Village Scribes: Galilean Conflicts and the Social Setting of Q* [Minneapolis: Fortress Press, 2001], 97–155; John Dominic Crossan and Jonathan L. Reed, *Excavating Jesus: Beneath the Stones, Behind the Text* [San Francisco: Harper Collins, 2001]). It would be interesting to see whether such responses were replicated in other places where cities were founded (as opposed to simply renamed, which surely would not have resulted in the same impact).

[59] Braund, *Rome and the Friendly King*, 79.
[60] *P. Tebt.* 33. See Braund, *Rome and the Friendly King*, 79.
[61] Josephus, *A. J.* 15.192–201.
[62] See Saller, *Personal Patronage*, 71, for examples of Roman clients naming the Emperor in their wills.
[63] Braund, *Rome and the Friendly King*, 129–30, offers a translation of this inscription.

Rome. Attalus bequeathed his entire kingdom to Rome as he had no heirs to whom to pass it. It appears that Attalus would rather have left the kingdom to Rome than let it fall into the hands of local opposition, despite the fact that locals are indigenous and Rome foreign. This of course speaks volumes to the close relationship of loyalty shared between Rome and some of its client-kings. That opposition to the throne was behind some royal wills bequeathing everything to Rome becomes clear in a third example discussed by Braund. When Nicomedes IV of Bithynia left his kingdom to Rome upon his death in 74 B.C.E., Braund suggests that Rome moved in fairly quickly. This was likely the result of the fact that Mithridates VI Eupator of neighbouring Pontus had clear designs on Bithynia—twice Mithridates had displaced Nicomedes and each time Nicomedes was replaced by Roman power. In fact, within a year of Nicomedes' death, Mithridates was already moving on Bithynia, prompting Rome to respond quickly and decisively. Leaving kingdoms to Rome was an act of loyalty because there were other options available, and because it implied that the land was better off in Roman control than in the control of even local opposition, let alone in the hands of foreign enemies. In other words, loyalty to Roman political patronage precluded the banding together of local enemies to fight a common foreign enemy.

It appears that in each of these cases, a kingdom was bequeathed to Rome because there was no heir to take over. In a related way, Rome might also be named as a guardian (*tutela*) in cases where the heir was too young to rule.[64] In both cases, there appear to be quite utilitarian reasons for these client-kings placing Rome in such a prominent position in their wills. Does this practicality undermine the role of loyalty in such instances? While there is certainly a practical aspect to this phenomenon, it is not mere practicality that has Rome inheriting the kingdoms of its client monarchs. It is important to keep in mind that naming guardians for one's heirs in a will was common among many strata of society, and that these guardians could be foreigners as well as locals.[65] That this was common practice is what makes the royal wills of the Principate significant. When Roman client-kings had no heir or no one fit yet to rule, Rome was always named as the one to rule or the one to choose a *tutela* for the young heir. In no instance is another party chosen. Clearly then, such wills were more than just functional, which they certainly were; they were also honouring towards Rome and must be understood as an element of the expression of client-loyalty. In other words, when a client-king needed someone to take over and protect the status of the kingdom, the wills we

---

[64] Braund, *Rome and the Friendly King*, 136–44, discusses several examples.
[65] See Braund, *Rome and the Friendly King*, 145–49.

possess suggest that their patron Rome was always chosen. Braund concludes that "The royal wills of the Principate were both a part of this relationship [namely, client–patron between emperor and king] and an expression of it."[66] Royal wills were therefore part of a client-king's opportunity, when the need arose, to offer one last expression of loyalty towards Rome.

Loyalty was a critical element in Roman political patronage, and since this was an honour and shame culture, this loyalty was, in fact it had to be, expressed outwardly and publicly. Hence we are left with a number of material realia that attest to the expression of loyalty towards that supreme of human patrons, the Roman emperor. It is worth reiterating at this point that while we do have evidence, ostensibly, of actual *feelings* of goodwill and friendship, loyalty was not an emotional state but a state of relationship. In other words, how one *felt* about the Emperor as patron was irrelevant; one was required to *act* in a manner that connoted loyalty. We have no way of knowing, for the most part, whether or to what extent the acts of loyalty observed above were attended by sincere feelings of affection, but thankfully we do not need to know. It is enough to point to actions and expressions that reflect loyalty without knowing anything else about the relationship between client and political patron. We shall return to these points below after discussing philosophical loyalty.

Imperial loyalty reveals little that allows us to connect patronage and conversion, but it is immensely useful as a way of illustrating the central importance of loyalty within patronage and benefaction. Loyalty was expressed creatively, in keeping with the obligation of any client to honour any patron or benefactor. This creativity tells us a great deal about the importance of loyalty—there were so many ways to express loyalty because there had to be. And as we shall see below, the centrality of loyalty to patronage is in no way unique to imperial patronage. It will not, of course, be expressed in the same means everywhere, and in some instances loyalty will be more exclusive than in other instances, but these are all simply variations on a theme.

5.2.2 Manumission Loyalty

Manumission was a common Roman practice.[67] Though most of the data used to discuss manumission is Roman in provenance, we are probably safe to

---

[66] Braund, *Rome and the Friendly King*, 155.
[67] A. M. Duff, *Freedmen in the Early Roman Empire* (Cambridge: W. Heffer & Sons, Ltd., 1958), though it is overstating the evidence to suggest that manumission was wildly

expect that even though material evidence of Greek manumission lacks strict numerical equivalence, in addition to the fact that it lacks many of the explicit legal aspects of its Roman counterpart, in a broad sense the two were similar.[68] As a rule, the closer the contact between slave and master the more likely it was that manumission would occur.[69] Slaves in fields or mines were unlikely to be manumitted because they rarely came into contact or had personal interaction with their master, and probably because it was the less educated, less articulate, and less talented slaves who were sent out to work in such environments in the first place. According to Treggiari, "Barbarian slaves, unskilled or savage, could expect nothing better than the mines, or the *latifundia*, where life was notoriously hard, men were expendable, and there was little hope of manumission."[70] Slaves that remained in the *familia*, on the other hand, usually had talents that served the *familia*, and thus both for reasons of these talents and by virtue of their close proximity and perhaps

out of control or excessively common (see Thomas E. J. Wiedemann, "The Regularity of Manumission at Rome," *CQ* 35 [1985]: 162–75).

[68] The issues surrounding whether manumission was unknown or uncommon in a classical Greek setting need not delay us here. Fisher admits on occasion that evidence concerning Greek manumission can be scarce, but he is able to show that what was true of Roman manumission was also true of classical Greek manumission. This is especially the case with respect to the fact that a manumitted slave was not entirely free, but through the *paramon*-clause still owed their former master, who becomes their patron, and that that relationship therefore involves loyalty (N. R. E. Fisher, *Slavery in Classical Greece* [London: Bristol Classical Press, 1998]). For further illustration of manumission in Greek settings see Benjamin Nadel, "Actes d'affranchissement des esclaves du royaume de Bosphore et les origines de la manumissio in ecclesia," in *Symposion 1971: Vorträge zur griechischen und hellenistischen Rechtsgeschichte* (ed. H. J. Wolff, D. Norr and J. Modrzejewski; Köln: Böhlau Verlag, 1975), 265–91; Keith Hopkins and P. J. Roscoe, "Between Slavery and Freedom: On Freeing Slaves at Delphi," in Hopkins, *Conquerors and Slaves* (Cambridge: Cambridge University Press, 1978), 133–71; Linda Collins Reilly, *Slaves in Ancient Greece: Slaves from Greek Manumission Inscriptions* (Chicago: Ares Publishers, 1978); J. Albert Harrill, *The Manumission of Slaves in Early Christianity* (HUT 32; Tübingen: J. C. B. Mohr [Paul Siebeck], 1995); E. Leigh Gibson, *The Jewish Manumission Inscriptions of the Bosporus Kingdom* (TSAJ 75; Tübingen: J. C. B. Mohr [Paul Siebeck], 1999); J. Andrew Overman, "Jews, Slaves, and the Synagogue on the Black Sea: The Bosporan Manumission Inscriptions and Their Significance for Diaspora Judaism," in *Evolution of the Synagogue: Problems and Progress* (ed. H. C. Kee and L. H. Cohick; Harrisburg, Pa.: Trinity Press International, 1999), 141–57.

[69] G. Alföldy, "Die Freilassung von Sklaven und die Struktur der Sklaverei in der römischen Kaiserzeit," *Rivista Storica dell' Antichità* 2 (1972): 97–129, cites that 98 % of extant manumission inscriptions reflect the setting of the *familia urbana*.

[70] Susan Treggiari, *Roman Freedmen During the Late Republic* (Oxford: Clarendon Press, 1969), 9.

relationship with their master, manumission was granted more frequently to nurses, teachers, artists, *amanuenses*, accountants, cooks, child-minders, dressmakers, treasurers, wardrobe masters and the like.

The various explanations for why manumission was so popular, the different ways in which slaves were manumitted, and the attempts of the state occasionally to intervene in manumission customs need not concern us here.[71] Of greater interest is the continuing relationship of the freedman or freedwoman to his or her former master. This relationship was governed, both in law and by custom, by the bond of loyalty. Loyalty here must be distinguished from obedience, though this is not necessarily easily done since one of the duties of the freedperson was frequently described as *obsequium*. Obedience from a slave was required by virtue of their being the property of the slave-owner. *Obsequium* from a freedperson, on the other hand, was the result of loyalty to their former master. While loyalty and good conduct were shared concerns of both slave and freedperson, the resulting portrait of each was different, in part because the loyalty in each case had different motivations.[72] This different motivation is obvious and self-explanatory when one realises that manumission was likely the one thing every slave hoped a master might grant him or her—it was the highest form of benefaction a slave owner could grant a slave. Bradley calls it an "unassailable fact" that "setting a slave free was an act of *indulgentia*, the conferment of a *beneficium*."[73] Through the benefaction of manumission the relationship between slave and slave-owner was changed from master–servant to that of patron-benefactor and client. And yet, we should not think by this that the freedperson was entirely free; a freedperson continued to live under the authority of the former master. It was the most structured and limited form of patron-benefactor and client relationship. According to Duff, "While this authority was not considered to be exactly that of a master over a slave, it was a power which could be enforced, and one which it was generally unwise to attempt to evade."[74] Hence, *obsequium* is a fitting word to describe the duty of freedperson to a patron—it was an obedience that was supposed to be grounded in loyalty and gratitude for the profound benefaction of freedom from bondage and (at least part of) the stigma associated with slavery. Even if there was

---

[71] For this information, see Fabre, *Libertus*; Treggiari, *Roman Freedmen*; and Duff, *Freedmen*.

[72] Fabre, *Libertus*, 232.

[73] K. R. Bradley, *Slavery and Society at Rome* (Cambridge: Cambridge University Press, 1994), 165. For *beneficium* see *Digest* 1.1.4.

[74] Duff, *Freedmen*, 36.

still a certain stigma to being a former slave, the benefaction of manumission brought a considerable improvement in social status, often in the form of citizenship, and an opportunity to become wealthy, as we shall see in Petronius's *Satyricon* shortly.

The gratitude and loyalty of freedmen to their patrons was a topic of heated debate in Roman legal circles on more than one occasion. Augustus' *Lex Aelia Sentia* of 4 C.E. refers to punishment for disloyal freedmen. Suetonius relates Claudius' order that freedmen who were disloyal and ungrateful be made slaves again (*Claud.* 25). And within Greek law, re-enslavement was an option for a slave who had failed to fulfil the expectations of loyalty and gratitude.[75] In fact, the very topic of re-enslaving the ungrateful freedperson occasioned a debate in Nero's Senate (Tacitus, *Ann.* 26–27). But it appears to have been decided that with too much left to the discretion of a patron, the rights of freedmen in general were at risk, and thus cases of re-enslavement had to be considered each on their own merit. Nonetheless, Hadrian sent disloyal clients off to the imperial quarries, and under the Antonines the disloyal freedperson risked being beaten (a reminder of their servile origins). Another way in which freedperson loyalty was reflected in the legal system resides in the fact that a client could not bring a law suit against a patron, or charge him or her with fraud or for complaints of injury save for the most serious kind.

In general, however, the loyalty of freedperson to patron was legislated far less than it was simply expected (and received). Loyalty was expressed in a number of ways, some quite in keeping with what we already know of patronage and benefaction in general, such as following a patron around town and attending public appearances. Treggiari also suggests that in addition freedpersons could serve as brokers between their patrons and those looking for benefactions, they could protect the reputation of the patron after death, and from slander while their patron was alive by attacking opponents. Loyalty is taken to an extreme, though according to the elder Pliny an honourable extreme and not a ridiculous one, when a freedman throws himself on the funeral pyre of his master despite being the sole heir of his master's property (*Nat.* 7.122). It was common for slaves to be manumitted for the sole purpose of inflating one's gallery of clients. Senators, for example, who found they were lacking in clients to follow them around town might "satisfy their vanity" by releasing a number of slaves: "this was not merely a concession to an irksome convention; it pleased the patron's vanity to have

---

[75] S. Scott Bartchy, *ΜΑΛΛΟΝ ΧΡΗΣΑΙ: First Century Slavery and 1 Corinthians 7:21* (SBLDS 11; Missoula: Society of Biblical Literature, 1973), 49.

a throng of clients paying the official morning call (*salutatio*), joining his procession to the city and applauding his legal speeches or his literary recitations."⁷⁶ This might also happen on the death-bed (or in a will where manumission was effective upon the death of the master), *manumissio testamento*, in order to ensure an impressive gathering of grieving clients at the funeral. The number of freed slaves at a patron's funeral represented a claim to honour concerning both the patron's wealth and his or her humanity. The fact that Augustus limited the age at which a master could manumit and the numbers of slaves that could be freed at a time can be interpreted as evidence that manumission for vanity was creating problems in the city.⁷⁷

Another form of the expression of loyalty between freedperson and client is found in the changing of one's name.⁷⁸ Our field of evidence for this data is funerary inscriptions, which of course presents methodological challenges all its own. Nonetheless, this is the data we have to work with, and from which several facts can be drawn. It was the privileged of the free-born to identify themselves with reference to one's tribe. According to Duff, and echoed by others, "After being freed, the slave would generally take the *praenomen* and the *nomen* of his patron, while he would retain his servile name as his *cognomen*."⁷⁹ So, in probably the most famous example, Marcus Tullius Cicero's slave Tiro became Marcus Tullius Tiro upon his manumission. Likewise, it was the domain of the free-born to identify their father on their funerary inscriptions, but freedpersons would identify their patron instead, or as Duff calls the freedperson's patron, their "legal father." The relationship between family vocabulary and patronal vocabulary has been noted before in these pages, but here it takes on a certain vitality. Fabre too noticed the parallelism between the way in which sons and freedmen identified themselves in funerary inscriptions. He claims, very importantly, that "Ce parallélisme n'est pas

---

⁷⁶ Duff, *Freedmen*, 18.
⁷⁷ Duff, *Freedmen*, 31–32. The *Lex Aelia Sentia*, 4 C.E., restricted, among other things, the age at which a slave owner could free slaves (20 years old). The *Lex Fufia Caninia*, 2 B.C.E., restricted the percentage of slaves from among a slave-owner's holdings that could be freed. On the other hand, Wiedemann warns against such an interpretation, though it seems in this case he is being excessively cautious with the evidence ("Regularity of Manumission," 168).
⁷⁸ The nomenclature of freedpersons is covered in the greatest detail by Fabre, *Libertus*, 23–121; Treggiari, *Roman Freedmen*, 250–51; Duff, *Freedmen*, 52–57; and within the context of imperial manumission P. R. C. Weaver, *Familia Caesaris: A Social Study of the Emperor's Freedmen and Slaves* (Cambridge: Cambridge University Press, 1972), 20–92.
⁷⁹ Duff, *Freedmen*, 52.

simplement formel: il souligne la place du *patronus* par rapport à l'affranchi, au même titre que celle du *pater* par rapport au *filius*."[80] Yet the relationship of son, freedman, and slave for that matter, while each of them is roughly analogous to each other vis-à-vis the *paterfamilias*, should not be confused for the others. A freedman and a son were not social equals, nor were they characterised by the same relationship to the legal and real father, respectively. The freedman's relationship to his former owner was as to a patron; of course a freedperson was not the master's son, nor was a man's son one of his clients, despite the fitting analogies that arise occasionally. For a freedperson to assume the name and share in the identity of their former owner is an expression of loyalty, it is not a literal adoption into the family.[81] Taking on a patron's name marked a freedperson, but it also marked the generous and humane person who beneficently manumitted that person, and this of course brought honour onto the patron and former master.[82]

In general, however, it appears that freedperson loyalty to a patron had more to do with a generally positive action than with a set of particular or concrete tasks. Obviously freedpersons were discouraged from suing their patrons and encouraged to honour them in public, but it is the sentiment that lies behind such actions that Fabre claims are the central measurement of freedperson loyalty. Fabre emphasises a generally good disposition towards the patron as the central characteristic of freedperson loyalty. He finds a number of terms that are used, usually by patrons, to describe the loyal freedperson. The central term is *fides* (trust, faith, loyalty), around which many others revolve: *obsequium* (obedience), *humanitas* (civility), *politesse*

---

[80] Fabre, *Libertus*, 114.
[81] Fabre, *Libertus*, 111.
[82] While name change in the context of manumission should be seen as an expression of loyalty, in this instance it is probably not appropriate to associate it with conversion. In other contexts, however, name change can be an indicator both of loyalty and, importantly, of conversion. Horsley concludes that in a number of cases, a change in name can be used as a marker for religious conversion (G. H. R. Horsley, "Name Change as an Indication of Religious Conversion in Antiquity," *Numen* 34 [1987]: 1–17). For instance, while theophoric names given at birth might say nothing (or little) about an adult's cultic loyalties, theophoric names adopted by adults almost certainly does. A particularly revealing example derives from one Simut, who in a lengthy inscription pledged exclusive loyalty (interesting for that reason too!) to his patron God Mut (Horsley, "Name Change," 6). The case of Paul's name change from Saul, is different, since it is not a theophoric name, but a name change that marks a change in status or ontology along the lines of the characters of the Hebrew Bible who encountered God (Abram, Sarai, Jacob [though Israel could be considered a theophoric name]).

(courtesy), *pietas* (piety, loyalty).[83] These are all very vague, but they serve to highlight the general emphasis on positive qualities. They are also perfectly in keeping with the expectations of patronage and benefaction, in that they are qualities that, when directed at the patron, are signs of loyalty or gratitude and that, when practised away from the patron, reflect well on him or her.

The epitaphs of freedpersons are a rich source for examples of expressions of honour from freedperson to patron. Indeed, according to Duff, "Brief memorials of patron's benevolence or freedman's loyalty abound among inscriptions."[84] We find in Latin inscriptions a fairly stable range of terms that refer to and reflect positively on the patron. Several inscriptions refer to the *Patrono bene merenti*, roughly, "for a patron deserving of merit" (*CIL* 6.18048, 18136, 18188). Sometimes this phrase is not enough, and greater honour and loyalty is expressed by using superlatives, as in *[dul]cissimo bene merenti* (*CIL* 6.18156), or with words like *amico optimo* (*CIL* 6.18109). Other superlatives and phrases that are used of patrons include *patrono i[ndulgen]tissimo* (*CIL* 6.18072), *patrono rarissimae* (*CIL* 12.2956), and *patrono optimo* (*CIL* 9.3922; 11.3892). Two inscriptions are of particular value for the degree to which they seem to eclipse others in their expression of honour and loyalty; *CIL* 2.4405 has an extended honorary reference with the words *patrono honestissimae et optimae de meritae*, and ILS 6348 offers, *patrono inimitabili largissimo, cuius facta enrari non passant*, "To a patron inimitable and most generous, whose deeds are beyond all narration."[85] The freedperson's epitaph served as a means and a locale for expressing loyalty and gratitude to a patron.

Comments concerning the loyalty of freedpersons to their patrons can be found in literary sources as well. For instance, in several letters to his friends Cicero refers to the very quality of freedmen with which we are concerned. In a letter of recommendation that Cicero himself admits is more detailed than normal, Cicero refers to his freedman C. Avianius Evander, a sculptor, with great enthusiasm to his friend Sulpicius (*Fam.* 13.21). He opens by claiming that his freedman was always well disposed towards Cicero, presumably referring to a period when Evander was still a slave. He expresses confidence

---

[83] Fabre finds other terms, less commonly, that refer to specific characteristic of certain freedpersons: *temperantia* (self-control), *prudens* (intelligent), *modestia* (restraint), *probitas* (honesty), and *frugi* (virtuous). These and the others are discussed in Fabre, *Libertus*, 233–38.

[84] Duff, *Freedmen*, 101.

[85] Translation of Duff, *Freedmen*, 102. In an interesting and not entirely expected twist, patrons are also known to have written inscriptions recognising the loyalty and gratitude of their clients (see Duff, *Freedmen*, 102).

that this client would recommend *himself* to Sulpicius perfectly well, but feels the need to make explicit the excellent qualities of loyalty that Evander and his own freedman, C. Avianius Hammonius, have consistently shown to their patron Cicero. Concerning Hammonius, Cicero writes, "not only has he won my approval by his remarkable sense of duty and loyalty (*officio et fide*) to his patron, but he has also conferred great obligations upon myself, and in my days of greatest trouble he stood by me as faithfully and affectionately as if it were I who had manumitted him" (*Fam.* 13.21.2). So much of what we have just learned about manumission and loyalty is explicitly represented in this text. Cicero's name is reflected in his freedman's name and Evander's name in *his* freedman's name. Evander treats and serves Cicero with respect and loyalty, and the freedman's own freedman also treats Cicero with service and respect.

In two letters, Cicero refers in passing to similar positive qualities of the freedmen of his friends. In a letter of exhortation to M. Marcellus (*Fam.* 4.9), Cicero regrets that he had not sent a letter initially with Marcello's freedman, Theophilus. Cicero has been very impressed with this freedman because of the loyalty and goodwill (*fides . . . benevolentiaque*) he shows towards his patron. Also, in one of his many letters to Appius Claudius Pulcher (*Fam.* 3.6), Cicero again mentions in passing an exchange with Pulcher's freedman, Phania, which confirms for Cicero the man's fidelity (*fidelitas*). The fact that Cicero does not go on at length concerning the loyalty of any of these freedmen suggests that he is not consumed with the topic of freedman loyalty. On the other hand, the fact that he is able to draw attention to this quality of the men so briefly yet forcibly suggests that the quality was well known, though worthy of noting nonetheless.

A final literary example of manumission loyalty worth noting comes from Petronius's *Satyricon*. In the *Satyricon*, one of Petronius's characters, the wealthy and corpulent freedman Trimalchio, tells of his transition from slavery to manumission (*Sat.* 57). Several points are worth pausing on. Trimalchio claims that he was a prince who sold himself into slavery in order to gain Roman citizenship, and then eventually bought his manumission. Trimalchio speaks about his hopes for how the benefaction of manumission will change his life. He claims that he can walk proud (bare headed), that he will owe no one, and that he hopes he will never be jeered at. He honours his master (quite possibly deceased at this point) in two ways in this speech. In the first, he claims that through forty years of slavery no one knew whether he was slave or free, surely a reference to being treated with respect and dignity by his master and perhaps even like a son. Trimalchio honours his master a second time with the claim that he was "a fine dignified man whose little finger was worth more than your whole body." It is striking then that the expectations and practice of a freedman honouring and expressing loyalty towards his patron can be found even in works such as the *Satyricon*, since this suggests a level of concern with loyalty at the cultural level, and not only in concrete life.

The freed slave, then, was still obligated to his or her former owner. The relationship, because of the profound benefaction of manumission, was that of patron and client, no longer strictly that of master and slave. But the freedperson was expected, both socially and legally, to be loyal and grateful to his or her former owner, and we have seen in this section that this was commonly done in a number of ways. What makes manumission loyalty interesting is not only that freedpersons behaved in ways that expressed loyalty to their patron, for in this they share the concerns of all clients. What is also of interest is that there was such a marked concern that the loyalty be expressed, that it not be forgotten or, worse, neglected. We might conclude, even, that loyalty was the defining characteristic of a freedperson's relationship with and response to a patron, since it appears on several occasions to have been of far greater concern than was typical in patron-benefactor and client relations.

Understanding manumission loyalty helps us to understand ancient conversion for a number of reasons. First, it amply illustrates the extent to which loyalty was a central feature of the patron-benefactor and client relationship. While in no other setting did people seriously consider legislating loyalty, the general importance of loyalty we see here is echoed everywhere else. But manumission loyalty offers a number of parallels to conversion, especially with the language of slavery, being a slave of a god, and with the language of freedom and salvation. Finally, manumission loyalty helps us to understand conversion within the patron-benefactor and client relationship because the shared rhetoric and expression of loyalty, and the practice of the changing of names as a change in social and legal status. We shall see, however, that philosophical loyalty provides not only additional parallels to the rhetoric of loyalty, but also a closer model for how conversion, and especially I think conversion to the Jesus movement, actually happened.

5.2.3 Philosophical Loyalty

In chapter three I established that the philosopher, and sometimes philosophy itself, can be referred to in the terms and framework of ancient patronage, especially when it comes to accounting for the benefactions gained from philosophy and from the philosopher. So, for instance, Seneca's protreptic epistle (*Ep.* 90) talks about the part played by philosophy in the progress of humanity in terms of all the things that philosophy confers:

> She shows us what things are evil and what things are seemingly evil; she strips our minds of vain illusion. She bestows upon us a greatness which is substantial, but she represses the greatness which is inflated, and showy but filled with emptiness; and she does not permit us to be ignorant of the difference between what is great and what is swollen; nay, she delivers to us the knowledge of the whole of nature and of her own nature. She discloses to us what the gods are and of what sort they are; what are the nether gods, the household deities, and the protecting spirits. (*Ep.* 90.28)[86]

These features of philosophy are benefactions because their intent is salvation. These sorts of benefactions that derive from philosophy are not ends in themselves; the goal is not knowledge for the sake of knowledge. Rather, the goal is to be saved, terminology found in abundance for instance in Cebes' philosophical ruminations in his *Tabula*.[87] Seneca's list of benefits given above is by far not a unique description of the advantages that the philosophical life, that faithfulness to philosophical teaching, bestows upon the willing and devoted. We can therefore talk about the philosopher-patron.

Not only are philosophers and philosophy imagined to be benefactors, but adherents, or worshipers, resemble clients in their honouring conduct towards the patron-philosopher. In this section we are interested in the place of loyalty in this particular patronal relationship. As I said above, patronal loyalty is not synonymous with exclusivity. In many forms of patronage and benefaction the question of exclusivity is left open: literary patronage, social (general) patronage, some manumission relationships, and political patronage all allow for one to have multiple patrons. With philosophical patronage, the question of exclusivity is more complex. It was far more common, and understandable, for philosophical loyalty to be exclusive. Now, this was not the case universally, but very typically. It is worthwhile attempting to understand what about philosophical loyalty encouraged exclusivity.

There is likely something to the nature of the ancient philosophies that encouraged exclusive loyalty where it was unnecessary in other forms of

---

[86] Translation is that of R. M. Gummere of Seneca's *Epistulae Morales* II (LCL 77).
[87] J. T. Fitzgerald and L. Michael White, *The Tabula of Cebes* (Chico: Scholars Press, 1983).

patronage. Ancient cultic life was largely about ritual, and about honouring the gods in one way or another in an attempt to secure future benefactions from them. Philosophy, conversely, taught a disciple important lessons about life and the world. Philosophy provided a world view while cult probably did not to the same extent, and these world views tended to be mutually exclusive of one another. In actuality, there was *some* overlap between a few of the philosophies (Platonism and Stoicism), but generally speaking we should think of the philosophies as offering different and competing answers to similar questions. This is what stood behind the distinction Nock made between philosophy and cult with respect to conversion. Nock's treatment of conversion to philosophy touches on the aspect of loyalty, though he uses other terminology to describe it.

Nock's famous distinction was between adherence and conversion, which required or resulted in exclusive commitment. The former was a loose and free relationship while the latter was marked by emotion and, significantly, exclusive loyalty.[88] Nock explains this loyalty by associating it with the emotional bond that is established by philosophy's redirection of right thoughts and beliefs, but it more likely has to do with the mutually exclusive nature of the philosophies themselves. Exclusivity in philosophical loyalty is to be accounted for in the nature of ancient philosophy in sharp contrast to the nature of ancient cult and other forms of patronage. As Nock has said, "Adhesion to Socrates somehow meant giving your soul to him."[89] We should understand 'giving one's soul' as an expression of exclusive loyalty, a common expectation among the Graeco-Roman philosophies. This certainly explains Alcibiades's proclamation of loyalty to Socrates: "From this day onward it must be the case that I am your attendant, and that you must always have me in attendance on you" (Ps-Plato, *Alc. maj.* 135D).

The most recent and explicit treatment of the topic of philosophical loyalty has been done by David Sedley.[90] Sedley claims that "what gives philosophical movements their cohesion and identity is less a disinterested quest for the truth than a virtually religious commitment to the authority of a founder figure."[91] In many cases this appears to have been combined with a loyalty

---

[88] Arthur D. Nock, *Conversion: The Old and the New in Religion from Alexander the Great to Augustine of Hippo* (London: Oxford University Press, 1933), 181.

[89] Nock, *Conversion*, 166.

[90] D. Sedley, "Philosophical Allegiance in the Greco-Roman World," in *Philosophia Togata: Essays on Philosophy and Roman Society* (ed. M. Griffin and J. Barnes; Oxford: Clarendon, 1989), 97–119.

[91] Sedley, "Philosophical Allegiance," 97. This sentiment is echoed also by Andrew D. Clarke, *Secular and Christian Leadership: A Socio-Historical and Exegetical Study of*

also to a body of canonical texts—the writings of Epicurus and the founding fathers Metrodorus, Polyaenus and Hermarchus for the Epicureans (*Kuriai Doxai*) and Zeno for the Stoics. Sedley claims that it was equally unthinkable for either Stoics or Epicureans to challenge or criticise the teachings of either of their founder figures.[92] He calls this a "loyalty to scriptures" and he considers it "integral to the philosophical enterprise."[93] Loyalty to a person or the person's writing were synonymous with many types of philosophical patronage.

Sedley's primary example of philosophical textual loyalty is the Epicurean Philodemus of Gadara. According to Sedley, Philodemus represents two levels of loyalty: he is painstakingly loyal to Epicurus, but also to his own teacher Zeno of Sidon. Evidence of the latter can be found in Philodemus' approval of the way Zeno challenged the authenticity of some writings attributed to important Epicurean figures. The desire to mark some writings as inauthentic, Sedley suggests, is evidence of a loyalty to authentic tradition. To distinguish authentic from inauthentic writings is an act of piety in that it is a result of loyalty to a tradition.[94] Evidence of Philodemus' loyalty to Epicurus is seen in his practice of textual criticism. Sedley suggests that Philodemus' library shows evidence of Epicurean manuscripts being compared as a way of dealing with textual or interpretive problems. Loyalty to both figures simultaneously is seen through Philodemus' debate concerning whether sophistic rhetoric was an expertise (τέχνη), contained in his *Rhetorica*, in which Philodemus defers constantly to the authority of the founder and of Zeno. For instance, Philodemus' loyalty is made explicit when he writes, "But now let us move on to showing that it is not the case that while we call sophistic rhetoric an expertise the founders of our sect say the opposite; and that it is not just we, but they too, who call political rhetoric a kind of research and observation developed by practice."[95] Philodemus' loyalty to Epicurus

---

1 Corinthians 1–6 (AGJU 18; Leiden: E. J. Brill, 1993), 94; and Bruce W. Winter, *Philo and Paul Among the Sophists* (Cambridge: Cambridge University Press, 1997), 129.

[92] Interestingly, however, among the Stoics there appears to have been no hesitation to challenge each other and even the teachings of their greatest teachers (Sedley, "Philosophical Allegiance," 98, 104–17).

[93] Sedley, "Philosophical Allegiance," 100. See also H. Gregory Snyder, *Teachers and Texts in the Ancient World: Philosophers, Jews and Christians* (London: Routledge, 2000), 5, who also includes Jews and the early Christian communities among those who practice loyalty to textual traditions.

[94] Snyder, *Teachers and Texts*, 50–53.

[95] Philodemus, *Rhetorica* IIa 43.26ff.; translation of Sedley, "Philosophical Allegiance," 109–10.

the founder and Zeno the teacher is evident in Philodemus' method of argumentation and reliance on a near canonical authority of Epicurean texts.

Remaining in the realm of Epicureanism we find another expression of loyalty to the philosophic patron, one that has all the bearings of a hymn in its beauty and profundity of expression. We find it as the proem of Lucretius' third book of *De rerum natura*. It is worth quoting at length, noting both what Lucretius attributes to Epicurus, as well as the honourable titles he uses and the explicit expressions of loyalty:

> O you who first amid the darkness were able to raise aloft a light so clear, illumining the blessings of life, you I follow, O glory of the Grecian race, and now on the marks you have left I plant my own footsteps firm, not so much desiring to be your rival, as for love, because I yearn to copy you: for why should a swallow vie with swans, or what could a kid with its shaking limbs do in running to match himself with the strong horse's vigour? You are our father (*pater*), the discoverer of truths, you supply us with a father's precepts, from your pages, illustrious man, as bees in the flowery glades sip all the sweets, so we likewise feed on all your golden words... Thereupon from all these things a sort of divine delight gets hold upon me and a shuddering, because nature thus by your power has been so manifestly laid open and uncovered in every part. (*De rerum natura* 3.1–30)[96]

Lucretius credits Epicurus with all sorts of benefactions, and here powerfully proclaims his desire to imitate him, not to challenge him. Are we to understand that to challenge would be to express something less than loyalty? It is certainly arguable that this is precisely the point he wishes to make. His hymn to Epicurus, as Sedley observed above, has a "religious" tenor to it, and its expression of unwavering and fervent loyalty certainly adds to that sense. Notably, this passage stands out even among others of Lucretius' expressions of praise to Epicurus. Three other times in *De rerum natura* Lucretius praises Epicurus (1.62–79; 5.1–54; 6.1–42), yet none of these parallels the intensity of the above quoted passage. At 5.14–21, Lucretius claims that the benefactions of Ceres (corn) and Liber (liquor), though great, can be done without, whereas for the good life the benefaction of Epicurus (a purged mind) cannot be done without, a sentiment that he repeats at the start

---

[96] Lucretius, *De rerum natura* (trans. W. H. D. Rouse and M. F. Smith; Cambridge: Harvard University Press, 1975).

of his sixth book. Four times, then, Lucretius pauses to praise Epicurus and to shower him with honouring words recognising the great benefaction that has come to humanity because of his teachings, and in one of these (3.1–30), he does so with a depth and beauty that is hymnic. There is no mistaking where Lucretius' philosophical loyalties lie, and that, one would have to conclude, was precisely the point.

Our tripartite topics of patronage, loyalty, and conversion converge in a number of fascinating examples from philosophy. Philosophical conversion, as we are about to see, is marked by a change in loyalty, and a change in the patronal relationship. We look first to the conversion of Antiochus of Ascalon.[97] Antiochus was a second century B.C.E. Academic sceptic trained under the tutelage of Philon of Larissa, the last of the Scholarchs of the Academy. Starting in the third century B.C.E. the Academy had seen the introduction and increasing influence of scepticism (also known as Pyrrhonism). According to Cicero, Antiochus continued within this sceptic Academic tradition for an unusually long number of years (*Acad. post.* 63, 69), suggesting an equally uncommon degree of loyalty to his teacher Philon. At some point, however, Antiochus abandoned his teacher, openly criticising him. The *Sosus* affair marks Antiochus' break with this former teacher (or at the least, his expression of that break), and his complete break with the institution followed shortly thereafter.

Very little is known about Antiochus or Philon, about what caused the break, and about what Philon's response was, since none of the primary sources survives. It seems that Antiochus attempted to inaugurate something of a revitalisation movement that sought to return the Academy to its Platonic and Aristotelian foundations. Antiochus called his ideas a return to the Old Academy, and claimed that Philon's were a New Academy too much under the influence of scepticism, and thus, according to Antiochus, different and in no way continuous with Platonic or Aristotelian dogma. Unlike Philodemus then, Antiochus was more loyal to the founder figures than to his present teacher, since in the *Sosus* he explicitly rejected the teaching and position of Philon.[98]

The question of what exactly it was to which Antiochus converted is as vexed as any other questions concerning his life. On the one hand, he repre-

---

[97] John Glucker, *Antiochus and the Late Academy* (Hypomnemata 56; Göttingen: Vandenhoeck and Ruprecht, 1978); J. Barnes, "Antiochus of Ascalon," in *Philosophia Togata*, 51–96.

[98] For an account of what the *Sosus* contained, see Barnes, "Antiochus of Ascalon," 70–76.

sented himself as loyal to the Old Academy, that is to the traditions of Plato and Aristotle. Yet, many observers both ancient and modern note that Antiochus' ideas are barely distinguishable from Stoicism.[99] Barnes proclaims that "it seems clear that Antiochus thought of himself as a champion of the Porch," but asks immediately, "how can he have professed himself both an Old Academic and a Stoic?"[100] Are we here dealing with an example of non-exclusive loyalty in a philosophical setting? Or did Antiochus in fact convert to Stoicism from the Academy? Neither option is satisfactory. Rather, Antiochus, likely through his interactions with Stoics like Sosus (who bears the name of Antiochus' move against Philon) and others, discovered that in many ways Stoic ideology derived from and was more closely related to Plato and Aristotle as were many positions of the new sceptical Academy.[101] Antiochus' return to the Old Academy had an ally in the Stoics.

What is most revealing about the story of Antiochus' conversion, that is his break with his teacher Philon, is that conversion here marks a change in loyalty. Antiochus also obviously had a change of mind. Had Antiochus remained loyal to Philon and the New Academy but merely held other opinions or worked towards change from within, it is doubtful we would have come to consider this a conversion. In fact, it is doubtful we would even have record of the disagreement. But it is the change in *loyalty*, that is the disloyalty expressed to Philon and loyalty expressed to Aristotle (or ancient tradition), not the change of opinions or the clashing of ideas that marks this as a conversion. The change in loyalty, marked above all by a show of disloyalty, marks the conversion of Antiochus out of the New Academy. Most certainly, Philon was outraged by the affront (cf. Augustine, *Acad*. 3.41), and undoubtedly, the blatant show of disloyalty that the *Sosus* affair represented would have ensured the relationship between the two men was permanently severed.[102]

---

[99] Glucker, *Antiochus*, 27.
[100] Barnes, "Antiochus of Ascalon," 79.
[101] Barnes, "Antiochus of Ascalon," 75.
[102] This raises the question: if loyalty was such a strong expectation of philosophical patronage especially, how was Antiochus' criticism of and conversion from Philon viewed? Little is known about the views of Antiochus' contemporaries, but we do know that by the first-century Plutarch was critical of Antiochus. For more detail, see Jeffrey W. Tatum, "Plutarch on Antiochus of Ascalon: *Cicero* 4,2," *Hermes* 129 (2001): 139–42. We should keep in mind that it is precisely because loyalty was such a strong expectation of patronage that signs of disloyalty such as this from Antiochus are significant. Their significance is what makes them useful in a discussion of loyalty.

A similar story of philosophic conversion and changing loyalty emerges from the biography of the third-century Neoplatonist Porphyry. Porphyry preserved, edited, and arranged the surviving works of his famous teacher Plotinus in a collection of books known as the *Enneads*. The preface to this collection is a *bios* of Plotinus, much like we still find in anthologies of famous writers' works. What is striking about Porphyry for our purposes is that he was not always a student of Plotinus. Porphyry began his study under the Platonist rhetorician and philosopher Cassius Longinus. Little is known about Longinus, or really about Porphyry's relationship with him. But we can learn about their parting of ways from Porphyry's *Life of Plotinus*, from which we glean the general framework of Porphyry's philosophical relationships: Porphyry started his study with Longinus and yet moved to study with Plotinus for five years in the 260s C.E. (*Vit. Plot.* 4–5).

What Porphyry says *about* Plotinus is of little importance here. Needless to say, his act of writing this *vita* of Plotinus is a clear expression of loyalty and honour. He writes, in keeping with the appropriate tenor of the genre, to honour and promote the memory and teachings of his teacher. He tells us that Plotinus was mild, gentle, kind, and charming, that he was tireless and always on guard for the purity of his soul (23). Porphyry also calls Plotinus the "foremost critic of our time" (20), and refers to those who venerated Plotinus, appearing to count himself among them (7, 12).[103] He also claims that there was more to Plotinus in terms of intellectual character at birth than many achieve in adulthood, and thus was able to transcend the spasms that wracked his ill body towards his death (10). Remarkably, perhaps to lend his work some semblance of objectivity, Porphyry notes that Plotinus, though a genius, was not equally the genius in all his work. Work undertaken while still immature philosophically and later while ill reflected a "lesser genius" (6).

We glean from this work some of the details of Porphyry's changing philosophical relationship. Plotinus and Longinus were adversaries (19–21); each (and their disciples) knew of the other's work and disliked it. Once when something of Longinus was read aloud to Plotinus, he concluded that "Longinus is a philologist ... but no philosopher" (14), slighting the man with the charge that his philosophical writing was too encumbered with ornamental word-play and not rich enough in its depth of learning. When Porphyry was loyal to Longinus, he carried on a volley of attacks and defences with one of Plotinus' disciples, Amelius (*Vit. Plot.* 18), in which he represented and was

---

[103] The translations here and below are from the translation and excellent commentary of Mark Edwards, *Neoplatonic Saints: The Lives of Plotinus and Proclus by their Students* (Liverpool: University of Liverpool Press, 2000).

loyal to the teachings of Longinus. Yet, it was during this exchange that Porphyry changed his position on the matters they were debating. He left Longinus to join Plotinus with an embarrassing admission of error and entry into Plotinus' circle. Porphyry cites a letter in which Longinus expresses the hope that Porphyry would return to him, and bring with him copies of Plotinus' work which he can read closely in order to attack.[104] Longinus appeared to hope that Porphyry would act as a spy in an enemy camp. In other words, Longinus hoped that Porphyry's change in loyalty was only for appearances, and that by working from within he would eventually prove loyal to him after all. But that was not to be. Eventually Longinus accepted the loss of Porphyry in a letter, writing that Porphyry "made no small effort to imitate Plotinus and [preferred] to take him rather than myself as his mentor" (*Vit. Plot.* 20). This fate would have been sealed by a final act of disloyalty: Porphyry's publication of a writing in criticism of his former teacher Longinus, referred to in the *Vita* (*Vit. Plot.* 20).

Here, as in the example of the Academic Antiochus, philosophical conversion is measured by loyalty, that is by one's intellectual and physical relationship with respect to a teacher. When Porphyry was loyal to Longinus, he wrote in defence of his ideas against Plotinus and was at Longinus' side, or in his circle of disciples. When Porphyry left, Longinus hoped Porphyry would return to him (physically, as well as intellectually no doubt) but Porphyry remained in the circle of Plotinus, loyal to him by proximity as well as intellectually. What is more, like Antiochus, Porphyry publicly challenged the teachings of Longinus, indicating for all to see that he had renounced his former position and teacher in favour of a new teacher. The conversion of Porphyry, as with Antiochus, is to be measured on the canon of loyalty, for it is the stark change of loyalty involved in the change of philosophical allegiance that, by all accounts, marks it as conversion. Edwards, for instance, translates Porphyry's description of the Roman senator Rogatanius to Plotinus' ways as a "conversion" because of the nature of philosophical loyalty (*Vit. Plot.* 7).[105] Porphyry's word here is ἀποστροφή, which we easily associate with the Greek vocabulary of conversion, to turn away from previous ways of doing things. Though this is a description of the Roman senator, we can be certain that Porphyry included himself in that camp of men who had abandoned a previous teacher (or life without a teacher at all as the case could often be) to express loyalty in action, word, and thought to their new teacher and philosophical patron.

---

[104] Edwards, *Neoplatonic Saints*, 34 n. 195.
[105] Edwards, *Neoplatonic Saints*, 16 n. 87.

Conversion in philosophy is expressed above all in terms of loyalty to the teacher and that teacher's doctrines. Diogenes Laertius relates that many were attracted to the Megarian school of which Stilpon, a well known predecessor of the Cynics and Stoics in the Socratic tradition, was the last head. Diogenes Laertius writes that "nearly the whole of Greece was attracted to him and joined the school of Megara" (2.113). Note here not the exaggerated number but that conversion to the school was expressed in terms of *joining* and thus of loyalty. Diogenes goes on to describe a number of people whose loyalties changed and who converted to the school: two followers of Theophrastus lost two followers to Stilpon, Aristotle a Cyrenaic philosopher also lost two, Aristides a dialectician lost one, and he goes on. Even two people who had initially openly criticised Stilpon, came to side with him and "hold to him with zeal" (2.114). These people all pledged loyalty to Stilpon and his teachings which would have meant simultaneously not criticising him and not following another. One could not serve two philosophical masters at the same time because their messages and world-views were usually, or they strived to be, mutually exclusive and unique. Because of the exclusive loyalty of philosophical patronage, however, we are given more explicit examples of something we did not get with other forms of patronage, namely evidence of *disloyalty*, and thus of conversion. Philosophical conversion necessarily involved disloyalty to someone while in the process of expressing loyalty to a new teacher. While loyalty is not a unique feature of philosophical patronage (neither disloyalty), many have noticed that philosophical loyalty takes on something of a "religious" (in the modern sense of the word) intensity that is less typical of other forms of patronal loyalty. But nonetheless, all these ways and means for expressing loyalty to a patron are simply variations on a theme. Though different in degree, united they represent a central feature of the patron-benefactor and client relationship. What remains, then, as our final task is to offer some concluding observations and remarks on the nature of loyalty and what it can tell us about ancient conversion.

5.3 Loyalty, Conversion, and Paul

The primary benefits to be gained from introducing loyalty into the patronage–conversion equation, especially concerning Paul's conversion, are three-fold. First, loyalty avoids the modernistic tendencies of psychologisation, yet as a phenomenon, it cannot possibly have been devoid of psychological elements (as if anything ever actually is). Secondly, our previous insight that ancient conversion is about the relationship between two parties and not about the internal measure of emotional tumult is confirmed by an analysis of ancient loyalty. Thirdly, we are able to relate an obvious feature of Paul's letters to his conversion—namely his tenacious loyalty first to the tradition of his forefathers and subsequently to the Jesus movement and what *he* in particular understood as the key benefactions to be gained from joining that movement. Let us look at each of these three benefits in turn.

Loyalty is measured in one way and one way alone—externally. This is not to say that loyalty did not have other aspects, some of them internal and emotional, but what we are dealing with here is how it was measured or assessed, not in how it was experienced. The ancients recognised that loyalty could not be measured in terms of internal features because these were inaccessible to the outside observer. Internal measures of loyalty, as we have seen, could not be legislated and they could not even be assumed. That is to say, one's true opinion of another party could not be known, and thus was not only not a reliable measure of loyalty, but appears to have been unnecessary as a measure of loyalty. Conversely, loyalty was an action, or perhaps more precisely it was a type of action: one that functioned to honour another person, in the examples we have limited our study to, a patron. And yet, having said that, it also appears that loyalty could be accompanied by sincere feelings of affection, friendship, and respect. It would be difficult to argue that in some of our cases of loyalty, we are not also dealing with sincere affection shared between two parties, and therefore that loyalty cannot also have an emotional component. But the key term is 'also.' Loyalty is primarily about the action and is measured primarily in terms of appropriate conduct. It is, or it can be, secondarily about the feelings that might attend such a relationship. But what is most helpful about loyalty is that it is not primarily emotional and for this reason works against the psychologising tendencies of the modern cultural framework.

Building from here, we can say then that conversion in the ancient world is framed and measured likewise. Conversion may well have been attended by some sincere emotional phenomena, but it was measured first and foremost by the actions of loyalty and by the change in the patronal relationship. The primary focus is on the external relationship with the patron—an emperor, a god, a philosopher, even a philosophy; the primary focus is not on internal emotional phenomena. Even piety in antiquity, the term εὐσέβεια, was not a state of mind or proper reflection on God, but the appropriate actions directed towards God or a god. When Lucius converts to Isis, the primary measure of that is his obvious change in loyalty in her favour. When Alcibiades converts to Socrates, that is measured and expressed in terms of loyalty and commitment. Finally, when Antiochus converts from one form of the Academy to another, it is expressed in terms of disloyalty and new loyalty, each of which are measured not by the opinions/convictions held but by the public airing of them and subsequent physical departure from a former teacher and his teachings. We can well imagine that there were emotional aspects and sincere feelings in the experiences of these figures, but it is the manifestation of loyalty in actions and conduct that gives substance to the change that has taken place. What makes loyalty most useful then for understanding ancient conversion is that it adds "life" or "dynamism" to the portrait of ancient conversion that might have been too sterile for some. There is likely a dominant sense that conversion can never be a staid and dispassionate decision, but rather that it must include an emotional component. Our look at ancient conversion has shown first that in fact there does not *have* to be an emotional component to conversion, secondly that the primary component is loyalty expressed outwardly, and third, that despite this there *can be* emotional elements to the experience.

Finally, it is evident throughout Paul's letters that loyalty is an important feature of Paul's relationship with his God. Malina and Neyrey, in fact, show that "loyalty" is a key feature not only of patronage, but also of ancient life and ancient personality in general.[106] Hofstede too claims that "Loyalty to the group is an essential element of the collectivist family," though he would say the same of collectivist cultures in general.[107] Loyalty is part of the socialisation of people from the ancient Mediterranean. Their temporal frame, to recall the material on Kluckhohn and Strodtbeck from Chapter One, was past oriented— their life was structured by past tradition and they sought to imitate the great figures of the past. This is obvious in the handing down of the Law and old lore, but tradition need not even be old. According to Malina and Neyrey,

> Paul appeals to just this point when he prefaces his account of the Eucharist (1 Cor. 11:23) and the resurrection (15:3) with an appeal to traditional authority, "I hand on . . . what I received." He expects the church to "maintain the traditions even as I have delivered them to you" (1 Cor. 11:2).[108]

---

[106] Malina and Neyrey, *Portraits of Paul*, 164–69.
[107] Geert Hofstede, *Culture's Consequences: Comparing Values, Behaviors, Institutions, and Organizations Across Nations* (2nd ed.; Thousand Oaks: Sage Publications, 2001), 229.
[108] Malina and Neyrey, *Portraits of Paul*, 164–65.

Rituals and ceremonies in past-oriented cultures serve to give value to the past, the loyalty to the past is expected; apparently Paul (or somebody in the Jesus movement) denigrated disloyalty to past traditions when he encountered it (1 Cor 14:33–36).[109]

Loyalty, for Paul and his people at least, was also an important element of their cultic associations—they were after all monotheists.[110] Monotheism is an expression of exclusive loyalty. Those who followed the God of Israel as well as members of the Jesus movement stood out because of their loyalty to their divine patron. And the injunction to loyalty was divinely sanctioned in the first and second of the Ten Commandments (Exod 20:4–6): make no idols, worship no other, fear God but count on steadfast love for ever for loving God and keeping God's commandments, and of course all this is contained in the frequently repeated Shema Yisrael.

It is clear from Paul's abundant use of the πιστ- root words that loyalty was of central interest to Paul. Faith for Paul is not only often synonymous with allegiance or faithfulness, it is also an expression of exclusive loyalty. Rom 1:25, 28 condemns those who fail to acknowledge the creator, the supreme benefactor, and even worse those who serve and worship instead anything or anyone else. At Rom 1:31, in a list of characteristics of such people, Paul calls them ἀσυνθέτους (disloyal). Disloyalty to Paul's God, as with disloyalty to any patron, carries severe consequences. In the first half of Romans, Paul seems to be constantly making a point, then back-tracking, working himself into a corner, then fighting to get out. In each case, this has to do with the value of the Law. It appears throughout these passages that Paul is struggling to express loyalty to God in a new way (law-free salvation) without expressing disloyalty to God for the previous gift of the Law. On the one hand he claims that "the law is holy and the commandment holy and just and good" (Rom 7:12), which honours God for a previous benefaction. Yet he is convinced that the law is no longer necessary soteriologically. How can Paul argue that the law was a benefaction from God but that the supersession of it was also a benefaction from the same God? These are the issues of loyalty, which are the result of a conversion that involved the same divine patron, that Paul is struggling to work out.

---

[109] So Malina and Neyrey, *Portraits of Paul*, 165.
[110] Or more precisely, henotheists, since they did not deny the existence of other gods, but thought they were pathetic and weak in the face of their more powerful and awesome god. Henotheism in fact reflects an even greater degree of loyalty to a divine patron than monotheism, since it starts from the position that there are other divine patrons, but chooses allegiance to just one.

We see features of Paul's loyalty within his conversion passages as well. In the previous chapter we noted Paul's references to his harassment of the early Jesus movement—Gal 1:13–14 and Phil 3:5–6. Numerous attempts have been made to explain Paul's persecution, mostly having to do with the Jesus movement preaching a salvation apart from the law,[111] but occasionally having to do simply with its teaching.[112] What unites any such explanations is the presentation of Paul as loyal and zealous to the traditions of his elders. At Gal 1:14, Paul connects his zeal for the traditions of his fathers to his harassment of the ἐκκλησία of God, and he does likewise at Phil 3:6—as to zeal, a pursuer of the ἐκκλησία. In fact, the ζηλ- root words (ζῆλος, ζηλωτής, ζηλόω) are all representative of loyalty—Paul's zeal is related to, or an expression of, his loyalty.[113] And zeal is often associated with philosophical loyalty, since it is ideally embedded in the behaviour of the philosophical disciple: ζηλωτής and μαθητής are interchangeable in some instances for Dio Chrysostom (*1 Regn.* 38; *4 Regn.* 122; *Hom. Socr.* 1, 3, 5). And blasphemy, for which members of the Jesus movement are depicted as being punished (Acts 6:8–15; 26:11), needs to be understood as an expression of disloyalty. For Paul, then, loyalty to a new tradition is a central characteristic of what he preaches to his new communities, and of what motivates him. Conversion to this movement means no less amount of loyalty than what he exhibited while ἐν τῷ Ἰουδαϊσμῷ.

Given the central importance of loyalty within the institution of patronage and benefaction, we can attribute Paul's palpable concern for loyalty (in others and in himself) to the ways in which his "religious" perspective as a whole is framed in the discourse of divine patronage and benefaction. His divine patron is the lone God of Israel, and to that God he was and is still fiercely loyal. Paul's conversion is expressed in terms of these features: the rhetoric of patronage and benefaction and the loyalty of the client/worshiper to the divine patron.

We have come across several close and useful analogies for understanding how Paul fits within this context of patronage, conversion, and loyalty. Lucius's conversion to Isis is most clearly about loyalty. She gives him the benefaction of salvation from his predicament, and he responds by pledging (and thus expressing) his loyalty to her, illustrated abundantly in the praise

---

[111] G. Bornkamm, *Paul* (trans. D. M. G. Stalker; Minneapolis: Fortress Press, 1971), 15.
[112] Arland J. Hultgren, "Paul's Pre-Christian Persecutions of the Church: Their Purpose, Locale, and Nature," *JBL* 95 (1976): 97–111.
[113] On the relationship between zeal, patronage, and loyalty, see Mott, "The Power of Giving and Receiving," 65, 70; Clarke, *Secular and Christian Leadership*, 99–101; Winter, *Philo and Paul*, 129–32.

he heaps on her, in his desire to move ever deeper into her mysteries, and above all in his desire to become one of her priests. But since Lucius's conversion involves a change in gods, it is not as close an analogy to Paul who retained the same patron in his conversion. Here the examples of philosophical loyalty provide a closer analogy it seems to Paul's conversion. Recall that Antiochus and Porphyry each left one philosopher for another, yet each remained loyal to the same over-arching philosophy. Antiochus remained loyal to the Aristotelian Academy, but he left Philon, who seems to function as broker seeking to bring disciples (clients) closer to salvation. Likewise, Porphyry converted from one broker to another but remained loyal to the ultimate patron, Plato and, in this case, Neoplatonism. Antiochus' and Porphyry's conversions involved a change in loyalty from one (philosophical) broker to another but they stayed with the same patron. This sounds remarkably like Paul's situation, so again we are drawn back to the question of who/what functioned as Paul's broker prior to Jesus. It is difficult to establish the answer to this question; for instance, could the Law function as a broker or could only sentient beings like humans or angels fill this role?

Despite this, we can see that loyalty remains a defining characteristic of Paul, and in keeping with his Jewish identity, that loyalty is exclusive and not to be shared among more than one divine patron. That Paul so uses the rhetoric of patronage and benefaction in his descriptions of his conversion suggests that Paul, like his Graeco-Roman and Hellenistic Jewish peers, understood his God to be his patron or benefactor, that he understood himself to be a client of God, and that he knew what this required of him in that position. Paul's concern for loyalty to God and to the powerful new broker supplements the details offered by the framework of patronage and benefaction. The loyalty of Paul to his new broker and his new understanding of his divine patron also offers an emotional component to Paul's conversion that modern sentiment may still require, yet it emphasises above all that Paul's conversion was about (and is explicitly expressed as) the relationship between Paul and his divine patron. That is to say, Paul's conversion, as with Antiochus's, Porphyry's, or Lucius's, may well have been attended by emotions, but their conversions are marked first and foremost with reference to the change in the patronal relationship, by expression that marked them as clients, and by actions of loyalty to that new patron.

We might stop at this point to consider why Paul converted, for it might be charged that if one removes the psychological elements from Paul's conversion, there is no satisfactory way to account for the event. But is this actually the case? Psychological approaches do not account for *why* Paul converted, at least that was rejected from Pauline scholarship long ago in the form of psychological categories like guilt and disaffection; rather psychological approaches simply cast the experience in psychological terms. They usually describe the conversion, but do not explain it. The *why* of Paul's conversion has always vexed scholarship, but the approach outlined in this work actually provides us with *both* a way of describing the event and of accounting for it. In the simplest possible terms, Paul converted because of a benefaction, namely the benefaction he received in the vision. What the phenomenon actually is, when Paul gets his vision or Aristides his call, is beyond the scope of this study. The results of these wide-spread occurrences, however, are remarkably consistent. As with other visions of gods in general in the Graeco-Roman world, loyalty (even in a newly expressed form) was the result of the vision Paul received from his God. Paul converted because God called him to do so in the form of a vision.

What makes Paul's loyalty unique is that it appears to borrow features from several different types of patronal loyalty. His loyalty that derives from having received a vision and encounter with the divine resembles the experience of many other recipients of divine revelations and visitations. His exclusively expressed loyalty, one could argue, is borrowed from philosophical loyalty, the nature of which required solitary allegiance. The fact that Paul's conversion did not in fact involve a change in patrons is borrowed both from manumission patronage, in which a slave becomes a client because of the benefaction of manumission, and from some forms of philosophical patronage, in which a disciple remains within a school of philosophy (the "patron") but changes teachers (the broker).

In general terms, the results of this study suggest that people converted because of the benefactions they received unannounced (such as an appearance from a god or call from a literary patron) or because of the benefactions they stood to gain by being loyal to a patron first. One might be attracted to a patron, human or divine, because of the benefactions that were promised—enlightenment, a certain view of the world, gnosis, the good life, insurance in daily life against hunger, poverty, or personal danger, salvation, and so on. Or one might be attracted because of what one saw manifest in those who were already loyal—a sunny disposition in the face of hardship, restoration of health, etc. Sometimes, mostly in the cases of the philosophies, the attraction might be understood as intellectual—a certain teaching impressed them—, but even here we must understand teachings as benefactions, for what they offered a disciple was a *better* way of getting through the day and through life.

5.4 Conclusion

Loyalty is the dynamic that animates a model of ancient conversion based on patronage and benefaction. Where one might be concerned that conversion within the patronage and benefaction framework involved solely the balance sheet of expenses and revenues, the existence and expectation of loyalty shows us there was more at stake than just that. People were bound to others in relationships of patronage, and in every instance loyalty motivated action. Conversion, a change in the patronal relationship, would have involved simultaneous acts of disloyalty and loyalty—disloyalty to a former patron, loyalty to a new patron. Each of these can be understood analogously with honour and dishonour—disloyalty is dishonouring, loyalty honouring, and thus, the stakes in conversion were high. In the human realm, though disloyalty could get one killed, it was typically less risky than that, involving instead the loss of benefactions and perhaps an inability to attract future benefactors. In the realm of Graeco-Roman cult, disloyalty was atypical because loyalty was not exclusive. Where disloyalty figured most prominently was in philosophical patronage and in the divine patronage of the Hellenised Jews and the Jesus movement. Here we can see clearly that loyalty and disloyalty were tied up in the experience of conversion, and when the rest of that experience is also coined in the language of patronage and benefaction, a pattern of ancient religion begins to emerge that incorporates the entirety of the first-century Mediterranean. Paul's zealous behaviour both before and after his conversion is explicitly related to loyalty to his divine patron. Paul's conversion and expression of loyalty draws syncretistically from two primary resources—his Jewish monotheistic loyalty to a single god, not terribly common among his Graeco-Roman peers, and his exclusive loyalty to a teacher more common among the philosophies. Despite obvious differences among Hellenistic Jewish, mystery, Jesus movement, and Graeco-Roman cults, they are united by a similar framework of divine patronage and benefaction, one in which the gods are treated as patrons, worshipers act as clients, and conversion entails pledges of loyalty and, where warranted, acts of disloyalty.

Conclusion

Anthropology, it might be said, is the study of humans being human. As such, it has had to deal constantly with the realisation while we are all human we are all human *differently*. And it is culture and context that make all the difference. Of course, anthropologists are not the only ones capable of recognising cultural difference; the work of New Testament scholars spans a similarly massive cultural breech, and this has certainly forced them to acknowledge similar issue of differences. And yet for some reason, it is assumptions of sameness and not difference that have long informed New Testament approaches to conversion. My suggestion in this work is that these assumptions of sameness, when it comes to conversion at least, are likely the result of the pervasive influence of psychology that is a cultural characteristic of the modern Western world. While New Testament scholarship has long recognised difference, perhaps the explicit reliance on an anthropological understanding of cultural difference is what is needed in order to take that extra step in understanding the full implications of this difference. This has certainly been the experience of, and accounts for the popularity of the work of, scholars like J. H. Elliott, Bruce Malina, Jerome Neyrey, J. J. Pilch, and a growing number of others.

This is a study of the differences that cultural difference makes with respect to conversion. But I have not asked, as others have, how people convert, what they convert to, under what conditions they convert, what leads them to convert, or similar questions. My focus has been on how *we* (as a culture) talk about, how we understand, how we frame the conversion experience, both of ourselves and others. In Chapter One I establish that psychology provides that framework for our assumptions and our discourse on conversion. I go on from there to show a number of reasons why, when it comes to understanding and talking about the conversion experience among first-century Mediterraneans, the modern psychological framework is not, indeed *cannot* be, helpful. Though the discovery of cultural difference in New Testament studies is not new, it seems that the full implications of this have been left untapped. In other words, we are obligated to ask: if ancient and modern people were human differently, how will this affect our assumptions about human experience and motivation? Conversion is probably not even the most pressing topic on which we would do well to exercise such an understanding.

There are several reasons why our approach to understanding ancient conversion has to change. The first is that we are a modern and Western culture attempting to read and understand the experiences of an ancient and Mediterranean culture. The significance of this is not only temporal and geographical, but also cultural. Culture is like language in that cultural institutions and values make actions meaningful just as grammar and syntax make strings of words meaningful. Culture is to actions as grammar and syntax are to words. With a lexicon, someone with as little as the Greek alphabet can look up words and see their range of meanings, but without a knowledge of Greek grammar and syntax, the strings of words *mean* nothing, they cannot become sentences. Likewise, an outside observer can observe activity and perhaps can recognise (sometimes only apparently) familiar behaviour, but without sufficient knowledge of the cultural details, the *meaning* of this behaviour is lost on the observer. Worse still is when an observer believes (s)he has understood an action but has only done so by using her or his own cultural referents analogically (ethnocentrism).

The primary cultural difference on which I have focused concerns different constructions of the self, of self-understanding and of the relationship between the self and others. Each culture constructs its own sense of self and self-identity, and this has an impact on how its individuals experience life and construct reality. The Mediterranean allocentric self does not understand herself, her world, or her relationship to others in the same way as does the Western idiocentric self. An understanding or framing of the conversion experience that is predicated on a particular construction of the self, it goes without saying, is going to lead to distortion, anachronism, and ethnocentrism if applied uncritically to a different construction of the self.

The second reason our approach to ancient conversion has to change is that our approach is too often accidentally (and frequently deliberately) psychological. The Western idiocentric self has made possible an understanding of human behaviour and experience that is self generated. Emotions and mental cognitive fluctuations originate within the self and the subconscious overrides the conscious experience of the world. This results in a view of conversion the defining characteristic of which is its emotional tumult and the individual introspective experience. What is wrong with this is emphatically not that ancient conversion cannot have involved emotional tumult nor that the ancient were incapable of introspection, but that psychological experiences, like the emotions and emotional states, are not easily exported across cultural boundaries. In other words, whatever emotional tumult existed in ancient conversion cannot be understood using Western emotional tumult as an analogy.

A modern understanding of conversion also tends to make these emotional categories central to the definition of conversion, rather than peripheral even if important aspects of conversion. Another result of the psychological approach to conversion is that it makes conversion almost exclusively introspective and personal. Introspection and personal reflection, however, are characteristics of the idiocentric self. This too is not meant to convey the impression that the ancients were incapable or distrustful of introspection—witness the entire philosophical tradition—, but that their social experience was not overridden by their internal one. Said another way, their behaviour as individuals was governed less by internal than by external forces.

The final problem with our modern approach to understanding conversion is how it combines the emphasis on the emotional with a psychological perspective. This is evidenced in our collective (that is cultural) tendency to draw a strong distinction between emotion and thought. While both derive from within the person, 'emotion' is said to be uncontrollable, chaotic, wild, involuntary, and irrational; at its worst it overrides reason, and controls and dominates us. Conversely, 'thought' is said to be the binary opposite of all these things; it is rational, thoughtful, and most importantly, unemotional.[1] By stressing the emotional and psychological features of conversion, the psychological approach tends to highlight certain features of it to the exclusion of others: conversion is thought to be beyond us to understand; conversion happens to us, we do not usually choose it. We would not likely call conversion irrational, but possibly a-rational.

But the ancient conversion experience would have been framed not within the religious experience of the idiocentric psychological self, but the dyadic (sociocentric, allocentric, collectivistic) experience of an unbounded self. This dyadic self operated in a world with different cultural values, which we should fully expect to give different meaning to experiences which might appear to be similar to modern experiences.

Using the model of patronage and benefaction to understand ancient conversion has many things to recommend it. In the first place, it frames conversion in terms that the ancients themselves used. Of course, much can be gained by using a non-native or external framework for understanding the

---

[1] See Catherine Lutz, "Emotion, Thought, and Estrangement: Emotion as a Cultural Category," *Cultural Anthropology* 1 (1986): 287–309.

experiences of other people (known anthropologically as the etic approach), but in this case the terms we use are so infused with cultural assumptions and features that their cross-cultural use is rendered highly ineffective. What I have sought to do here is to strike a balance between what Clifford Geertz called "experience near" and "experience distant" concepts. Geertz warns against exclusive reliance on one or the other.

> Confinement to experience-near concepts leaves an ethnographer awash in immediacies as well as entangled in vernacular. Confinement to experience-distant ones leaves him stranded in abstractions and smothered in jargon. The real question . . . is what roles the two kinds of concepts play in anthropological analysis. To be more exact: How, in each case, should they be deployed so as to produce an interpretation of the way a people live which is neither imprisoned within their mental horizons, an ethnography of witchcraft written by a witch, nor systematically deaf to the distinctive tonalities of witchcraft as written by a geometer?[2]

We avoid these pitfalls by using categories and a framework that the ancient writers so relied upon, coupled with our propensity for constructing models from observable data. Patronage and benefaction is an external phenomenon, and the fact that the ancients framed their understanding of conversion in this way needs to be fully developed. It says something significant about the different ways in which our two cultures (our own and that of the New Testament) understand, measure, and talk about the experience of conversion.

The prevalence of the rhetoric of patronage and benefaction in discourse about the gods tells us the obvious: they saw their gods as patrons and benefactors and their own conduct as clients. But it also tells us that this must be our starting point for any analysis of ancient conversion. Ancient people had a consistent set of conventions that they used within their interaction with their gods as well as within their descriptions of these actions to others. I have grouped these conventions together as examples of the rhetoric of patronage and benefaction. They include the call of the patron, the philosopher and philosophy as patron, prayer, praise, and proselytism, patronal synkrisis, and finally the term χάρις. These conventions appear both in writing

---

[2] C. Geertz, "From the Native's Point of View: On the Nature of Anthropological Understanding," in *Culture Theory: Essays on Mind, Self and Emotion* (ed. R. A. Shweder and R. A. LeVine; Cambridge: Cambridge University Press, 1984), 123–36, this quote p. 124.

about human patrons and divine patrons and, as I show in Chapter Four, they appear in Paul's conversion passages.

What can we know about Paul's conversion from this fact? Admittedly, not everything. But we can know with certainty that he did not think of his own conversion as modern Western individualists think of theirs. His conversion, like so many others, was the result of a divine patron making a benefaction to a human in and through a vision and calling. Does this require us to take literally that God appeared to Paul? Not exactly, but it does require us to take literally *Paul's claim* that this happened. And in this we treat Paul's claim no differently than we treat Aristides' claim or the claims of the others called and healed by Asclepius. The question is not *whether* these claims to calls and healings and divine benefactions are real, but *what* these claims reveal about ancient religion and culture.

We know that Paul's conversion had to do with his entering into a new form of relationship with a patron, since in this case he did not change patrons. Conversion that involved a change in the patronal relationship rather than a wholesale change in patrons was, as we saw, not the most common form of conversion, but neither was it the experience of Paul alone. And finally we know that Paul's conversion, like all others of his day, was marked by the expression of loyalty. Loyalty is a fundamental part of the patron–client relationship. Loyalty might be thought of as, in the language of electricity, the current that passed between patron and client; it was the charge that gave the institution life. Loyalty is, therefore, what was at stake in conversion; and, as we saw, the stakes were often high because loyalty was the enervating force in the relationship. Without loyalty, patronage and benefaction was as lifeless as an unplugged appliance.

We can say too then of Paul's conversion that just because it was framed in the context of the patron–client relationship of exchange and reciprocity in no way can be taken to mean that it was an undynamic change. Yes, we should assume that conversion in the ancient Mediterranean context involved the balance sheet of benefactions and reciprocity, but a knowledge of the animating role of loyalty illustrates that there was more at stake than only this. Loyalty also encourages us not to assume that ancient people were motivated solely on a principle of rational choice ('What's in it for me'), which a model of patronage and benefaction without loyalty might allow. Above all, however, what an understanding of loyalty and its relationship to patronage and benefaction tells us about conversion is that it was primarily external, that it was primarily marked by action, and that it was not primarily an internal, personal and introspective experience.

Conclusion

Before drawing this work to a close, I would like to add a few very brief comments concerning a theoretical issue undergirding much of what I have done here, and suggest from there an area for fruitful future research. In the fields of history and sociology a debate has raged concerning the motivations of human action. Traditionally, the debate has swung between two poles: structure vs. agency (also known or described as reification vs. psychologism, determinism vs. voluntarism, emergence vs. reductionism, holism vs. individualism, and macro vs. micro). These two poles represent different ways of accounting for human action. The structures of society compel (passive) humans towards certain predictable actions, or the agency (creative will) of humans makes them active (not passive) participants in the choices they make at any given moment. Recent work in historical-sociology has begun to see that in fact nothing is gained from preserving these binary opposites, and some have begun working out how these two work in dialectic with each other. There is, in short, human agency within structurally and culturally imposed limitations.

In terms of the present work, I have definitely privileged 'structure' over 'agency.' Ancient patronage and benefaction provide the structure within which, I have presupposed (though also illustrated), human actions are predictable and explainable and agency is non-existent. Conversely, modern approaches to conversion, with their psychologising framework, could be said to privilege the 'agency' of humans—the individual's freedom to create and re-create her own structures. This brings up a series of questions that would benefit from future analysis. To what extent has the emphasis on structure throughout this work been dictated by the collectivistic culture and its sources? Does the 'agency' component of the structure–agency dialectic presuppose an individualistic agent? A convincing argument could probably be made that it does. If this is so, since the ancient Mediterranean was a collectivistic culture (as opposed to an individualistic one), is personal and creative agency so limited as to reduce the quality of the dialectical relationship? In short, would there have been much of a structure–agency dialectic at work in the ancient Mediterranean, or will we find there mostly 'structure'?

Bibliography

Aarde, Andries van. *Fatherless in Galilee: Jesus as a Child of God*. Harrisburg, Pa.: Trinity Press International, 2001.

———. "Jesus as a Fatherless Child." Pages 65–84 in *The Social Setting of Jesus and the Gospels*. Edited by Wolfgang Stegemann, Bruce J. Malina, and Gerd Theissen. Minneapolis: Fortress Press, 2002.

Adkins, Arthur W. M. *Merit and Responsibility: A Study in Greek Values*. Oxford: Clarendon Press, 1960.

Alexander, Loveday. "Paul and the Hellenistic Schools: The Evidence of Galen." Pages 60–83 in *Paul in his Hellenistic Context*. Edited by Troels Engberg-Pedersen. Minneapolis: Fortress Press, 1995.

Alföldy, Geza. *The Social History of Rome*. Translated by David Braund and Frank Pollock. London: Routledge, 1988.

———. "Die Freilassung von Sklaven und die Struktur der Sklaverei in der römischen Kaiserzeit." *Rivista Storica dell' Antichità* 2 (1972): 97–129.

Alkana, Joseph. *The Social Self: Hawthorne, Howells, William James, and Nineteenth-Century Psychology*. Lexington: The University Press of Kentucky, 1997.

Alter, Margaret G. *Resurrection Psychology: An Understanding of Human Personality Based on the Life and Teachings of Jesus*. Chicago: Loyola University Press, 1994.

Anderson, F. C. "The Call of Saul of Tarsus." *Expository Times* 42 (1930–1931): 90–92.

Anderson, R. Dean. *Glossary of Greek Rhetorical Terms: Connected to Methods of Argumentation, Figures and Tropes from Anaximenes to Quintilian*. Contributions to Biblical Exegesis and Theology 24. Leuven: Peeters, 2000.

———. *Ancient Rhetorical Theory and Paul*. Revised ed. Contributions to Biblical Exegesis and Theology 18. Leuven: Peeters, 1996.

Ando, Clifford. *Imperial Ideology and Provincial Loyalty in the Roman Empire*. Berkeley: University of California Press, 2000.

Andrews, M. E. "The Conversion of Paul." *Journal of Bible and Religion* 9 (1941): 147–54.

Apuleius. *Metamorphoses*. Translated by John Arthur Hanson. Loeb Classical Library 44, 453. Cambridge, Mass.: Harvard University Press, 1989.

Arichea Jr., Daniel C. "Translating 'Grace' (*Charis*) in the New Testament." *Bible Translator* 29 (1978): 201–206.

Aristides. Edited by Wilhelm Dindorf. 3 vols. Leipzig: Weidmann, 1829. Reprint: Hildesheim: Georg Olms Verlagsbuchhandlung, 1964.

Aristotle. *Rhetoric*. Translated by John Henry Freese. Loeb Classical Library 193. Cambridge, Mass.: Harvard University Press, 1926.

Arnal, William E. *Jesus and the Village Scribes: Galilean Conflicts and the Social Setting of Q*. Minneapolis: Fortress Press, 2001.

Arnaoutoglou, I. "Associations and Patronage in Ancient Athens." *Ancient Society* 25 (1994): 5–17.

Arnim, Hans von, ed. *Stoicorum Veterum Fragmenta*. Lipsiae: Aedibus B. G. Teubneri, 1903–1924.

Ascough, Richard S. "Benefaction Gone Wrong: The 'Sin' of Ananias and Sapphira in Context." Pages 91–110 in *Text and Artifact in the Religions of Mediterranean Antiquity: Essays in Honour of Peter Richardson*. Edited by Stephen G. Wilson and Michel Desjardins. Waterloo: Wilfred Laurier University Press, 2000.

———. "The Thessalonian Christian Community as a Professional Voluntary Association." *Journal of Biblical Literature* 119 (2000): 311–28.

———. *What Are They Saying About the Formation of Pauline Churches?* New York: Paulist Press, 1998.

———. "Voluntary Associations and Community Formation: Paul's Macedonian Christian Communities in Context." Ph.D. dissertation, University of St. Michael's College, Toronto School of Theology, 1997.

Ash, Mitchell G., and William Ray Woodward. *Psychology in Twentieth-Century Thought and Society*. Cambridge: Cambridge University Press, 1987.

Attridge, Harold W. *The Interpretation of Biblical History in Antiquitates Judaicae of Flavius Josephus*. Missoula: Scholars Press, 1976.

Aubin, Paul. *Le problème de la "conversion". Étude sur un terme commun à l'hellénisme et au christianisme des trois premiers siècles*. Théologie historique 1. Paris: Beauchesne, 1963.

Aune, David E. "Human Nature and Ethics in Hellenistic Philosophical Traditions and Paul: Some Issues and Problems." Pages 291–312 in *Paul in his Hellenistic Context*. Edited by Troels Engberg-Pedersen. Minneapolis: Fortress Press, 1995.

———. "Romans as a Logos Protreptikos." Pages 278–96 in *The Romans Debate*. Edited by Karl P. Donfried. Revised edition. Peabody: Hendrickson, 1991.

Austin, R. "Empirical Adequacy of Lofland's Conversion Model." *Review of Religious Research* 18 (1977): 282–87.

Babcock, William S. "MacMullen on Conversion: A Response." *The Second Century* 5 (1985–1986): 82–89.

Badian, Ernst. *Foreign Clientelae (264–70 B.C.)*. Oxford: Oxford University Press, 1958.

Bailey, Cyril. *Epicurus: The Extant Remains*. Oxford: Clarendon Press, 1926. Reprint: Hildesheim: Olms, 1970.

Bainbridge, William S. "The Sociology of Conversion." Pages 178–91 in *Handbook of Religious Conversion*. Edited by H. Newton Malony and Samuel Southard. Birmingham: Religious Education Press, 1992.

Barclay, William. *The New Testament: A New Translation*. 2 vols. London: Collins, 1968.

Barnes, Jonathan. "Antiochus of Ascalon." Pages 51–96 in *Philosophia Togata: Essays on Philosophy and Roman Society*. Edited by Miriam T. Griffin and Jonathan Barnes. Oxford: Clarendon Press, 1989.

Barr, James. *The Semantics of Biblical Language*. Oxford: Oxford University Press, 1961.

Barrett, Charles Kingsley. *Paul: An Introduction to his Thought*. Louisville: Westminster/John Knox Press, 1994.

———. *A Critical and Exegetical Commentary on the Acts of the Apostles*. International Critical Commentary on the Holy Scriptures of the Old and New Testaments. Edinburgh: T&T Clark, 1994.

———. *A Commentary on the Second Epistle to the Corinthians*. Harper/Black New Testament Commentaries. New York: Harper and Row, 1973.

———. *The Signs of an Apostle*. London: Epworth Press, 1970.

———. *A Commentary on the First Epistle to the Corinthians*. Harper/Black New Testament Commentaries. New York: Harper and Row, 1968.

Bartchy, S. Scott. *First-Century Slavery and the Interpretation of 1 Corinthians 7:21*. SBLDS 11. Missoula: Society of Biblical Literature, 1973.

Bartolomé, J. J. "'Soy lo que soy por gracia de Dios' (1 Cor 15:10): La Experiencia de la Gracia como Clave para la Comprehension de Pablo." *Estudios Biblios* 57 (1999): 125–46.

Barton, S. C. "Social-Scientific Criticism." Pages 277–89 in *Handbook to Exegesis of the New Testament*. Edited by Stanley E. Porter. Leiden: E. J. Brill, 1997.

Batten, Alicia. "God in the Letter of James: Patron or Benefactor?" Paper presented at the annual meeting of the Society of Biblical Literature, Toronto, 2002.

Beare, Francis Wright. *A Commentary on the Epistle to the Philippians*. Black's New Testament Commentaries. London: A&C Black, 1959.

Beaude, Pierre-Marie. "Psychologie et exégèse paulinienne." Pages 101–18 in *Paul de Tarse*. Edited by Jacques Schlosser. Lectio divina 165. Paris: Éditions du Cerf, 1996.

Beck, Norman A. "The Lukan Writer's Stories about the Call of Paul (Acts 9:1–19a; 22:3–21; 26:1–32)." Pages 213–18 in *Society of Biblical Literature 1983 Seminar Papers*. Edited by Kent Harold Richards. Chico: Scholars Press, 1983.

Beck, Roger. "The Mithras Cult as Association." *Studies in Religion/Sciences Religieuses* 21 (1992): 1–13.

Becker, Jürgen. *Paul: Apostle to the Gentiles*. Translated by O. C. Dean Jr. Louisville: Westminster/John Knox Press, 1993.

Bee-Schroedter, Heike. *Neutestamentliche Wundergeschichten im Spiegel vergangener und gegenwärtiger Rezeption: Historisch-exegetische und empirisch-entwicklungspsychologische Studien*. Stuttgarter biblische Beiträge 39. Stuttgart: Katholisches Bibelwerk, 1998.

Behm, J. "μετανοέω." Pages 975–1008 in vol. 4 of *Theological Dictionary of the New Testament*. Edited by Gerhard Kittel and Gerhard Friedrich. Translated by G. W. Bromiley. 10 vols. Grand Rapids: Eerdmans, 1964.

Behr, Charles A. *Aelius Aristides and The Sacred Tales*. Amsterdam: Adolf M. Hakkert, 1968.

Beker, J. Christiaan. *Paul the Apostle: The Triumph of God in Life and Thought*. Philadelphia: Fortress Press, 1980.

Benedict, Ruth. *The Chrysanthemum and the Sword: Patterns of Japanese Culture*. Rutland, Vt.: C. E. Tuttle, 1946.

Berger, Klaus. *Historische Psychologie des Neuen Testaments*. Stuttgart: Katholisches Bibelwerk, 1991.

Berger, Peter L. *The Sacred Canopy: Elements of a Sociological Theory of Religion*. Garden City, N. Y.: Doubleday, 1967.

Berger, Peter L., Brigitte Berger, and Hansfried Kellner. *The Homeless Mind: Modernization and Consciousness*. New York: Random House, 1973.

Berger, Peter L., and T. Luckmann. *The Social Construction of Reality: A Treatise in the Sociology of Knowledge*. Garden City, N. Y.: Doubleday, 1966.

Bertram, G. "στρέφω." Pages 714–29 in vol. 7 of *Theological Dictionary of the New Testament*. Edited by Gerhard Kittel and Gerhard Friedrich. Translated by G. W. Bromiley. 10 vols. Grand Rapids: Eerdmans, 1964.

Best, Ernest. *Second Corinthians*. Atlanta: J. Knox Press, 1987.

―――. "A Damascus Road Experience." *Irish Biblical Studies* 7 (1985): 2–7.

―――. *A Commentary on the First and Second Epistles to the Thessalonians*. Black's New Testament Commentaries. London: Adam & Charles Black, 1972.

———. *The Letter of Paul to the Romans*. Cambridge Bible Commentary: New English Bible. Cambridge: Cambridge University Press, 1967.

Betz, Hans Dieter. *Galatians: A Commentary on Paul's Letter to the Churches in Galatia*. Hermeneia. Philadelphia: Fortress Press, 1979.

Bevan, Edwyn R. "Mystery Religions." Pages 83–115 in *The History of Christianity in the Light of Modern Knowledge: A Collective Work*. London: Blackie and Sons, 1929.

———. *Later Greek Religion*. The Library of Greek Thought 9. London: Dent, 1927.

———. "Hellenistic Popular Philosophy." Pages 79–107 in *The Hellenistic Age: Aspects of Hellenistic Civilization*. Edited by John B. Bury. Cambridge: Cambridge University Press, 1923.

Bligh, John. *Galatians: A Discussion of St. Paul's Epistle*. Householder Commentaries 1. London: St. Paul Publications, 1969.

Boas, Franz. *The Mind of Primitive Man*. New York: MacMillan, 1911.

Bock, Philip K. *Rethinking Psychological Anthropology: Continuity and Change in the Study of Human Action*. New York: W. H. Freeman, 1988.

Bockmuehl, Markus N. A. *A Commentary on the Epistle to the Philippians*. Black's New Testament Commentaries. London: A&C Black, 1997.

Boissevain, Jeremy Fergus. *Friends of Friends: Networks, Manipulators, and Coalitions*. New York: St. Martin's Press, 1974.

Bolt, Peter G. "The Philosopher in the Hands of an Angry God." Pages 327–43 in *The Gospel to the Nations: Perspectives on Paul's Mission*. Edited by Peter Bolt and Mark Thompson. Downers Grove, Ill.: InterVarsity Press, 2000.

Borg, Marcus J. *Conflict, Holiness and Politics in the Teachings of Jesus*. New York: Edwin Mellen Press, 1984.

Borgen, Peder, Kåre Fuglseth, and Roald Skarsten. *The Philo Index: A Complete Greek Word Index to the Writings of Philo of Alexandria*. Grand Rapids: Eerdmans, 2000.

Bornkamm, Günther. *Paul*. Translated by D. M. G. Stalker. Minneapolis: Fortress Press, 1971.

Boyarin, Daniel. *A Radical Jew: Paul and the Politics of Identity*. Berkeley: University of California Press, 1994.

Bradley, Keith R. *Slavery and Society at Rome*. Cambridge: Cambridge University Press, 1994.

———. *Slaves and Masters in the Roman Empire: A Study in Social Control*. Oxford: Oxford University Press, 1987.

Brandon, Samuel George Frederick. *Time and Mankind: An Historical and Philosophical Study of Mankind's Attitude to the Phenomena of Change*. London: Hutchinson, 1951.

Braund, David C. "Client Kings." Pages 348–49 in *Oxford Classical Dictionary*. Edited by Simon Hornblower and Antony Spawforth. Oxford: Oxford University Press, 1996.

———. *Rome and the Friendly King: The Character of the Client Kingship*. London: Croom Helm, 1984.

Bremer, J. M. "Greek Hymns." Pages 193–215 in *In Faith, Hope and Worship: Aspects of Religious Mentality in the Ancient World*. Edited by Hendrik S. Versnel. Studies in Greek and Roman Religion 2. Leiden: E. J. Brill, 1982.

Bruce, Frederick Fyvie. *The Acts of the Apostles: The Greek Text with Introduction and Commentary*. 3rd ed. Grand Rapids: Eerdmans, 1990.

———. *Philippians*. New International Biblical Commentary 11. Peabody: Hendrickson, 1989.

_____. *The Epistle to the Galatians: A Commentary on the Greek Text*. The New International Greek Testament Commentary. Grand Rapids: Eerdmans, 1982.
_____. *1 and 2 Corinthians*. New Century Bible 49. London: Oliphants, 1971. Reprint: The New Century Bible Commentaries. Grand Rapids: Eerdmans, 1980.
_____. *Paul: Apostle of the Heart Set Free*. Grand Rapids: Eerdmans, 1977.
Bryant, Joseph M. *Moral Codes and Social Structure in Ancient Greece: A Sociology of Greek Ethics from Homer to the Epicureans and Stoics*. New York: State University of New York Press, 1996.
Burke, Mariann. *Advent and Psychic Birth*. New York: Paulist Press, 1993.
Burkert, Walter. *Greek Religion*. Translated by John Raffan. Cambridge: Harvard University Press, 1985.
Burton, Ernest de Witt. *A Critical and Exegetical Commentary on the Epistle to the Galatians*. International Critical Commentary. Edinburgh: T&T Clark, 1921.
_____. "Saul's Experience on the Way to Damascus." *Biblical World* 1 (1893): 9–23.
Butt, M. Munawar. *Psychology, Sin & Society: An Essay on the Triumvirate of Psychology, Religion, and Democracy*. Lanham: University Press of America, 1992.
Byrne, Brendan. *Romans*. Sacra Pagina 6. Collegeville: Liturgical Press, 1990.

Caird, George Bradford. *Paul's Letters From Prison: Ephesians, Philippians, Colossians, Philemon*. New Clarendon Bible. New Testament. Oxford: Oxford University Press, 1976.
Callan, Terrance D. *Psychological Perspectives on the Life of Paul: An Application of the Methodology of Gerd Theissen*. Studies in the Bible and Early Christianity 22. Lewiston, N. Y.: Edwin Mellen Press, 1990.
Campbell, Barth L. *Honor, Shame, and the Rhetoric of 1 Peter*. Atlanta: Scholars Press, 1998.
Campbell, John Kennedy. *Honour, Family and Patronage*. Oxford: Oxford University Press, 1964.
Cancik, Hubert. "Lucian on Conversion: Remarks on Lucian's Dialogue *Nigrinos*." Pages 26–48 in *Ancient and Modern Perspectives on the Bible and Culture: Essays in Honor of Hans Dieter Betz*. Edited by Adela Yarbro Collins. Atlanta: Scholars Press, 1998.
Capps, Donald. *Jesus: A Psychological Biography*. St. Louis: Chalice Press, 2000.
Carney, Thomas F. *The Shape of the Past: Models and Antiquity*. Lawrence, Kansas: Coronado Press, 1975.
_____. *The Economies of Antiquity*. Lawrence, Kansas: Coronado Press, 1973.
Carrington, Philip. *The Early Christian Church*. 2 vols. Cambridge: Cambridge University Press, 1957.
Cawkwell, G. L. "Isocrates." Pages 769–71 in *The Oxford Classical Dictionary*. Edited by Simon Hornblower and Antony Spawforth. Oxford: Oxford University Press, 1996.
Cerfaux, Lucien. *The Christian in the Theology of St. Paul*. Translated by Lilian Soiron. New York: Herder and Herder, 1967.
Charlesworth, Martin Percival. "Some Observations on Ruler-Cult, Especially in Rome." *Harvard Theological Review* 28 (1935): 5–44.
Cheek, J. L. "Paul's Mysticism in the Light of Psychedelic Experience." *Journal of the American Academy of Religion* 38 (1970): 381–89.
Childs, Hal. *The Myth of the Historical Jesus and the Evolution of Consciousness*. SBL Dissertation Series 179. Atlanta: Society of Biblical Literature, 2000.

Chow, John K. *Patronage and Power: A Study of Social Networks in Corinth*. Journal for the Study of the New Testament Supplement Series 75. Sheffield: Sheffield Academic Press, 1992.

Chrysostom, Dio. *Dio Chrysostom*. Translated by James Wilfred Cohoon. Loeb Classical Library 257, 339, 358, 376, 385. Cambridge, Mass.: Harvard University Press, 1961.

Cicero, Marcus Tullius. *De inventione. De optimo genere oratorum Topica*. Translated by H. M. Hubbell. Loeb Classical Library. London: Heinemann, 1949.

_____. *Letters to his Friends*. Translated by W. Glynn Williams. Loeb Classical Library. Cambridge, Mass.: Harvard University Press, 1958.

_____. *De oratore*. Translated by E. W. Sutton. Completed and Introduced by H. Rackham. Loeb Classical Library. Cambridge, Mass.: Harvard University Press, 1959.

_____. *De officiis*. Translated by Walter Miller. Loeb Classical Library. Cambridge, Mass.: Harvard University Press, 1961.

_____. *Rhetorica ad Herennium*. Translated by Harry Caplan. Loeb Classical Library. Cambridge, Mass.: Harvard University Press, 1964.

_____. *Letters to Atticus*. Translated by D. R. Shackleton Bailey. 2 vols. Loeb Classical Library. Cambridge, Mass.: Harvard University Press, 1999.

Citroni, M. "Patronage, Literary." Pages 1124–26 in *The Oxford Classical Dictionary*. Edited by Simon Hornblower and Antony Spawforth. Oxford and London: Oxford University Press, 1996.

Clark, Andrew C. "Apostleship: Evidence from the New Testament and Early Christian Literature." *Vox Evangelica* 19 (1989): 49–82.

Clark, W. H. "William James: Contributions to the Psychology of Religious Conversion." *Journal of Religion and Psychical Research* 3 (1980): 287–96.

Clarke, Andrew D. *Secular and Christian Leadership: A Socio-Historical and Exegetical Study of 1 Corinthians 1–6*. Arbeiten zur Geschichte des antiken Judentums und des Urchristentums 18. Leiden: E. J. Brill, 1993.

Clarke, M. L. "Poets and Patrons at Rome." *Greece and Rome* 25 (1978): 46–54.

Cohen, Shaye J. D. "Was Judaism in Antiquity a Missionary Religion?" Pages 14–23 in *Jewish Assimilation, Acculturation and Accommodation*. Edited by Menachem Mor. Lanham: University Press of America, 1992.

Cole, Robert A. *The Letter of Paul to the Galatians*. The Tyndale New Testament Commentaries 9. Grand Rapids: Eerdmans, 1989.

Collins, Raymond F., and Daniel J. Harrington. *First Corinthians*. Sacra Pagina Series 7. Collegeville, Minn.: Liturgical Press, 1999.

Conzelmann, Hans. *1 Corinthians: A Commentary on the First Epistle to the Corinthians*. Translated by James W. Leitch. Hermeneia. Philadelphia: Fortress Press, 1975.

_____. "χάρις κτλ." Pages 372–402 in vol. 9 of *Theological Dictionary of the New Testament*. Edited by Gerhard Kittel and Gerhard Friedrich. Translated by G. W. Bromiley. 10 vols. Grand Rapids: Eerdmans, 1964.

Cooper, J. C. "Conversion." Pages 224–25 in *The Dictionary of Bible and Religion*. Edited by William H. Gentz. Nashville: Abingdon, 1986.

Corley, B. "Interpreting Paul's Conversion—Then and Now." Pages 1–17 in *The Road From Damascus: The Impact of Paul's Conversion on his Life, Thought, and Ministry*. Edited by Richard N. Longenecker. Grand Rapids: Eerdmans, 1997.

Cotter, Wendy. "The Collegia and Roman Law." Pages 74–89 in *Voluntary Associations in the Graeco-Roman World*. Edited by John S. Kloppenborg and Steven G. Wilson. New York: Routledge, 1996.

Countryman, L. W. "Patrons and Officers in Club and Church." Pages 135–43 in *Society of Biblical Literature 1977 Seminar Papers*. Edited by Paul J. Achtemeier. Missoula: Scholars Press, 1977.

Cousar, Charles B. *Galatians*. Interpretation: A Bible Commentary for Teaching and Preaching. Atlanta: John Knox Press, 1982.

Craddock, Fred B. *Philippians*. Interpretation: A Bible Commentary for Teaching and Preaching. Atlanta: John Knox Press, 1985.

Craffert, P. F. "Paul's Damascus Experience as Reflected in Galatians 1: Call or Conversion?" *Scriptura* 29 (1989): 36–47.

Cranfield, Charles Ernest Burland. *A Critical and Exegetical Commentary on the Epistle to the Romans*. 2 vols. International Critical Commentary. Edinburgh: T&T Clark, 1975, 1979.

Crook, Zeba Antonin. "The Divine Benefactions of Paul the Client." *Journal of Greco-Roman Christianity and Judaism* (Forthcoming).

_____. "Paul's Praise and Riposte of the Thessalonians." *Biblical Theology Bulletin* 27 (1997): 153–63.

Crossan, John Dominic, and Jonathan L. Reed. *Excavating Jesus: Beneath the Stones, Behind the Text*. San Francisco: HarperCollins, 2001.

Curtius, Ernst Robert. *European Literature and the Latin Middle Ages*. Translated by Willard R. Trask. Princeton: Princeton University Press, 1953.

Cutton, George B. *The Psychological Phenomena of Christianity*. New York: Charles Scribner's Sons, 1908.

Czachesz, I. "Socio-Rhetorical Exegesis of Acts 9:1–30." *Communio Viatorum* 37 (1995): 5–32.

Danker, Frederick W. "Associations, Clubs, Thiasoi." Pages 501–503 in vol. 1 of *Anchor Bible Dictionary*. 6 vols. Edited by David Noel Freedman. New York: Doubleday, 1992.

_____. "Paul's Debt to the De Corona of Demosthenes: A Study of Rhetorical Techniques in Second Corinthians." Pages 262–68 in *Persuasive Artistry: Studies in New Testament Rhetoric in Honour of George A. Kennedy*. Edited by Duane Frederick Watson. Journal for the Study of the New Testament Supplement Series 50. Sheffield Academic Press: Sheffield, 1991.

_____. *A Century of Greco-Roman Philology: Featuring the American Philological Association and the Society of Biblical Literature*. Atlanta: Scholars Press, 1988.

_____. *Benefactor: Epigraphic Study of a Graeco-Roman Semantic Field*. St. Louis: Clayton Publishing House, 1982.

Danker, Frederick W., ed. *A Greek-English Lexicon of the New Testament and Other Early Christian Literature*. Chicago: University of Chicago Press, 2000.

Danker, Frederick W., and Robert Jewett. "Jesus as the Apocalyptic Benefactor in Second Thessalonians." Pages 486–98 in *The Thessalonian Correspondence*. Edited by Raymond F. Collins. Bibliotheca Ephemeridum Theologicarum Lovaniensium 87. Leuven: Leuven University Press, 1990.

Davies, D. M. "Free From the Law: An Exposition of the Seventh Chapter of Romans." *Interpretation* 7 (1953): 156–62.

Davies, Stevan L. *Jesus the Healer: Possession, Trance, and the Origins of Christianity*. New York: Continuum, 1995.

Davis, John. *The People of the Mediterranean*. London: Routledge and Kegan Paul, 1977.

de Ste Croix, G. E. M. "Suffragium: From Vote to Patronage." *The British Journal of Sociology* 5 (1954): 33–48.

Deer, Donald S. "Whose Faith/Loyalty in Revelation 2.13 and 14.12?" *The Bible Translator* 38 (1987): 328–30.

Deissmann, Adolf. *Paul: A Study in Social and Religious History*. Translated by William E. Wilson. New York: Harper and Brothers, 1957.

———. *Light from the ancient East*. Translated by Lionel R. M. Strachan. New York: Harper & Brothers, 1927.

Demosthenes. *Works*. Translated by J. H. Vince. Loeb Classical Library. Cambridge, Mass.: Harvard University Press, 1962.

des Places, Edouard. *La Religion Grecque: Dieux, cultes, rites et sentiment religieux dans la Grèce antique*. Paris: Éditions A. et J. Picard et Cie, 1969.

deSilva, David A. *Perseverance in Gratitude: A Socio-Rhetorical Commentary on the Epistle to the Hebrews*. Grand Rapids: Eerdmans, 2000.

———. "Patronage and Reciprocity: The Context of Grace in the New Testament." *Ashland Theological Journal* 31 (1999): 32–84.

———. "Exchanging Favor for Wrath: Apostasy in Hebrews and Patron–Client Relationships." *Journal of Biblical Literature* 115 (1996): 91–116.

DeWitt, Norman Wentworth. *St. Paul and Epicurus*. Toronto: The Ryerson Press, 1954.

Dittenberger, Wilhelm. *Orientis graeci inscriptiones selectae. Supplementum Sylloges inscriptionum graecarum*. 2 vols. Lipsiae: S. Hirzel, 1903.

Dittenberger, Wilhelm, and Friedrich Freiherr Hiller von Gaertringen. *Sylloge Inscriptionum Graecarum*. 4 vols. 3rd ed. Lipsiae: S. Hirzel, 1915.

Dodd, Charles Harold. "The Mind of Paul: A Psychological Approach." *Bulletin of the John Rylands Library* 17 (1933): 91–105.

———. *The Epistle of Paul to the Romans*. London: Hodder & Stoughton, 1932.

Dominian, Jack. *One Like Us: A Psychological Interpretation of Jesus*. London: Darton Longman and Todd, 1998.

Donaldson, Terence L. *Paul and the Gentiles: Remapping the Apostle's Convictional World*. Minneapolis: Fortress Press, 1997.

———. "Israelite, Convert, Apostle to the Gentiles: The Origin of Paul's Gentile Mission." Pages 62–84 in *The Road From Damascus: The Impact of Paul's Conversion on his Life, Thought, and Ministry*. Edited by Richard N. Longenecker. Grand Rapids: Eerdmans, 1997.

Donfried, Karl P. "The Cults of Thessalonica and the Thessalonian Correspondence." *New Testament Studies* 31 (1985): 336–56.

Doughty, D. J. "The Priority of ΧΑΡΙΣ: An Investigation of the Theological Language of Paul." *New Testament Studies* 19 (1973): 163–80.

Douglas, W., and J. R. Scroggs. "Some Social Scientific Perspectives." Pages 115–34 in *Papers from the National Faith and Order Colloquium*. Edited by W. A. Norgren. Indianapolis: Council on Christian Unity, 1966.

Drewermann, Eugen. *Jesus von Nazareth: Befreiung zum Frieden*. Zürich: Walter-Verlag, 1996.

———. *Discovering the God Child Within: A Spiritual Psychology of the Infancy of Jesus*. Translated by Peter Heinegg. New York: Crossroad, 1994.

Duff, Arnold Mackay. *Freedmen in the Early Roman Empire*. Oxford: Clarendon Press, 1928. Repr. Cambridge: W. Heffer & Sons, 1958.

Dunn, James D. G. "Paul's Conversion—A Light to Twentieth Century Disputes." Pages 77–93 in *Evangelium – Schriftauslegung – Kirche: Festschrift für Peter Stuhlmacher zum 65. Geburtstag*. Edited by Scott J. Hafemann, Otfried Hofius and Jostein Ådna. Göttingen: Vandenhoeck & Ruprecht, 1997.
_____. *A Commentary to the Epistle to the Galatians*. Black's New Testament Commentaries 9. London: A&C Black, 1993.
_____. *Romans*. 2 vols. Word Biblical Commentary 38. Waco, Texas: Word, 1988.
Durkheim, Émile. *The Elementary Forms of the Religious Life*. London: G. Allen & Unwin, 1915.

Ebeling, Gerhard. *The Truth of the Gospel: An Exposition of Galatians*. Translated by D. Green. Philadelphia: Fortress Press, 1985.
Edelstein, Emma J., and L. Edelstein. *Asclepius: A Collection and Interpretation of the Testimonies*. 2 vols. New York: Arno Press, 1975.
Edgar, Campbell Cowan. *Zenon Papyri in the University of Michigan Collection*. University of Michigan Studies. Humanistic Series 24. Ann Arbor: University of Michigan Press, 1931.
Edlund, I. E. "Invisible Bonds: Clients and Patrons Through the Eyes of Polybios." *Klio* 59 (1977): 129–36.
Edwards, Mark. *Neoplatonic Saints: The Lives of Plotinus and Proclus by their Students*. Liverpool: University of Liverpool Press, 2000.
Eisenstadt, Schmuel R., and Luis Roniger. "Patron–Client Relations as a Model of Structuring Social Exchange." *Comparative Studies in Society and History* 22 (1980): 42–77.
_____. *Patrons, Clients and Friends: Interpersonal Relations and the Structure of Trust in Society*. Cambridge: Cambridge University Press, 1984.
Elazar, Daniel J. *Covenant and Polity in Biblical Israel: Biblical Foundations and Jewish Expressions*. London: Transaction Publishers, 1995.
Ellingsworth, Paul. "More About Faith: Synopsis of a Discussion Between Daniel D. Arichea and Eugene Botha." *The Bible Translator* 38 (1987): 330–32.
Elliott, John H. *What is Social-Scientific Criticism?* Guides to Biblical Scholarship. Minneapolis: Fortress Press, 1993.
_____. "Patronage and Clientism in Early Christian Society: A Short Reading Guide." *Forum* 3 (1987): 39–48.
_____. "Social-Scientific Criticism of the New Testament and its Social World." *Semeia* 35 (1986): 1–33.
Engberg-Pedersen, Troels. "Ephesians 5,12–13: ἐλέγχειν and Conversion in the New Testament." *Zeitschrift für die neutestamentliche Wissenschaft und die Kunde der Älteren Kirche* 80 (1989): 89–110.
Erchak, Gerald M. *The Anthropology of Self and Behaviour*. New Brunswick, N. J.: Rutgers University Press, 1992.
Erskine, Andrew. "The Romans as Common Benefactors." *Historia* 43 (1994): 70–87.
Esler, Philip F., ed. *Modelling Early Christianity: Social-Scientific Studies of the New Testament in its Context*. London: Routledge, 1995.

Fabre, Georges. *Libertus: Recherches sur les Rapports Patron–Affranchi à la fin de la République Romaine*. Rome: École Française de Rome, 1981.
Falls, Thomas B. *The Writings of Saint Justin Martyr*. New York: Christian Heritage, Inc., 1948.

Fee, Gordon D. *The First Epistle to the Corinthians*. New International Commentary on the New Testament. Grand Rapids: Eerdmans, 1987.
_____. *Paul's Letter to the Philippians*. New International Commentary on the New Testament. Grand Rapids: Eerdmans, 1995.
_____. *Philippians*. IVP New Testament Commentary Series 11. Downers Grove, Ill.: InterVarsity Press, 1999.
Feldman, Louis H. "Was Judaism a Missionary Religion in Ancient Times?" Pages 24–37 in *Jewish Assimilation, Acculturation and Accommodation*. Edited by Menachem Mor. Lanham: University Press of America, 1992.
Ferguson, Everett. *Backgrounds to Early Christianity*. 2nd ed. Grand Rapids: Eerdmans, 1993.
Ferguson, John. *The Religions of the Roman Empire*. Ithaca: Cornell University Press, 1970.
Ferm, Robert O. *The Psychology of Christian Conversion*. Old Taplan, N. J.: Revell, 1959.
Finley, Moses I. *Ancient History: Evidence and Models*. London: Chatto and Windus, 1985.
Fisher, Nicolas R. E. *Slavery in Classical Greece*. London: Bristol Classical Press, 1998.
_____."Greek Associations, Symposia, and Clubs." Pages 1167–97 in *Civilization of the Ancient Mediterranean*. Edited by Michael Grant and R. Kitzinger. New York: Scribner's, 1988.
_____. "Roman Associations, Dinner Parties, and Clubs." Pages 1199–1225 in *Civilization of the Ancient Mediterranean*. Edited by Michael Grant and R. Kitzinger. New York: Scribner's, 1988.
Fitzgerald, John T. *Cracks in an Earthen Vessel*. Society of Biblical Literature Dissertation Series 99. Atlanta: Scholars Press, 1988.
Fitzgerald, John T., and L. Michael White. *The Tabula of Cebes*. Chico: Scholar Press, 1983.
Fitzmyer, Joseph A. *The Acts of the Apostles*. Anchor Bible 31. New York: Doubleday, 1998.
_____. *Romans: A New Translation With Introduction and Commentary*. Anchor Bible 33. New York: Doubleday, 1993.
_____. *The Gospel According to Luke*. 2 vols. Anchor Bible 28. Garden City, N. Y.: Doubleday, 1981.
Fortes, Meyer. *Oedipus and Job in West African religion*. Cambridge: Cambridge University Press, 1959.
Foss, Sonja K., Karen A. Foss, and Robert Trapp, *Contemporary Perspectives on Rhetoric*. 2nd edition. Prospect Heights, Ill.: Waveland Press, 1995.
Foucart, Paul-François. *Des associations religieuses chez les Grecs—thiases, éranes, orgéons, avec le texte des inscriptions relatives à ces associations*. Paris: Klincksieck, 1873. Reprint New York: Arno Press, 1975.
Frame, James Everett. *A critical and exegetical commentary on the Epistles of St. Paul to the Thessalonians*. International Critical Commentary. Edinburgh: T&T Clark, 1912.
Franzmann, John William. "The Early Development of the Greek Concept of 'Charis'." Ph.D. dissertation, University of Wisconsin, 1972.
Fredriksen, Paula. "Paul and Augustine: Conversion Narratives, Orthodox Traditions and the Retrospective Self." *Journal of Theological Studies* 37 (1986): 3–34.
_____. "Augustine and his Analysts: The Possibility of a Psychohistory." *Soundings* 61 (1978): 206–27.
Freud, Sigmund. "A Religious Experience." Pages 243–46 in *Collected Papers 5*. Edited by James Strachey. New York: Basic Books, 1959.

_____. *The Origins of Religion: Totem and Taboo, Moses and Monotheism and Other Works*. Translated from the German under the general editorship of James Strachey. The present volume edited by Albert Dickson. Pelican Freud Library 13. London; New York: Penguin, 1990.

Freyburger, Gérard. *Fides: Étude sémantique et religieuse depuis les origines jusqu'à l'époque augustéenne*. Collection d'Études anciennes. Paris: Société d'Édition «Les Belles Lettres», 1986.

Fung, Ronald Y. K. *The Epistle to the Galatians*. Translated by H. Zylstra. New International Commentary on the New Testament. Grand Rapids: Eerdmans, 1953.

Gager, John G. "Some Notes on Paul's Conversion." *New Testament Studies* 27 (1980–1981): 697–704.

Gale, Richard M. *The Divided Self of William James*. Cambridge: Cambridge University Press, 1999.

Galipeau, Steven A. *Transforming Body and Soul: Therapeutic Wisdom in the Gospel Healing Stories*. Jung and Spirituality. New York: Paulist Press, 1990.

Garrett, Susan. "Sociology of Early Christianity." Pages 89–99 in vol. 6 of *Anchor Bible Dictionary*. 6 vols. Edited by David Noel Freedman. New York: Doubleday, 1992.

Gaventa, Beverly R. "Conversion." Pages 1131–33 in vol. 1 of *Anchor Bible Dictionary*. Edited by David Noel Freedman. New York: Doubleday, 1992.

_____. "Galatians 1 and 2: Autobiography as Paradigm." *Novum Testamentum* 28 (1986): 309–26.

_____. *From Darkness to Light: Aspects of Conversion in the New Testament*. Philadelphia: Fortress Press, 1986.

_____. "Paul's Conversion: A Critical Sifting of the Epistolary Evidence." Ph.D. dissertation, University of Michigan, 1978.

Geertz, Clifford "On the Nature of Anthropological Understanding." *American Scientist* 63 (1975): 47–53.

_____. *The Interpretation of Cultures: Selected Essays*. New York: Basic Books, 1973.

Gellner, Ernest, and John Waterbury, eds. *Patrons and Clients: In Mediterranean Societies*. London: Gerald Duckworth, 1977.

Gelzer, Matthias. *The Roman Nobility*. Translated by Robin Seager. New York: Barnes & Noble, 1969.

Gibson, E. Leigh. *The Jewish Manumission Inscriptions of the Bosporus Kingdom*. Texte und Studien zum Antiken Judentum 75. Tübingen: J. C. B. Mohr (Paul Siebeck), 1999.

Gibson, Richard J. "Paul and the Evangelization of the Stoics." Pages 309–26 in *The Gospel to the Nations: Perspectives on Paul's Mission*. Edited by Peter Bolt and Mark Thompson. Downers Grove, Ill.: InterVarsity Press, 2000.

Glad, Clarence E. *Paul and Philodemus: Adaptability in Epicurean and Early Christian Psychagogy*. Supplements to Novum Testamentum 81. Leiden: E. J. Brill, 1995.

Glucker, John. *Antiochus and the Late Academy*. Hypomnemata 56. Göttingen: Vandenhoeck and Ruprecht, 1978.

Gold, Barbara K. *Literary Patronage in Greece and Rome*. Chapel Hill and London: University of North Carolina Press, 1987.

Goodman, Martin. *Mission and Conversion: Proselytizing in the Religious History of the Roman Empire*. Oxford: Clarendon Press, 1994.

_____. "Jewish Proselytizing in the First Century." Pages 53–78 in *The Jews Among Pagans and Christians in the Roman Empire*. Edited by Judith Lieu, John North and Tessa Rajak. New York: Routledge, 1992.

Gordon, R. "The Veil of Power: Emperors, Sacrificers and Benefactors." Pages 201–31 in *Pagan Priests: Religion and Power in the Ancient World*. Edited by Mary Beard and John North. London: Duckworth, 1990.

Gottwald, Norman K. *The Tribes of Yahweh: A Sociology of the Religion of Liberated Israel, 1250–1050 B.C.E.* Maryknoll, N. Y.: Orbis Books, 1979.

Grayston, Kenneth. *The Letters of Paul to the Philippians and to the Thessalonians*. Cambridge Bible Commentary. London: Cambridge University Press, 1967.

Grenfell, Bernard P., and Arthur S. Hunt. *The Oxyrhynchus Papyri*. 66 vols. Egypt Exploration Society. Graeco-Roman Memoirs. London: Egypt Exploration Society, 1898–1999.

Griffin, Christine. "More Than Simply Talk and Text: Psychologists as Cultural Ethnographers." Pages 17–30 in *Culture in Psychology*. Edited by Corinne Squire. London: Routledge, 2000.

Guthrie, D. *Galatians*. London: Nelson, 1969.

Haenchen, Ernst. *The Acts of the Apostles: A Commentary*. Translated by B. Noble et al. Philadelphia: Westminster Press, 1971.

Hagendijk, R., and H. Helms. "De invloed van de psychologie op andere disciplines: een kwantitatieve verkenning." *Nederlands Tijdschrift voor de Psychologie en haar Grensgebieden* 50 (1995): 257–66.

Hands, Arthur R. *Charities and Social Aid in Greece and Rome*. Aspects of Greek and Roman Life. London: Thames and Hudson, 1968.

Hanson, Kenneth C. "Greco-Roman Studies and the Social-Scientific Study of the Bible. A Classified Periodical Bibliography." *Forum* 9 (1993): 63–119.

Hanson, Kenneth C., and Douglas E. Oakman. *Palestine in the Time of Jesus: Social Structures and Social Conflicts*. Minneapolis: Fortress Press, 1998.

Harkins, Jean, and Wierzbicka, Anna (eds.). *Emotions in Crosslinguistic Perspective*. Berlin: Mouton de Gruyter, 2001.

Harland, Philip H. *Associations, Synagogues, and Congregations: Claiming a Place in Ancient Mediterranean Society*. Minneapolis: Fortress Press, 2003.

_____. "Honours and Worship: Emperors, Imperial Cults, and Associations at Ephesus (first to third centuries C.E.)." *Studies in Religion* 25 (1996): 319–34.

Harrill, J. Albert. *The Manumission of Slaves in Early Christianity*. Hermeneutische Untersuchungen zur Theologie 32. Tübingen: J. C. B. Mohr (Paul Siebeck), 1995.

Harris, Grace Gredys. "Concepts of Individual, Self, and Person in Description and Analysis." *American Anthropologist* 91 (1989): 599–612.

Harris, Marvin. "History and Significance of the Emic–Etic Distinction." *Annual Review of Anthropology* 5 (1976): 329–50.

Harrison, James R. *Paul's Language of Grace in its Graeco-Roman Context*. Wissenschaftliche Untersuchungen zum Neuen Testament 2.172. Tübingen: Mohr Siebeck, 2003.

_____. "Paul's House Churches and the Cultic Associations." *Religious Studies Review* 58 (1999): 31–47.

_____. "Benefaction Ideology and Christian Responsibility for Widows." Pages 106–16 in *New Documents Illustrating Early Christianity: A Review of the Greek

Inscriptions and Papyri published 1984–85. NewDocs 8. Edited by S. R. Llewelyn. Grand Rapids: Eerdmans, 1998.
Hatch, Edwin. *The Influence of Greek Ideas on Christianity*. The Hibbert Lectures. London: Williams and Norgate, 1891.
———. *The Organization of Early Christian Churches: Eight Lectures*. Bampton Lectures. London: Rivingtons, 1881.
Hays, Richard B. *First Corinthians*. Interpretation 53. Louisville: Westminster/John Knox Press, 1997.
———. *The Faith of Jesus Christ: An Investigation of the Narrative Substructure of Galatians 3:1–4:11*. Chico: Scholars Press, 1983.
Headland, Thomas N., Kenneth Lee Pike, and Marvin Harris, eds. *Emics and Etics: The Insider/Outsider Debate*. Frontiers of Anthropology 7. Newbury Park, Calif.: Sage Publications, 1990.
Hebert, G. "'Faithfulness' and 'Faith'." *Theology* 58 (1955): 373–79.
Hedrick, C. W. "Paul's Conversion/Call: A Comparative Analysis of the Three Reports in Acts." *JBL* 100 (1981): 415–32.
Heikkinen, J. W. "'Conversion': A Biblical Study." Pages 92–114 in *Papers from the National Faith and Order Colloquium*. Edited by W. A. Norgren. Indianapolis: Council on Christian Unity, 1966.
Heinze, R. "Fides." *Hermes* 64 (1929): 140–66.
Heisig, J. W. "Psychology of Religion." Pages 57–66 in *Encyclopedia of Religion*. Edited by Mircea Eliade. New York: MacMillan, 1987.
Hellegouarc'h, Joseph. *Le vocabulaire latin des relations et des partis politiques sous la république*. Paris: Société d'Édition «Les Belles Lettres», 1963.
Hendrix, H. L. "Benefactor/Patron Networks in the Urban Environment: Evidence From Thessalonians." *Semeia* 56 (1991): 39–58.
Herman, Ellen. *The Romance of American Psychology: Political Culture in the Age of Experts*. Berkeley: University of California Press, 1995.
Hermogenes. *Hermogenes' On Types of Style*. Chapel Hill: The University of North Carolina Press, 1987.
Hewitt, Joseph William. "The Terminology of 'Gratitude' in Greek." *Classical Philology* 22 (1927): 142–61.
Hobbs, T. Raymond. "Reflections on Honor, Shame, and Covenant Relations." *Journal of Biblical Literature* 116 (1997): 501–503.
Hock, Ronald F. *The Social Context of Paul's Ministry: Tentmaking and Apostleship*. Philadelphia: Fortress Press, 1980.
Hofstede, Geert. *Culture's Consequences: Comparing Values, Behaviors, Institutions, and Organizations Across Nations*. 2nd ed. Thousand Oaks: Sage Publications, 2001.
Homans, Peter. *Jung in Context: Modernity and the Making of a Psychology*. Chicago: University of Chicago Press, 1979.
Hooker, Morna D. "ΠΙΣΤΙΣ ΧΡΙΣΤΟΥ." *New Testament Studies* 35 (1989): 321–42.
Hopkins, Keith. *Conquerors and Slaves*. Sociological Studies in Roman History 1. Cambridge: Cambridge University Press, 1978.
Horace. *Satires; Epistles; and Ars poetica*. Translated by H. Rushton Fairclough. Loeb Classical Library 194. Cambridge, Mass.: Harvard University Press, 1991.
Horrell, David G., ed. *Social-Scientific Approaches to New Testament Interpretation*. Edinburgh: T&T Clark, 1999.

Horsley, G. H. R. "Name Change as an Indication of Religious Conversion in Antiquity." *Numen* 34 (1987): 1–17.

Horsley, Greg H. R. (ed.). *New Documents Illustrating Early Christianity: Linguistic Essays. NewDocs* 5. North Ryde, Australia: Ancient History Documentary Research Centre, Macquarie University, 1989.

———. *New Documents Illustrating Early Christianity: A Review of the Greek Inscriptions and Papyri Published in 1979. NewDocs* 4. North Ryde, Australia: Ancient History Documentary Research Centre, Macquarie University, 1987.

———. *New Documents Illustrating Early Christianity: A Review of the Greek Inscriptions and Papyri Published in 1978. NewDocs* 3. North Ryde, Australia: Ancient History Documentary Research Centre, Macquarie University, 1983.

———. *New Documents Illustrating Early Christianity: A Review of the Greek Inscriptions and Papyri Published in 1977. NewDocs* 2. North Ryde, Australia: Ancient History Documentary Research Centre, Macquarie University, 1982.

———. *New Documents Illustrating Early Christianity: A Review of the Greek Inscriptions and Papyri Published in 1976. NewDocs* 1. North Ryde, Australia: Ancient History Documentary Research Centre, Macquarie University, 1981.

Horsley, Richard A. *1 Corinthians*. Abingdon New Testament Commentaries. Nashville: Abingdon Press, 1998.

Horsley, Richard A., ed. *Paul and Empire: Religion and Power in Roman Imperial Society*. Harrisburg, Pa.: Trinity Press International, 1997.

Howard, George. "The 'Faith of Christ'." *Expository Times* 85 (1974): 212–15.

———. "Notes and Observations on the Faith of Christ." *Harvard Theological Review* 60 (1967): 459–84.

Hui, C. Harry, and Marcelo J. Villareal. "Individualism–Collectivism and Psychological Needs." *Journal of Cross-Cultural Psychology* 20 (1989): 310–23.

Hultgren, A. J. "The Pistis Christou Formulation in Paul." *Novum Testamentum* 22 (1980): 248–63.

———. "Paul's Pre-Christian Persecutions of the Church: Their Purpose, Locale, and Nature." *Journal of Biblical Literature* 95 (1976): 97–111.

Hunt, Arthur S., and Campbell Cowan Edgar. *Select Papyri*. Loeb Classical Library 266. London: W. Heinemann, 1932.

Hurtado, Larry W. "Convert, Apostate, or Apostle to the Nations: The 'Conversion' of Paul in Recent Scholarship." *Studies in Religion/Sciences Religieuses* 22 (1993): 273–84.

Iamblichus. *Les Mystères d'Égypte*. Translated by Edouard des Places. Collection des universités de France. Paris: Société d'Édition «Les Belles Lettres», 1989.

Inglis, G. J. "St. Paul's Conversion in his Epistles." *Theology* 34 (1937): 214–28.

———. "The Problem of St. Paul's Conversion." *Expository Times* 40 (1928–29): 227–81.

Isocrates. *Isocrates*. Translated by George Norlin. Loeb Classical Library. Cambridge: Harvard University Press, 1980.

Jaeger, Werner. *Early Christianity and Greek Paideia*. Carl Newell Jackson Lectures. Cambridge: Harvard University Press, 1961.

———. *Aristotle: Fundamentals of the History of his Development*. Translated by Richard Robinson. Oxford: Clarendon Press, 1948.

James, William. *The Varieties of Religious Experience*. New York: Penguin, 1902.

Johnson, Cedric B., and H. Newton Malony. *Christian Conversion: Biblical and Psychological Perspective*. Rosemead Psychology Series. Grand Rapids: Zondervan, 1982.

Jordan, Mark D. "Ancient Philosophic Protreptic and the Problem of Persuasive Genres." *Rhetorica* 4 (1986): 309–33.

―――――. "Philosophic 'Conversion' and Christian Conversion: A Gloss on Professor MacMullen." *The Second Century* 5 (1985–86): 90–96.

Joubert, Stephan. "One Form of Social Exchange or Two? 'Euergetism,' Patronage and Testament Studies." *Biblical Theology Bulletin* 31 (2001): 17–25.

―――――. "Coming to Terms with a Neglected Aspect of Ancient Mediterranean Reciprocity: Seneca's views on benefit exchange in *De Beneficiis* as the framework for a model of social exchange." Pages 47–63 in *Social Scientific Models for Interpreting the Bible: Essays by the Context Group in Honor of Bruce Malina*. Edited by John J. Pilch. Biblical Interpretation Series 53. Leiden: E. J. Brill, 2001.

―――――. *Paul as Benefactor: Reciprocity, Strategy and Theological Reflection in Paul's Collection*. Wissenschaftliche Untersuchungen zum Neuen Testament 2.124. Tübingen: J. C. B. Mohr (Paul Siebeck), 2000.

―――――. "Managing the Household: Paul as *Paterfamilias* of the Christian Household Group in Corinth." Pages 213–33 in *Modelling Early Christianity: Social-Scientific Studies of the New Testament in its Context*. Edited by Philip F. Esler. London: Routledge, 1995.

Judge, Edwin Arthur. "The Early Christians as a Scholastic Community." *Journal of Religious History* 1 (1960–61): 125–37.

―――――. *The Social Pattern of Christian Groups in the First Century; Some Prolegomena to the Study of New Testament Ideas of Social Obligation*. London: Tyndale, 1960.

Jung, Carl Gustav. *Psychology and Religion: West and East*. Translated by R. F. C. Hull. Bollingen Series 20. New York: Pantheon Books, 1958.

Justman, Stewart. *The Psychological Mystique*. Rethinking Theory. Evanston: Northwestern University Press, 1998.

Kähler, Christoph. *Jesu Gleichnisse als Poesie und Therapie: Versuch eines integrativen Zugangs zum kommunikativen Aspekt von Gleichnissen Jesu*. Wissenschaftliche Untersuchungen zum Neuen Testament 78. Tübingen: J. C. B. Mohr (Paul Siebeck), 1995.

Kee, Howard C. "Pauline Eschatology: Relationships with Apocalyptic and Stoic Thought." Pages 135–58 in *Glaube und Eschatologie: Festschrift für Werner Georg Kümmel zum 80. Geburtstag*. Edited by Erich Grässer and Otto Merk. Tübingen: J. C. B. Mohr (Paul Siebeck), 1985.

Keller, Fred S. *The Definition of Psychology*. New York: Appleton-Century-Crofts, 1973.

Kennedy, George A. *The Art of Rhetoric in the Roman World, 300 B.C.–A.D. 300*. A History of Rhetoric, vol. 2. Princeton: Princeton University Press, 1972.

Kille, D. Andrew. *Psychological Biblical Criticism*. Guides to Biblical Scholarship, edited by Gene M. Tucker. Minneapolis: Fortress Press, 2001.

Kim, Seyoon. *The Origin of Paul's Gospel*. Grand Rapids: Eerdmans, 1981.

―――――. "'The grace that was given to me. . .': Paul and the Grace of his Apostleship." Pages 50–59 in *Die Hoffnung festhalten*. Edited by Gerhard Maier. Neuhausen-Stuttgart: Hänssler-Verlag, 1978.

Kirk, J. Andrew. "Apostleship Since Rengstorf: Towards a Synthesis." *New Testament Studies* 21 (1975): 249–64.

Kirner, Guido O. "Apostolat und Patronage (I): Methodischer Teil und Forschungsdiskussion." *Zeitschrift für Antikes Christentum* 6 (2002): 3–37.

Klauck, Hans-Josef. *The Religious Context of Early Christianity: A Guide to Graeco-Roman Religions*. Translated by Brian McNeil. Edinburgh: T&T Clark, 2000.

Kloppenborg, John S. "Edwin Hatch, Churches and *Collegia*." Pages 212–38 in *Origins and Method: Towards a New Understanding of Judaism and Christianity: Essays in Honour of John C. Hurd*. Edited by Bradley H. McLean. Journal for the Study of the Old Testament Supplement Series 86. Sheffield: JSOT Press, 1993.

———. "Collegia and *Thiasoi*: Issues in Function, Taxonomy and Membership." Pages 16–30 in *Voluntary Associations in the Graeco-Roman World*. Edited by John S. Kloppenborg and Steven G. Wilson. New York: Routledge, 1996.

Kloppenborg, John S., and Steven G. Wilson, eds. *Voluntary Associations in the Graeco-Roman World*. New York: Routledge, 1996.

Kluckhohn, Florence Rockwood, and Fred L. Strodtbeck. *Variations in Value Orientations*. Evanston, Ill.: Row, Peterson and Company, 1961.

Knox, John. *Chapters in a Life of Paul*. New York: Abingdon Press, 1950.

Konstan, David. "The Emotions of the Ancient Greeks—Anger and Hatred." *Unpublished Paper* (2001).

———. "The Emotions of the Ancient Greeks—Jealousy." *Unpublished Paper* (2001).

Konstan, David, Diskin Clay, Clarence E. Glad, Johan C. Thom, and James Ware. *Philodemus: On Frank Criticism*. Society of Biblical Literature Texts and Translations 43; Graeco-Roman Religion Series 43. Atlanta: Scholars Press, 1998.

Krentz, Edgar, John Koenig, and Donald Juel. *Galatians*. Augsburg Commentary on the New Testament. Minneapolis: Augsburg Publishing House, 1985.

Lausberg, Heinrich. *Handbook of Literary Rhetoric: A Foundation for Literary Study*. Translated by Matthew T. Bliss, Annemiek Jansen and David E. Orton. Edited by David E. Orton and R. Dean Anderson. Leiden: E. J. Brill, 1998.

Lehmeier, Karin. "Gemeinschaft nach dem oikos-Modell: Philodem und Paulus im Vergleich." Pages 107–21 in *Text und Geschichte: Facetten theologischen Arbeitens aus dem Freundes- und Schülerkreis*. Edited by Stefan Maser and Egbert Schlarb. Marburg: N.G. Elwert, 1999.

Lemche, Niels Peter. "From Patronage Society to Patronage Society." Pages 106–20 in *The Origins of the Ancient Israelite States*. Edited by Volkmar Fritz and Philip R. Davies. Journal for the Study of the Old Testament Supplement Series. Sheffield: Sheffield Academic Press, 1996.

———. "Kings and Clients: On Loyalty Between the Ruler and the Ruled in Ancient 'Israel'." *Semeia* 66 (1994): 119–32.

Leuba, James H. *The Psychology of Religious Mysticism*. New York: Harcourt Brace, 1925.

———. *The Psychological Origin and the Nature of Religion*. Religions Ancient and Modern. London: Constable, 1921.

———. *A Psychological Study of Religion, its Origin, Function, and Future*. New York: MacMillan, 1912.

———. "A Study in the Psychology of Religious Phenomena." *American Journal of Psychology* 5 (1896): 309–85.

LiDonnici, Lynn R. *The Epidaurian Miracle Inscriptions: Text, Translation and Commentary*. Texts and Translations 36; Graeco-Roman Religion Series 11. Atlanta: Scholars, 1995.

Lifton, Robert Jay. *History and Human Survival*. New York: Random House, 1970.
Lightfoot, Joseph B. *Epistle to the Galatians*. London: MacMillan and Co., 1856.
Lightstone, Jack N., and Canadian Corporation for Studies in Religion. *Mishnah and the Social Formation of the Early Rabbinic Guild: A Socio-rhetorical Approach*. Studies in Christianity and Judaism 11. Waterloo: Published for the Canadian Corporation for Studies in Religion = Corporation canadienne des sciences religieuses by Wilfrid Laurier University Press, 2002.
Lindsay, Dennis R. *Josephus and Faith: Πίστις and Πιστεύειν as Faith Terminology in the Writings of Flavius Josephus and in the New Testament*. Arbeiten zur Geschichte des antiken Judentums und des Urchristentums 19. Leiden: E. J. Brill, 1993.
Lips, Hermann von. "Der Apostolat des Paulus—ein charisma? Semantische Aspekte zu charis–charisma und anderen Wortpaaren im Sprachgebrauch des Paulus." *Biblica* 66 (1985): 305–43.
Llewelyn, Stephen R., ed. *New Documents Illustrating Early Christianity: A Review of the Greek Inscriptions and Papyri Published in 1984–85*. NewDocs 8. Grand Rapids: Eerdmans, 1998.
Llewelyn, Stephen R., and Rosalinde Kearsley, eds. *New Documents Illustrating Early Christianity: A Review of the Greek Inscriptions and Papyri Published in 1982–83*. NewDocs 7. North Ryde, Australia: Ancient History Documentary Research Centre Macquarie University, 1994.
Lofland, John. "'Becoming a World Saver' Revisited." *American Behavioral Scientist* 20 (1977): 805–18.
Lofland, John, and Rodney Stark. "Becoming a World-Saver: A Theory of Conversion to a Deviant Perspective." *American Sociological Review* 30 (1965): 862–74.
Lohfink, Gerhard. *The Conversion of St. Paul: Narrative and History in Acts*. Translated by Bruce J. Malina. Chicago: Franciscan Herald Press, 1976.
Long, Anthony A. *The Hellenistic Philosophy: Stoics, Epicureans, Sceptics*. 2nd ed. Berkeley: University of California Press, 1986.
Longenecker, Bruce W. "ΠΙΣΤΙΣ in Romans 3:25: The Neglected Evidence for the 'Faithfulness of Christ'." *New Testament Studies* 39 (1993): 478–80.
Longenecker, Richard N. *Galatians*. WBC 41. Waco, Texas: Word, 1990.
Longenecker, Richard N., ed. *The Road From Damascus*. Grand Rapids: Eerdmans, 1997.
Louw, Johannes P. *Semantics of New Testament Greek*. Philadelphia: Fortress Press, 1982.
Lucretius Carus, Titus. *De rerum natura*. Translated by W. H. D. Rouse and Martin Ferguson Smith. 2nd ed. Loeb Classical Library. Cambridge, Mass.: Harvard University Press, 1982.
Lutz, Catherine. "Emotion, Thought, and Estrangement: Emotion as a Cultural Category." *Cultural Anthropology* 1 (1986): 287–309.

MacDonald, P. S. "Philosophical Conversion." *Philosophy and Theology* 10 (1997): 303–27.
Mack, Burton L. *The Christian Myth: Origins, Logic, and Legacy*. New York: Continuum, 2001.
Mack, Burton L., and Vernon K. Robbins. *Patterns of Persuasion in the Gospels*. Sonoma: Polebridge Press, 1989.
MacMullen, Ramsay. "Conversion: A Historian's View." *The Second Century* 5 (1985–86): 67–81.
———. *Christianizing the Roman Empire: A.D. 100–400*. New Haven: Yale University Press, 1984.

―――――. "Two Types of Conversion to Early Christianity." *Vigiliae Christianae* 37 (1983): 174–92.

―――――. "The Epigraphic Habit." *American Journal of Philology* 103 (1982): 233–46.

―――――. *Paganism in the Roman Empire*. New Haven: Yale University Press, 1981.

―――――. *Roman Social Relations, 50 B.C. to A.D. 284*. New Haven: Yale University Press, 1974.

Malherbe, Abraham J. "Conversion to Paul's Gospel." Pages 230–44 in *The Early Church and Its Context: Essays in Honor of Everett Ferguson*. Edited by Abraham J. Malherbe, Frederick W. Norris and James W. Thompson. Supplements to Novum Testamentum 90. Leiden: E. J. Brill, 1998.

―――――. *Paul and the Popular Philosophers*. Minneapolis: Fortress Press, 1989.

―――――. *Paul and the Thessalonians: The Philosophic Tradition of Pastoral Care*. Philadelphia: Fortress Press, 1987.

Malik, Rabia. "Culture and Emotions: Depression Among Pakistanis." Pages 145–62 in *Culture in Psychology*. Edited by Corinne Squire. London: Routledge, 2000.

Malina, Bruce J. "'Let Him Deny Himself' (Mark 8:34 & par): A Social Psychological Model of Self-Denial." *Biblical Theology Bulletin* 24 (1994): 106–19.

―――――. *The New Testament World*. Louisville: Westminster/John Knox Press, 1993.

―――――. "Is There a Circum-Mediterranean Person: Looking for Stereotypes." *Biblical Theology Bulletin* 22 (1992): 66–87.

―――――. "Dealing with Biblical (Mediterranean) Characters: A Guide for U.S. Consumers." *Biblical Theology Bulletin* 19 (1989): 127–41.

―――――. "Patron and Client: The Analogy Behind Synoptic Theology." *Forum* 4 (1988): 2–32.

―――――. *Christian Origins and Cultural Anthropology: Practical Models for Biblical Interpretation*. Atlanta: John Knox Press, 1986.

―――――. "Religion in the World of Paul." *Biblical Theology Bulletin* 16 (1986): 92–101.

―――――. "What is Prayer?" *The Bible Today* 18 (1980): 214–20.

―――――. "The Individual and the Community—Personality in the Social World of Early Christianity." *Biblical Theology Bulletin* 9 (1979): 126–38.

Malina, Bruce J., and Jerome H. Neyrey. *Portraits of Paul: An Archaeology of Ancient Personality*. Louisville: Westminster/John Knox Press, 1996.

―――――. "First-Century Personality: Dyadic, not Individual." Pages 67–96 in *The Social World of Luke–Acts*. Edited by Jerome H. Neyrey. Peabody: Hendrickson, 1991.

Malinowski, Bronislaw. *Magic, Science and Religion: and Other Essays*. Boston: Beacon Press, 1948.

―――――. *The Foundations of Faith and Morals: An Anthropological Analysis of Primitive Beliefs and Conduct with Special Reference to the Fundamental Problems of Religion and Ethics*. London: H. Milford and Oxford University Press, 1936.

Malone, Peter. *The Same as Christ Jesus: Gospel and Type*. London: St. Paul's, 2000.

Manson, William. "Grace in the New Testament." Pages 33–60 in *The Doctrine of Grace*. Edited by William Thomas Whitley. London: SCM Press, 1932.

Marshall, I. Howard. *1 and 2 Thessalonians*. Grand Rapids: Eerdmans, 1983.

Marshall, Peter. *Enmity in Corinth: Social Conventions in Paul's Relations with the Corinthians*. WUNT 2.23. Tübingen: J. C. B. Mohr (Paul Siebeck), 1987.

Martens, John W. "Romans 2:14–16: A Stoic Reading." *New Testament Studies* 40 (1994): 55–67.

Martial. *Epigrams*. Translated by Walter Charles Alan Ker. Loeb Classical Library. London: W. Heinemann, 1919.
Martin, Dale B. *Slavery as Salvation: The Metaphor of Slavery in Pauline Christianity*. New Haven: Yale University Press, 1990.
Martin, Luther H. "The Anti-Individualistic Ideology of Hellenism." *Numen* 41 (1994): 117–40.
Martin, Ralph P. *Philippians*. London: Oliphants, 1976.
Martyn, J. Louis. *Galatians*. Anchor Bible 33A. New York: Doubleday, 1997.
Maslow, Abraham H. *Religious Values, and Peak-Experiences*. The Kappa Delta Pi Lecture Series. Columbus: Ohio State University Press, 1964.
Mason, Steve. "*PHILOSOPHIAI*: Graeco-Roman, Judean and Christian." Pages 31–58 in *Voluntary Associations in the Graeco-Roman World*. Edited by John S. Kloppenborg and Steven G. Wilson. New York: Routledge, 1996.
Matera, Frank J., and Daniel J. Harrington. *Galatians*. Sacra Pagina Series 9. Collegeville, Minn.: Liturgical Press, 1992.
Matlock, R. Barry. "Detheologizing the ΠΙΣΤΙΣ ΧΡΙΣΤΟΥ Debate: Cautionary Remarks from a Lexical Semantic Perspective." *Novum Testamentum* 42 (2000): 1–23.
Mauss, Marcel. "A Category of the Human Mind: The Notion of Personhood; the Notion of the Self." Pages 1–25 in *The Category of the Person: Anthropology, Philosophy, History*. Edited by M. Carrithers, S. Collins and S. Lukes. Cambridge: Cambridge University Press, 1985.
McCready, Wayne O. "EKKLESIA and Voluntary Associations." Pages 59–73 in *Voluntary Associations in the Graeco-Roman World*. Edited by John S. Kloppenborg and Steven G. Wilson. New York: Routledge, 1996.
McKnight, Scot. *Turning to Jesus: The Sociology of Conversion in the Gospels*. Louisville: Westminster/John Knox Press, 2002.
McLean, Bradley H. *An Introduction to Greek Epigraphy of the Hellenistic and Roman Periods from Alexander the Great down to the Reign of Constantine (323 B.C.–A.D. 337)*. Ann Arbor: University of Michigan Press, 2002.
———. "The Place of Cult in Voluntary Associations and Christian Churches on Delos." Pages 186–225 in *Voluntary Associations in the Graeco-Roman World*. Edited by John S. Kloppenborg and Steven G. Wilson. New York: Routledge, 1996.
McLean, Bradley H., ed. *Origins and Method: Towards a New Understanding of Judaism and Christianity: Essays in Honour of John C. Hurd*. Journal for the Study of the Old Testament Supplement Series 86. Sheffield: JSOT Press, 1993.
Mead, Margaret. *Sex and Temperament in Three Primitive Societies*. New York: William Morrow, 1935.
———. *Coming of Age in Samoa: A Psychological Study of Primitive Youth for Western Civilization*. New York: W. Morrow, 1928.
Meeks, Wayne A. *The First Urban Christians: The Social World of the Apostle Paul*. New Haven: Yale University Press, 1983.
Mendenhall, George E. *Law and Covenant in Israelite and the Ancient near East*. Pittsburgh: The Presbyterian Board of Colportage, 1955.
Miller, John W. *Jesus at Thirty: A Psychological and Historical Portrait*. Minneapolis: Fortress Press, 1997.
Mitford, T. B. "A Cypriot Oath of Allegiance to Tiberius." *Journal of Roman Studies* 50 (1960): 74–79.
Moffatt, James. *Grace in the New Testament*. New York: Ray Long and R. R. Smith, 1932.

Momigliano, Arnaldo. "How Roman Emperors Became Gods." *American Scholar* 55 (1986): 181–93.

Montgomery, James A. "Hebrew *Hesed* and Greek *Charis*." *Harvard Theological Review* 32 (1939): 97–102.

Morris, Brian. *Anthropology of the Self: The Individual in Cultural Perspective*. Boulder, Colo.: Pluto Press, 1994.

Morris, Leon. *The First and Second Epistles to the Thessalonians*. Rev. ed. New International Commentary on the New Testament. Grand Rapids: Eerdmans, 1991.

Moscovici, Serge, and Gabriel Mugny. *Psychologie de la conversion: Études sur l'influence inconsciente*. Fribourg: Delval, 1987.

Mott, Stephen Charles. "Greek Ethics and Christian Conversion: The Philonic Background of Titus II 10–14 and III 3–7." *Novum Testamentum* 20 (1978): 22–48.

⸺⸺. "The Power of Giving and Receiving: Reciprocity in Hellenistic Benevolence." Pages 60–72 in *Current Issues in Biblical and Patristic Interpretation*. Edited by Gerald F. Hawthorne. Grand Rapids: Eerdmans, 1975.

⸺⸺. "The Greek Benefactor and Deliverance from Moral Distress." Ph.D. dissertation, Harvard University, 1971.

Moussy, Claude. *Gratia et sa famille*. Paris: Presses universitaires de France, 1966.

Moxnes, Halvor. "Patron–Client Relations and the New Community in Luke–Acts." Pages 241–68 in *The Social World of Luke–Acts: Models for Interpretation*. Edited by Jerome H. Neyrey. Peabody: Hendrickson, 1991.

Munck, Johannes. *Paul and the Salvation of Mankind*. Translated by Frank Clarke. Atlanta: John Knox Press, 1977.

Murphy-O'Connor, Jerome. *Paul: A Critical Life*. New York: Oxford University Press, 1996.

⸺⸺. *I Corinthians*. New Testament Message 10. Wilmington, Del.: Michael Glazier, 1979.

Mynarek, Hubertus. *Jesus und die Frauen: Das Liebesleben des Nazareners*. Frankfurt am Main: Eichborn, 1995.

Nadel, Benjamin. "Actes d'affranchissement des esclaves du royaume de Bosphore et les origines de la manumissio in ecclesia." Pages 265–91 in *Symposion 1971: Vorträge zur griechischen und hellenistischen Rechtsgeschichte*. Edited by Hans Julius Wolff, Dieter Norr and Joseph Modrzejewski. Köln: Böhlau Verlag, 1975.

Neyrey, Jerome H. "Josephus' Vita and the Encomium: A Native Model of Personality." *Journal for the Study of Judaism in the Persian, Hellenistic, and Roman Periods* 25 (1994): 177–206.

Neyrey, Jerome H., ed. *The Social World of Luke–Acts: Models for Interpretation*. Peabody: Hendrickson, 1991.

Nida, Eugene A. *Toward a Science of Translating: With Special Reference to Principles and Procedures Involved in Bible Translating*. Helps for Bible Translators 8. Leiden: E. J. Brill, 1964.

Nida, Eugene A., and Johannes P. Louw. *Lexical Semantics of the Greek New Testament*. Atlanta: Scholars Press, 1992.

Nilsson, Martin P. *Greek Piety*. Translated by Herbert J. Rose. The Norton Library 265. New York: Norton, 1969.

Nock, Arthur D. *Early Gentile Christianity and its Hellenistic Background*. Harper Torchbooks. The Cloister Library. New York: Harper & Row, 1964.

_____. *Conversion: The Old and the New in Religion from Alexander the Great to Augustine of Hippo*. London: Oxford University Press, 1933.
Nolland, John L. "Luke's Use of Charis." *New Testament Studies* 32 (1986): 614–20.
_____. "Grace as Power." *Novum Testamentum* 28 (1986): 26–31.

Oates, John F., et al. *Checklist of Editions of Greek Papyri and Ostraca*. 3rd ed. Bulletin of the American Society of Papyrologists Supplements 4. Chico: Scholars Press, 1985.
Ober, Josiah. *Mass and Elite in Democratic Athens*. Princeton: Princeton University Press, 1989.
O'Brien, Peter Thomas. *The Epistle to the Philippians: A Commentary on the Greek Text*. The New International Greek Testament Commentary. Grand Rapids: Eerdmans, 1991.
Oliensis, Ellen. *Horace and the Rhetoric of Authority*. Cambridge: Cambridge University Press, 1998.
Olivier, H. "God as Friendly Patron: Reflections on Isaiah 5:1–7." *In die Skriflig* 30 (1996): 39–58.
O'Rourke, John J. "Pistis in Romans." *Catholic Biblical Quarterly* 35 (1973): 188–94.
Osiek, Carolyn. *Philippians, Philemon*. Abingdon New Testament Commentaries. Nashville, Tenn.: Abingdon Press, 2000.
_____. *Galatians*. New Testament Message 12. Wilmington, Del.: Michael Glazier, 1980.
Overman, J. Andrew. "Jews, Slaves, and the Synagogue on the Black Sea: The Bosporan Manumission Inscriptions and Their Significance for Diaspora Judaism." Pages 141–57 in *Evolution of the Synagogue: Problems and Progress*. Edited by Howard Clark Kee and Lynn H. Cohick. Harrisburg, Pa.: Trinity Press International, 1999.

Page, Denys L. *Select Papyri: Literary Papyri, Poetry*. Loeb Classical Library. Cambridge, Mass.: Harvard University Press, 1970.
Paloutzian, Raymond F., S. L. Jackson, and J. E. Crandall. "Conversion Experience, Belief System, and Personal and Ethical Attitudes." *Journal of Psychology and Theology* 5 (1977): 103–109.
Pavlock, Barbara. "Horace's Invitation Poems to Maecenas: Gifts to a Patron." *Ramus* 11 (1982): 79–98.
Peace, Richard V. *Conversion in the New Testament: Paul and the Twelve*. Grand Rapids: Eerdmans, 1999.
Peristiany, John George, ed. *Honor and Shame: The Values of Mediterranean Society*. Chicago: University of Chicago Press, 1966.
Perkins, Pheme. *The Johannine Epistles*. Wilmington, Del.: Michael Glazier, 1979.
Pilch, John J. "Psychological and Psychoanalytical Approaches to Interpreting the Bible in Social-Scientific Context." *Biblical Theology Bulletin* 27 (1997): 112–16.
_____. *Introducing the Cultural Context of the New Testament*. Hear the Word, vol. 2. New York: Paulist Press, 1991.
_____. *Galatians and Romans*. Collegeville Bible Commentary 6. Collegeville, Minn.: Liturgical Press, 1983.
Pitt-Rivers, Julian. "Honor and Social Status." Pages 19–77 in *Honor and Shame: The Values of Mediterranean Society*. Edited by J. G. Peristiany. Chicago: University of Chicago Press, 1966.

Plevnik, J. "Paul's Appeal to His Damascus Experience and 1 Cor 15:5–7: Are They Legitimations?" *Toronto Journal of Theology* 4 (1988): 101–11.
Pliny the Elder. *Natural History*. Translated by H. Rackham, W. H. S. Jones & D. E. Eichholz. 10 vols. Loeb Classical Library. Cambridge, Mass.: Harvard University Press, 1940–1963.
Pliny the Younger. *Letters*. Translated by William Melmoth and W. M. L. Hutchinson. Loeb Classical Library. London: W. Heinemann, 1915.
Plummer, Alfred. *A Commentary on St. Paul's Epistle to the Philippians*. London: Robert Scott, 1909.
Plutarch. *Lives*. Translated by Bernadotte Perrin et al. 11 vols. Loeb Classical Library. London: W. Heinemann, 1914–1926.
_____. *Moralia*. Translated by Frank Cole Babbitt. Loeb Classical Library. 13 vols. Cambridge, Mass.: Harvard University Press, 1969.
Poland, Franz. *Geschichte des griechischen Vereinswesens*. Leipzig: B. G. Teubner, 1909.
Polanyi, Karl. *Primitive, Archaic, and Modern Economies: Essays of Karl Polanyi*. Edited by George Dalton. New York: Doubleday, 1968.
Porter, Stanley E. *Handbook of Classical Rhetoric in the Hellenistic Period, 330 B.C.–A.D. 400*. Leiden: E. J. Brill, 1997.
Poster, Carol. "The Affections of the Soul: *Pathos*, Protreptic, and Preaching in Hellenistic Thought." Pages 23–37 in *Paul and Pathos*. Edited by Thomas H. Olbricht and Jerry L. Sumney. Atlanta: Society of Biblical Literature, 2001.
Pötscher, Walter. *Theophrastos 'Peri Eusebeias': Griechischer Text, herausgegeben, übersetzt und eingeleitet*. Leiden: E. J. Brill, 1964.
Price, Simon R. F. *Rituals and Power: The Roman Imperial Cult in Asia Minor*. Cambridge: Cambridge University Press, 1984.
_____. "Gods and Emperors: The Greek Language of the Roman Imperial Cult." *Journal of Hellenic Studies* 104 (1984): 79–95.
_____. "Between Man and God: Sacrifice in the Roman Imperial Cult." *Journal of Roman Studies* 70 (1980): 28–43.

Quincy, J. H. "Greek Expressions of Thanks." *Journal of Hellenic Studies* 86 (1966): 133–58.

Radford, John. "Psychology." Pages 689–94 in *The Social Science Encyclopedia*. Edited by A. Kuper and J. Kuper. London: Routledge, 1996.
Rambo, Lewis R. *Understanding Religious Conversion*. New Haven: Yale University Press, 1993.
_____. "The Psychology of Conversion." Pages 159–77 in *Handbook of Religious Conversion*. Edited by H. N. Malony and S. Southard. Birmingham: Religious Education Press, 1992.
_____. "Conversion." Pages 73–79 in *Encyclopedia of Religion*. Edited by Mircea Eliade. New York: MacMillan, 1987.
_____. "Current Research on Religious Conversion." *Religious Studies Review* 8 (1982): 146–59.
Reichardt, Michael. *Psychologische Erklärung der paulinischen Damaskusvision: Ein Beitrag zum interdisziplinären Gespräch zwischen Exegese und Psychologie seit dem 18. Jahrhundert*. Stuttgarter Biblische Beiträge 42. Stuttgart: Katholisches Bibelwerk, 1999.
Reid, W. S. "Psychology of Conversion." *Evangelical Quarterly* 28 (1956): 33–42.

Reilly, Linda Collins. *Slaves in Ancient Greece: Slaves from Greek Manumission Inscriptions.* Chicago: Ares Publishers, 1978.

Remus, Harold R. "Voluntary Associations and Networks: Aelius Aristides at the Asclepeion in Pergamum." Pages 146–75 in *Voluntary Associations in the Graeco-Roman World.* Edited by John S. Kloppenborg and Steven G. Wilson. New York: Routledge, 1996.

Rengstorf, Karl Heinrich. *A Complete Concordance to Flavius Josephus.* 5 vols. Leiden: E. J. Brill, 1973.

———. "ἀποστέλλω/ἀπόστολος." Pages 398–447 in vol. 1 of *Theological Dictionary of the New Testament.* Edited by Gerhard Kittel and Gerhard Friedrich. Translated by G. W. Bromiley. 10 vols. Grand Rapids: Eerdmans, 1964.

———. *Apostleship.* Translated by J. R. Coates. Bible Key Words. London: Adam and Charles Black, 1952.

Reumann, John. "'Stewards of God'—Pre-Christian Religious Application of *Oikonomos* in Greek." *Journal of Biblical Literature* 77 (1958): 339–49.

Rich, J. "Patronage and Interstate Relations in the Roman Republic." Pages 117–35 in *Patronage in Ancient Society.* Edited by Andrew Wallace-Hadrill. London: Routledge, 1989.

Richardson, Peter. *Herod: King of the Jews and Friend of the Romans.* Columbia: University of South Carolina Press, 1996.

Rieff, Philip. *The Triumph of the Therapeutic: Uses of Faith after Freud.* Chicago: University of Chicago Press, 1987.

———. *Freud, the Mind of the Moralist.* 3rd ed. Chicago: University of Chicago Press, 1979.

Robbins, Vernon K. *The Tapestry of Early Christian Discourse: Rhetoric, Society and Ideology.* London: Routledge, 1996.

———. *Exploring the Texture of Texts: A Guide to Socio-Rhetorical Interpretation.* Valley Forge, Pa.: Trinity Press International, 1996.

———. *New Boundaries in Old Territory: Form and Social Rhetoric in Mark.* Emory Studies in Early Christianity 3. New York: P. Lang, 1994.

———. *Ancient Quotes & Anecdotes: From Crib to Crypt.* Foundations & Facets. Sonoma, Calif.: Polebridge Press, 1989.

———. *Jesus the Teacher: A Socio-Rhetorical Interpretation of Mark.* Philadelphia: Fortress Press, 1984.

Robert, L. "Théophanie de Mytilène à Constantinople." *Comptes rendus de l'Académie des Inscriptions et Belles-Lettres* (1969): 42–64.

Robertson, Archibald, and Alfred Plummer. *A Critical and Exegetical Commentary on the First Epistle of St. Paul to the Corinthians.* International Critical Commentary. Edinburgh: T&T Clark, 1911.

Rodd, Cyril S. "On Applying a Sociological Theory to Biblical Studies." *Journal for the Study of the Old Testament* 19 (1981): 95–106.

Roetzel, Calvin. *Paul: The Man and the Myth.* Minneapolis: Fortress Press, 1999.

Rohrbaugh, Richard L., ed. *The Social Sciences and New Testament Interpretation.* Peabody: Hendrickson, 1996.

Rollins, Wayne G. *Soul and Psyche: The Bible in Psychological Perspective.* Minneapolis: Fortress Press, 1999.

Rollinson, Philip B., and Richard Geckle. *A Guide to Classical Rhetoric.* Signal Mountain, Tenn.: Summertown, 1998.

Rosaldo, Michelle Z. "Toward an Anthropology of Self and Feeling." Pages 137–57 in *Culture Theory: Essays on Mind, Self and Emotion*. Edited by Richard A. Shweder and Robert A. LeVine. Cambridge: Cambridge University Press, 1984.

Rubenstein, Richard L. *My Brother Paul*. New York: Harper and Row, 1972.

Rudd, Niall. *The Satires of Horace*. Cambridge: Cambridge University Press, 1966.

Sahlins, Marshall. *Stone Age Economics*. New York: Aldine Publishing Company, 1972.

Saller, Richard P. "Patronage and Friendship in Early Imperial Rome: Drawing the Distinction." Pages 49–62 in *Patronage in Ancient Society*. Edited by Andrew Wallace-Hadrill. London: Routledge, 1989.

———. *Personal Patronage under the Early Empire*. New York: Cambridge University Press, 1982.

Sanders, Ed P. *Paul and Palestinian Judaism: A Comparison of Patterns of Religion*. Philadelphia: Fortress Press, 1977.

Sanders, Jack T. *Charisma, Converts, Competitors: Societal and Sociological Factors in the Success of Early Christianity*. London: SCM Press, 2000.

Sandmel, Samuel. *Judaism and Christian Beginnings*. New York: Oxford University Press, 1978.

Schenkeveld, Dirk M. "Philosophical Prose." Pages 195–264 in *Handbook of Classical Rhetoric in the Hellenistic Period, 330 B.C.–A.D. 400*. Edited by Stanley E. Porter. Leiden: E. J. Brill, 1997.

Schmithals, Walter. *The Office of Apostle in the Early Church*. Translated from the German by John E. Steely. Nashville: Abingdon Press, 1969.

Schwartz, S. "Josephus in Galilee: Rural Patronage and Social Breakdown." Pages 290–306 in *Josephus and the History of the Greco-Roman Period: Essays in Honour of Morton Smith*. Edited by Fausto Parente and Joseph Sievers. Studia Post-Biblica 41. Leiden: E. J. Brill, 1994.

Scott, J. C. "Patronage or Exploitation?" Pages 21–39 in *Patrons and Clients in Mediterranean Society*. Edited by Ernest Gellner and John Waterbury. London: Duckworth, 1977.

Scroggs, Robin. "Psychology as a Tool to Interpret the Text." *The Christian Century* 99 (1982): 335–38.

———. "The Sociological Interpretation of the New Testament: The Present State of the Research." *New Testament Studies* 26 (1980): 164–79.

———. "The Heuristic Value of a Psychoanalytic Model in the Interpretation of Pauline Theology." *Zygon* 13 (1978): 136–57.

———. *Paul for a New Day*. Philadelphia: Fortress Press, 1977.

Sedley, D. "Philosophical Allegiance in the Greco-Roman World." Pages 97–119 in *Philosophia Togata: Essays on Philosophy and Roman Society*. Edited by Miriam T. Griffin and Jonathan Barnes. Oxford: Clarendon Press, 1989.

Segal, Alan F. "Conversion and Messianism: Outline for a New Approach." Pages 296–340 in *The Messiah: Developments in Earliest Judaism and Christianity*. Edited by James H. Charlesworth. Minneapolis: Fortress Press, 1992.

———. *Paul the Convert: The Apostolate and Apostasy of Saul the Pharisee*. New Haven: Yale University Press, 1990.

Segall, Marshall H., Pierre R. Dasen, John W. Berry, and Ype H. Poortinga. *Human Behavior in Global Perspective*. New York: Pergamon Press, 1990.

Seid, Timothy W. "Synkrisis in Hebrews 7: The Rhetorical Structure and Strategy." Pages 322–47 in *The Rhetorical Interpretation of Scripture: Essays from the 1996 Malibu Conference*. Edited by Stanley E. Porter and Dennis L. Stamps. Journal for the Study of the New Testament Supplement Series 180. Sheffield: Sheffield Academic Press, 1999.

Seneca, Lucius Annaeus. *Moral Essays*. Translated by John W. Basore. Loeb Classical Library. Cambridge, Mass.: Harvard University Press, 1928.

Sevenster, Jan N. *Paul and Seneca*. Supplements to Novum Testamentum 4. Leiden: E. J. Brill, 1961.

Shweder, Richard A. *Thinking Through Cultures: Expeditions in Cultural Psychology*. Cambridge, Mass.: Harvard University Press, 1991.

Silva, Moisés. *Biblical Words and their Meaning: An Introduction to Lexical Semantics*. Grand Rapids: Zondervan Publishing House, 1983.

Simkins, Ronald A. "Patronage and the Political Economy of Monarchic Israel." *Semeia* 87 (1999): 123–44.

Snyder, H. Gregory. *Teachers and Texts in the Ancient World: Philosophers, Jews and Christians*. Religion in the First Christian Centuries, edited by Deborah Sawyer and John Sawyer. London: Routledge, 2000.

Spilsbury, P. "God and Israel in Josephus: A Patron–Client Relationship [Ant 1–11]." Pages 172–91 in *Understanding Josephus: Seven Perspectives*. Edited by Steve Mason. Journal for the Study of Pseudepigrapha Supplement Series 32. Sheffield: Sheffield Academic Press, 1998.

Squire, Corinne. "Introduction." Pages 1–16 in *Culture in Psychology*. Edited by Corinne Squire. London: Routledge, 2000.

Stannard, David E. *Shrinking History: On Freud and the Failure of Psychohistory*. New York: Oxford University Press, 1980.

Starbuck, Edwin Diller. *The Psychology of Religion*. New York: Charles Scribner's Sons, 1899.

Stark, Rodney. *The Rise of Christianity: A Sociologist Reconsiders History*. Princeton: Princeton University Press, 1996.

Stegemann, Ekkehard W., and Wolfgang Stegemann. *Urchristliche Sozialgeschichte: Die Anfänge im Judentum und die Christusgemeinden in der mediterranen Welt*. Stuttgart: Kohlhammer, 1995; ET *The Jesus Movement: A Social History of Its First Century*. Translated by O. C. Dean. Jr. Minneapolis: Fortress Press, 1999.

Stendahl, Krister. *Paul Among Jews and Gentiles*. Philadelphia: Fortress Press, 1976.

―――. "Paul and the Introspective Conscience of the West." *Harvard Theological Review* 56 (1963): 199–215.

Stevenson, T. R. "Social and Psychological Interpretations of Graeco-Roman Religion: Some Thoughts on the Ideal Benefactor." *Antichthon* 30 (1996): 1–18.

―――. "The Ideal Benefactor and the Father Analogy in Greek and Roman Thought." *Classical Quarterly* 42 (1992): 421–36.

Stowers, Stanley K. *Letter Writing in Greco-Roman Antiquity*. Library of Early Christianity, edited by Wayne A. Meeks. Philadelphia: Westminster Press, 1986.

―――. "Social Status, Public Speaking and Private Teaching." *Novum Testamentum* 26 (1984): 59–82.

―――. "The Social Sciences and the Study of Early Christianity." Pages 149–81 in vol. 5 of *Approaches to Ancient Judaism*. Edited by William Scott Green. Chico: Scholars Press, 1983.

Sumney, Jerry L. "Paul's 'Weakness': An Integral Part of his Conception of Apostleship." *Journal for the Study of the New Testament* 52 (1993): 71–91.
Syme, Ronald. *The Roman Revolution*. Oxford: Clarendon Press, 1939.
———. "The Allegiance of Labienus." *Journal of Roman Studies* 28 (1938): 113–25.

Tarachow, S. "St. Paul and Early Christianity." *Psychoanalysis and the Social Sciences* 4 (1955): 223–81.
Tatum, Jeffrey W. "Plutarch on Antiochus of Ascalon: *Cicero* 4,2." *Hermes* 129 (2001): 139–42.
Taylor, B. "Recollection and Membership: Converts' Talk and the Ratiocination of Commonality." *Sociology* 12 (1978): 316–24.
Taylor, G. M. "The Function of ΠΙΣΤΙΣ ΧΡΙΣΤΟΥ in Galatians." *Journal of Biblical Literature* 85 (1966): 58–76.
Taylor, Nicholas H. "Paul's Apostolic Authority: Autobiographical Reconstruction in Gal 1:11–14." *Journal of Theology for Southern Africa* 83 (1993): 65–77.
Theissen, Gerd. *Psychological Aspects of Pauline Theology*. Translated by John P. Galvin. Edinburgh: T&T Clark, 1987.
Thiselton, Anthony C. *The First Epistle to the Corinthians*. New International Greek Testament Commentary. Grand Rapids: Eerdmans, 2000.
Thurén, Lauri. *Derhetorizing Paul: A Dynamic Perspective on Pauline Theology and the Law*. Harrisburg, Pa.: Trinity Press International, 2002.
———. "'By Means of Hyperbole' (1 Cor 12:31b)." Pages 97–113 in *Paul and Pathos*. Edited by Thomas H. Olbricht and Jerry L. Sumney. Atlanta: Society of Biblical Literature, 2001.
Tod, Marcus N. *Sidelights on Greek History: Three Lectures on the Light Thrown by Greek Inscriptions on the Life and Thought of the Ancient World*. Oxford: Basil Blackwell, 1932.
Tomlin, Graham. "Christians and Epicureans in 1 Corinthians." *Journal for the Study of the New Testament* 68 (1997): 51–72.
Toren, Christina. "Psychological Anthropology." Pages 456–61 in *Encyclopedia of Social and Cultural Anthropology*. Edited by Alan Barnard and Jonathan Spencer. London: Routledge, 1996.
Torrey, E. Fuller. *Freudian Fraud: The Malignant Effect of Freud's Theory on American Thought and Culture*. New York: Harper Collins, 1992.
Travisano, R. V. "Alternation and Conversion as Qualitatively Different Transformations." Pages 594–606 in *Social Psychology Through Symbolic Interaction*. Edited by Gregory Prentice Stone and Harvey A. Farberman. Waltham, Mass.: Ginn-Blaisdell, 1970.
Treggiari, Susan. *Roman Freedmen During the Late Republic*. Oxford: Clarendon Press, 1969.
Triandis, Harry C. "The Self and Social Behavior in Differing Cultural Contexts." *Psychological Review* 98 (1989): 506–20.
Triandis, Harry C., et al. "An Emic–Etic Analysis of Individualism and Collectivism." *Journal of Cross-Cultural Psychology* 24 (1993): 366–83.
Turner, Max. "Modern Linguistics and the New Testament." Pages 146–74 in *Hearing the New Testament*. Edited by Joel B. Green. Grand Rapids: Eerdmans, 1995.

Vaage, Leif E. *Galilean Upstarts: Jesus' First Followers According to Q*. Valley Forge: Trinity Press International, 1994.

van Straten, F. T. "Gifts for the Gods." Pages 65–151 in *Faith, Hope and Worship: Aspects of Religious Mentality in the Ancient World*. Studies in Greek and Roman Religion 2. Edited by Hendrik S. Versnel. Leiden: E. J. Brill, 1982.
Vanhoye, Albert. "Personnalité de Paul et Exégèse paulinienne." Pages 3–15 in *L'Apôtre Paul: personnalité, style et conception du ministre*. Edited by Albert Vanhoye. Bibliotheca Ephemerides theologicae Lovanienses 72. Leuven: Peeters, 1986.
Versnel, Hendrik S. "Religious Projection: A Hellenistic Instance." Pages 25–39 in *Religious Transformations and Socio-Political Change: Eastern Europe and Latin America*. Edited by Luther H. Martin. Religion and Society 33. Berlin/New York: Mouton de Gruyter, 1993.
_____, "Religious Mentality in Ancient Prayer." Pages 1–64 in *Faith, Hope and Worship: Aspects of Religious Mentality in the Ancient World*. Edited by Hendrik S. Versnel. Studies in Greek and Roman Religion 2. Leiden: E. J. Brill, 1982.
_____, ed. *Faith, Hope and Worship: Aspects of Religious Mentality in the Ancient World*. Studies in Greek and Roman Religion 2. Leiden: E. J. Brill, 1982.
Veyne, Paul. *Bread and Circuses: Historical Sociology and Political Pluralism*. Translated by Brian Pearce. London: Penguin Press, 1990.
Vincent, Marvin R. *A Critical and Exegetical Commentary on the Epistles to the Philippians and to Philemon*. International Critical Commentary. Edinburgh: T&T Clark, 1897.
Vitz, Paul C. *Psychology as Religion: The Cult of Self-Worship*. Grand Rapids: Eerdmans, 1977.

Wallace-Hadrill, Andrew. "Patronage in Roman Society." Pages 63–87 in *Patronage in Ancient Society*. Edited by Andrew Wallace-Hadrill. London: Routledge, 1989.
_____, ed. *Patronage in Ancient Society*. Leicester-Nottingham Studies in Ancient Society 1. London: Routledge, 1989.
Waltzing, Jean-Pierre. *Étude historique sur les corporations professionelles chez les Romains depuis les origines jusqu' à la chute de l'Empire d'Occident*. 4 vols. Mémoires couronnés par l'Académie royale des Sciences, des Lettres et des Beaux-Arts de Belgique 50. Bruxelles; Louvain: F. Hayez, 1895, 1896, 1899, 1900.
Watson, Alan. *Jesus: A Profile*. Athens: University of Georgia Press, 1998.
Watson, Nigel M. "'The Philosopher Should Bathe and Brush his Teeth'—Congruence Between Word and Deed in Graeco-Roman Philosophy and Paul's Letters to the Corinthians." *Australian Biblical Review* 42 (1994): 1–16.
Weaver, Paul R. C. *Familia Caesaris: A Social Study of The Emperor's Freedmen and Slaves*. Cambridge: Cambridge University Press, 1972.
Weinfeld, M. "*Berit* – Covenant vs. Obligation." *Biblica* 56 (1975): 120–28.
Weiss, Johannes. *Earliest Christianity: A History of the Period A.D. 30–150*. Translated by Frederick C. Grant. New York: Harper and Row, 1959.
Welles, C. Bradford. *Royal Correspondence in the Hellenistic Period*. New Haven: Yale University Press, 1934.
Whitby, Mary. *The Propaganda of Power: The Role of Panegyric in Late Antiquity*. Mnemosyne, bibliotheca classica Batava. Supplementum 183. Leiden: E. J. Brill, 1998.
White, J. M. "Psychological Anthropology." Pages 687–88 in *The Social Sciences Encyclopedia*. Edited by A. Kuper and J. Kuper. London: Routledge, 1996.
Wiedemann, Thomas E. J. "The Regularity of Manumission at Rome." *Classical Quarterly* 35 (1985): 162–75.

Wierzbicka, Anna. *Emotions across Languages and Cultures.* Cambridge: Cambridge University Press, 1999.
Wilken, Robert L. *The Christians as the Romans Saw Them.* New Haven: Yale University Press, 1984.
_____. "Collegia, Philosophical Schools and Theology." Pages 268–91 in *The Catacombs and the Colosseum: The Roman Empire as the Setting of Primitive Christianity.* Edited by Stephen Benko and John J. O'Rourke. London and Valley Forge: Oliphants, 1972.
Williams, Sam K. *Galatians.* Abingdon New Testament Commentaries 9. Nashville: Abingdon Press, 1997.
Wilson, Steven G. "Voluntary Associations." Pages 1–15 in *Voluntary Associations in the Graeco-Roman World.* Edited by John S. Kloppenborg and Steven G. Wilson. New York: Routledge, 1996.
Winden, Jacobus C. M. van. *An Early Christian Philosopher: Justin Martyr's Dialogue with Trypho, Chapters One to Nine. Introduction, Text and Commentary.* Philosophia Patrum 1. Leiden: E. J. Brill, 1971.
Winter, Bruce W. *Philo and Paul Among the Sophists.* Cambridge: Cambridge University Press, 1997.
_____. *Seek the Welfare of the City: Christians as Benefactors and Citizens.* Grand Rapids: Eerdmans, 1994.
_____. "Is Paul Among the Sophists?" *Reformed Theological Review* 53 (1994): 28–38.
_____. "'The Seasons' of this Life and Eschatology in 1 Corinthians 7:29–31." Pages 323–34 in *Eschatology in Bible & Theology: Evangelical Essays at the Dawn of a New Millennium.* Edited by Kent E. Brower and Mark W. Elliott. Downers Grove, Ill.: InterVarsity Press, 1993.
_____. "The Public Honoring of Christian Benefactors: Rom 13.3–4 and 1 Peter 2.14–15." *Journal for the Study of the New Testament* 4 (1988): 87–103.
Witherington, Ben. *The Gospel of Mark: A Socio-Rhetorical Commentary.* Grand Rapids: Eerdmans, 2001.
_____. *The Acts of the Apostles: A Socio-Rhetorical Commentary.* Grand Rapids: Eerdmans, 1998.
_____. *Grace in Galatia: A Commentary on St. Paul's Letter to the Galatians.* Edinburgh: T&T Clark, 1998.
_____. *Conflict and Community in Corinth: A Socio-Rhetorical Commentary on 1 and 2 Corinthians.* Grand Rapids: Eerdmans, 1995.
Woodward, William R. "Professionalization, Rationality, and Political Linkages in Twentieth Century Psychology." Pages 295–309 in *Psychology in Twentieth-Century Thought and Society.* Edited by Mitchell G. Ash and William R. Woodward. Cambridge: Cambridge University Press, 1987.
Worthington, Ian, ed. *Persuasion: Greek Rhetoric in Action.* London: Routledge, 1994.
Wuellner, Wilhelm. "Biblical Exegesis in the light of the History and Historicity of Rhetoric and the Nature of the Rhetoric of Religion." Pages 492–513 in *Rhetoric and the New Testament: Essays from the 1992 Heidelberg Conference.* Edited by Stanley E. Porter and Thomas H. Olbricht. Journal for the Study of the Old Testament Supplement Series 90. Sheffield: Sheffield Academic Press, 1993.
Wykoff, Elizabeth. *Greek Tragedies*, vol. 1. Edited by D. G. Green and R. Lattimore. Chicago: University of Chicago Press, 1960.

Xenophon. *Memorabilia; Oeconomicus; Symposium, Apology*. Translated by E. C. Marchant and O. J. Todd. Loeb Classical Library. Cambridge, Mass.: Harvard University Press, 1992.

Yrizarry, Nathan, David Matsumoto, Chikako Imai, Kristie Kooken, and Sachiko Takeuchi. "Culture and Emotion." Pages 131–47 in *Cross-Cultural Topics in Psychology*. Edited by Leonore Loeb Adler and Uwe P. Gielen. Westport, Conn.: Praeger, 2001.

Index of Primary Sources

1. Hebrew Bible

Genesis		Isaiah	
6:8	99–100	6:6–8	100, 176
32:11	109	49:1	176

Exodus		Jeremiah	
2:16–20	82	1:4–19	100, 176
20:4–6	245	1:5	176

Numbers		Ezekiel	
14:19	109	2:1–3:11	100, 176

Deuteronomy		Jonah	
33:12	181	1:1–3	100, 176
		4:2	109

1 Samuel		Hosea	
3:2–4:1	100, 176	1:2	100

Psalms		Amos	
12:6 (LXX)	80	7:15	100
13:6	80		
56:3 (LXX)	80		
57:3	80		
77:11 (LXX)	81		

2. Apocrypha / Pseudepigrapha

Acts of John		2 Baruch	165
41–42	27		

2 Maccabees

4:2	81
6:13	81
9:26	81
10:38	81

3 Maccabees

3:19	81
6:24	81

4 Maccabees

8:6	81
8:17	81

Sirach

15:12–13	211
15:15	211

Wisdom of Solomon

11:1–14	129
11:4	128
11:5	81, 129
11:13	81, 129
16:1–4	129
16:2	81
16:5–14	129
16:11	129, 130
16:15–29	129
16:24	81, 129
17:1–18:4	129
18:2	82
18:5–25	129
19:1–12	129

3. New Testament

Matthew

10:16	167
13:41	167
21:33–46	168
23:23	213
23:34	167, 171
24:45	212
25:21	212

Mark

1:45	115
2:2	115
3:9	115
12:1–12	168

Luke

1:28	112
1:30	144
1:46–55	112
1:67–79	112
2:28–32	111
2:40	144
2:52	144
4:22	133, 144
6:32	144
6:33	144
6:34	144
10:3	167
12:42	160, 212
16:1–8	160
17:19	144
19:14	166
19:17	212
20:9–19	168

John

1:14	144
1:16	144
1:17	144

Acts

2:47	144
4:33	144
6:7	210
6:8	144
6:8–15	247
7:10	144
7:46	144
8	29
8:3	173
9	28
9:1	173
9:3–9	151
10	29
11:23	144
13:43	144
14:3	144
14:26	144
15:11	144
15:40	144
16:15	213
18:27	144
20:24	134, 144
20:32	144
22	28
22:4	173
22:6–11	151
24:27	144
25:3	144
25:9	144
26	28
26:10–11	173–74
26:11	247
26:12–18	151

Romans

1:5	143, 145
1:6–7	175
1:7	143
1:8	146, 214
1:18–32	187
1:21	146
1:23	187
1:25	246
1:26	187
1:28	246
1:31	246
3:3	214
3:24	143, 145
4:4	143
4:16	143
5:2	143, 145
5:15	143
5:17	143, 145
5:20, 21	143
6:1, 14, 15	143
6:17	136, 142
7	19, 20, 23
7:12	246
7:13	172
7:22	19
7:25	136, 142
8:18–30	175
9:24	175
10:2–4	151
11:5, 6	143
12:3	143, 145, 147
12:6	143
14:6	146
15:15	143, 145, 147
16:20	143

1 Corinthians

1:2	175
1:3	143
1:4	143, 146, 172
1:5	172
1:7	172
1:9	175
1:14	146
2:2	172
2:3	172
3:10	143, 145, 147
4:2	212
4:8–13	172
6:12	172
7:8	21
8:6	187
9:1	8, 151, 152, 155–69, 171
9:16	159

9:16–17	8, 151, 155–69	**Galatians**	
9:17	160	1:3	143, 174
10:30	143	1:6	143
11:2	172, 245	1:6–7	213
11:23	245	1:11–17	8, 23, 151, 152, 170–79, 182
12:31	173	1:13	172, 173, 182
12:58	173	1:13–14	171, 247
13	173	1:13–16	171
13:18	146	1:14	182, 247
14:33–36	246	1:15	143, 145, 147, 164, 171, 175, 177
15:3	245	1:15–16a	171
15:8	152, 156, 157, 171	1:15–16	169, 171
15:8–10	8, 151, 155–69	1:16	169
15:9	172	1:17	152
15:10a	157	1:23	172
15:10	113, 143, 145, 147, 157, 158	1:23–24	171
15:57	136, 143	2:9	143, 145, 147
16:3	143	2:21	143
16:23	143	3:9	151
		5:4	143
		5:16–23	187
2 Corinthians		5:22	213
1:2	143, 145	6:18	143
1:8	173		
1:12	143		
1:15	143	**Ephesians**	
2:14	136, 143	1:1	213
3:4–4:6	151	1:2	144
4:15	143, 145, 146	1:6	144
5:16	151	1:7	144
6:1	143	2:5	144
8:1	143, 145	2:7	144
8:4	143, 145	2:8	144
8:6	143, 145	3:1–13	151
8:7	143, 145	3:2	144
8:9	143, 145	3:7	144
8:16	143	3:8	144
8:19	143, 145	4:7	144
9:8	143	4:29	144
9:11	146	6:21	213
9:12	146	6:24	144
9:14	143		
9:15	143		
10:3–6	188	**Philippians**	
12:9	143	1:2	143
13:13	143	1:3	146

New Testament

1:7	143
1:15–17	180
1:28	180
3	182
3:2	180
3:4b–11	8, 23, 151, 153, 179–86
3:5–6	247
3:6	182, 247
3:7	181
3:9	182
3:18	180
4:6	146
4:8–9	187
4:23	143

Colossians

1:2	144, 213
1:4	213
1:6	144
1:7	213
1:23–29	151
3:16	144
4:15	68
4:16	144
4:18	144

1 Thessalonians

1:1	143
1:2	146, 172
1:3	172
1:8	172
2:1–12	188, 190
2:3	146
2:8	172
2:9	172
3:9	146
3:10	172
4:1	213
5:18	146
5:28	143

2 Thessalonians

1:2	144
1:4	213
1:12	144
2:16	144
3:18	144

1 Timothy

1:2	144
1:12	144
1:14	144
6:9–10	212
6:11	212
6:21	144

2 Timothy

1:2	144
1:3	144
1:9	144
2:1	144
2:22	212
4:22	144

Titus

1:4	144
2:11	131, 144
3:3–7	130
3:3	130
3:4	131
3:7	131, 144
3:15	144

Philemon

2	143
4	146
25	143

Hebrews

2:9	144
4:16	144
10:29	144
10:38	213
12:15, 28	144
13:7	213
13:9, 25	144

James

4:1–6	142
4:3	143
4:6	144

1 Peter

1:2, 10, 13	144
2:19, 20	144
3:7	144
4:10	144
5:5, 10, 12	144

2 Peter

1:2	144
3:18	144

2 John

1:3	144

3 John

5	212

Jude

4	144

Revelation

1:4	144
2:13, 19	213
13:10	213
14:12	213
22:21	144

4. Early Christian Writings

Acts of Paul and Thecla	19

Augustine

Acad. (*Against the Academics*)	
3.41	240

Barnabas

5:11	172

Justin

Dial. (*Dialogue with Trypho*)	
1.3	101

5. Graeco-Roman Literary Sources

Aeneas

22.15–18	210
22.15	211
22.16	211
22.17	211

Apuleius

Metamorphoses (*The Golden Ass*)

11.5	123
11.19	123
11.25	79
13	113
15	113

Aristides

Asclepius

44.2	78

Sacred Tales

2.292.14	97, 175

2.294.8	78	*Fam. (Epistulae ad Familiares)*	
4.322.1–2	111	3.6	233
4.323.14	78	4.9	233
4.329.16	78	13.21	232
4.330.13–16	111	13.21.2	233
4.337.11	78	20.1	121, 184
4.341.3	97	20.4	121
4.345.14	97, 175	73.10	121

Speech for Asclepius
37.1–7   111
39.19   78
40.1–2   111
40.6–8   113

Fin. (De finibus)
3.31   188

Off. (De officiis)
2.15   70

Aristotle

Eth. nic. (Nicomachean Ethics)
4.2   61
4.3   61
1162a.6   76

Part. or. (Partitiones oratoriae)
9   204, 208

Planc. (Pro Plancio)
80   209

Rhet. (Rhetoric)
1368a (19–23)   117

Tusc. (Tusculanae disputationes)
5.5   103

Cassius Dio
58.4.5   218

Cleanthes (*SVF*)

Hymn to Zeus
1–7   102
34–38   102–103

Cebes
Tabula
10   106, 130

Demosthenes

Cor. (De corona)
18.80   166
18.107   166

Cicero

Acad. post. (Academica posteriora = Lucullus)
63   239
69   239

3 Olynth.
3.26   210

Arch. (Pro Archia)
3.5–6   94
10.26   94
11.27   75

Dio Chrysostom

1 *Glor.* (*De gloria* 1 – Oration 66)
2   68

1 *Regn.* (De regno 1 – Oration 1)
38   209, 247

2 *Regn.* (*De regno* 2 – Oration 2)
75   110

3 *Regn.* (*De regno* 3 – Oration 3)
86   211
88   211

4 *Regn.* (*De regno* 4 – Oration 4)
22   110
122   247

Borysth. (*Borysthenetica* – Oration 36)
35–36, 60   110

Dei cogn. (*De dei cognitione* – Oration 12)
21   76
27–28   76
32   76
39   76

De leg. (*De lege* – Oration 75)
6   71
7   68

Hom. Socr. (*De Homero et Socrate* – Oration 55)
1   247
3   247
5   247

Diodorus Siculus
Library of History
1.70.6   141
3.21.5   141
3.73.6   141
36.3.3   141

Diogenes Laertius
Lives (*Lives of Eminent Philosophers*)
2.48   107
2.113   243
2.114   243
4.16   126
7.87–89   188

Dionysius of Halicarnassus
Ant. rom. (*Antiquitates romanae*)
5.21.3   140
9.59   166

Epictetus
Diatr. (*Diatribai* – *Dissertationes*)
1.4.29   103
1.4.32   76, 109
1.10.3   109
2.6.9   188
2.23.5   109
3.22.23   167
3.22.74   167
3.23.46   167
4.1.91–98   109
4.4.7   109
4.5.9   109
4.7.9   109
4.8.31   167

Euripides
Bacchae
319–321   78

Iphigenia in Tauris
l.14   134

Herodotus
Historiae
1.21   166
4.136   135

Hesiod
Op. (*Opera et dies*)
190   133

Homer
Il. (*Iliad*)
14.183   133

Graeco-Roman Literary Sources

Od. (Odyssey)		16.212	84
1.346	209	18.181	68, 83
8.175	133		
8.464ff.	109	*B. J. (Bellum judaicum)*	
		1.215	83
		1.388	84
## Horace		2.607	84
Ep. (Epistulae)		3.400–403	83
1.7.8–9	75	3.459	84
1.7.9	71	4.113	84
2.1.103–107	71	4.622	83
		7.71	84
Sat. (Satirae)			
1.1.9–10	71	*Vita*	
2.6.16ff.	75	7–12	30
6.45	96	16	68, 83
6.62–63	96	244	84
		259	84

Isocrates
Evag. (Evagoras – Oration 9)
39   118

Juvenal
Sat. (Satirae)
5.80–85   185

Josephus

A. J. (Antiquitates judaicae)		### Lucian	
1.8	83	*Double Indictment*	
1.229	85	17	126–27
2.89	160		
2.196	85	*Nigrinus*	
2.261–263	83	1	125
3.300	84		
3.459	83	### Lucretius	
4.212	85	*De Rerum Natura*	
4.316	84	1.62–79	238
4.317	84	3.1–30	238
4.318	84	5.1–54	238
4.319	84	5.14–21	238
5.115	84	6.1–42	238
6.60	85		
8.111	85		
9.93	84	### Lysias	
12.200	160	*Speeches*	
15.192–201	224	19.32	211
16.98	84		
16.146–147	83		

Martial

Ep. (*Epigrams*)
2.18	71
2.57	71
5.19	120–21
6.2	121
6.48	71
9.88	95
10.82	71
11.24	75

Menander

Fragment	127

Pausanias

Hist.
9.60.3	134

Petronius

Sat. (*Satyricon*)
57	233

Philo

Abr. (*De Abrahamo*)
268	211

Cher. (*De cherubim*)
122–123	88

Decal. (*De decalogo*)
165–167	71

Deus (*Quod Deus sit immutabilis*)
107	85

Ebr. (*De ebrietate*)
32	87, 142

Her. (*Quis rerum divinarum heres sit*)
32	87

Leg. (*Legum allegoriae*)
3.76	86, 142
3.77–78	86, 142
3.215	87, 142

Migr. (*De migratione Abrahami*)
73	87, 142

Mut. (*De mutatione nominum*)
24	86, 142

Opif. (*De opificio mundi*)
23	87, 142
77	86

Plant. (*De plantatione*)
85–89	87
125–131	111
126–131	112

Praem. (*De praemiis et poenis*)
126	142

Sacr. (*De sacrificiis Abelis et Caini*)
57–58	88
60	87
127	87

Sobr. (*De sobrietate*)
55	87

Virt. (*De virtutibus*)
180	130
182	130

Philodemus

Rhet. (*Volumina rhetorica*)
IIa 43.26ff.	237

Plato

Apol. (*Apologia*)
36b	160

Charm. (*Charmides*)
155A	107

Graeco-Roman Literary Sources

Euthyd. (Euthydemus)
275A   106

Resp. (Respublica)
498a   160
7   25
7.518   106

Theaet. (Thaetetus)
144D   107

Pliny the Elder
Nat. (Naturalis historia)
7.117   110
7.122   229

Pliny the Younger
Ep. (Epistulae)
1.1   95
3.8   74
10.4   73
10.5   73
10.51   71

Pan. (Panegyricus)
5.6–8   120
95.4   120

Plutarch
E Delph. (De E apud Delphos)
384E   70

Is. Os. (De Iside et Osiride)
351C–351D   76
356A–B   76
361C   79
377A   109
379D   109

Superst. (De superstitione)
169F–170A   209

Polybius
Hist. (Historiae)
1.31.6   140
20.11.10   140
21.18–19   141
21.19.10   141
30.31.7   140

Porphyry
Vit. Plot. (Vita Plotini)
4–5   241
6   241
7   241, 242
10   241
12   241
14   241
18   241
19–21   241
20   241, 242
23   241

Propertius
El. (Elegiae)
3.9.43–44   75

Pseudo-Libanius
Ἐπιστολιμαῖοι Χαρακτῆρες
64   72

Pseudo-Plato
Alc. maj.
135D   108, 236

Quintilian
Inst. (Institutio oratoria)
2.4.21   117

Sallust

Bell. Cat. (*Bellum Catilinae*)
19	206

Bell. Jug. (*Bellum jugurthinum*)
71	205–207

Seneca

Ben. (*De beneficiis*)
1.1.1	69
1.2.4	70
1.4.2	69
1.5.3–6	70
1.10.4	72
1.10.5	76
2.1.1–4	76
2.11.3	71
2.11.5	159
2.17.7	159
2.19.2	160
2.23.1–2	71
2.24.4	71
2.30.2	159
2.34.2	69
2.34.5	70
2.35.3	70
3.8.2	159
3.8.3	70, 98
3.15.4	76
3.25	205
4.3.2	109
4.3.3	76
4.5	76
4.18.1	69, 72
4.26.1	76
4.28	76
4.28.1	76
5.7.2	159
5.8.2	71
6.4.1	160
7.30.4–5	76
7.31.2–4	76
7.32	76

Ep. (*Epistulae morales*)
10.2–4	187
39.6	188
81.7	69
90.1	106
90.12	128
90.24	128
90.28	235
90.35	128
90.44	128
90.46	128

Sidonius

Ep. 1.1   95–96

Sophocles

Aj. (*Ajax*)
713	209

Ant. (*Antigone*)
292	209

Oed. col. (*Oedipus coloneus*)
l. 41	24–25

Oed. tyr. (*Oedipus tyrannus*)
596–598	73
1438–1439, 1442–1443	210

Stobaeus

Ecl. (*Eclogae*)
2.7.6	188

Suetonius

Aug. (*Divus Augustus*)
60	223

Claud. (*Divus Claudius*)
25	229

Tacitus			Thucydides	
Ann. (Annales)			*Pel. (History of the Peloponnesian War)*	
26–27		229	3.95.1	133
			4.51	211
			6.12	135
Terence				
Andr. (Andria)			Virgil	
29–30		207	*Georg. (Georgica)*	
33		207	3.41	95
155–169		207		
Theocritus			Xenophon	
Idyll		94	*Hell. (Hellenica)*	
			2.4.30	211
Theognis			*Mem. (Memorabilia)*	
Elegiac Poems			1.2.61	107
1319		135	1.3.1	107
			4.8.11	107
			Oec. (Oeconomicus)	
			1.1	160

6. Inscriptions

BGU		CIRB (IBosp)	
I 19.21	141	38	221
IV 1085.5	141	1046	221
		978	221
CIL			
2.4405	232	*IAssos*	
6.18048	232	19	78
6.18072	232	20	78
6.18109	232		
6.18136	232		
6.18156	232	*IBM*	
6.18188	232	IV 1032	68
9.3922	232	IV 1034	114
11.3892	232		
12.2956	232	*IDelos*	
		IV1519	78

IV1520	78	51.26	160
IV1521	72	248	72
IV1778	78		
IV2325	78		

SEG

II 821	76, 131
II 821.11	131
IX 7	221, 224
XI 948	72
XXIV 1100	72
XXVIII 1033	211

IG

II² 1297.16	209
II² 1283.27	209
II² 1327.28	209
II² 4473	111
II² 4636	114
IV² 126	124
XI⁴ 1299	78
XI⁴ 1299.29–36	111
XII⁹ 899	72
XIV 966	98

SIG

1173	98

SIG²

814.2	209

IGRR

3.137	222

SIG³

721	72

IKret

I 17	124

Syll³

162.18–19	136
226.15	136
282.26–27	136
285.22–23	136
356.25–27	136
365	78
374.50–51	136
391.13	136
485.27	136
587	141
613.36–37	136
615.10	136
645.79–80	136
708.25, 30	78
709.45	136
709.47	78
731.18	136
731.19	78
1098.54–55	136
1172.9–10	78

IKyme

30 (=*NewDocs*) 1.2	78

ILS

6348	232

ISardH

4	215

NewDocs

1.2	78
1.10–21	76
1.11–12	131
3.10	211

OGI

50.12	160

7. Papyri

P. Agon.		*P. Mich. Zen.*	
6	209	23.4	167
		78.1	167
		98.4	167
P. Fay.			
124.16	109	*P. Oxy.*	
		939.6	135
P. Giss.		963.6	109, 135
1.17.6	109	963	135
		1021.17–18	135
		11.1381	156
P. Grenf.		1197.13	167
68	140	1381.145–167	99
92.9	135	*P. Petr.*	
		1.29.2	109
P. Hib.			
1.79.6	109	PSI	
		1.94.6	109
P. Lips.			
I 34.21	135	*P. Tebt.*	
		24.62	161
P. Lond.		27.21	161
3.1178.14	209	33	224

Index of Names and Subjects

Anthony, Mark 83
Asclepius 5, 78, 98, 99, 101, 111, 113, 114, 123–24, 127, 157, 159, 175, 185, 196, 255
Associations 60, 63, 65, 66, 70, 76–78, 94, 111, 113, 125, 142
Augustus (Octavian) 84, 146, 220, 222, 223, 224, 230

Benefaction, see *Patronage and Benefaction*
Brokerage 72–73, 74, 76, 79, 84, 94, 100, 103, 111, 115, 122, 159, 170, 171, 174, 175, 180, 186, 194, 195, 217, 248, 249

Caesar, C. Iulius 110, 120, 121, 218–19
Caesarea Maritima 222, 223
χάρις 7, 92, 113, 132–48, 156, 157, 161, 163–64, 170, 171, 179, 254
    meanings 132–36, 140–48
    in the New Testament 143–44
    theological interpretations 136–39, 147, 163–64
χάρ- root words 80, 86, 87, 140, 141, 142, 145
Claudius, Tiberius 209, 229
Clientage 62–63, 64, 92
    gratitude 71, 72, 75, 78, 83, 85, 88, 108, 109, 111, 112, 114, 116, 117, 119, 122, 125, 127, 130, 134, 135–36, 139, 140, 141, 145, 149, 150, 180, 184, 159, 209, 215, 223, 228, 229
    ingratitude 62, 69, 71, 72, 88, 136, 216
    of gods 76, 78, 112, 122–24, 157, 158, 184, 248
    of humans 70–72, 75, 78, 191, 207, 208, 215, 228, 234
    see *Rhetoric of Patronage*

Colour
    and culture 42–43
Conversion
    philosophical conversion 92, 104–105, 188, 191–92, 236
    psychological approaches 2–4, 22–27, 150, 153–54, 196–97, 200, 248, 251
    sociological approaches 13, 28–31
    theological approaches 13
Covenant 79, 99, 100, 194, 214, 219
Cross-cultural psychology
    and Paul 17–21, 193
    assumptions 32–33, 45–46
    critique 31–47
Cynics/Cynicism 31, 108, 115, 116, 167, 168, 187–88, 189

Dionysus 78, 111, 141
Discipleship 6, 58, 70, 78, 92, 101, 107, 108, 112, 124, 126–27, 149, 192, 235–36, 247, 249
δωρ- root words 83, 84, 85, 86, 98, 142

Elyot, Sir Thomas 202
Emotions
    and loyalty 199, 200, 204, 205, 207, 208, 212, 214
    as a measure of psychological phenomena 4, 15, 23, 25–26, 27, 153–54, 172, 174, 200, 252, 253
    cultural specificity 39–47, 252
    repression 21
Epicurus/Epicureanism 31, 105, 115, 128, 237
Ethnolinguistics 43–44
εὐεργ- root words 80, 81, 82, 83, 84, 85, 86, 87, 134, 139, 141, 142, 145
Exchange, see *reciprocity*
Exploitation 62, 63, 65

Fictive-Kinship 68, 110

Herod 82, 84, 220
Honour and Shame 3, 36, 43, 45, 51, 67–68, 71, 97, 184, 226, 244, 250

Individualism 2, 3, 13, 14, 22, 24, 26, 30–31, 33, 34, 35–36, 37, 38, 39, 41, 47, 48, 49; see also *personality*
Isis 5, 76, 101, 111, 113, 116, 123, 131, 156, 157, 224, 247

Kinship 10, 40, 56, 68, 110

Loyalty 9, 24, 61, 34, 114, 117, 123, 142, 149, 180, 203
   and emotion 243–44, 228
   and monotheism 211, 213, 214, 215, 246
   and naming 201–14, 215, 222, 230–31
   and Paul 174, 177, 182, 195, 255
   disloyalty 174, 201, 205, 206, 211, 213, 216, 229, 240, 242, 243, 246, 250
   fides 201–208, 210, 211, 215, 219, 231 233
   language of 204, 209–13, 214
   manumission loyalty 200, 226–34
   philosophical loyalty 24, 25, 101, 104, 108, 117, 125, 190–91, 192, 200
   imperial loyalty 200, 207–26

Maecenas 75, 95, 96, 175
Metanoia 130, 191, 192

Nero, Claudius 83, 209, 229

Obligation 7, 19, 59, 63, 64, 66, 69, 70, 74, 76, 78, 79, 85, 96, 99, 114, 122, 140, 159–60, 161, 163, 204, 217, 218, 226, 233, 234

Patron Evangelisation 7, 112, 114

Patronage and Benefaction 4–8, 191, 214
   acts of 58, 60, 66, 68–70, 76, 83, 156–57, 161, 249
   and apostleship 143, 158, 159, 164–69, 170
   and divine patronage and benefaction 79–88
   and friendship language 54, 66, 69, 70, 73, 74, 79, 84, 96, 142
   and generalized reciprocity 57, 58, 64, 98
   and honour and shame 58, 61, 63, 64, 67, 70, 71, 77, 78, 82, 88, 102, 113, 119, 159, 174, 175, 177, 183, 193, 194, 200, 216, 239, 250
   and philosophy, see *Philosophy*
   defined 68–76
   divine Patronage and Benefaction 5, 58, 74, 76–88, 92, 97–99, 112, 122–24, 129, 156–58, 171, 175, 176, 193–94, 211, 214, 216, 247, 254
   euergetism 61, 62, 64–65
   gift vs. benefaction 55, 56–58, 61, 64, 66, 71, 83, 84, 86, 88, 89, 99, 107, 109, 132, 133, 135, 138, 140, 142, 143, 144, 148, 164, 224, 246
   imperial patronage 58, 60, 140
   literary patronage 58, 70, 71, 74–75, 94–97
   patronage vs. benefaction 59–66
   social patronage 67, 70, 75, 235
Personality
   bounded vs. unbounded 26, 33, 253
   idiocentric vs. allocentric 35, 37, 47, 252
   individualistic vs. collectivistic 13, 33, 35
   monadic vs. dyadic 33, 48, 253
Philosophy
   and Paul 186–90
   philosopher as patron 6, 8, 58, 70, 92, 100, 103, 106, 107, 108, 115, 124–28, 149, 186, 190, 191, 192, 234, 239

philotimia 63, 68
Physiognomics 48
Piety 21, 26, 81, 118, 183–84, 209, 232, 237, 244
πιστ- root words 204, 209–13, 215, 246
Plato/Platonism 25, 105, 106, 107, 236, 240, 248
Pompey 74, 122, 207, 218–19
Prayer, see *rhetoric of patronage*
Psychological Biblical Criticism 17
Psychology
    and conversion, see *Conversion*
    and Jesus 17, 18
    and Paul 17–21
    and shame 45
    and Torah observance 19–20
    anger 21, 41, 43
    defined 15
    depression 42
    in W. James 22–24
    in R. MacMullen 26–27
    in A. D. Nock 24–26
    influence on New Testament studies 17–22
    influence on the West 15–17
    introspection 2–3, 22–23
    jealousy 43
    relation to individualism 13, 14, 36
Pyrrhonism 239

Reciprocity
    balanced 55, 56
    familial 56
    generalized/general 51, 54–55, 64, 135, 149, 185
    market exchange 57
    negative 55
Rhetoric of Patronage
    call 5–6, 92, 93–94, 107, 171, 174–77, 254
    philosophical persuasion 6, 92, 100, 104, 254
    prayer, praise, proselytism 6, 92, 103, 108–12, 112–17, 159, 165–66, 173, 194, 195, 215, 254
    see *Synkrisis*

Sarapis 78, 97, 185
Self 2, 41, 44
    construction of the self 3, 14, 24, 33, 34–38, 42, 47, 48, 50, 252
    divided self 22, 23–24
    see also *personality*
Socio-Cultural institutions 10, 67–68
Stereotyping 48
Stoics/Stoicism 101, 102, 168, 187–88, 189, 236, 240
Synkrisis 7, 81, 92, 117–32, 150, 171, 180–83, 184, 254

Tiberius, Claudius Nero 218, 221
Titus, Flavius Vespasianus 84, 217
Trajan 73, 74, 84, 120

Values Oritentation Model (VOM) 13, 34–35
Vespasian 83, 84, 217
Votive offerings 114

Zeal 43, 115, 123, 178, 181, 182, 247, 250
Zeus 102, 111, 125

Index of Modern Authors

Aarde, A. van	18	Braund, D. C.	140, 219, 220, 221, 222, 223, 224, 225–26
Alexander, L.	101, 190–91		
Alföldy, G.	227	Bremer, J. M.	111
Alter, M. G.	18	Bruce, F. F.	152–53, 164, 166
Anderson, R. D.	105, 118	Bryant, J. M.	31
Ando, C.	219	Burke, M.	18
Arnal, W. E.	224	Burkert, W.	101
Arnaoutoglou, I.	94, 142	Burton, E. de Witt	152, 154, 166
Attridge, H. W.	80, 82		
Aune, D. E.	187	Callan, T.	18
		Campbell, J.	68
Badian, E.	220	Cancik, H.	126
Barclay, W.	212–13, 214	Capps, D.	17
Barnes, J.	239, 240	Carney, T. F.	69
Barr, J.	137–38, 139, 146, 166	Carrington, P.	20
Barrett, C. K.	152, 166	Cawkwell, G. L.	118
Bartchy, S. S.	229	Charlesworth, M. P.	76, 109
Batten, A.	60, 62, 63, 64, 65	Cheek, J. L.	28
Beare, F. W.	184	Childs, H.	17
Beaude, P.-M.	19	Chow, J. K.	53, 132
Bee-Schroedter, H.	18	Citroni, M.	74, 94
Behr, C. A.	78	Clack, F. L.	36
Beker, J. C.	153	Clark, A. C.	166
Benedict, R.	16	Clarke, A. D.	236, 247
Berger, K.	19	Collins, R. F.	162
Betz, H. D.	152	Conn, W. E.	28
Bligh, J.	152	Conzelmann, H.	139, 152, 162
Boas, F.	16	Cousar, C. B.	152
Bock, P. K.	16, 50	Craddock, F. B.	153
Bockmuehl, M. N. A.	153, 179, 183	Crandall, J. E.	28
Boissevain, J.	73	Crook, Z. A.	188
Bolt, Peter G.	187	Crossan, J. D.	161, 224
Borg, M. J.	18	Curtius, E. R.	95
Borgen, P.	85	Cutton, G. B.	19, 28
Bornkamm, G.	247		
Bourne, E. J.	37–38	Danker, F. W.	53, 59, 78, 98, 113, 131, 132, 142, 148
Boyarin, D.	177		
Bradley, K. R.	228	Davies, D. M.	20
Brandon, S. G. F.	16	Davies, S. L.	18

Davis, J.	69	Gibson, R. J.	187–88, 190
Deer, D. S.	213	Glad, C. E.	187
Deissmann, A.	25, 154	Glucker, J.	239, 240
des Places, E.	101	Gold, B. K.	74, 94, 95
deSilva, D. A.	54, 73, 74, 132, 142	Goodman, M.	115–16, 165
DeWitt, N. W.	186	Griffin, C.	36, 47
Dindorf, W.	78	Guthrie, D.	152
Dodd, C. H.	19–20		
Dominian, J.	18	Haenchen, E.	174
Donaldson, T. L.	165, 176, 194	Hagendijk, R.	14
Doughty, D. J.	137	Hand, A. R.	71
Drewermann, E.	18	Hanson, K. C.	68, 142
Duff, A. M.	226–27, 228, 230, 232	Harland, P. H.	77, 78, 215
Dunn, J. D. G.	188	Harrill, J. A.	227
Durkheim, E.	16	Harris, G. G.	48
		Harrison, J. R.	60, 66, 72, 80, 85,
Ebeling, G.	152		132, 135, 145, 146, 168
Edelstein, E. J.	99, 111, 114, 124	Hays, R. B.	152, 162, 213
Edelstein, L.	99, 111, 114, 124	Hebert, G.	213
Edwards, M.	241, 242	Heinze, R.	204
Eisenstadt, S. R.	58	Heisig, J. W.	17
Elazar, D. J.	79	Hellegouarc'h, J.	69, 203–204, 207, 208
Ellingsworth, P.	209	Helms, H.	14
Elliott, J. H.	53, 70, 71, 132, 251	Herman, E.	14
Erchak, G. M.	34	Hewitt, J. W.	135, 136
Evelyn-White, H. G.	134	Hobbs, T. R.	79
		Hock, R. F.	166
Fabre, G.	208, 228, 230, 231, 232	Hofstede, G.	13, 35, 37, 38, 245
Fee, G. D.	152–53, 162, 167, 168,	Hooker, M. D.	213
	180, 181, 183, 185, 189	Hopkins, K.	227
Ferguson, E.	191	Horsley, G. H. R.	78, 231
Ferm, R.	23, 28	Horsley, R. A.	54, 132
Fisher, N. R. E.	227	Horsley, R. H.	152
Fitzgerald, J. T.	188–89, 235	Howard, G.	213
Fortes, M.	39–40	Hultgren, A. J.	174, 213, 247
Franzmann, J. W.	135	Hurtado, L. W.	165
Frazer, G.	39		
Freud, S.	16	Inglis, G. J.	28
Freyburger, G.	204, 205		
Fung, R. Y. K.	152, 177–78	Jackson, S. L.	28
		Jaeger, W.	191
Gager, J. G.	28	James, W.	2, 16, 22–25
Gale, R. M.	23	Johnson, C. B.	28, 213
Galipeau, S. A.	18	Jordan, M. D.	104, 106, 191
Gaventa, B. R.	9–10, 22, 28–31	Joubert, S.	60–65, 68, 207
Geertz, C.	37, 254	Jung, C. G.	16
Gibson, E. L.	227		

Index of Modern Authors

Kee, H. C.	186
Keller, F. S.	15
Kennedy, G. A.	108
Kille, D. A.	17
Kim, S.	151, 152, 153, 164, 166
Kirk, J. A.	166
Kirner, G. O.	168
Kittel, G.	137
Klauck, H.-J.	101, 102
Kloppenborg, J. S.	77
Kluckhohn, F. R.	34–35, 245
Knox, J.	154
Konstan, D.	42–43
Kuhn, Thomas	29
Lausberg, H.	118
Lehmeier, K.	187
Lemche, N. P.	79, 215, 219
Leuba, J. H.	16
Leung, K.	36
Lightfoot, J. B.	152, 166
Lindsay, D. R.	210
Longenecker, B. W.	187, 213
Louw, J. P.	133, 134, 136, 139, 140, 209
Lutz, C.	253
MacDonald, P. S.	191
MacMullen, R.	2, 22, 26–27, 67
Malherbe, A. J.	154, 187, 188, 191
Malik, R.	41–42, 51
Malina, B. J.	35, 47–49, 53, 67, 132, 209, 245, 246, 251
Malinowski, B.	16
Malone, P.	17
Malony, H. N.	28
Manson, W.	136, 137–38
Martens, J. W.	187
Martin, D. B.	161
Martin, R. P.	184
Martyn, J. L.	147, 172, 177
Maslow, A. H.	16
Mason, S.	125
Matlock, R. B.	213
Mauss, M.	36, 47
McKnight, S.	23
McLean, B. H.	77, 111, 114, 222
Mead, M.	16

Mendenhall, G. E.	79
Miller, J. W.	18, 147
Miller, M. S.	147
Mitford, T. B.	221–22
Moffatt, J.	136, 137–38
Moore, R. L.	19
Morris, B.	34
Moscovici, S.	28
Mott, S. C.	68, 70, 71, 76, 130, 137, 142, 169, 216, 247
Moussy, C.	69
Moxnes, H.	53, 73, 74, 111, 132
Mugny, G.	28
Munck, J.	153
Murphy-O'Connor, J.	20–21, 152, 153
Mynarek, H.	18
Neyrey, J. H.	35, 48–49, 82, 209, 245, 246, 251
Nida, E. A.	133, 134, 139, 140, 209
Nock, A. D.	2, 22, 24–27, 116, 125, 191, 236
Oakman, D. E.	68, 142
Ober, J.	142
O'Brien, P. T.	153, 189
Olivier, H.	79
O'Rourke, J. J.	213
Osiek, C.	184–86
Overman, J. A.	227
Page, D. L.	127
Paloutzian, R. F.	28
Perkins, P.	212
Pilch, J. J.	35, 47, 251
Pitt-Rivers, J.	67
Plummer, A.	152, 154
Polanyi, K.	54
Poster, C.	105
Pötscher, W.	109
Price, S. R. F.	37, 76, 109
Quincy, J. H.	135
Rambo, L. R.	22, 23, 28
Reed, J. L.	224
Reichardt, M.	19, 20

Reid, W. S.	28	Tarachow, S.	19, 28
Reilly, L. C.	227	Tatum, J. W.	240
Rengstorf, K. H.	82, 166, 167	Taylor, G. M.	213
Reumann, J.	160–61	Taylor, N. H.	152
Rich, J.	218, 220	Theissen, G.	20
Richardson, P.	220	Thiselton, A. C.	162, 163
Robbins, V. K.	107	Thurén, L.	172–73
Robert, L.	74	Tod, M. N.	77
Robertson, A.	152, 154	Tomlin, G.	187
Roetzel, C.	166	Travisano, R. V.	29
Rollins, W. G.	17	Treggiari, S.	227, 230
Roniger, L.	58	Triandis, H. C.	35, 36
Rosaldo, M. Z.	41–45	Tucker, G. M.	17
Roscoe, P. J.	227	Turner, M.	147, 148
Rubenstein, R. L.	20, 28		
		Vaage, L. E.	166, 167
Sahlins, M.	54–55, 56	Vanhoye, A.	18
Saller, R. P.	58, 69, 74, 142, 217, 218, 224	Versnel, H. S.	86, 109, 117
Sanders, E. P.	194	Villareal, M. J.	36
Schenkeveld, D. M.	104, 105, 106	Vincent, M. R.	153
Schmithals, W.	166		
Schwartz, S.	82	Wallace-Hadrill, A.	69, 217
Sedley, D.	190, 236–37	Watson, A.	18, 187
Segal, A. F.	10, 22, 28–31, 153, 165, 177	Weaver, P. R. C.	230
Segall, M. H.	32	Weinfeld, M.	79
Seid, T. W.	118	Weiss, J.	191
Sevenster, J. N.	186, 190	White, J. M.	16
Shweder, R. A.	32, 33, 37–38, 41, 47	White, L. M.	235
Simkins, R. A.	79	Wiedemann, T. E. J.	227, 230
Snyder, H. G.	100, 237	Wierzbicka, A.	43–44
Spilsbury, P.	79, 82, 85	Wilken, R. L.	186, 192
Stannard, D. E.	46, 47	Williams, S. K.	178
Starbuck, E. D.	16	Wilson, S. G.	77
Stegemann, E. W.	56–58	Winden, J. C. M. van	101
Stegemann, W.	56–58	Winter, B. W.	187, 237, 247
Stendahl, K.	2–3, 30, 49, 176, 181	Witherington, B.	173
Stevenson, T. R.	110	Woodward, W. R.	14
Stowers, S. K.	190	Wuellner, W.	105, 108
Straten, F. T. van	109, 114	Wundt, W.	15
Strodtbeck, F. L.	34–35, 245	Wykoff, E.	209
Sumney, J. L.	166		
Syme, R.	217, 218–19	Yrizarry, N.	39